SET into SONG

Ewan MacColl, Charles Parker, Peggy Seeger
and the Radio Ballads

PETER COX

In memory of
Ewan MacColl, 1915–1989
Charles Parker, 1919–1980

And in celebration of
Peggy Seeger, born 1935

Published by Labatie Books
www.setintosong.co.uk

© Peter Cox, 2008

All rights reserved. No part of this publication may be reproduced, stored in a retrieval system, or transmitted, in any form or by any means, electronic, mechanical, photocopying, recording or otherwise, without prior permission, in writing, from the publisher.

Project management by the Cambridge Editorial Partnership Ltd
Design by Paul Barrett Book Production, Cambridge
Printed by Piggott Black Bear, Cambridge

ISBN 978-0-9551877-1-1

By the same author: Sixty Summers – English Cricket since World War 2

For *Angela*, without whose encouragement this book would not have been possible.

Contents

Preface iv
Acknowledgements v

Chapter 1   Prologue – Dear Ewan   1
Chapter 2   The Red Megaphone – Jimmie Miller   4
Chapter 3   An Officer and a Gentleman – Charles Parker   19
Chapter 4   Dancing on the Staves – Peggy Seeger   28
Chapter 5   Man of Many Parts – From Theatre to Folk Song   36
Chapter 6   Riding the Engine – The Ballad of John Axon   49
Chapter 7   BBC Voices – Documentaries Before the Radio Ballads   62
Chapter 8   Muck Shifting – Song of a Road   72
Chapter 9   From Microphone to Broadcast – Engineering the Programmes   86
Chapter 10 The Big Catch – Singing the Fishing   96
Chapter 11 Another Bloody Working-Class Epic – The Big Hewer   108
Chapter 12 Radio on the Cheap – Birmingham Ballads and The Body Blow   117
Chapter 13 Growing Pains – Centre 42 and On the Edge   131
Chapter 14 Boxing Clever – The Fight Game   142
Chapter 15 Killed at the Crossroads – Travelling People   154
Chapter 16 The Word Hewers – Finding the Voices   165
Chapter 17 The Song Smith – Setting Speech into Song   173
Chapter 18 Trickling Marbles – The Sounds of the Radio Ballads   185
Chapter 19 Old Hands and Young Voices – The Performers   201
Chapter 20 From Ballads to Banners – Charles Parker, 1964–80   219
Chapter 21 Ballads of Accounting – Ewan MacColl and Peggy Seeger, 1964–89   235
Chapter 22 Different Therefore Equal – Peggy Seeger   247
Chapter 23 Sound in Vision – Three Radio Ballads on Film   259
Chapter 24 A New Generation – The 2006 Radio Ballads   268

Endnotes – Major Sources   284
List of Illustrations   289
Picture Acknowledgements   290
Simplified Timeline   290
Index   291

Preface

In a chilly church in Maida Vale, in late January 1958, a group of musicians and singers assembled to record an unusual radio programme. The popularity of radio would soon be irreversibly usurped by television, but not quite yet. When in July of that year the resulting *Ballad of John Axon* was finally broadcast, after a prolonged battle both with primitive technology and the programme's detractors within the BBC, it was universally acclaimed by reviewers. Although the BBC, perturbed by the instant success of independent television when it began in Britain in 1955, was already siphoning money away from radio, television as yet offered poor competition. But by 1964, when the team were producing their eighth and last programme, the picture had changed completely. Living rooms began to be dominated by the new box in the corner, and radio, with its demand that listeners create their own images, was in rapid retreat.

The three people who came together to create the Radio Ballads formed an unlikely team. Ewan MacColl was a playwright and actor who had recently turned his back on 20 years of pioneering radical theatre to concentrate on folk song. Charles Parker was a former wartime submarine commander now making radio programmes for the BBC. Peggy Seeger was a much younger American musician, born into a family steeped in music. Seeger's college education had been abruptly ended, Parker had a Cambridge degree, MacColl had left school at 14. MacColl was a Communist and an atheist, Parker was Christian and a conservative, Seeger had little interest in politics. They brought contrasting backgrounds and personalities, but complementary talents. Without any one of them the programmes probably couldn't have been made, and certainly wouldn't have been as successful. What they did have in common was a desire for perfection and a determination to achieve it. The obstacles they faced were formidable, and the series very nearly foundered before it began.

So why write a book about a largely forgotten series of radio programmes nearly 50 years old? What possible interest could they have for us today? Before these programmes were made, radio and TV in Britain rarely featured real people talking about their own lives. The Radio Ballad creators made listener and programme-maker alike realise that 'ordinary' people can tell extraordinary stories. That to do them justice, scripts, actors and narrator are not only unnecessary: they're inadequate. Yet these aren't just pioneering documentaries. Woven into the stories are carefully crafted songs, written by Ewan MacColl after long study of the vocabulary and vocal rhythms of the speakers. Their words are literally 'Set into Song', as the preamble to each programmes announces. They are set into music by Peggy Seeger, and finally set into sound, onto tape repeatedly chopped and spliced into its final form, by Charles Parker, a man convinced he could combine tape recorder and radio into an art form.

When I started researching the book, armed with an out-of-date list of phone numbers, I didn't quite realise the extent of the old folk singer network. Nor did I expect the enthusiastic reception and help I would receive from everyone who had taken part in the programmes, from retired radio producers and engineers to old folk singers and even older jazz musicians, many of them still performing at over 80. All were eager to recall their part in making the Radio Ballads, usually an intensely exhausting but exhilarating week under Charles Parker's direction and Peggy Seeger's banjo-neck baton. This book is for them.

Acknowledgements

The book is designed for the general reader. For those who wish to pursue an interest in the Radio Ballads, the book's website, www.setintosong.co.uk, shows footnotes, a full list of sources, the complete text of the programmes, and an opportunity to buy the Topic Records release of the CDs. On the website readers will have an opportunity to comment, criticise and correct. In a book of this kind, dependent on individual memories as well as written sources, conflicting interpretations are inevitable. You have only to compare the recall of Ewan MacColl and Bert Lloyd to the same events – such as their first meeting – to understand the dilemma. Great stories abound, most of them based on fact, but often embroidered in the retelling.

The principal source for the period of the Radio Ballads is the Charles Parker Archive in Birmingham, which holds the copious files he kept on each of the programmes, as well as on every aspect of his working life until his death in 1980. This has been supported and maintained by the energetic Charles Parker Trust. In addition, the Ewan MacColl/Peggy Seeger Archive at Ruskin College, Oxford, keeps track of their joint working until the death of Ewan MacColl in 1989. The BBC Archive at Caversham records the BBC employment of all three. The Archive of the English Folk Dance and Song Society (EFDSS) contains much invaluable material on their participation in the folk song revival. The help of those in the Archives has been unstinting: my thanks to the teams led by Fiona Tait, Valerie Moyses, Jeff Walden and Malcolm Taylor.

Thanks to: the BBC for permission to quote material; Peggy Seeger and Ian Campbell for permission to quote from their unpublished writings; Peggy Seeger and publishers EMI, Harmony Music and Stormking Music for permission to quote copyrighted lyrics; Jill Donnellan to quote from Philip Donnellan's unpublished autobiography 'Corporation Street'; Amber Good to quote from her thesis 'Lady, What Do You Do All Day?'. Thanks to Currency Press, Hutchinson, Methuen, Northway Publications, Oak Publications, OUP, Scarlet Press, Sidgwick and Jackson, Victor Gollancz, Wiley Blackwell and The Women's Press for permission to quote text.

I have listed in the Endnotes all the many people who so willingly contributed interviews, and I thank them all, especially for their buoyant and infectious enthusiasm. Foremost among them is Peggy Seeger herself, who not only spent three days going over the Radio Ballads in detail but also read and advised on the complete manuscript. Sheelagh Neuling read and corrected several versions of the text, and her research, support, and constructive criticism have been invaluable. I'd like, too, to thank Fred McCormick for both his advice and his jazz intelligence network, which unearthed several of the original participants with the help of Louis Lince. Thanks to Pam Bishop and Paul Long for their enthusiastic support at the Birmingham end, and to Brian Pearson for the extended loan of his *Festival of Fools* scripts. Thanks to Hazel Hardy for tracking down Fitzroy Coleman, and to Ann Bates and Iris Porter for their help. I'm also in debt to everyone who read all or sections of the text: Angela Cox, Mike McHugh, Fred McCormick, Patrick McNeill, Ted Power, Dave Arthur, John Tams, Eileen Whiting, Matthew Parker, Sara Parker and Ian Parr. I'm especially grateful to Charles Parker's daughter Sara, a distinguished radio feature-maker in her own right, for her advice and support from the outset. Rosalind Horton and Sue Ecob, of the Cambridge Editorial Partnership, have again kept me as close to the straight and narrow as they could.

Finally, a book about radio programmes is seriously hampered if you can't listen to them. Fortunately you can: if you don't already have some or all, they're available from this book's own website, www.setintosong.co.uk, and at www.topicrecords.com. I'm grateful to Tony Engle of Topic for his efforts with the BBC to ensure that the Radio Ballad CDs are now once more available.

CHAPTER 1

Prologue
Dear Ewan

Dear Ewan

I have an idea for a radio ballad which is absolutely up your street … a dramatic ballad treatment of the story of John Axon, the Stockport engine driver recently awarded the George Cross posthumously for staying in the cab of a run-away goods train until it crashed and he was killed.

CHARLES PARKER, 12 JULY 1957

The man who started his letter with these words was a gangling red-bearded BBC radio producer in Birmingham. Charles Parker had been a wartime submarine commander, who subsequently studied History at Cambridge before taking a job with the BBC North American service. He was a devout Christian whose politics could then be described as caring Conservative. What enthused him was making much more out of radio, still the dominant communications medium in the late 1940s and early 1950s. In particular he wanted to capture in home and workplace the rich voices of real people, rather than lose their vibrancy and authenticity in the mouths of actors in the studio. The voices of working people and their varied dialects were rarely heard over the airwaves at that time. By 1957, when he was with BBC Midlands, his abiding passion for sound had been further stimulated by the recent arrival of the new 'midget' portable tape recorder. Midget for the 1950s, anyway.

The letter was addressed to a man ostensibly as different as it was possible to be, apart from the red beard. In 1929, at the age of 14, Ewan MacColl had left school in a Salford where unemployment was on its inexorable rise towards the 30 per cent it reached two years later. A failure at school, he managed to find just three jobs, the longest lasting a year. But he read voraciously in public libraries, and became an active Communist, a lifelong fighter against injustice. He revealed a talent for singing and writing, and by the time he was 16 he had started a street theatre group called the Red Megaphones. He was married before he was 21 to Joan Littlewood, who became one of the great theatrical innovators of the 20th century.

With Littlewood he spent the rest of the 1930s acting, writing, singing, on stage and for BBC radio, as well as using theatre to campaign against poverty, support the poor and unemployed in Britain, and oppose the rise of fascism in Europe. About his own war he spoke little, but he emerged from it to continue writing imaginative plays and performing for the roving Theatre Workshop that he and Joan ran. When Charles met him on one of his radio programmes in the mid 1950s, Ewan had given up the theatre – though it stayed deep in his bones – and was creating a new career as one of the main instigators of the so-called Folk Song Revival.

When Charles and Ewan had been working on that 'radio ballad' programme on and off for four months, a third person joined them. Peggy Seeger came from a New England family steeped in music. Now 22, younger than Ewan by 20 years, she had met him in England two years earlier in a basement flat in Chelsea. She had been called up while in a Denmark youth hostel, recruited for a television play because of her skill on the five-string banjo. She and Ewan had an instant meeting of minds, of singing and of songwriting, so when she returned from another continental sojourn in January 1958 her musical skill made her the ideal person to help Ewan set to music the songs he'd written for the new programme. Self-taught musically as in everything else in his life, Ewan was nevertheless floundering when it came to creating musical accompaniment.

When they had spent several days rehearsing and recording the programme, Charles Parker came away with a mass of assorted reel-to-reel tapes, voice and music separate from sound effects. But on trying to combine them into the coherent hour they'd planned, he found himself facing a technical nightmare, with flawed tapes, some running at different speeds. In the following weeks, night after illicit night, he slipped into a studio and worked on what he could retrieve. If genius is an infinite capacity for taking pains, he became an editing genius in those weeks. So, in that make-it-up-as-we-go-along manner, three remarkable people came together in a creative partnership that exploited to the full their very different talents.

Before we examine how that first programme started its journey, let's go back to track the route each of them took to that BBC studio in January 1958, when the first Radio Ballad, *The Ballad of John Axon*, was created.

CHAPTER 2

The Red Megaphone
Jimmie Miller

I remember ... coming in when Jimmie was there with four or five other boys. I listened to him from behind the door – he was laying the law down, stuff he'd read in books. He was about eight.

He stayed up reading till midnight often as a boy. I never made his bed but there was a book under the pillow ... He was only nine when he started to write. I watched him from day to day and knew that he'd be a writer. Writing stories for the school, here and there, and I read them all.

EWAN MACCOLL'S MOTHER BETSY MILLER,
RECORDED BY CHARLES PARKER IN 1962

What made Ewan MacColl tick? Fascinated by and distinctly in awe of him, in 1962 Charles Parker went down to Ewan and Peggy's new home in Beckenham to interview Betsy Miller. Ewan's mother was a tiny but formidable Scot, who was instinctively severe on every other woman in her only child's life, if not on the men. Ostensibly Charles was interviewing her about her own early life for the sixth Radio Ballad, on teenagers, but the recording shows he was also eager to pick her brains about her son's childhood.

The man we know as Ewan MacColl was born Jimmie Miller in Salford, near Manchester, suitably enough on Burns Day, 25 January 1915. He was Betsy and William Miller's third child, but only one other had lived for long, and that 'darling boy' had died before he was three. Betsy had also miscarried twice, so it's no surprise that she was fiercely proud and protective of her only surviving child. The Millers had been born in Scotland into poor working-class families, he in Stirlingshire, she in Auchterarder in Perthshire, from where she'd been sent into domestic service at the age of 12. Will Miller was by trade an iron moulder and developed a recurrent asthma worsened by the often vile conditions in the foundries in which he worked. A horrified Jimmie saw them for himself when as a boy he took in his father's lunch, and he was later to liken the foundry to Dante's Inferno. Sixty years later he wrote 'My Old Man':

> My old man was a union man, skilled in the moulding trade;
> In the stinking heat of the iron foundry my old man was made.
> Down on his knees in the moulding sand,
> He wore his trade like a company brand.
> One of the Cyclops' smoky band, yes, that was my old man.

Will Miller was a working-class intellectual, a militant union man with much to be outspoken about, and many of his jobs were short-lived as a consequence. Encouraged to come to Lancashire by Betsy's sister, who had moved there, the couple came down from Scotland and settled eventually in a street of grim and grimy back-to-backs in Salford. In the summer of 1912 Will went with some of Betsy's family to Australia for his health, leaving her behind with their first child. He found work in a foundry in the naval dockyard on Cockatoo Island in Sydney Harbour but, before he could call for his family to join him, his inevitable participation in a long-running union dispute saw his entry permit revoked. He was back after less than a year, his short-lived son dead, and Jimmie was born 18 months later. From 1913 until 1925 Will was in work more often than not, but in that year his health deteriorated severely, and as unemployment and his asthma worsened he would find work only sporadically in the time left to him.

The union's funds paid him eight to nine shillings a week unemployment money, very much less than he would have earned as a skilled foundry worker. Betsy did her best to make up the shortfall, initially by taking in laundry. To the young Jimmie the house seemed always filled with washtubs and the smell of hot linen, and he recalls coming home at dusk to see her standing ironing by the dim light of the fire, singing old Scots songs from her childhood. But the shortage of money soon obliged her to be up before dawn, taking the tram into Manchester to clean offices. She was tough, still alive at over 90, when her son wrote 'Nobody Knew She Was There':

> Working shoes are wrapped in working apron,
> Rolled in an oilcloth bag across her knees;
> The swaying tram assaults the morning,
> Steely blue-grey day is dawning,
> Draining the last few dregs of sleep away.

For Ewan, his father's work had dignity, but hers was an insult. From those office floors, 'cleaning the same wide sweep each day anew', she would hurry across town to scrub the houses of the better off, making in all just two shillings and sixpence a day. Once Jimmie was invited in and given a cast-off coat. The feeling of humiliation so incensed him it stayed with him for years. Occasionally Betsy would come back with a bag of chicken bones. Chicken was unknown in working-class homes, which seems startling today when factory-raised chicken is a cheap staple. Somehow this emphasises the grinding poverty more starkly than the familiar picture of parallel terraces of identical smoke-blackened two-up, two-down houses, bare floors, a single cold tap, a coal fire, a tin tub, and an outside privy. Terraces that faced each other across 28 feet of cobbled street.

Childhood

Children played, argued, fought, sang and grew up in those streets. Jimmie did too, but his mother's fiercely protective nature ensured the best for her only child, and in a way set him apart: she dressed him so smartly that at primary school he came to be called Jimmie the Toff. From an early age there was an odd contradiction in his inner life. As soon as he could read he devoured books at home and absorbed his father's radical ideas and ideals. But like many bright yet disadvantaged boys Jimmie disliked school, and he didn't prosper. He was thrashed for reading Darwin's *Origin of Species* beneath his desk, a book bought by his father from a barrow in Pendleton Market. Told one day to bring in an apple to draw, he was ridiculed by the teacher because, with none in the house, he turned up with an onion, filched from a stall on the way to school. Such humiliations corrode, and while his passion for reading, his writing and his enthusiasm for political argument were growing, what he was being taught at school by often hostile teachers seemed to him increasingly irrelevant.

His political education began early. He remembered being hoisted on his father's shoulders among the masses packed at a rally for Sacco and Vanzetti – 'two Italian folk, working class like you, son, and like me.' Immigrants to America accused of armed robbery, they became an international cause célèbre in the 1920s. He listened with fascination to his father's intense and profound political debates with other working-class intellectuals at places like the Workers' Arts Centre. Here Will would sit over a beer with those of a similar political disposition and argue for hours over fine philosophical points, Engels v Feuerbach, or the works of the American rationalist Robert Ingersoll, in great debates that were almost theatrical. Ewan said, 'They would quote from Tom Paine as though he was a contemporary.'

Jimmie's informal musical education began early too, absorbed from his parents and from the streets. Betsy and Will had an apparently inexhaustible fund of Scots songs that Jimmie would memorise without conscious effort. In his early days in Scotland Will had supplemented his income in pubs and music halls as 'Wally MacPherson, a Fellow of Infinite Jest'. At the Workers' Arts Centre he could hold the floor and even silence the clack of snooker balls by standing at the bar, singing all the verses of some long Scots ballad. Betsy, too, had a fine voice, with perfect pitch maintained until old age – in a Pete Seeger home movie of 1961, when she was 75, she sings in a voice that is weak, but still pure. Pete, Peggy's much older half-brother, described being intensely moved by Betsy and Ewan's singing of 'A Wee Drappie O't'. In Salford, Hogmanay parties lured Jimmie back from bed down to the stairs long after bedtime to listen to their often bawdy songs into the small hours. Song was everywhere. He later described the singing streets of his childhood:

> Of course there was tremendous entertainment in the street, with mass unemployment everywhere. In summer especially in good weather singers would arrive around 11 am, street singers with the technique to make the verse of a song last all the way from the top to the bottom of the street. Fifteen Welsh miners singing, say, 'David of the White Rock'. Choirs of fishermen from Grimsby or Hull. Blokes who played the bones, two bones held between the fingers sounding like castanets, spoons, barrel organs, piano accordions. I've even known guys come round the streets with a piano on a handcart. Clog dancers ... Songbook sellers, 100–300 songs very poorly printed. They'd go down the streets singing them as though it was one continuous song!

It was as though he resisted being taught – he'd learn everything for himself. Straight after his 14th birthday in early 1929 he joined the hopeless army of school leavers with little prospect of a job: since the General Strike in 1926 unemployment had doubled. Intermittent jobs – in a wire-drawing mill until he pinned a scurrilous '151st' psalm to the noticeboard, a textile magazine about to go bust, and as an apprentice car mechanic – all petered out in turn. His prime consolation was the public library, where, he told the BBC radio producer Geoffrey Bridson later:

> The old men are standing against the pipes to get warm, all the newspaper parts are occupied, and you pick a book up. I can remember then that you got the smell of the unemployed, a kind of sour or bitter-sweet smell, mixed in with the smell of old books, dust, leather and the rest of it. So now if I pick up, say, a Dostoyevsky – immediately with the first page, there's that smell of poverty.
>
> I went through a phase in the 1930s when I literally read anything I could get my hands on. I could read Swinburne one week and Langland the next, and I found that for certain types I had a photographic memory almost, so that I could sit down and read *The White Devil* perhaps a couple of times and know most of the main parts; the same with *King Lear*. I could remember large passages of them.

He read a girlfriend's *King Lear* 'as she was undressing', as he said with a typical flourish, and he wrote her essay for her. Leaving school had unleashed his hunger for knowledge (and women). He soon discovered John Stuart Mill and Tom Paine, then Engels and Lenin, who gave his radical instincts a historical underpinning. Engels' *The Peasant War in Germany* deeply impressed him. A need for action as well as learning was answered through a lodger, Charlie Harrison, a Communist Party branch organiser, and soon Jimmie joined the youth wing of the CP, able to convince them he was as old as the minimum 16. Charlie had a gramophone and a stack of opera records, and hearing Jimmie's wittily accurate mimicry of them he suggested he should join the Clarion Players, a socialist drama group. He began with them by performing Upton Sinclair's play *The Singing Jailbirds*, set in California – 'We speak to you from jail today, six hundred union men.' So in the same year the twin motors of revolutionary politics and the theatre powered him up, and would propel Jimmie through the 1930s and for the rest of his life.

Dirty Old Town

Soon his life was transformed from one where he had to find ways to fill his time to one that was a rush from morning to night. On a street corner he sold the new Communist *Daily Worker*, the forerunner of today's *Morning Star*. As young as 15 he began to write pieces for radical factory papers in the party's office in Ancoats, and there he would set to at whatever work needed doing.

A 'proper' education might have been a hindrance in his writing, because for his simple articles and songs to sound plausible to factory workers he had to get the wording just right, to know an industrial worker's terminology. They were blunt pieces of political satire, but they were effective.

Unemployment accentuated the North/South divide. To Geoffrey Bridson, a left-wing radio producer from the middle-class Lancashire seaside town of Lytham, Manchester was 'a grimy and despondent city wallowing in the backwash of the Cotton slump. During the slow strangulation of the Cotton trade, the city had an almost embattled air – that of the waning capital of a grimly autonomous Northern republic.' The writer JB Priestley talked of 'sooty dismal little towns, and still sootier grim fortress-like cities.' Another BBC man, sent to Birmingham, had in three months seen just two men begging, and no bands of unemployed. On his first stroll in Manchester he saw 'hundreds of men, the good tough Northern brand of English, sitting or wandering about, workless.'

Salford itself seemed little more to Jimmie than a gigantic slum, a landscape where 'everything offended the eye.' The Millers' Coburg Street was in a network of identical roads bounded by the canal and the River Irwell, a 'quiet oleaginous sump with a scum of coloured oil and grease', where if you fell in you were said to asphyxiate before you drowned. Bordering the canal opposite were a glassworks, a small mill, a finishing mill, a bleaching mill, all dating from the late 18th century, and each had its unique smell. Salford was where Engels stayed in 1842–4 before writing *The Condition of the English Working Class*, in which he described most houses there as unfit for human habitation. Jimmie famously recalled it later in song:

> I found my love by the gasworks croft,
> Dreamed a dream by the old canal;
> Kissed my girl by the factory wall.
>   Dirty old town, dirty old town.

To Jimmie and Bob Goodman, the close friend with whom he strode the streets delivering radical literature and running errands for the CP, Salford seemed little different a century later. 'Engels was our mate … he walked the same streets, looked on the same factories, same mills, knew the same kind of people … There, look – that's the place Engels mentions in that letter to Marx.' (Well, in fact it had been pulled down, but why let that spoil a good story?) As ardent hill walkers Jimmie and Bob were thrilled to learn that Engels had taken his sweetheart Mary Burns to a little place outside Marple they knew from their hikes. Engels, too, had been keen to escape from the 'wretched, damp, filthy cottages … the streets which surround them … usually in the most miserable and filthy condition.'

I'm going to take a good sharp axe
Shining steel tempered in the fire;
We'll chop you down like an old dead tree.
   Dirty old town, dirty old town.

This became Jimmie's creed. He was unashamedly out to change the world – there was plenty to change. Betsy said she and Will once saw him in St Peter's Square in Manchester on a soapbox lecturing to 1000 people, with policemen listening for anything 'seditious'. Will laughed – 'he's got it right'. In the autumn of 1931 the National Government (the Labour Party was emasculated because it could only rule with the support of the Liberals) responded to the spiralling costs of the unemployed by cutting their benefit by ten per cent. The Family Means Test deprived nearly a million of the poor of their benefit payments. A public protest meeting was called in Salford for 1 October 1931. *Love on the Dole*, the outstandingly successful novel by Walter Greenwood, a Salford door-to-door salesman earning 28 shillings a week, uses the meeting as a centerpiece. That day became notorious for unprovoked police brutality, begun by a horseback charge. Ewan takes four pages to describe it in his autobiography *Journeyman*, such an impact did it have on the 16-year-old Jimmie. A literal impact, for he and his companion Nellie Wallace lay bleeding on Salford Town Hall steps, struck while holding a banner. Jimmie escaped arrest, but his friend Eddie Frow was one of several imprisoned.

Nellie Wallace was a miner's daughter, an ex-weaver, who by then was acting with Jimmie in the Red Megaphones, a street theatre group of young unemployed activists he'd formed with others after a split in the Clarion Players. By his own admission they were not very good collaborative scriptwriters, and even worse actors, a pale amateurish imitation of the German Blue Blouse agitprop groups that were their inspiration. Nevertheless they cobbled together a first show on May Day 1931. Soon they had the perfect cause close at hand. The devastation of an ageing textile industry was exacerbated by the attempts of increasingly desperate employers to wring more out of their workers. The four-loom weavers' strike was a direct result. Each employee looked after four looms, often ancient machines dating back to Victorian times, and constantly had to stop to mend snapped threads. The employers' decision to require them to supervise <u>eight</u> looms each brought a surge of rolling strikes. Two thirds of all the days lost to strikes in Britain at the turn of the 1930s were in the weaving industry. Nellie's inside knowledge of the trade helped Jimmie write sketches and songs that spoke directly to the textile workers, using tunes familiar to them. They performed them to strikers, and at factory gates from the back of a cart, touring the mills of Lancashire. They used megaphones to be heard by a huge mass of strikers awaiting a food convoy assembled by South Wales miners.

It seems extraordinary now that singing in the open air was against the law. No air could be more open than that above the hills of Derbyshire, where Jimmie and his friends rambled and sang. Jimmie's songwriting then was never anything he agonised over, and many of the early songs, like the sketches, are raw polemics. But they came easily to him, never more so than when he was out walking. He would stride out ahead, inventing songs as he went, as Natt Frayman remembered: 'Hello, Jimmie's off again.' He was making up new song lyrics constantly, instantly – so much so that when hikers heard the original words they assumed someone had pinched Jimmie Miller's tune. One such was 'Mass Trespass 1932', using the tune of 'Road to the Isles', and, yes, Jimmie had found a fresh-air cause. Like his more famous 'Manchester Rambler', also written when he was 17, it was a protest against the private ownership of moorland, often by those who also owned the factories. Despite an Access to the Mountain Bill over 40 years old, less than one per cent of the High Peak was accessible to the public. That we can all walk there now is due to hiking activists like Benny Rothman, who organised the Kinder Scout mass trespass of 1932. Jimmie's energetic publicity ensured the attention of the press when a Derby Assize jury packed with landowners sentenced Rothman and four others, none older than 23, to several months hard labour for riotous assembly and assault. Widespread reporting of this harsh justice helped to change the law – eventually.

Radio

It was Jimmie's singing that gave his career an unexpected and vital turn. Early in 1934 he was spotted singing Border ballads to the queue outside the Paramount Cinema in Manchester. Kenneth Adam was a *Manchester Guardian* journalist who later joined BBC radio and ultimately became Director of Television. On Adam's advice, Jimmie went to audition for Archie Harding, an Oxford-educated socialist banished to BBC's Northern Region for an outspoken *United Europe* programme the previous New Year's Eve. This had so enraged the Polish ambassador that he demanded heads should roll: Harding's rolled to Manchester. The BBC's overlord, John Reith: 'You're a very dangerous man, Harding. I think you'd be better off up in the North, where you can't do so much damage.' In Harding's renegade view all broadcasting was propaganda, because if it didn't attack the anomalies of capitalism it became propaganda in tacit support of them. Reith had sent him to fertile territory. Archie Harding was to preside over a brilliant period in broadcasting history.

From 1933–9 the unpaid radical theatre would be the centre of Jimmie Miller's life, while his radio work would give him employment and entry to another world. Within weeks of Archie Harding's arrival in Manchester he'd recruited Jimmie Miller as his 'Northern voice' in Geoffrey Bridson's *May Day in England*. Jimmie read an extract from Bridson's unemployment poem 'Song for the Three Million'. Bridson describes him 'snarling out in seething anger [in] a vigorously proletarian voice that must have rattled the coffee cups in sitting-rooms all over the country.'

> Cut the cost somehow, keep the balance whole;
> Men are in the making, marching for the dole.

Marching on Manchester a few months later was a young actress of 19 to whom Harding had awarded a prize for verse-speaking at the Royal Academy of Dramatic Art, the most prestigious London drama school. A small, feisty, gap-toothed Londoner, brought up by a single mother, she was as far from the typical RADA entrant as could be imagined in those days. She soon despised the place and the theatre it set out to train her for. Only the fascinating movement classes inspired by the theories of the German émigré Rudolph Laban had interested her. After a year she walked out, and most of the way towards Liverpool to 'stow away to the New World.' After a typically picaresque journey, sleeping under hedges and catching pneumonia, she was actually working as a charwoman in Burton-on-Trent to earn some cash, when a letter with a radio contract found its way to her from Archie Harding. Her name was Joan Littlewood, and her new world was Manchester.

As she tells it in her gloriously gossipy *Joan's Book*, with its great chunks of recreated dialogue that have the ring – if not the precision – of truth, she was being taken to the canteen on arrival at the BBC in Manchester when she was disconcerted by a Voice booming out over the loudspeakers. In her memory 60 years later it becomes:

> Eighty two thousand cast iron segments from Ilkeston, five hundred and ninety four thousand, five hundred and eighty bitumen-grommeted boltings, one hundred and thirty tons of iron washers. My guide explained: 'Archie's rehearsing Bridson's *Tunnel*. We've been at it all day. The King's opening the new Mersey Tunnel next Wednesday … the Voice is Jimmie Miller. You should try these scones.'

Jimmie's first experience of Joan was identical – her voice before her face. He describes how he was prompted by Archie Harding to listen to it – 'the most beautiful and compelling voice I had ever encountered' – also coming over the BBC loudspeakers. They didn't meet for several weeks, but when they did they stayed up all night in exhilarating discussion, finding their views on life and the theatre coincided on almost every point. Joan knew immediately that Jimmie's agitprop was for her – actors male and female in blue overalls, just a different hat and voice to change a character, simple props. Not the ASM (assistant stage manager) of the local repertory theatre with occasional acting parts, which is what she found herself doing. Jimmie thought her a superb actress in the making:

She was able to invest even the smallest walk-on with the deep shining passion of real art ... But she didn't look the way actresses were supposed to look ... she made no attempt to conceal her opinions about the level of production and acting ... and could be dangerously and woundingly outspoken ... That deep velvety voice could be wonderfully soothing one moment, and the next dismissing you as a lousy piss-kitchen.

For her Jimmie Miller was an inspiration – 'he had a way of talking to you that knocked you down.' By then the Red Megaphones had disbanded and reassembled as Theatre of Action, and Joan took time off from her unimaginative repertory theatre to invigorate their faltering start. By his own admission Jimmie was desperately inexperienced as a director, but Joan soon displayed her brilliant theatrical instincts.

Theatre of Action

Theatre of Action had been constituted as a club, which enabled them to avoid sending their scripts in advance to the Lord Chamberlain's office, a censorship process that was not abandoned in Britain till 1968. After *Fire Sermon*, a version of TS Eliot's *The Waste Land*, came *Newsboy*, a reworking of a long American poem about a news vendor's awakening to the iniquities of big business. It was followed by *John Bullion*, about the arms trade, a short and bewilderingly surreal 'ballet with words'. 'The finest piece of expressionistic craft seen in Britain', said the *City News* of its performance at the Round House in Ancoats. But in early 1935 *Draw the Fires*, by the exiled German Ernst Toller, was not a success. A play about a mutiny, suitably enough, it became a fraught joint exercise with the professionals from the repertory theatre, who Jimmie, Joan and Toller regarded as decidedly <u>un</u>professional. That persuaded Joan to join Theatre of Action full-time.

In August 1935 they toured a series of Lancashire towns with Clifford Odets' *Waiting for Lefty*, about the previous year's New York taxi strike. Its success in attracting more, and more varied, recruits to the group was double-edged. Some of these, often older people with a middle-class background, were unconvinced either by the attempt to preach to uninterested working-class audiences, or by Jimmie and Joan's distinctly dictatorial approach. In fact Theatre of Action was on the verge of a split when the pair were offered places at the Moscow Academy of Cinema and Theatre. Among their teachers would be Stanislavski, Eisenstein and Meyerhold, magical theatrical names.

By now they were lovers, and lack of money had obliged Joan to move in with Jimmie's parents. Betsy Miller, thin and bent, affected by the chronic skin disease psoriasis, didn't take to Joan: 'Betsy would always speak of the class enemy, and that meant everyone but Jimmie and her husband.' Will Miller told Joan that Betsy 'would take the skin off her back for Jimmie', one of the few things he did say, for 'he'd hardly breath to speak.' His depression was so severe that one Sunday he was found only just in time to stop him gassing himself. Betsy turned on Joan in her own anguish, but was later astute enough to spot Joan's pregnancy before she herself did, which led to a London backstreet abortion, illegal and squalid. Betsy wanted the pair married, but Joan was adamantly against it. Soon after her 21st birthday, though, she yielded, Jimmie ultimately persuading her that it would be more prudent if they arrived in the Soviet Union married. Not that she gave in without a flaming row in the street, mind, one 'that came to blows', settled according to her by an amused driver who stopped his tram and came over to separate them. At Pendleton Town Hall Joan, who wouldn't wear rings, was obliged to borrow one from one of the two witnesses for the few minutes of the ceremony. And so on 2 November 1935 the 20-year-old 'radio features writer' James Henry Miller married the 21-year-old 'actress (stage)', Maudie Joan Littlewood. They never referred to themselves as man and wife, but as 'co-workers'.

Back to Radio

Then the promised Soviet visas failed to come through, they cut short an attempt to start a theatre school in London, and a few months later were back in Manchester. There they were met by a timely bequest of £100 in the will of Jimmie's uncle, a Glasgow butcher. They moved with the Millers to a house in Fallowfield, and immediately got more work from the BBC. Harding and Bridson were delighted to see them back. They loved their voices, apart from anything else. In a verse play of Bridson's called *Prometheus the Engineer* back in 1934 Jimmie had played a militant workers' leader. Unfortunately the nation never heard the muscular verse that made exciting listening, said Bridson: 'belted out by MacColl and others above the steady roar of the machines.' It was banned as 'dangerously seditious'. Harding had pushed the script upstairs, cautious after being upbraided again by Reith for actually putting hunger marchers on the air without having censored their criticisms of the government. Such were the times.

Joan and Jimmie became friends with a young producer, an unaffected Oxford graduate from London, Olive Shapley, who was another early pioneer of the use of real Northern voices in radio features. For *Homeless People*, broadcast in September 1938, her *Radio Times* article averred: 'You will hear no BBC voices at all.' Working opposite Jimmie was the young Yorkshire actor Wilfred Pickles, recording testimony on a tour of doss-houses, children's homes, Seamen's Institutes and Street Missions. With powerful simplicity, Jimmie's introduction to *Homeless People* ran:

> Do you know what happens to you if you apply for a night's lodging in a casual ward? To begin with you're booked in: then you're searched to make sure you

have no money (at least no more than a shilling); then you get your supper, you're given a bath and you go to bed. Next morning you get another meal and two ounces of cheese to take away with you. You can't come back within a month; if you do, you have to stay four days and work in the institution. Normally you sleep in a dormitory ... a big, bare room, the floor scrubbed to whiteness, smelling faintly of disinfectant – and then lie there all morning. Men of all ages and types. War heroes who have never won back to work and security since 1918. Young lads tramping, perhaps from Glasgow to London, still young and silly enough to have hope and trust. Old men lying like sacks or heaps of rags on the hard floor – no mattresses, no covering.

It ends:

We came out into the bustle and light of Saturday evening shopping in Newcastle – gleaming fruit and succulent meat and melting pastries; soft beds and rich carpets; warm bright clothes and strong, shapely shoes – all this a few feet away behind frail pieces of glass, yet as inaccessible to those lying on the Refuge floor as if they had been stars in the sky.

That was the painful reality of Northern life they were trying to reveal, and Jimmie was fighting to end. Joan worked with Olive Shapley on *Classic Soil*, a quote from Engels – Manchester was the 'classic soil' where capitalism flourished. It was unstinting in its depiction of inner-city misery. Olive later described the result in an unnecessary tone of apology as 'probably the most unfair and biased programme ever made by the BBC.' Asked by Olive to find a pregnant woman to describe what it was like to bring new life into Manchester in 1939, Joan arrived in the BBC studio with <u>eight</u>, some with small children, to tell their stories. This was rare reality, as was a terrible sequence of the voice of a mother, numb with grief, watching her 14-year-old daughter waste away from consumption in a damp tenement block.

Olive describes driving Jimmie and Joan in her battered open-top car to France, where they slept in a tent. The car broke down. After they'd got it fixed, they arrived in Paris with Joan performing an impromptu pantomime as she sat on the luggage at the back of the car, to the delight of passers-by. They promptly ran out of money, but earned enough to get back by working in a restaurant, Jimmie singing to the guitar for tips, while Joan and Olive washed up at the back.

Another producer with whom they worked was the poet John Pudney, who preferred to dispense with narration altogether. For Pudney, Jimmie wrote or co-wrote a series of programmes: on the Chartist underground press; on Seafarers; an early experimental blend of songs and emigrants' voices; and a foray into the traditional music of immigrant societies in the North of England. Less successful was an ambitious piece for the centenary of the Chartists' petition for universal suffrage in May 1938. Jimmie found it difficult to write sketches with convincing dialogue, or a marching song that the young Benjamin Britten could put music to. Pudney had to step in and rescue it, a chastening experience. Still, it was some consolation that a man like Pudney had chosen to commission as a writer a 23-year-old who had left school at 14, and Ewan learned an instructive lesson from it.

Theatre Union

After a lull, the couple had restarted their theatrical career in 1937 with a play by Hans Schlumberg to mark Manchester's annual Peace Week. In *Miracle at Verdun* the dead of World War I return from their graves to inspect the results of their sacrifice. To perform it Jimmie and Joan attracted a new set of actors: each directed alternate scenes, and they played to packed houses at the Lesser Free Trade Hall. Back in business, now as 'Theatre Union', they adapted a play by Lope de Vega, a Spanish contemporary of Shakespeare, never before performed in Britain. A great success, it was to support the International Brigade, for which over 500 Britons would die fighting in the Spanish Civil War on the side of the elected Republican government. Another innovation in their support was a series of pageants in which Paul Robeson took part. Among the war dead were Jimmie's friends Alec Armstrong and Bob Goodman. To honour them Jimmie adapted 'Jamie Foyers', a song his mother had sung about a Scots soldier who had died in the Napoleonic Wars over 100 years earlier:

> He's gone frae the shipyard that stands on the Clyde –
> His hammer is silent, his tools laid aside;
> To the wide Ebro river young Foyers has gone
> To fecht by the side o' the people of Spain.

Theatre Union, still an amateur group but with Harold Lever (later a post-war Labour cabinet minister) as business manager, had a formidably professional approach. Rehearsing five nights a week, they took on Jaroslav Hasek's witty anti-war satire *The Good Soldier Schweik*, about a dumb-insolent Czech soldier in World War I. Jimmie dramatised the German translation, they managed to create a revolving stage at the Lesser Free Trade Hall to cope with the many scene changes, and Joan described it later as their most successful play ever. By now it was 1939, the war was looming, and they decided to orchestrate a 'Living Newspaper' production which would catalogue what they saw as the shamefully feeble response of the Western democracies to the rise of Fascism.

They scavenged every possible source, assisted by journalists who shared their views (many on right-wing newspapers), and in March 1940 mounted a breathtaking multi-media performance at the Round House in Ancoats. *Last Edition* had five separate stages, dance sequences, a novel electronic news display, impersonations of living people (actually banned then), and nightly changes of content. Fast and furious and funny, it was a spectacular synthesis of all they'd learned. The *Manchester Guardian*:

> The acting and production are of such quality that weak spots go unnoticed in a pervading sense of urgency, relieved at times by an interval of delightful fantasy and witty satire, rising on occasions to a climax of startling emotional force.

Closed Down

Living Edition toured into Lancashire through March and April, with standing ovations every night. But with men from Special Branch often in the audience, it was only a matter of time before the police closed it down, and by a grim irony it was on the day of the German invasion of France, 13 May. Miller and Littlewood were arrested, found guilty at the end of May for mounting an unlicensed performance, fined and bound over to 'keep the peace' for a year. 'That's what we've been trying to do', said Jimmie. Some of the younger members of Theatre Union left after their parents had been leaned on by the police. Soon afterwards, when the pair turned up to act in an Olive Shapley children's play, they were barred from entering the BBC: they were on a blacklist. Unable to perform, Theatre Union spent the second half of 1940 studying and teaching across Lancashire, with the remaining men anxiously scanning the post for their call-up papers. Jimmie created a lengthy reading list, Joan got some journalism work, and they secretly rehearsed an adaptation of Aristophanes' *Lysistrata*, but their cast leached away.

In July 1940 Jimmie Miller got his own call-up papers. Posted to Richmond in the Yorkshire Dales for basic training, he loathed it, his misery relieved only by Theatre Union friends arriving each weekend with food parcels from Betsy, and by getting some free time to write. Despite his antipathy to army life and the loss of freedom, he was described as a model soldier by the regiment's lieutenant colonel. It was a query from MI5, keeping tabs on him, that brought that observation, its positive tone doubtless helped by the songs and sketches he produced for a concert party, including 'Browned Off', which included verses like:

> The medical inspection, boys, is just a bleedin' farce –
> He gropes around your penis and he noses up your arse –
> For even a private's privates boys, enjoy no privacy –
> You sacrifice all that to save democracy.

His basic training complete, a weekend's leave at the end of September allowed him to join the remnants of Theatre Union in a show to raise funds for the *Daily Worker*, still defiantly printing. Finally closed down a few months later, it was supporting the Communist Party's line of <u>opposing</u> the war against Nazism as an 'imperialist adventure', forced into that uneasy position at the start of the war by the Nazi/Soviet Ribbentrop Pact. Jimmie was shuttled around a circuit of northern barracks while awaiting a posting, and took a medical, which he failed for reasons unknown. He was posted to the 10th Battalion of the King's Regiment, one due for Home Duties. Not therefore destined to fight abroad, he was sent to Derby on 11 December 1940.

At some point in the following week he disappeared.

CHAPTER 3

An Officer and a Gentleman
Charles Parker

I found early on that the only way in which a microphone could be got near enough ... without halting the flow, was for me to approach as unobtrusively as possible with the equipment slung well behind my back, advancing the microphone diffidently towards the source of sound, but myself ignoring the microphone and by refusing to comment on it either in speech or in facial expression, convincing the victim that I was just rather rude and perhaps slightly odd.

CHARLES PARKER, FROM AN INTERNAL BBC MEMO, 1952

I'd say to him, Charles, go home pretty soon ... 'Oh, yes, I will, I'll just finish.' I'd get home, about an hour later, when I was cooking, I'd pick up the telephone: 'Charles, you'll ruin it, you'll go over the top with it. GO HOME.'

PEGGY BROADHEAD, CHARLES'S BOSS FROM 1948–53, SPEAKING IN 2007

At the BBC in the early years after the war, Charles Parker's background seemed to epitomise that of the typical producer. Wartime submarine commander, 'good' war, History at Cambridge, and the accent to go with it. He differed from the stereotype, though, by being enthusiastically religious, and by being Conservative in politics, if not in his humane outlook. Many of the post-war broadcasters who hadn't already entered the war with left-wing views certainly tended to acquire them. As with the pre-war Manchester producers such as Olive Shapley, exposure to the post-war hardships of many working people served to accentuate that leaning.

Few who knew Charles Parker realised that his background hadn't been as privileged as his headline CV implied. He had been born in 1919, son of a disabled railway clerk who made a living tramping the streets of Bournemouth, selling paraffin from a handcart. He had died when Charles was seven. His mother, the daughter of a railway worker, had been in domestic service when they married, and later kept a boarding house. For her, cleanliness was next to godliness, a lesson the young Charles absorbed. His father's father had been a seed merchant's clerk in Wisbech, in Cambridgeshire. Theirs was not the grinding poverty of the industrial North, true. But if Charles was to escape a humdrum existence it would have to be by his own efforts.

The first step was to win a scholarship to the local grammar school in Bournemouth. Afterwards, a place at university for someone in his financial position was out of the question, so at 18 he got a job in the metallurgy lab at the National Physical Laboratory in Teddington, down by the Thames in London's western suburbs. Like many in his position, while there he studied in the evening for an Engineering degree at a London Technical Institute. He was about to return for his third year when war was declared.

Submariner

Charles had loved sailing since he was a boy and had worked in a boatyard in the Solent in his school holidays. Before the war he'd joined the RNVR, the naval volunteer reserve, so when it began he was called up. Like so many, afterwards he would speak only sparely about that period. We do know that he started as a signalman in a minesweeper and saw action at Dunkirk. He was plagued in later life by nightmares following an incident during the evacuation, when his vessel couldn't pick up burned and drowning Indian soldiers whose ship had been blown up alongside his own. He was commissioned as a sub lieutenant in 1940, and for a year was in destroyers before going into submarines – not ideal for a man of well over six foot, who became known as 'Dip-Rod' Parker, constantly bent double. In submarines he saw action with HMS *Porpoise* in the Mediterranean off the North African coast, including escorting relief convoys under continuous fire through the notorious 'bomb alley' to the strategic and beleaguered island of Malta.

In the North Atlantic in 1943 he was promoted temporary lieutenant on HMS *Sceptre*, towing the new 'X-craft' that successfully attacked the battleship *Tirpitz* off the coast of German-held Norway. The tense and protracted operation involved snaking through fiercely defended Norwegian fjords at night. This action and others won him the DSC (Distinguished Service Cross) the following year. The X-craft, better known as midget submarines, were small four-man craft with a short range that had to be towed silently close to their target so that they could lay depth charges, and be picked up later. Sometimes. It was extremely hazardous for everyone. The citation read:

> For outstanding efficiency and devotion to duty in HMS *Sceptre* during eight war patrols, in which five enemy ships have been sunk and one damaged and in which two successful operations with X-craft have been carried out. Lieutenant Parker has been First Lieutenant throughout this time and has been partly responsible for the training of the crew. His handling and control of the submarine, not only under difficult attack conditions but also under the more difficult conditions of counter attack has been uniformly excellent. In the X-craft operations, it fell to him to make nearly all the arrangements for the towing and recovery of the X-craft, and the success of these operations was largely due to his outstanding zeal and devotion to duty. Working with the Engineer Officer, he has always kept the submarine in the highest possible state of efficiency in spite of adverse conditions, and of long periods away from base.

In March 1945 he took over HMS *Umbra*, becoming the only ex-RNVR officer to command a sub. His colleagues remember him telling how, off the coast of Egypt, he had shelled King Farouk's pink confection of a palace in error during a firing practice. A typical story against himself, as was the one he told of hearing a local dignitary at Scapa Flow in Orkney, when Charles went back to the naval base to make a radio programme after the war. The man was complaining about a 'bloody idiot' submarine commander who had inadvertently sent a torpedo towards the town. Charles didn't let on it was him, a mistake when cleaning torpedo tubes. He rarely spoke about his successes, nor about what gave him nightmares.

The war widened his horizons. Rather than finishing his Engineering degree he took advantage of a scheme set up for returning officers and won a place at Queens' College Cambridge to study History, specialising in the USA. With him went his wife Phyllis (Phyl), who he'd married in 1944 in full naval dress uniform, with the dangling sword he was unused to wearing 'threatening his manhood', as he later remarked. While at Cambridge he was bitten by the theatre bug. He acted whenever he could for the college, directed their 400th-anniversary production of *As You Like It* in the college cloisters, and appeared for the Cambridge Footlights in its tentative post-war resurrection, the annual Cambridge revue which would later launch the

1960s satirists. With the Oxford Marlowe Society he took Webster's Jacobean tragedy *The White Devil* to Berlin. They were there in the breath-holding days of 1948 when the Russians blockaded the divided city, which was relieved ultimately by the Allied Berlin airlift.

Into the BBC

Graduating 'with astonishment', as he said in an early CV, he eschewed the teaching career that he'd originally planned at the end of the war, and applied to join the BBC. They took him on in November 1948, and after induction training and a brief spell in the European Service he joined the North American arm as a talks producer in March 1949. He was 30 a month later. At that time the North American Service (NAS) was based in Great Castle Street in central London, and its brief was to create programmes that would interest US and Canadian radio stations. The NAS attracted an eclectic mix of 'rugged individualists', as their Australian boss Peggy Broadhead put it. Among her 'boys' was Tony Benn, later to be a minister in the 1960s Labour government of Harold Wilson – 'Tony immatures with age', said Wilson. Benn would later become an articulate and tireless left-wing scourge of all governments everywhere. Charles's views would in due course be close to Tony Benn's, but not yet.

Charles was essentially a jobbing producer, creating radio programmes designed for a North American audience. He produced plays, covered industrial fairs, Christmas traditions – anything with a religious component gravitated towards him and became a speciality – and duty stuff like the world of the Women's Institute and their agricultural work. Having had enough of such fare, and after being turned down for a transfer to Nigeria in 1951, he tapped an old naval colleague for a chance to take one of the rare new mobile tape recorders on the annual race round Fastnet Rock, not something for the faint-hearted. The resulting programme, like almost all in this period, has been wiped, but circulating round the BBC for years was a tape he made of crew members being sick (including, it must be said, himself). The indelible picture it conjures up is of Charles leaning over with a 'Just vomit a little closer to the mike, would you, old boy.'

A vivid memory of Charles at that time comes from a fellow radio man who would later move into television, Philip Donnellan. Later a great friend, indeed soulmate, he first met him in 1950, after being warned that he was difficult:

> We met a tall rather gangling figure with a lock of gingery hair over his eyes and … beard below scarred cheeks. He was enthusiastic and punctilious about the simple recording we had to do … I was in a good position to note his mannerisms: head on one side, attention riveted on what his informant had to

say; the rather elaborate use of a bony hand and fingers to unlock, almost, what he was trying to obtain. I thought he had difficulty in asking precisely formulated questions: he seemed to use a method of challenging the interviewee's ideas – and it worked. In casual talk afterwards I found him efficient, pleasant and slightly unusual, no more than that. I could not understand why I had been warned that he was difficult.

Charles was creating a reputation for eccentricity. Peggy Broadhead recalls an occasion at the end of 1951 when Charles's wife Phyl called her to say he'd sustained a head injury and wouldn't be able to go down to RAF Brize Norton to record American airmen for the traditional pre-Christmas broadcast. Perturbed – Charles never missed an assignment – she went round to his flat in Charlotte Street to find a gaunt face and tattered beard surrounded by a mass of bloodied bandage. The tailor living below, his child's nights and his own rendered sleepless by Charles's night-time pacing, had ambushed him on the stairs and smashed a teapot over his head. Peggy went off to make the programme with Eamonn Andrews, later a big name in television.

Broadhead remembers Charles as eager, imaginative, excitable, and increasingly fascinated by the voices of 'real' people, as opposed to actors speaking their words. Charles and the others were allowed a free rein – 'The essence of the North American Service was that we had all come in through our own doors.' Broadhead saw her job as one of tugging at the reins only when their enthusiasm for novelty ran away with them, as it could easily do in Charles's case. She had a shrewd eye for what their North American customers would just about accept. Unfortunately, she said wistfully, this did not include an army of Hoovers advancing on New York City, in a programme Charles planned on the Revolt of the Machine. She had been prepared to run with that one, but New York wasn't. Charles's enthusiasm, then and later, meant he was inclined to arrive unannounced at someone's home late in the evening, bursting to talk about something he was doing.

> One night he was beguiling us all, and missed the last train, so we bedded him down in front of the fire. He was a long man. Later my five-year-old arrived crying, having gone down to find a naked man thrashing about in the midst of a nightmare.

Charles relished the occasional chance to visit the US, get out and about and record real people's voices, the 'actuality' in BBC jargon. The US, which unlike Britain was dominated by commercial radio, led by the innovative Columbia Broadcasting System (CBS), was increasingly attracted to outside broadcast programmes that used mobile recording equipment. Pioneered in Germany before the war, AEG's Magnetophon tape recorder had been much refined after being enthusiastically adopted by the Nazis. In dollar-starved post-war Britain mobile recording equipment was hard to get hold of, and Charles was fascinated by the prospect. EMI's Midget was a home-grown version, late on the scene and expensive at £100, and the BBC had only six available by 1952. They were earmarked for the Indian Service and for the Helsinki Olympics, but Charles wangled the loan of a rare new American Stencil-Hoffman Midget from friends in CBS. He got a chance to use it when assigned to record the crowd at the annual agricultural Royal Show for a 15-minute feature that July. In the period between her accession and her coronation the public was eager to see the new Queen, and she attracted huge crowds through which Charles pressed, trying to record real voices as inconspicuously as possible.

Afterwards he wrote a three-page memo of his experience, trying to interest his NAS colleagues (and doubtless support his lobbying for their own kit). 'I cannot express strongly enough my conviction' – Oh yes he could – 'that the use of this equipment can give a quite new dimension to the actuality feature, and I personally am very excited by the possibilities.' His enthusiasm and engaging naivety shine through in the extract that heads this chapter, which continues:

> I soon found that an invaluable refinement was to simulate a hearing aid by running the lead from the playback equipment to an improvised deaf-aid ear piece, and this seemed to be the most successful. The whole secret seems to be in the approach to the victim and in the positioning … so that he never has a clear view of the recording box, but only of the microphone and the deaf-aid mock-up. This may appear to be rather suspect ethically…

Indeed it was, but he did at least seek the victim's permission afterwards. He goes on to describe his day with great relish, particularly his 'tragic failure to record the Queen's arrival' because a new tape reel hadn't engaged properly, and his falling backwards in a surging press of people onto a pram containing a sleeping infant 'which did not even wake up.' (One imagines students in a modern Media Studies course being asked to comment on the use of the words 'diffidently', 'victim', 'ethically' and 'unobtrusively' in the whole extract, especially given the massive microphone he was wielding.)

This piece goes on to provide copious advice to the BBC Engineering department on how to use the recording equipment. It illustrates his growing compulsion to achieve spontaneity of recording, an intense desire for perfection of recorded sound, and an enthralled technical curiosity that would enable him to overcome the horrendous difficulties set to plague the British counterpart of the American recorder he'd cadged. The EMI Midget was boxy, unwieldy, double its size and a third heavier. These notes were just a sighting shot for the ten-year siege that he would undertake of the engineers' stubborn defences, with mounting exasperation. Whole filing cabinets would be filled with his advice…

That Royal Show programme in 1952 was one of a series of 15-minute features he was engaged in for a series called *London Column*. Week in, week out, he was out and about, with the same challenging deadlines as a journalist but with a decidedly more nerve-racking climax, as every item went out live, as much of the BBC's radio output did then. Being a perfectionist meant that he was constantly working late as well as traipsing all over the country. In a fortnight in the spring of 1951 he had clocked up 120 hours unpaid 'overtime', which he used as a basis for a time-in-lieu request. There weren't to be many such extra holidays in later years, but Phyl had recently given birth to their daughter Sara, whose arrival elicited a classic first-child response in a letter to one of his many American ex-servicemen friends:

> But what an extraordinarily hopeful thing it is to have a small baby in the house. It brings a blessed sense of proportion into one's being. The nightmare fantasies of the future fade before the immediate necessity of feeding the little brat at 2 o'clock in the morning, and despair for humanity just cannot compete with one's fascinated awareness of a dawning intelligence in this scrap of humanity. As you can imagine, Sara has got me just where she wants me. [Later] Sara has just started to walk … at present she shows no signs of taking after her father except for a raging temper. [Later still] Sara is now quite unbelievably enchanting and too believably infuriating by turn.

The family man was 34 when he applied for promotion to Senior Features Producer in BBC Midlands in September 1953. Three earlier transfer applications had been turned down since 1950. In one of them he'd expressed his enthusiasm for recording actuality simply: 'My duties with NAS have taken me more and more out into the field, producing the actuality type of programme most suited for North America, and I have found myself presenting sound-pictures … exclusively in terms of actuality.' But by 1953 this had extended to a clear view that radio could emulate some of the techniques of the pioneering documentary film-makers:

> I believe that the documentary idea of Grierson and Rotha is valid for the radio feature, that 'creative editing' can apply to sound actuality as to film actuality; that the function of the documentary should be the interpretation of society to itself … and I believe that this can yet be done in terms of true 'entertainment' in its widest sense.

He had begun to see what could be achieved on film, and saw no reason why he couldn't apply the same technique on radio. The reference to 'entertainment' was to convey the impression that he had his feet on the ground, and was not just a dilettante out to make arty minority programmes. He convinced the Head of BBC Midlands Region Programmes, Denis Morris, and his deputy David Gretton, and he started working for them in Birmingham in January 1954. Gretton's letter of congratulation concluded with 'at last you will be able to get down to real features without feeling constricted by the short wave medium's grass roots requirements.' But for Charles they weren't mutually exclusive.

Birmingham

Charles and Phyl eventually found a flat to rent in the Birmingham district of Harborne, where he entered enthusiastically into the life of the parish church. During the next four years he made 42 major features for radio, a few that were not broadcast, and a couple for television. Many of these programmes would sow seeds of more ambitious ventures later. Among them were features about a miner going to work, the deaf, Lowestoft trawler men, Offa's Dyke, a village bus, guitar teaching, foreign students and a Wisbech gypsy. Typical of his desire to test the midget recorder's capabilities was a 1954 broadcast, *The Polar Bears' Picnic*, about a military exercise on Salisbury Plain, where Charles spent four days eavesdropping with his recorder. Introducing it in the *Radio Times*, he said: 'I wanted to catch the territorial soldier on the job … wanted to overhear – and record for you to share – everything, from the General outlining his plans … to a private's … earthy observation on the slit trench.' Unfortunately the equipment couldn't cope, and Donnellan describes helping him assemble the programme from 'the tattered shreds of conversations, and weave them into a compelling garment of sound.' He was working on the edge – he was the kind of man who would use every spare minute titivating an ambitious programme until he was (sometimes) satisfied – and he was meeting all kinds of people. One of them was a man named Ewan MacColl.

Charles had for some time had a growing interest in folk song. In 1942, in a Lebanon hotel for a spell recovering from sandfly fever, 'surrounded by Druze princesses protected by bodyguards with six-foot scimitars', he met a group of roistering American airmen who had mistakenly tried to bomb his submarine a few weeks before. They intrigued him with their own traditional songs, like 'Casey Jones' – 'The fact that you could actually sing about railway engineers was incredible … I used to regret bitterly the fact that I was not American and therefore could never live.' As he said ruefully later, all he had were dreadful things like 'Farmer Brown he had an old Sow', and music-hall songs. He had thought that English folk song no longer existed, but later came across some while picking through the BBC's invaluable sound library, much in demand because BBC recordings were the cheapest way for a producer to add music to programmes. He was enthralled by Isla Cameron singing 'Queen Jane', and by MacColl's barnstorming 'Eppie Morrie', sung at a speed that would get it on a three-minute 78 rpm disc. At the BBC Charles had used the Irish piper and folk song collector Seamus Ennis on some of his *London Column* pieces, though when he proposed a programme using Seamus for rural songs and Ewan for urban, he was warned off using MacColl, who was on an unofficial BBC blacklist again. (This man is dangerous. He may alter your opinions.)

He eventually met Ewan when producing a programme on experimental theatre, and told him he was longing to get his teeth into something worthwhile. Superficially they were as different as could be, the Marxist and the Christian Conservative, but, although radio was hardly Ewan's major preoccupation at this point, they shared a desire to make imaginative yet 'true' radio programmes, and a fascination for the human voice. The portable tape recorder, however clunky and unreliable, was nevertheless allowing Charles to get out into homes and factories. But was BBC radio prepared to be imaginative? Could it afford the investment in time and money, when television was starting to tug at its purse strings? Fortunately, he had a sympathetic boss, who was prepared to give an imaginative producer his head. Charles wanted to emulate in radio the reality that he was just starting to see on television. He was casting around for a subject to experiment with when he heard about a train driver awarded the George Cross for bravery.

So it was that on 12 July 1957 he sounded out Ewan MacColl. The idea piqued Ewan's interest, but they couldn't meet until he returned from a Moscow youth festival. He was about to fly there with Theatre Workshop, a group now run solely by Joan Littlewood. He was no longer married to her, but to Jean Newlove, the company's dance teacher, who was also in the party. A third woman came along, too, on a more protracted journey among hundreds of young musicians, first on an overcrowded boat, then for three days on a train in which 'singers and musicians hung from luggage racks.' Her name was Peggy Seeger.

CHAPTER 4

Dancing on the Staves
Peggy Seeger

I would like to communicate to her the intense comradeship that I feel with her now – married as she was to a man 15 years her senior, constantly impatient to get to composing, endlessly trying to get across to her children as a person and being rejected not by their direct lack of interest but by any child's preoccupation with its own life.

PEGGY SEEGER SPEAKING OF HER MOTHER,
UNPUBLISHED WRITINGS, 1992

Whenever Pete came down we got off school. My mother reckoned he was as good an education for us as the teachers. Mike and I would sit while he played the banjo, putting our fingers on the strings to see what would happen. He was in his early twenties at the time and never got annoyed.

PEGGY SEEGER, IBID, 1992

In June 1935, a few months before Jimmie Miller married Joan Littlewood, Ruth Crawford Seeger gave birth in New York to her second child Margaret, known ever after as Peggy. At that moment Ruth's husband Charles Seeger was picking blueberries on a farm 60 miles away to make ends meet, and it was several weeks before they were back together, living in a trailer on a ridge at his parents' farm, coping with dirty nappies and no running water. They were consigned to the trailer rather than the farmhouse because Charles's parents disapproved of this, his second marriage. He was already 49, and had three boys by his first wife, Constance: Charles and John were grown-up, and the young Pete Seeger was 16. He had been four years old when his parents' marriage broke up – and was promptly sent away to school. He survived rather well in the circumstances.

Seasonal fruit picking for a few extra dollars sounds rather like a symptom of American rural poverty, a variant of the British urban version that Jimmie Miller had lived through in the same period. Indeed, the terrible blight that had swept the American South and Mid-West, exemplified by the familiar images of desperate dustbowl homesteaders, was only just being tackled by President Roosevelt's 'New Deal' government. In his State of the Union address that January the President had proposed a twin programme for emergency public employment in the cities and in rural areas. The rural Resettlement Administration (RA) was designed to move destitute 'sharecroppers' and unemployed miners into refugee camps, there to re-equip them for a new life. Its enlightened head, Rexford Tugwell (known as Rex the Red to the right-wing opponents who engineered his downfall two years later) set up a Special Skills division, aimed at fostering art and music recreation to create a sense of community in these 'colonies'.

However, Charles and Ruth Seeger were not the rural poor, but the urban educated, suddenly short of work and money. Charles was a professor of music, and (using a pseudonym) the part-time music critic for the *Daily Worker*, the American equivalent of the Communist newspaper that Jimmie Miller had sold at factory gates. Charles had lost his main teaching job, more because his music was too radical than because his politics were – though this would become a problem 20 years later – and for a spell had been living on money from occasional jobs and handouts from friends. He and Ruth were almost broke. He had paid for his boys to go to boarding school, and Pete remembers once coming home from vacation and lending his father five dollars to buy milk for Peggy's older brother Mike, then a baby. Charles could stump up enough for rent and food but little else. But late in 1935 came an invitation to set up the RA music programmes, so ending a tough year for the family on a more optimistic note.

That new job was a dramatic turning point. Quite apart from keeping his new young family afloat, it signalled an abrupt change in his musical interests, as well as those of Ruth and his son Pete. Charles Seeger arrived in Washington to take up the new job with a somewhat elitist belief that traditional music had died out in America by 1900. Throughout the South he visited homesteads and camps set up by the Federal government for the hungry and dispossessed, like the one in which Johnny Cash was brought up in Arkansas. Seeger was surprised and delighted to find folk song was alive and well. He acquired an early sound recording machine, which cut grooves in aluminium discs, to make field recordings for the musicians he was hiring to work in the camps.

The Seegers and Traditional Music

Thus began the Seeger family's great love affair with traditional music, the music that Peggy grew up with. That summer the 17-year-old Pete accompanied Charles and Ruth to one of the burgeoning traditional music festivals, at Asheville in North Carolina, and described it as 'visiting a foreign country ... past wretched little cabins with half-naked children peering out of the door.' There he heard the legendary five-string banjo player Samantha Bumgarner, and set out to learn the instrument he would later master and popularise in the post-war American folk song revival. One-year-old Peggy didn't hear it quite yet: she was parked in a nursing home at a dollar a day. Ruth too was eager to absorb this music, new to her, and worked in the field with her husband whenever she could.

Peggy's mother embraced this change to her own musical direction. As a promising young avant-garde composer, she had been the first woman to win a Guggenheim music scholarship to Europe. Keen to be taught by Charles Seeger, she had ignored his initial rejection – he didn't think much of women composers – and had browbeaten him into taking her on as a student and amanuensis. They fell in love, and moved in together when she was 30, in 1931, the year in which ten years of constant composing had culminated in her *String Quartet*, then much admired in 'modern' music circles. To Peggy later this music was simply alien. She couldn't understand how the woman she knew as a mother could create something like 'someone crying, someone beating on the walls.' Her mother was 'the folk song lady', and one who was far too sane to have produced something so disconcertingly scary.

From 1936 Peggy's mother turned from composing atonal music to become that folk song lady. During the period she described herself as 'composing babies', she went on to teach music while managing a household of three children under five, often with the help of babysitters running a 'combined drugstore and hospital ward'. But above all she was transcribing traditional music. She was astonishingly painstaking, listening to scratchy aluminium field recordings brought to life by a sharpened cactus needle, endlessly replaying tricky swooping phrases till she got them right. For the father-and-son team of John and Alan Lomax, who were busy recording for the Folk Song Archive at the Library of Congress, she transcribed over 200 songs, eventually published in 1941 as *Our Singing Country*. After the war, with Charles she transcribed and arranged over 100 more for voice and piano for the Lomaxes' *Folk Song USA*. Then she branched out on her own with *American Folk Songs for Children* and *Animal Folk Songs for Children*, inventive piano arrangements of songs she'd listened to countless times, in countless versions.

As Pete said, the Seegers and the Lomaxes were 'high on dreams of how this music would capture the heart of America.' As Mike and Peggy grew older their mother recruited them into the book-making process. No longer the 'golden-haired tot with the high voice, which when excited would go through the ceiling', for whom Pete remembered playing the banjo and singing whenever he stopped over, Peggy was learning transcription at the age of nine. At 11 she was transcribing for Ben Botkin's *Western Treasury* for a nickel a song. The family had no radio, nor later did they have television, but they made music together at weekends. Peggy and Mike would learn new songs and trade them with Pete's whenever he dropped by. Pete, the 'tall exotic half-brother, with his long, long-necked banjo and his big, big feet stamping at the end of his long, long legs.' Often he'd come with his musical friends, who would jam late at night, fall asleep in front of the fire, and confront the young Seeger children with a tangle of sprawled bodies and instruments in the morning.

Among Pete's fellow musicians passing through would be Woody Guthrie, hardly bigger than Peggy, the massively imposing Leadbelly, in prison for murder when first recorded by Alan Lomax, and Aunt Molly Jackson. Pete had started The Almanac Singers in 1940 to sing labour songs, and moved on to form The Weavers with Woody Guthrie. They sold millions in their heyday from 1949–52, starting with Leadbelly's 'Goodnight Irene'. Pete wrote or co-wrote 'Where Have All the Flowers Gone'; 'Turn, Turn, Turn'; 'We Shall Overcome'; and 'If I Had a Hammer', all such iconic songs of peace and protest that many people don't know who wrote them. 'If I Had a Hammer' is innocent to us now, but it was controversial because back then, as Pete said, 'only Commies used words like peace and freedom.' Actually part of the household was Elizabeth Cotten, recruited as a Saturday help after she'd found the eight-year-old Peggy lost and wandering on the wrong floor of a department store. The floors were segregated, black from white.

'Libba' Cotten was a black singer who, at the age of 11, had written 'Freight Train', which many years later would be a success in a skiffle version for Lonnie Donegan. Libba's singing was in such demand by the Seeger children that Mike and Peggy would do the clearing up for her so she could sing and play her guitar. And yet, according to Peggy:

She had been ordered by the church to lay her guitar down by the riverside when she gained puberty. And she did. Let it alone for over fifty years ... I don't know how long Libba listened to us before that day when Mike walked into the kitchen and found her playing the guitar, left-handed without having re-strung it – index finger swinging away doing the job of the thumb, thumb relegated to finger-dom. That's how we heard 'Freight Train' for the first time. Mike was fascinated and learned to play exactly as Libba played, left-handed and without re-stringing the guitar. I waited till he had it, transferred it to the right hand and then we were 'Freight Train' mad.

The Working Mother

In the early post-war period Peggy's mother was working a 14-hour day, away teaching students of composition, giving lessons to children with 'fingers like cooked macaroni', and at home working on her transcriptions till late into the night. By then she had four children, and Peggy, not yet a teenager, would get the youngsters' breakfast and lunch ready before she went to school. Her mother would have the supper menu written out, and Peggy would have to shop for it. 'She'd run the whole thing like a battle, with notes saying: Peggy get two chickens, Mike you're making dinner so peel the onions. We're having chicken cacciatore in *Joy of Cooking* p225.' Peggy would cycle off down to the shops, or walk there pulling an old wooden wagon, sometimes loaded with a younger sister. Charles was by this time over 60, still working but not the main breadwinner, content as most men then were (then?) to have the world arranged for his comfort. Nevertheless he was proud of his wife's achievements and supported her in every sphere except the domestic.

And he supported his musical children: 'What my father gave me was a freedom to do what I wanted. That was quite unusual in those days.' He played dual piano with Peggy, sitting together at one piano, or each at one of the two grands, 'bashing away at piano versions of the Beethoven symphonies. If I came to a part that was difficult he just sat and let me work it till I got it.' Her mother had originally taught her the piano in an engaging and unorthodox style, such as:

> Playing the 'Irish Washerwoman' in every key on the piano (including two Turkish modes) and explaining the circle of fifths, resolutions, cadences, sight-reading ... But when it came to playing the piano and practising when I knew she was in earshot, I couldn't ... She was the best teacher of music I've ever come across, and yet I couldn't learn piano from her.

Her mother's musical energy and enthusiasm still coursed through the house, though. For Peggy: 'The music came right into us, we osmosed it.

I can still sit there listening to music, seeing it on the staff line, all the sharps and flats, dancing on the staves.' By the time Peggy was a teenager she played piano, guitar and banjo, as did the equally talented Mike. She had to overcame the stage fright that afflicted her at 15 when she entered a talent show at her High School: 'Fear flooded my entire being; my voice developed a brilliant but uncontrollable vibrato; my lungs shrank to half an inch in diameter.' She swore she would never sing for a living, an oath she soon broke, fortunately for this story. She and Mike would sing and conduct folk song sessions to help publicise their mother's books in department stores and schools, and as teenagers they recorded an album for Folkways.

But with no warning, in the space of a year their lives began to fall apart. In 1951, at the height of their success, Pete Seeger's Weavers were blacklisted by Senator McCarthy's House Un-American Activities Committee. Once openly radical too, in the 1930s Peggy's father had seen the danger and, fearing he'd lose his livelihood just as he was raising a second family, Charles Seeger moved to a safer haven as a supporter of Roosevelt's New Deal. Peggy later reflected:

> My parents were radical in a certain kind of way in the Thirties, tempered in the Forties, intimidated in the Fifties. I don't ever remember being disturbed, even by Hiroshima. We didn't talk politics as I remember at our table, and yet I was of a liberal family that was supposed to be progressive and supposed to be political.

'Progressive' was all right, but Charles was wary of hearing his politics called left-wing or revolutionary. When much later Ewan and her father started talking politics together she was astounded by her father's views. It made her bristle that he had never talked to her about it, angry that: 'He didn't want to prejudice my thinking. Bollocks. He prejudiced my thinking by his very manner, by our very way of life, by the place we lived, the social milieu that I now took for granted, that comfortable desert called middle-class suburbia.' And by having black servants (as he always had) who were treated courteously but not as part of the household.

Charles Seeger's past came back to bite him when in 1952 his passport was downgraded so he could only travel abroad on official business. The following February he had its renewal turned down on the grounds of Sedition, as a person 'supporting Communist movements', and, now 67 and with the writing blazoned on the wall, he retired from the Pan American Union, an organisation he'd worked for since 1941. McCarthy's witch-hunt was in full swing. But Charles hadn't shopped anyone (nor would Pete), as others like Burl Ives had. Ives cooperated with the Committee, and in consequence Peggy's mother had withdrawn from a joint book project with him. Later this 'rooting out of reds' would be the reason for their friend Alan Lomax's crucial spell in England.

Worse was to follow, much much worse. When Peggy was 14 her mother had started tentatively composing again in the evenings, her disturbing music floating up from the room below Peggy's. (Peggy had never even realised until then that her mother had composed anything at all significant before.) In 1952, with her first major work for 20 years, Ruth won a prize for new compositions. She had worked on it flat out despite feeling increasingly unwell. When her *Suite for Wind Quintet* was performed for the first time at the award ceremony that December, she accepted her prize shyly, wearing a black taffeta skirt that Peggy had made for her. Then, in February 1953 she discovered she had intestinal cancer. She ignored it for as long as she could. She went on teaching, started a flurry of new projects, and worked as intensively as ever to finish a new book, just as she visibly wasted away.

By November 1953 she was clearly dying. Peggy, away at Radcliffe College in Cambridge, Massachusetts, was summoned back and spent a last few days with her as she slipped away, drugged with morphine, uncomplaining. 'I sang to her conscious and I sang to her unconscious as dusk and dawn changed guard outside the windows.' Peggy was there when she died. On the same day Peggy and Mike were due to be at the Children's Book Fair at the Washington Post building, promoting their mother's *American Folk Songs for Christmas*. The book was another great success – for other people's Christmases. For Peggy 'the life went out of the household when she died. It just vanished.'

In September 1955 in Quebec City Peggy boarded a ship bound for Holland, accompanied by little more than her new long-necked Vega banjo. In the intervening period she had gone back to college at her father's insistence, and before long she had been joined in Cambridge by her father, her younger sisters, and her mother's huge grand piano. She kept house for this odd ménage for the academic year of 1954–5, but her father soon fell in love once more with a childhood sweetheart (after whom Peggy had been named) and moved in with her in California. He was now nearly 70, but his new wife's money made him financially secure and would help to bail out Peggy at crucial moments in the next couple of years. Peggy was packed off abroad alone to the Dutch university town of Leiden to live with one of Pete's elder brothers. The plan was that she would continue (in Dutch) with the Russian studies she had begun at Radcliffe, and then go back to college after a year in Europe.

On the Road

It didn't work out like that. The chemistry between the two sisters-in-law was not as it had been when Peggy was ten, and she and the banjo hit the road. In a Belgian snowstorm that winter she was given a lift, and promptly recruited, by a pastor who ran a home for Catholic children displaced by the war. He would go to East Germany, find them in camps set up in aircraft hangars, and bring back a dozen 12-year-olds to a Belgian village. Peggy was asked if she 'wanted to be their little mother', and puzzled over the period in retrospect, especially her slide towards Roman Catholic belief after long debates with the persistent priest. 'I guess I needed structure ... and he had a crush on me. But the boys were little Nazis.' She became the household skivvy and had to sleep in a vast double bed with the five girls. On the freezing afternoon walks she would be besieged by the pastor: 'That's the nunnery. If you stayed, I could head the monastery and you could head the nunnery.' She needed rescuing, and wrote to an American couple she had met on the boat. They drove up and took her back with them to Copenhagen, happily jammed under the luggage in their microscopic Fiat.

She was in Copenhagen in March 1956 when a call came through for her on the youth hostel phone. It was Alan Lomax, now in England, who had tracked her down via her father. The BBC needed someone for a televised version of the play *Dark of the Moon*, specifically someone who could play the five-string banjo, act a bit, and sing 'Barbara Allen'. Lomax told the producer he would dig out the best banjo player in Europe – 'Oh, he was always full of superlatives.' (He actually had something else in mind too, for he was starting a band and her banjo playing would be ideal for it.) He found her in a Danish youth hostel, and over 24 wearying hours later she arrived at Waterloo Station to a reassuring Lomax bear-hug. She was dishevelled and unwashed, with little more than the banjo and the clothes she stood up in. The clothes would have stood up of their own accord. Lomax's then girlfriend was a model, and she sluiced her down and spruced her up, put her long hair up in a lacquered beehive creation, and stood her in unfamiliar high heels. At 10.30 on 25 March 1956 she tottered into Alan Lomax's basement flat in Chelsea, and all heads turned. One head in particular.

CHAPTER 5

Man of Many Parts
From Theatre to Folk Song

A fine documentary play, dealing fearlessly and poetically with the crucial problems of our day ... Marlowe is in the wings ... Why is it being ignored?'

SEAN O'CASEY, THE IRISH PLAYWRIGHT,
ON READING EWAN MACCOLL'S *URANIUM 235* IN 1949

The main objective of the series was to show that Britain possessed a body of songs that were just as vigorous, as tough, and as down-to-earth as anything that could be found in the United States.

EWAN MACCOLL, IN *JOURNEYMAN*,
ON HIS 1953 RADIO SERIES *BALLADS AND BLUES*

MAN OF MANY PARTS – FROM THEATRE TO FOLK SONG

One of the entrepreneurial successes of the immediate post-war period in England was the holiday camp, an opportunity for cheap and cheerful holidays, fresh air and fun, for largely Northern working-class families. At the Butlin's camp in Filey, on the bracing Yorkshire coast, entertainment was laid on in a massive tent – ballroom dancing, music hall variety turns, wrestling. But whether you were a holidaying miner or a visiting *News Chronicle* reporter, the last thing you would be expecting after the wrestling was a radical theatre group playing Lorca, Molière and MacColl.

MacColl? Who was he? And a play about nuclear energy called *Uranium 235*? The reporter there that afternoon in the May of 1946 blinked in disbelief, but went back and described something very different from what he'd imagined, a 'theatrical event of the greatest importance.' The play's name hadn't been announced, which was probably as well, and the packed Butlin's audience took it as it came, as if it was a game of football, as Ewan would say later:

> They cheered, groaned, shouted their approval, and when one of the actors tried to make a planned interruption from the auditorium they howled him down... It was a triumph and a complete vindication of everything we had said about the theatre. A working-class audience could be won for a theatre which concerned itself with the social and political problems of our time ... what was regarded as wildly experimental by theatre buffs and representatives of the theatre establishment was accepted by our Butlin's audience as a perfectly sensible way of doing things. 'And the wonderful bare stage!' enthused our theatre friends. But it wasn't bare to our audience ... If there were moments when they regretted the absence of 'real' sets and stage furniture, there were other things to stimulate the imagination, such as the amplified sound of machines, passing cars, railway trains, explosions, whispering voices, announcements of news items ...

How does the new theatrical voice of Jimmie Miller, reborn as Ewan MacColl after the war, become the voice of the folk singer who Peggy Seeger met in a Chelsea basement ten years after his *Uranium 235* excited an afternoon audience at the seaside? He was still a theatre man through and through – Peggy would see him later that first day performing in the West End in a part that bridged his two worlds, the street singer in Bertolt Brecht's *Threepenny Opera*. But the theatre had been usurped in his affections by an interest long dormant. The British folk song revival was under way, and Ewan would play a crucial part in that national awakening.

After Jimmie Miller absconded from the army in December 1940 he turned up briefly at the home of his parents, where Betsy burned his uniform in the boiler and gave him her blessing, before he moved in with the Theatre Union actress Rosalie Williams. She was alone in a big Victorian house in the Manchester suburb of Urmston, vacated by parents who had gone to the USA. It became the unofficial wartime HQ for the company's dwindling remnants. Jimmie stayed there out of sight, reading as widely as ever and working on adaptations of plays. The German invasion of the Soviet Union in June 1941 soon changed the attitude of the Communist Party to the war and of the British government to the Soviet Union. Joan Littlewood was allowed back into the BBC, earning £10 a week making a series for Geoffrey Bridson (and discovering for herself the arcane art of tape splicing well before Charles Parker did). For Jimmie, though, to emerge after his desertion to fight what was now legitimised as a People's War was too dangerous. So he stayed put.

Understandably perhaps, the *Journeyman* of Jimmie Miller stops in 1939, restarting in 1945 with the birth of Ewan MacColl and of Theatre Workshop. The new group formed again around a Theatre Union nucleus of Joan Littlewood, Ewan MacColl, Rosalie Williams, its future archivist Howard Goorney, and a (necessarily) tireless young business manager, Gerry Raffles. With an uncertain future if he were ever recaptured by the military, probably a spell in prison and a tour of duty abroad, Jimmie Miller grew a startling red beard to go with his dark hair and re-emerged with a new name and a Scots identity. Ewan MacColl is an anglicisation of the name of a famous 19th-century Gaelic poet and songwriter who left his native Perthshire for Canada, Eoghan MacColla. Though the original MacColl translated it as Evan, Ewan is the name of two characters in Lewis Grassic Gibbon's *A Scots Quair* trilogy, a series Jimmie Miller had read avidly (one was a Communist, the other a deserter eventually shot.) You can see the connection, for Ewan, who considered himself another émigré, was always proud of his Scottish parentage. Moreover, the Scots literary scene had a tradition of pseudonyms: indeed, Grassic Gibbon itself was one.

Ewan MacColl and Theatre Workshop

The new Ewan MacColl wasn't finally clear of the old Jimmie Miller until April 1947. After the success of *Uranium 235* was repeated on a Scottish tour in the autumn of 1946, Theatre Workshop settled down to study and rehearse in the palatial surroundings of Ormesby Hall outside Middlesbrough. They were the unlikely guests of an amiable retired colonel, James Pennyman, and his theatre-fixated wife Ruth. Ewan had finished his adaptation of Aristophanes' *Lysistrata* in December 1946 when the military police finally caught up with him. Now what? Joan abandoned plans to accompany the group on a tour of West Germany, and stayed to fight for Ewan's cause for both personal and professional reasons – and to provide moral support for his new love. Ewan had by now fallen for the company's dance teacher Jean Newlove, as had Joan Littlewood for the young and handsome Raffles. Joan and Ewan were nevertheless still collaborating and on good terms – from the very start theirs had been a working partnership more than a domestic one.

Jean was stunned by the turn of events, having been entirely unaware of the threat hanging over him. Joan canvassed sympathetic MPs, and raised money for a psychiatrist. Ewan's court martial was set for 17 February, but was cancelled after the psychiatrist's report confirmed a form of epilepsy. Betsy Miller was convinced her son had 'played it up a treat' and diddled them, but Ewan never spoke or wrote of it, nor of the unpleasant 11 weeks that followed in a grim military hospital. He was at a low enough ebb anyway, in Joan's view genuinely suicidal for a time, and while awaiting the court martial he'd had to cope with his father's final physical disintegration and death. But in early April 1947 he was discharged after nearly four months in prison, and he could finally start his life again free from the fear of capture, if not from the taint of desertion.

Before we whisk Theatre Workshop from its peripatetic beginnings to its eventual home in the other Stratford, let's have a closer look at the startling success of *Uranium 235*. It will underline what <u>didn't</u> happen in British theatre afterwards. As soon as the prolonged war in the Far East had been abruptly terminated after the dropping of two atom bombs on Japan in August 1945, Ewan was persuaded to write a play to explain it all. *Uranium 235* owes its existence to Bill Davidson, an aircraft designer who ambled into a rehearsal one day. His interest was piqued and, given a problem that intrigued him, he designed and built a revolving stage using a novel system of tensioned wires, and stayed for three years. Typical of the brilliant eccentrics that Theatre Workshop attracted in those early days, he went on to fire Ewan's enthusiasm and tutor him on the history of the atom from Democritus to Einstein. Ewan found it hard, but he got there.

For a few weeks the world of the company becomes, in Joan Littlewood's words, 'a mass of electrons, protons and neutrons, and the millions of stars at night mere molecules in a Milky Way.' From that unpromising material Ewan fashions a dizzying two-hour play which Joan directs with her growing verve and assurance. Everyone plays a dozen parts. The first half is billed Democritus to Dalton, with mime, dance sequences, and a Chorus of Alchemists. (Democritus was an Athenian who came up with a remarkably prescient theory of atoms 2400 years ago, Dalton his 19th-century successor. Both thought atoms indestructible.) During the second half, Dalton holds forth at a roll of velvet to represent a lectern, held flat by two assistants squatting on empty air. The 'Release of Energy' becomes a whirling atomic ballet. A morality play interlude has Energy on a leash held by Greed, Lust and Death. A scene with Marie and Pierre Curie seems to Joan at first impossible, but she stages it as a waltz punctuated by verse, until Death slowly dances Pierre away. Bill Davidson plays the Scientist, who invites and answers impromptu questions from the audience.

Actor friends came to see it and were bowled over, and scientists who saw it couldn't fault it. At the end of the launch of the short version with which it opened in Newcastle the stage was besieged by fascinated young people. The Scots poet Hugh MacDiarmid (another Scots pseudonym – he began life as Christopher Grieve) called Ewan 'by far the most promising young dramatist writing in English … at the present time.' *Uranium 235* was later, for the normally hostile *Scotsman* newspaper, 'the only striking event' at Edinburgh's so-called People's Festival in 1951, where Ewan is described as 'the Picasso of Drama'. The festival was inspired by an uninvited trip to Edinburgh that Theatre Workshop had made in 1949, where they had become a much-admired alternative to the new International Festival of the Arts. This People's Festival was a forerunner of the annual Fringe that now transforms Edinburgh into a seething August of live events, outgrowing the international festival it had originally merely fringed. (Now it's peopled by Theatre Workshop's noisy sprawling grandchildren, most of them ignorant of their first illegal immigrant forebears.) In 1952 *Uranium 235* was brought to London by Michael Redgrave and Sam Wanamaker, two of the few Men of the Theatre who bothered with Theatre Workshop. Alan Lomax, just arrived from the USA, watched 'Ewan running through the history of science, leaning on the proscenium arch like Shaw but far more witty.'

The eminent Irish playwright Sean O'Casey enthused about *Uranium 235* when sent a copy of the script (thus he wasn't influenced by the brilliant staging). But his modern Marlowe, 'waiting in the wings', was to stay off-stage, despite a further plaudit from George Bernard Shaw, who called MacColl the only genius working in the theatre of the day – apart from himself. Perhaps it took one prolific polemicist to recognise another. Ewan later felt of his post-war plays that in each of them 'there are moments when the language takes off, comes alive, but they are only moments.' He could write brilliantly at his best, but reviewers not in tune with his politics could find his work heavy going. He had been trying to 'evolve a dramatic utterance which would crystallise, or at least reflect, a certain kind of working-class speech.' In the Radio Ballads he would in due course find that dramatic utterance in the mouths of working people themselves, and discover that for him song was a better vehicle with which to express it.

For eight years after the war Ewan acted as playwright and artistic director for Theatre Workshop, and frequently performed leading roles in their plays. Much of his writing was adaptations of, or new works based on, originals by Aeschylus, Aristophanes, Ben Jonson, Lorca and Molière – he cast his net wide. The endlessly travelling Theatre Workshop troupe had mixed success with these and with his own original plays – *Hell is What you Make it*, *Johnny Noble*, *The Flying Doctor*, *Landscape with Chimneys*, *The Other Animals*, *The Travellers*. The Arts Council, for whom Joan Littlewood reserved her most venomous scorn, simply refused to support them through all their years of touring – it's indicative of its mindset that it gave more to the Covent Garden Opera than to the whole of British Theatre. Theatre Workshop was acclaimed abroad, ignored at home. They were way ahead of anyone in Britain in their use of voice coaching, acting exercises based on Stanislavski, and the movement techniques pioneered by Rudolf Laban. They were creating the theatrical language we now speak. If they'd had greater support, who knows what would have happened to British theatre, and to Ewan.

If they'd had that greater support, they wouldn't have been constantly on the move looking for a new base, touring in places where they often had to perform miracles of improvisation to put on a show at all. The company was threadbare, its members often hungry, exhausted and ill. In the middle of one debilitating Welsh tour the wonderful 'Doc' Thomas took them in hand and doled out antibiotics and vitamin injections between his visits to grievously sick miners. (Ewan used him later in *The Big Hewer*.) In Britain they were helped by a few inspired individuals, but never by institutions. Abroad they were feted by both – though their touring had started inauspiciously in February 1947, with a cold and miserable trek through a still-devastated Germany in that vile winter. This tour was the one disrupted by Ewan's arrest, which to Gerry Raffles' annoyance kept Joan Littlewood in England, so neither of the company's theatrical twin engines were there. Half the company left after their return, and they had to retrench.

Those that stayed toured Czechoslovakia in 1948, a few months after the Communist takeover that February. Not surprisingly, Ewan's plays were always popular behind the Iron Curtain, but it was on the Swedish tour which immediately followed that they had their greatest success. Theatre Workshop played 16 sell-out shows, some in vast theatres, despite the fact that they performed everything in English. But Littlewood productions teemed with life and were visually vivid, so foreign audiences were captivated even when the play's themes provoked fierce debate, as they often did. One critic was amused by a beautifully dressed audience applauding 'Red propaganda'. The newspapers described a packed audience of reserved Swedes stamping with joy, and applauding with 'southern spontaneity':

> The means of expression, rhythm, movement, design of light and shade, the spoken word, all were worked together to create a liberating, expressive whole … The actors are like acrobats … *Johnny Noble* gripped the audience … concluded with an ovation. [They filled the 1200-seat Opera House in Stockholm, where] the storm of applause was fully justified … use of light is especially important, use of sound is wonderful, full of nuance … The performance has a richness and film-like quality.

So it was all the more galling, after they returned glutted with praise, to find the burghers of Little England still content with drawing-room comedy viewed through a proscenium arch, and the small target working-class audiences were rarely as excited as the Butlin's holidaymakers had been. It's a tragedy that, commonplace as it is to us now over 60 years later, the Theatre Workshop style took years to catch on. It wasn't until the late 1950s that their brand of theatre reached the populace at large – and the critics. That was long after the wandering Theatre Workshop of Butlin's and a trail of less welcoming venues had, after a fierce debate, found a permanent home in the run-down East End of London. The successes of Brendan Behan's *The Quare Fellow* and *The Hostage* were quickly followed by that of the 18-year-old Shelagh Delany's *A Taste of Honey* and Frank Norman's *Fings Ain't Wot They Used T'Be*. They were all new plays. The conventional wisdom today is that it was John Osborne's *Look Back in Anger* that revitalised the stagnant British theatre, and the Royal Court that began to foster new British writing. But in truth its roots lay in the Theatre Workshop and their hard years after the war.

The company had settled, like weary Travellers, at the Theatre Royal 'and Palace of Varieties' in Angel Lane at Stratford-atte-Bowe. Theatre and location sound exotic, but both were seriously run-down, as far as could be from the Stratford of Shakespeare. To Ewan MacColl, though, whose involvement had steadily reduced after they found a permanent home, they had been obliged to water down their heady brew to earn the approbation of the West End critics and theatre managements. The theatre hadn't captured his working-class audience – it was at home watching television. It would not be until the late 1960s that imaginative political and community theatre picked up where the early Theatre Workshop left off.

Ewan's disillusion isn't at all surprising. Although touring was exhausting, he still felt that their aim should be to take theatre to working people all over the country, so he was against its settlement in a London of which he was still suspicious. Gradually, for he hadn't stopped writing for them, he drifted away with little lasting rancour, though Joan was saddened and thought him a fool:

> One day ... [our] prime mover, inspiration, Daddy o't, walked out, quit, buggered off ... Theatre Workshop had been his life, his inspiration, his pride and joy, the vehicle for all his plays. Whether improvised in the back of a lorry or on some God-forsaken railway station, Jimmie's songs had always lifted our spirits.

It would gall him later that the eventual success came to 'Joan Littlewood's' Theatre Workshop. After 20 years at the heart of the movement his name had been quietly expunged from the record. (Given this, his sensitivity in later years to the expression 'Charles Parker's Radio Ballads' is hardly a surprise.) He came down to London with them, still supported them, adapting plays and putting on fund-raising concerts for the cash-strapped company, which for years remained solely dependent on box office receipts until 1955, when a few minuscule grants arrived. Jean Newlove would remain the company's choreographer for years. They had married in April 1949, and in July 1950

Hamish was born. A child changes perspectives, and Ewan was besotted with him. For Ewan too, it was undoubtedly his discovery that people would pay to hear him sing that weakened his enthusiasm for Theatre Workshop. Enter the folk singer.

The Folk Singer

In a BBC studio in February 1951 sits a larger-than-life figure, born in January 1915, womaniser, enthusiast, hugely knowledgeable, a man who 'gorges himself on ideas, concepts, systems, philosophies.' With him is Ewan MacColl. Ewan is not often swept off his feet by a man – he is just as likely to see him as a rival – but on this occasion he is taken by storm. Alan Lomax, an older but no less energetic version of the young man who collaborated with Peggy Seeger's mother before the war, has become an expert on folk music and much else besides. To Ewan this enormous Texan 'is big but not gigantic. The illusion of size is the result of his expansiveness and the warmth he generates. At times he gives the impression that he is expanding in front of your eyes.'

They hit it off instantly. Lomax described Ewan in turn as someone who could take an idea new to him, talk eloquently about it non-stop for half an hour, and emerge with a complete philosophy of a subject that he had known little about. His comment was less a criticism than admiration, and they were invigorated by each other's intellect and energy, and empathy with working people. Lomax had been recording American source singers in the field, and the recording process worked its magic on him:

> Every time I took one of those big, black, glass-based platters out of its box I felt that a magical moment was opening up in time ... For me, the black discs spinning in the Mississippi night, spitting the chip centripetally toward the center of the table ... heralded a new age of writing human history.

As well as being an indefatigable field recorder, he was an experienced and innovative radio programme maker. As early as 1941 Lomax had made a novel programme about a Tennessee valley about to be flooded for a dam, in which he recorded a local farmer talking to his friends, in a way that would anticipate Charles Parker and Ewan:

> For several days I let him do all the talking and make all the decisions about where we were to go and whom we were to talk to. Whenever he said anything that was particularly memorable, which I was unable to record, I tried later on to reproduce the circumstances of the statement, and to record it with the same emotion as he had originally.

Lomax's ability to help people be themselves in front of a microphone had deeply impressed Geoffrey Bridson, who described him as having a 'zest for living' and for his work. 'I never knew any American who more fully embodied the virtues – and the more engaging vices – of all his countrymen.' Later in the war Lomax produced *The Martins and the Coys*, a family rivalry piece with music by Burl Ives, Woody Guthrie and Pete Seeger, which found its way to British radio in wartime Manchester. It very much influenced Ewan's *Johnny Noble*.

After nearly two decades collecting folk songs in the USA, Lomax crossed the Atlantic with a new recorder he'd bought with the proceeds from the Weavers' first hit, whose copyright he shared with Leadbelly. 'In 1950 I set sail for Europe with a new Magnecord tape machine in my cabin and the folk music of the world my destination.' Lomax had blagged his way to a contract with Columbia to produce a 40-disc anthology of world music. It took eight years to produce just 18, but it was a landmark. It had the useful by-product of getting him out of McCarthy's firing line – anyone with anything to do with folk music was a prime target for his committee. The Weavers were by now in its sights. Ironically, Senator Joe McCarthy was thus in part responsible for the British folk revival.

Lomax tracked Ewan down after hearing of his fund of Scottish folk songs, and immediately began recording him. In the Durham town of Tow Law, as they rigged the night's set, he entranced the Theatre Workshop company by singing American folk songs, ballads and blues, chants and hollers, all collected in prison camp and workplace. This was compelling, and Ewan was hooked, spending much of the year debating with Lomax and listening to his massive music collection. Ewan was now meeting more people from outside the theatre. Through Lomax he met the Irish collector Seamus Ennis, met again Hamish Henderson, the Scottish folk song collector, and – eventually – one Albert Lancaster Lloyd.

AL Lloyd, or Bert Lloyd – or AL Bert, or AL Lewd as the fancy took him – was a journalist, writer and translator, a fellow Communist, and a friend of Peggy Seeger's father. He had picked up songs in outback Australia over several years, and had even signed on in a whaler, so his sea songs had the tang of authenticity. A 'walking toby jug', in Ewan's words, like him self-educated, an outstanding linguist with a remarkable ability to absorb new languages, it was he who had translated *Blood Wedding*, a play by Lorca that Littlewood planned to stage. Lloyd had been researching English folk song since before the war. As they had so much in common it was rather odd that he and Ewan had never met, but Lomax made sure they did, and their animated impromptu songfest outside the Theatre Royal, Stratford East, was only ended when a policeman moved them on. The debate continued across the months – Ewan 'believed from the outset there was a strong correlation between language and music. Bert wasn't convinced, but was eventually converted.'

Since before the war Bert Lloyd had been interested in working men's songs, and was now compiling a book of songs from coal miners, Come All Ye Bold Miners. In 1947 he had selected the songs for a Bridson radio programme, Johnny Miner (though the songs had original settings by the Hungarian émigré Matyas Seiber and weren't sung by folk singers). Bridson had to steer it through the flak from coal owners fighting the industry's nationalisation. There were far more mining songs than Ewan had realised, though he was able to contribute a few he knew. Alan Lomax was excited by the idea of a British folk song revival, seeing the 'waulking' song – a traditional Hebridean work song form, sung while women prepared tweed cloth – as an underlying form as powerful as the Blues. The combination of the two ideas of traditional and urban song was a potent mix for Ewan. Here was a form that was still living, and deeply imbued with the rhythms of working-class speech, a working man's culture that was lying hidden and waiting to be dug up. A seam was there to be mined, and Ewan and Bert took pick and shovel to it.

Ewan sang with Bert Lloyd at union meetings all over London, in an unprecedented but ultimately unsuccessful attempt to engage the leaders of the working class with their patrimony of song. But the unions had other preoccupations and, moreover, in Ewan's later view, they approached them several years too early – it had needed to come during the folk song revival, not before it could begin. The radio was a more fertile field. He had managed to get work for the BBC again in Manchester since 1948, a useful sideline in Children's Radio that allowed him to have fun creating new voices, not explicitly 'Northern' this time. Animals mostly, whose regional accents hadn't yet been pored over by anthropologists.

In 1953, however, he was allowed back on grown-up radio, with a series of six Saturday morning programmes with Alan Lomax exploring the roots of folk song in the English language. Produced by Denis Mitchell, *Ballads and Blues* was a breakthrough, reaching an eager audience and reaping a rich postbag. Ewan was even allowed on television (after an internal BBC argument) on Lomax's *Song Hunter* series. For one programme Lomax flew down twenty Hebridean women to illustrate the waulking song – testing the nerve and budget of its young producer, one David Attenborough. *Ballads and Blues* introduced Ewan to a gallery of musicians and contacts he'd use over the next 20 years: members of Humphrey Lyttleton's band, the Theatre Workshop graduate Isla Cameron and Seamus Ennis, as well as Alan Lomax and the old blues singer Big Bill Broonzy. The programmes didn't attract a particularly wide audience, but they enthused a generation of potential young singers. A key message for them to take away was that the British Isles had just as much traditional song as America for them to learn.

September 1953 was perhaps a pivotal moment. Ewan was in Edinburgh with Theatre Workshop, where the previous year they'd mounted an imaginative and well-reviewed production of his latest play, *The Travellers*. A driving political thriller set on a train hurtling across Europe to war, peopled with passengers of many nationalities and attitudes, its staging problems were solved by constructing the train down the main aisle of the auditorium, with the audience on raked seats at either side. Not the kind of thing you'd normally see in 1952. From that high point his play-writing energies began to wane. A year after the success of The Travellers, in the same Edinburgh venue he launched a series of Scottish traditional songs he had been working on for a Workers' Musical Association (WMA) anthology. It was a tour de force, a masterly unaccompanied solo concert, lasting three hours before a spellbound audience.

Here was an intellectually satisfying quest, and with it the emotional charge brought by an enthusiastic live audience. And he was brilliant at it. With Bert Lloyd, Isla Cameron, the guitarist Fitzroy Coleman, the jazz clarinet and saxophone player Bruce Turner, and the (actually the only) English concertina player Alf Edwards, he performed with increasing frequency. This loose 'Ballads and Blues' group performed a sell-out benefit concert for the Daily Worker in July 1954 at the new Royal Festival Hall on the South Bank. He described it as 'a fantastic success, and that's what launched the folk revival as far as the left wing were concerned. They didn't really understand it, mind.'

On the same bill was Ken Colyer's band. Colyer, according to Ewan, was the first to see the link between the blues and English folk music, which he loved though he never played it. He unwittingly pioneered the 'skiffle' craze in the intervals of his concerts, triggering a two-year explosion of interest in getting up and performing on instruments, often home-made, a trend of which Ewan approved. After all, working people were taking to a form of folk music. He hadn't yet met the woman who would listen incredulously when she first heard her very own Libba Cotten's Freight Train sung by Lonnie Donegan. How could he do that to it?

Ewan and Peggy

Early in 1956, at the time Donegan's version of the chain gang song 'Rock Island Line' entered the charts, Ewan – now almost a full-time singer and songwriter – was making a rare acting appearance in the West End. It was during the run that Ewan met Peggy Seeger, coiffed and made up by an expert, in Alan Lomax's basement flat in Chelsea. Peggy could barely see the man in the opposite corner for cigarette smoke. Her features, though, were clear enough to him. There was to be no Dark of the Moon – the play she had been summoned for had been cancelled – but instead a rehearsal for a new folk group that Lomax was forming, to be called The Ramblers. Banjo flying, she launched into 'The House Carpenter', and earned a smattering of applause, though not from Ewan, who sat leaning on his elbow in the opposite corner, chain smoking and regarding her intently. They were both now Ramblers. They talked, he offered her a complimentary ticket to watch him at the theatre. 'Complimentary anything, that was me. I had no money and was interested in everything.' That night she turned up at the theatre in her workaday clobber, hair tousled. His picture of her underwent an instant revision, but he became increasingly obsessed by her.

Ewan was appearing as the (definitive) street singer in the British premiere of Bertolt Brecht's *Threepenny Opera*. Directed by the American anglophile Sam Wanamaker (later to be the driving force behind the rebuilding of Shakespeare's Globe Theatre) and including Warren Mitchell in its cast, it had been a landmark production for the Royal Court theatre. It ran for several months at three venues, and had moved to the Comedy when Peggy saw it. 'I'd never been in that kind of theatre – plush seats, goodies being sold during the intervals, dressed-up people. Well, up goes the curtain and this beery, leery old man starts the show singing. What a lovely voice! I was entranced.'

O the shark has pretty teeth dear,
And he keeps them pearly white,
Just a jack-knife has MacHeath, dear,
And he keeps it out of sight.

'Then I realised it was Ewan, with his belly poking out and togged out in a torn shirt, a filthy stovepipe hat and ragged jacket! I was appalled at how such a change could be wreaked.' They met backstage, had a drink, and as he drove her back to the cheap room in Chelsea she'd rented he began to lay siege to her. She was flattered, intrigued, but a married man twice her age with a child? A shark with pretty teeth but nicotine-stained fingers? There was no way she was going to fall, she told herself. Yes, well.

The Ramblers were based in Manchester, making a six-part series for Granada television in the summer of 1956, and hoping to be Britain's answer to The Weavers. Their first broadcast took place the night before Peggy's 21st birthday. The long train journeys there and back each weekend gave Ewan and Peggy ample opportunity to talk and talk, and she too was in a whirl: 'Ewan and I courted all the way up and all the way back every week for 11 weeks.' Alan Lomax was in precisely the same state (and same age gap) with a young singer from Sussex, Shirley Collins, who was the other female singer in the group. With Ewan MacColl and Bert Lloyd, Fitzroy Coleman, Bruce Turner, the bass player Jim Bray, the session guitarist Bryan Daly, and a Nigerian drummer, they formed a ten-piece band. The line-up looks stuffed with brilliance to a modern eye, but it was over-rich, and Lomax's bluff American hoedown introductions set the tone. Considering his later interdict against those who sang outside their own tradition in his club, Ewan would have cringed at the American songs he sang (he even recorded the Merle Travis hit 'Sixteen Tons' that year). Peggy got a hay fever reaction to the straw bales that littered the set, and all in all, as she said, 'we didn't deserve to succeed, and we didn't.'

Peggy and Ewan became lovers. Jean found out, and there began a fraught period of nearly three years when neither woman could be sure which of them Ewan – 'frustration, exhilaration and guilt were my constant companions' – would eventually settle with. In late 1956 Peggy escaped from an increasingly untenable situation by taking a boat back to the USA, running the gauntlet of fierce Atlantic gales – 'the sickest I have ever been, and the longest I have ever been so sick.' Diverted to St John's Newfoundland by a strike in New York, she arrived on Christmas Eve 1956 to be met by customs officials who spent hours opening her suitcases, instruments – and motor scooter. After that it got better. While staying in California with her father, she made some radio appearances and secured an engagement in Chicago. Collecting her scooter from Philadelphia, she piled it high with suitcases and instruments, hit the road, and was swept along bare-headed in the slipstream of giant trucks. When the police stopped her she discovered that a car licence didn't allow her to ride a scooter, and that she was required to take their test there and then. This was a cinch for someone used to rush-hour London, and she wowed them by weaving her scooter and its teetering load expertly through their obstacle course. Now helmeted, she completed her 900-mile journey.

At a Chicago dive called the Gates of Horn owned by Albert Grossman, later to be the manager of Bob Dylan, she performed around midnight for three months, sharing the bill with Big Bill Broonzy. He was wonderful on stage, she said, and off it he sat in the bar with glasses of brandy which he drank neat, one after the other. As well as American folk songs she sang 'The First Time Ever', which Ewan had composed over the phone to her when she was in California and had needed a love song to sing on a radio show the following night. It's a song totally uncharacteristic of him back then. It describes how he felt at that first meeting, and he would never sing the song on stage. It was written for her, though it was others who would popularise it later. Ironically, as she said, she had not actually felt this way herself at that first meeting ...

> The first time ever I saw your face
> I thought the sun rose in your eyes,
> And the moon and the stars were the gifts you gave
> To the dark and empty skies my love,
> To the dark and empty skies.

CHAPTER 6

Riding the Engine
The Ballad of John Axon

Last week a technique and a subject got married, and nothing in radio kaleidoscopy, or whatever you care to call it, will ever be the same again. This was music with a purpose: its picture of a morning in winter, a family and friends, things to look forward to, a train, a broken brake, and a man staying on to die, was sharp and strange and powerful … Anecdote turned into song, song turned into the hiss of steam. It didn't, presumably couldn't, keep still for a minute.

PAUL FERRIS, THE OBSERVER, 1958

I broke in to the BBC in Broad Street every night at half past twelve when the night shift went on, took over the three tape machines there, and edited the programme till seven in the morning for about two months, when I did finally get it together, and was only rumbled on the last day, luckily.

CHARLES PARKER, INTERVIEWED BY TREVOR FISHER, 1971

Hugh Carleton-Greene, Director-General of the BBC through the 1960s, called *The Ballad of John Axon* 'the most originally conceived, the most brilliantly executed and the most moving radio programme I've ever heard.' In fact, it didn't turn out as originally conceived, it was executed after months of hard labour, and the BBC very nearly didn't broadcast it at all. When Charles Parker wrote to Ewan MacColl in July 1957 he had in his mind's ear a 1944 programme, part of a 26-week series produced by the legendary radio journalist Norman Corwin for CBS. Written by Millard Lampell and Earl Robinson, the writer of the song 'Joe Hill', and narrated in song by Burl Ives, it told the story of Abraham Lincoln's funeral train. Charles had wept when he first heard it.

> A lonesome train on a lonesome track,
> Seven coaches painted black.

Charles writes that the idea is still 'very much in embryo', but wants to sound Ewan out because it clearly hinges on his participation. We could have a British equivalent of *Lonesome Train*, he tells him, 'drawing its strengths from the tradition and pride of the railwayman, and from the work songs, of which [you are] such a master.' He envisages a shape built around the last journey of John Axon, giving a reiterated 'bass tune' of the doomed goods train working up to the climax, out of which he anticipates flashbacks into the dead man's life. From meetings with Axon's workmates they could create 'impressionistic dramatic vignettes to build up the character of the man.' He goes on to praise the music Ewan had written and performed for Denis Mitchell's recent television programme *Night in the City*. Mitchell is the radio producer who had made Ewan's *Ballads and Blues* series: he had since defected to television.

Charles clearly sees Ewan's participation as crucial, but flattery isn't necessary. In his reply Ewan is eager at the prospect of working on that kind of programme, and points out that he has already collected some old English railway songs with a 'somewhat vague notion of writing a ballad-opera on the subject', which could provide useful raw material. He won't, though, be able to start on it straight away. He's off to Moscow for five weeks with Jean (and Peggy…) and isn't due back till 25 August.

His support galvanises Charles, who replies immediately. Although he's tied up with a couple of programmes himself, he hopes to meet Axon's widow Gladys early in August to get her agreement, which is vital. He then goes on: 'Depending on the actuality characters themselves [BBC-speak for the real railwaymen] I am toying with the idea of using actuality recordings for the flash back sequences with yourself as the link between them and the dramatico-musical evocation of the goods train, but it will have to be actuality well up to Denis's standards before this could begin to work.' Denis

Mitchell has used 'actuality' impressively in his programmes, and Charles wants to try it here. So Charles at the outset has a pretty clear idea of the kind of programme he wants to make, in particular using actuality where he can, as well as actors.

A fortnight after the initial letter Charles interviews Gladys Axon with enough sensitivity that she agrees to the programme. He excitedly despatches a series of interview transcripts to Ewan, and meets him in London at the end of August. Two weeks later he formally commissions Ewan to 'compose and arrange music and lyrics for a railway ballad.' At the moment, he tells his BBC superiors, the programme is conceived as a 30-minute musical radio ballad of a somewhat unusual form, possibly involving a small amount of actuality (he knew they'd be nervous about actuality), but consisting largely of music and musical effects in a modern folk song idiom. Estimating 20–25 minutes of music, he suggests an initial fee for Ewan of 100 guineas, for at least two weeks' location research and four weeks of composition and experimental arrangement, with a specially recruited ensemble. No mention of Peggy at all, for she hadn't come back from Moscow. (In fact Ewan had fallen out with her there when she sang rousing American religious rather than political songs. She'd gone on to China against the 'advice' of the State department, and then to perform in Poland, where she said she nearly died of pneumonia, alone and freezing in a student dormitory. In effect it was an international crash course after her cloistered childhood.)

The decks cleared, the necessary footplate and guards' passes issued, Ewan and Charles arrange to go to Stockport late in October. In the run-up Charles sets himself to learn more about folk music, discovering that he can go to folk and jazz clubs virtually every night of the week in Birmingham. He writes to Ewan cadging a bed for the night after an event in London, and asks him for records of guitar technique. And for several days he's on a high, recording some 'very exciting actuality' from an old traveller in Wisbech, an ex-prize fighter with a 'wonderful sense of timing and instinctive feeling for words: "He hit me and the blood came into my mouth like liver – I was spitting it out in lumps".' Charles signs off 'Ha, life is good.'

At Edgeley railway sheds they enjoy themselves hugely. For someone like Charles in that era, a romantic about steam and mad about sound, the chance to mess about on and around trains seems to have brought out the small boy in him. Having budgeted for three or four days, they spend a fortnight there. Charles records every clank and hiss and whistle. Ewan recalls them recording on the footplate of a night goods train, bouncing up and down. until they had to change tapes – when if they were not careful they would have tape reeling out in the wind behind them. They take a room above a pub in Edgeley and interview the railwaymen there. They track workers through Edgeley railway yards for ten days till the men were 'absolutely sick' of them. Later Charles remembers vividly the moment he is knocked out by the words of the engine driver, about 'railways going through the back of the spine like Blackpool goes through rock.' He stays up after Ewan has returned, recording the Axon family among others, and discovering an earlier accident which Mrs Axon 'is anxious shouldn't be mentioned ... There's something especially terrifying about a locomotive collision. The sort of look they had in their eyes is the sort of look one sees in returning prisoners of war.'

Ewan took the 40 hours of actuality and set to work on it night and day. It wasn't going to be easy, and he was so amazed with it that he realised that he'd have to try a completely different approach. As he says in *Journeyman*:

> In that railway shed ... it was dark and gloomy, there was the constant hiss of steam ... and the great shuddering noises of the big steam locomotives starting in, and getting steam up. There was also a fair amount of shouting went on, so I began to see that the problem was a much bigger one than I had originally envisaged ... Previously, in any work I'd done for radio ... the way of using the material was merely to interrupt the programme at certain points and have the narrator sing [but] the impact of this great mass of material was staggering, and it was immediately apparent that what we had got in the can was a unique picture of a way of life, told in words which were themselves charged with the special kind of vitality which derives from involvement with a work process. Furthermore, it seemed to us that the railwayman's speech was full of the same kinds of symbols and verbal nuances which inform the ballads and folk songs of our tradition, and it was obvious that we could not rewrite it without reducing and falsifying it.

This was even better than they'd hoped, and from then on reliance on the richness of voices of working men and women became their creed. Combining the need to tell the story with the desire to have the best of the voices they'd collected, a pretty daunting task in itself, Ewan set to on the songs, and wrote them in ten days. Each was an 'extension of the actuality or a framework for it.' But he was disappointed by his rough assembly: 'I can still remember the feeling of excited anticipation when I pressed the playback switch on my Ferrograph. The excitement gave way to dismay. The programme in my head and the one on the tape were so far apart that I almost abandoned the project there and then.'

By his own admission he was floundering when it came to orchestration – all he knew was that he wanted a driving banjo to signify the train – until he was rescued when Peggy arrived back from Europe after Christmas. She was supposed to have participated in *Sing Christmas and the Turn of the Year*, an ambitious live countrywide recording on Christmas morning put together by Alan Lomax and produced by Charles, but she hadn't made it in time. Once back, she got a grip on the John Axon material, 'transforming it into a smoothly flowing whole', all carefully timed apart from some sections to be improvised, and the final version took shape. In fact her first mention in the correspondence is not until well after the recordings, when Charles has to badger for £35 for her contribution. She hadn't been signed up originally. Charles had already secured an extra 50 guineas for Ewan. (Weren't women worth guineas?)

When Charles first saw what Ewan had produced his reaction was 'What do you expect me to do with this?' He was expecting a normal script of 30–40 pages. What he got was nine pages of foolscap, with cue numbers for the voices and effects rather than the complete actuality. For a while he got cold feet, and no wonder. He had intended to use raw actuality, certainly, but this much? And some of Ewan's extracts were so short he worried whether they'd register on the listener's ear. But he was soon tremendously excited:

> For the first time you were telling a story without a narrator and without actors coming in, and being able to tell a story by context. After the crash ... you have simply some chords on the guitar, another verse of the ballad and then the entry of his fireman, saying it was still dark when they got to the shed that Sunday morning, and you realise it works. It works!

He got to work on splicing together the actuality around which they could build the music in the studio. But he soon realised what a huge task it was, aggravated by unexpected difficulties with variable recording speeds. He only had two days available for editing, explaining: 'It was half-cut, I mean, we only got about one third of the sequences edited crudely by the time we went into the studio ... I didn't get any sleep for about seven days, seven nights, you know ... [I created] a furore there by sleeping in the Red Cross room, never been heard of before ... If I'd slept with the Director General's wife I'd have been better received.' Nevertheless they were ready to rehearse in London in late January, shuttling between a studio and St Hilda's church in Maida Vale, where after a day's break they recorded the music component of the programme in two days, 26–27 January 1958.

Unlike the method they'd develop for the six final Radio Ballad programmes, the musicians and singers recorded 'blind' – they couldn't hear the recorded voices and sound effects they were playing over and between. Moreover, they behaved as jobbing musicians – there was little sense yet of a musical team. One of the instrumentalists from that programme, still alive in 2008, the fiddler Bob Clark, who had been to Moscow with Ewan, recorded his contribution totally unaware until two weeks later that Jim Bray had also been recording for *John Axon* – despite the fact that the pair of them roomed together in Soho. The double bass player Bray was to become a key part of the Radio Ballad ensemble, but it was Clark's only appearance before he went off round the world with a jazz trio to play on cruise ships.

Peggy laughed ruefully when she recalled her first stab at orchestration. 'Although I'd had some musical training at college … and I could transcribe anything, it was the first time I'd ever scripted for real.' Still only 22, she acquired a copy of a Henry Mancini book on composing and gave herself a crash course. She says she learned a vast amount on that original Radio Ballad. Her first orchestration draft took in only the songs themselves. 'Charles understood that the instrumentation I did was not enough. Every now and then he'd say we need a little twiddle here – Give us something, Bruce.' He realised they'd need occasional musical 'colour' as mood setting, behind a voice, or as a link. Only Alf Edwards, brilliant player of his array of concertinas and ocarinas, couldn't improvise, though he could 'write music as fast as anyone else could write English': he had a sheet music business. For the rest – particularly Bruce Turner on saxophone and clarinet, for whom she hardly needed to write out anything – improvisation was natural, as it was for Peggy herself on banjo and guitar.

As well as the musicians and Ewan, they had Bert Lloyd, whose voice, workaday but atmospheric, stood for the ordinary railwayman. For Fitzroy Coleman, an exquisite guitarist and singer from Trinidad, Ewan wrote an engine fireman's calypso in perfect idiom:

> Got me paddle iron, that's a ten foot spoon,
> Got me pricker and me dart like a long harpoon,
> Mama, I tell you positive,
> Going to serve me steam locomotive.

Stan Kelly-Bootle, an early computer pioneer and polymath, on his only Radio Ballad performance, sang 'Manchester Rambler', written when Ewan was 17. Another pre-written song, 'The Fireman's Not For Me', was given with some new verses to Isla Cameron, who had joined Theatre Workshop as a 16-year-old in the 1940s. It was the sole song for a woman, a piece spiced with innuendo about an engine driver who loved his engine more than her:

> He said my dear Molly 'Oh won't you be mine –
> Just give me the signal and let's clear the line.
> My fires they are burning, my steam it is high –
> If you don't take the brake off I think I shall die.'

Extra singers were brought in to complete a chorus line-up, including the roistering and unreliable Dominic Behan, before Ewan sacked him. They bashed out work songs, Ewan insisting that they mime shovelling coal as they did so:

RIDING THE ENGINE – THE BALLAD OF JOHN AXON

> Put your weight behind your shovel.
> From your middle swing.
> Swing your steel-bladed shovel!
> From your shoulders swing.

This is sung at a tempo that mimics the slow initial motion of the train. As the speed builds, the chorus quickens and the pace changes to the rocking rhythm of the train in full motion, written by a man who has made sure he, too, sweated on the footplate, shovelling that coal.

> Sweat on your back,
> Sweat in your eyes,
> Feed the fire,
> The steam'll rise.
> Bend and thrust,
> Twist and turn,
> There's nine tons of coal to burn.
> Breathing steam,
> Swallowing coal,
> Brace your legs to take the roll.

The thrust of the storyline is carried by Ewan's voice. He had the theatrical intelligence to know that he could maintain and build the tension despite telling the audience the ending right at the beginning, as the old ballads often did:

> John Axon was a railway man, to steam trains born and bred,
> He was an engine driver at Edgeley loco shed,
> For forty years he followed and served the iron way,
> He lost his life upon the track one February day.

There follows a spectacular 30-second crash. No suspense there, then. When Charles Parker first played out Ewan's concept with the tapes he doubted whether the programme could be carried without a narrator. But, through a series of scene-setting diversions – life in the railway yard as a spoken and sung recitative, the long years as a driver's fireman shovelling that coal, off on the Derbyshire hills where he met his wife – Ewan gradually returns us to that routine Saturday morning in February, and the minor irritation of a leaking steam brake pipe. A wait while the fitter fixes it, and the long slow haul at walking speed up to Bibbington Top, on a bright crisp morning. Then all hell breaks loose when the pipe fractures, as scalding steam fills the cab. They can't reach the driver's 'regulator' to close it down even with coats over their heads and a fire iron to reach it. 'You only had to put your face anywhere near and it would peel like an onion', says Ron Scanlon the fireman. Axon orders him to jump off, try to pin enough of the brakes down on the 33 loaded wagons to stop the train before the top of the hill (a forlorn hope with such an archaic and dangerous system) and warn the guard at the back. The last Ron sees is the train disappearing over the top and down the stretch to Chapel en le Frith, a little under three miles, over which the train will inexorably gather pace.

MacColl's voice and the music ratchet up the tension as the story unreels, and takes us down that doomed descent with Axon spreadeagled outside the cab. In the final section MacColl tries to recreate Axon's last thoughts, declaiming against the sound of the thundering train and a wailing trumpet:

All alone now. Ron's gone. On my own now, all the way, all the way.
Never make it. How far's all the way?
There's a gradient all the way into Whaley.
Seven mile gradient. One in seventy. One in sixty. One in fifty eight. WAIT!

Dove Holes passed.
Going too fast to see if they saw me hanging outside the cab.
Down the curving line, through the hill of limestone, Eaves Tunnel.

Was I born for this? To hang like a fly on an iron ball.
Helpless, on a moving wall.
To die, to end, in a welter of blood and oil. Twisted metal, splintered bone.

That twisted metal and splintered bone we can imagine all too easily in the climactic crash that follows. Ending the programme are the framing tones of the BBC announcer reading the letter to Gladys Axon that confirms the Queen's assent to her husband's George Cross. It guarantees we have a lump in the throat.

With the raw programme in the can Charles came back to Birmingham with a stack of about 30 tapes – music, railwaymen's voices, and sound effects – made incompatible by variable recording speeds, even on the Maida Vale machines, which had somehow got out of sync. He saw his great new concept crashing with his career in a mass of twisted tape: 'Then I had the problem of assembling the programme and it was just going to be impossible to do this in the normal facilities of studio time – normal nine-to-five working day, so…' He knew the night security man wouldn't give him away, but if caught he knew he risked the sack. 'Probably if the programme hadn't been finally successful, I would have been sacked.'

Charles had rescued the programme ultimately by speeding up and slowing down the editing machine <u>manually</u> at key moments. Down in London, Alan Ward, a radio engineer who would soon enter the story, remembers being told of 'this mad red-bearded producer in Birmingham who cut up recording tape and suspended it in his office from a washing line.' Nobody did that sort of thing. In the BBC tape was still intended as a more convenient replacement for acetate discs which deteriorated rapidly at each replay, not to be cut and spliced on <u>that</u> scale. It was, well, cheating.

When Charles was able to cut a demo tape to play to colleagues in the BBC, the response was lukewarm at best and hostile at worst. Nearly two months after the programme was recorded, the feature writer Sasha Moorsom writes in an internal review that 'the thread of the story is sometimes lost in the songs and background actuality.' That their density and construction required an unusually intense concentration was a constant theme in early responses to the Radio Ballads, one that was echoed in the audience research comments. You were either absolutely spellbound or you couldn't be bothered. The underlying problem, for listeners used to a story simply told from start to finish, lies in Ewan's espousal of the 'ballad form' in his construction. In a sung ballad, you don't tell the story straight out, but jump between present and past, dialogue and narrative, switch tenses, swap viewpoints. At worst it's a maddening jumble, at best it's brilliantly illuminating. Films have increasingly done it in recent years, but it was unfamiliar then.

One who couldn't stand it was the head of the Light Programme, George Camacho, who 'execrated' it, said Charles later: 'He described it as technique run riot.' And although Charles was supported 'through thick and thin' by the head of the Home Service, Ronald Lewin, and by Laurence Gilliam, the Head of Features in London, the piece was disliked by the producers in Gilliam's Features team. Gilliam wanted the name changed to The John Axon Story, and Charles had to fight to keep the word 'Ballad' on the card. 'One of these ridiculous things was this gulf between the London Features department, who were then sort of the aristocrats of the business, and … the regions … so I was very unpopular.'

On 22 March his script labelled 'final transmission tape as edited' ran to 40 seconds under an hour. It was no longer a 30-minute programme. But it wasn't final, and it wouldn't stay at an hour either. In this period the BBC pressed the Foreign Office successfully for Peggy, whose visa was about to run out, to secure just a month's extension to work on the changes needed to get it down to 45 minutes. (The recorded Topic version you can hear is the original hour.) It wasn't until 10 pm on 2 July 1957, over five months after the recording, that the 45-minute version of *John Axon* was broadcast on the Home Service, as Radio 4's predecessor was then called. A letter from Charles's fellow producer Douglas Cleverdon after the broadcast hints at what he must have gone through: 'I trust that this will be some slight salve for the lacerations that you endured so patiently at our hands.' He refers to the news that the BBC has chosen *The Ballad of John Axon* to be its entry for the Italia Prize of 1958, the prestigious award for European radio documentaries. The pain was worth it: the forced revision exercise was probably essential in enabling Charles to stand back from the results of his editing efforts and hear it as others did.

The press reaction was immediate and congratulatory. Those were the days when radio reviews received as much prominence as television, with column inches to match. Paul Ferris in the *Observer* gave it the review quoted at the chapter head, which continues: 'Ewan MacColl's words and music were enriched by the fragments of flat thin voice from the fireman and the quiet voice of Mrs Axon ... It was a brilliant success for the producer Charles Parker.' Later Ferris would say in his end-of-year review: 'For pure radio and pure pleasure in 1958, this was far and away the best piece of original writing and production. It was a new dimension, and there was nothing else quite like it all year.' Another plaudit came from Robert Robinson in the *Sunday Times*:

> As remarkable a piece of radio as I have ever listened to. It was not only skilful, it was honest ... The total effect was overwhelmingly convincing ... truthful as documentary, truthful as art ... One criticism – the tradition in which the ballad was sung seemed to be of American provenance ... at variance with the voices of singers and railwaymen. But I will not carp ... It worked, and worked magnificently. I congratulate all concerned.

This criticism of 'American influence' was taken on board by Ewan, but as Peggy said later: 'There <u>was</u> no English traditional music being played back then. It was all in dusty tomes in the British Library. That came later.' 'WLW' in the *Manchester Guardian* said this:

> The great danger of 'experimental' radio is that the experimenters may be so proudly intrigued with their new technique that the result for the audience is all elaborate means and no end. After the first ten minutes of John Axon one had one's doubts – too much seemed to be happening in too short a time. But as the story gathered speed and rattled on to its tremendous catastrophe the pulse caught up with the pounding rhythm and the mind caught on to what Ewan MacColl and Charles Parker had been driving at – something like the experience a drowning man is supposed to undergo in his last minutes ...

The other aim of the writers was to honour a hero of the people and the tradition of service out of which his heroism grew, and to do this in something like the idiom of the people, through a series of ballads and a curiously effective sort of recitative with folky overtones, linked by scraps of reminiscences and engine-shed lore ... It passed the test of 'experimental' radio by proving to be a powerfully effective way of telling the story. Peggy Seeger's orchestration of a weird folky combination of instruments was frequently brilliant and the songs themselves were direct and simple and never self-consciously 'folky' in their effect. But the really memorable bits of the programme were the gentle, reminiscing Northern voices of Axon's mates ... This really was some of the characteristic poetry of the idiom of the people.

An uncredited report in the *Stoke Evening Sentinel* made this shrewd point: 'The niceties of our present day code of courtesy require that we speak of the dead only in hushed tones as if we stand still at their open graves. To people of such reserve the ballad must have come like a ramrod blow from a locomotive's piston.' In the *New Statesman* Tom Driberg, the Labour MP and an active supporter of Theatre Workshop in its early days, went so far as to say:

A generation from now – I would even say centuries from now – listeners will surely still be moved by the recording of *John Axon*, a panegyric ... A great naturalness was achieved ... by a combination of art and artlessness. If less well done this could have been pretentious. This superb piece of radio ... is 'by' Ewan MacColl and Charles Parker, but one would like to give a long credit list of all involved in it.

The only discordant note was struck by the *Daily Mail*, which had got hold of a 'complaint' by railwaymen to whom the programme had been played, about the calypso. In fact the calypso was genuinely born out of a remark from an old driver with a mesmeric Lancastrian voice, Jack Pickford: 'I had a West Indian fireman with me, on long distance trains, and he's been as good a fireman as I've ever had on the job. He definitely has it in his blood, and he comes from Jamaica.' Although Adrian Clancy's *Mail* review was strongly supportive, and correctly reported that Gladys Axon not only approved but took part in it – 'a very good and fine tribute to my husband's work' – it received an editorial twist with a further piece under the heading:

IT'S DYNAMITE, SAY TWO RAILWAYMEN

Two engine drivers who worked with Driver Axon at Edgeley ... referred to a comment concerning colour and religion which was followed by a calypso and asked – 'What has this to do with John Axon? This is dynamite. It is a trimming that had no right to be in it ... Why was this controversy brought in?'

Why indeed, one might ask the *Mail*. Clancy reported that one railwaymen broke down and wept when he heard it, and other railwaymen were strongly supportive. It was a mark of Charles and Ewan's concern for authenticity that, whenever they could, they played the end result to the participants to gauge their reaction.

The journalists liked it, so did the railwaymen, so did Gladys Axon. What about the listening public? The BBC had pioneered an audience research panel before the war, to keep them in touch with Middle England (or at least Home Service listeners). For *John Axon* the audience reaction was mixed, with a sharp divide between enthusiasts and loathers, and little middle ground. For every 'Ambitious. Adventurous. Wonderfully unusual. A real break into a new art form. Unconventional, untraditional, but all completely right, nothing jarred', there was an 'I hope to calm down later … It, by its very method, smothered and almost buried the story, the heroic story – even cheapened the iron courage of the man by putting him on … with banjos, guitars and, worse still, calypsos.'

Of views of the music, these were typical extremes, from: 'Monotonous, a racket, un-British, a travesty of music unsuitable for the theme of tragedy', to 'Apt and varied, rhythmical and stimulating. Various instruments were used with clever effect.' But Charles will have been pleased by this one: 'The effects were terrifying and suggested the impending tragedy as no words could have. I felt I was riding that engine.'

It's no oversimplification to conclude that the audience split more or less down social fault lines – the research report includes the occupation of the respondent. For later Radio Ballads this blurs, perhaps as the listener's ear gets more attuned and the mind less startled. It's a telling point, though, that among the BBC's respondents was a loco driver – 'Please please re-broadcast this programme. A magnificent tribute to John Axon and all his fellow locomen … marvellously true and beautifully put over.' His view was reinforced by the wife of the railway accident clerk for the area where the tragedy happened: 'The railwaymen concerned in the mishap or having knowledge of it found the programme remarkably good, and a very new approach.' A warehouse salesman's wife made a point that delighted Charles: 'There would be no folk songs or stories or ballads at all if events in the past had not been given similar treatment.' Exactly.

Charles was by turns exultant and relieved at the Press reaction, and at the news that the BBC, earlier doubts emphatically dispelled, had chosen it as their entry for that year's Italia Prize. That led to a debate about possible improvements. The problem was that they would have to be done without Peggy. She had been living with Bert Lloyd's family in Greenwich, learning the fiddle, when she was shopped to the Home Office by the wife of a rival banjo player who knew her visa had expired. Given two days to leave the country, she slipped out, slipped back, was caught, spent a night in a cell and was deported, and she was then shuttled like a stateless person between France, Belgium and Holland before holing up in Paris. She was there on 2 July straining to hear the broadcast, as she told Charles in a postcard from Paris XVI, and in a subsequent letter:

> I cannot tell you what a pleasure it was to hear John Axon on the radio here in Paris. Every minute of work, every detail of its conception was a reward. I think we both grew up a little more then, yes? Cheers for the future! ... Keep the guitar going and don't forget your friend Peggy.
>
> I am deeply disappointed that we are not rerecording the programme – I have been spending the weeks (since I heard it faintly over the French radio) past just thinking, cursing myself for not doing a better job and hoping I could redeem some of the more serious faults with the arranging. But if that's how it is, I'll refer my improvements to the next show of its kind, which I hope we do together.

But that would depend on her. And Peggy was stuck in Paris, with no visa. If she returned to the US her passport would be impounded. And she was pregnant with Ewan's child.

CHAPTER 7

BBC Voices
Documentaries Before the Radio Ballads

We are now taking Regional listeners over to hear a talk on the larvae of the common logarithm; this will be followed by Precioso's Fugue No. 6 in G (Op. 28) played by the Hautchapean Ensemble...

In his continued determination to break away from the tyranny of the scripted programme Bridson put a group of Durham miners into the Newcastle studio and told them to talk ... After a few minutes I was sent in with a large piece of cardboard on which Bridson had hastily chalked 'Do not say BLOODY or BUGGER.'

OLIVE SHAPLEY, IN *BROADCASTING A LIFE*, 1996

Why did *The Ballad of John Axon* excite its radio reviewers so much in the summer of 1958? To listeners today hearing a Radio Ballad for the first time, the sense of novelty lies in the use of music and song helping to tell the story, and – when we stop to think about it – the lack of a spoken narration. And what jars to our ears is not the Lancashire dialect spoken by the railwaymen, but the classic BBC voice of the announcer. As much a dialect as Lancashire, it has now almost died out, but that was the typical sound of the BBC – the orotund tones of John Snagge giving the train's destination not as Arpley, but Arpleah.

So what was radio like then, what was the sound landscape in 1958? To start with you really had just four main channels to listen to. The BBC had three – the Home Service (with its regional variations), the Light Programme, and the Third Programme – though a few could pick up the embryo World Service. The fourth, catering for the growing number of pop music enthusiasts, was Radio Luxembourg, virtually the only commercial station then in existence available to British listeners.

The Birth of the BBC

For those of us for whom the BBC is a national institution, born long before we were, its origins seem rather odd. It was set up in 1922 simply because the manufacturers of the new radios, then called wireless sets even though they weren't, needed something to broadcast to induce the general public to buy them. The Post Office invited the manufacturers to form a limited company, financed by a licence fee augmented by royalties from the sale of the sets. The licence cost ten shillings a year, and it stayed at that figure till it was doubled to one pound at the end of World War II. There were heavy restrictions though: to appease the newspaper magnates, powerful then as now, news could only be broadcast once it had been printed. They could cover only educational and religious topics, plus entertainment and music, and at the beginning couldn't even start until 10.15 am.

The General Manager was the severe Presbyterian Major John Reith, who ensured that a puritan straitjacket would tightly restrain that 'entertainment', particularly on Sundays (broadcasts didn't begin then till after 12.30 pm, when church services were over), which allowed the few early pre-war independent stations to thrive. There was certainly radio drama, but it was hampered at first because poor reception made voices hard to discriminate. Initially there was very little written specifically for radio, but it took off once the BBC realised its potential as a medium for the imagination.

Drama had begun tentatively with simple adaptations of existing plays, but early in 1924 the producer Nigel Playfair asked Richard Hughes, later the author of *A High Wind in Jamaica*, to produce the first specific 'Listening' play. He tossed him a first line – 'The lights have gone out!' – and overnight Hughes wrote a play about an accident in a coal mine. That night he confronted all the issues of radio drama for the first time. *Danger* would have, in his words:

> total darkness; explosions and running water; the picks of the rescue team ... But all miners' voices would be hard to tell apart. Better a party of visitors – an old man, a young one, a girl ... With rehearsals and production however, a cold awakening! I had spread myself on sound effects without considering how they were to be done ... The primitive transmission of those days ... reduced all sounds to a single indistinguishable 'wump' which might be the buzzing of a gnat, the clash of swords, the roaring of Niagara or the shutting of a door. Moreover, the studio was a vast padded cell designed to make voices sound as if they were floating in outer space.

Playfair turned outer to inner space by getting the cast to speak with their heads in buckets so the audience could be convinced they were in a tunnel; assembled an impromptu Welsh choir from among unemployed miners singing for pennies in the London streets; put them in the corridor outside the studio singing continuously; and opened and shut the soundproofed door to cue them in and out. An explosion? Tricky – anything in the studio was out of the question. However, reporters had been assembled in a special room with its own loudspeaker to listen to the broadcast, and they couldn't be fobbed off with the feeble 'phut' that ordinary listeners would hear. So Playfair rigged up an impressive explosion in the room next door to them. No one twigged that the sound came through the wall, and the press were mighty impressed with this new sound play. Thus, bizarre as it was, radio drama, sound effects, and live music were combined for the first time. Charles Parker and Ewan MacColl would set themselves a different problem nearly 40 years later, using musical effects to recreate their pit in *The Big Hewer*.

BBC Manchester

By the time the BBC's new Manchester chief Archie Harding arrived in his Siberia in 1933, Reith had nurtured the fledgling BBC through a trial of its independence during the 1926 General Strike. With almost all newspapers off the streets, the Home Secretary Winston Churchill had wanted it to broadcast only government news bulletins, but Prime Minister Baldwin disagreed and Reith was allowed to broadcast his own. Critics on the Left regarded them as indistinguishable – who needs government bulletins when you've got Reith? But it was the birth of a crucial principle. Away from London and Reith, Harding set about encouraging his producers to create programmes about the world as it really was. His New Year's Eve 1932 programme that so affronted the Polish ambassador had used recent news reports from around the world, largely Europe, and two narrators – one factual, the other poetic.

His documentary feature *Crisis in Spain*, about the formation of the Spanish Republic in 1931, had been universally admired. To Ewan MacColl, Harding was the creator of a new art form, the radio feature. His 'early programmes were not only stylistically brilliant and innovative, they were also passionate political statements, vibrant with anger and impatience.' No wonder he was despatched north, and no wonder Ewan admired him.

The great advantage of being out of sight, if not entirely out of mind, was that Harding could turn Manchester into his laboratory for creating programmes about important events that could be heard by as many people as possible. Radio had now reached the whole country: 98 per cent could get a signal. To achieve his aim Harding employed three key figures, all as middle class as he was and university educated, but each with a radical leaning and a sympathy for working people: Geoffrey Bridson, Olive Shapley, and John Pudney (though strictly he was on loan from London). They complemented each other: Bridson was a poet first and playwright second, Pudney a journalist first and poet second, Shapley a historian with an abiding interest in people. Only Bridson was a Northerner, but his middle-class Formby was a world away from the Salford of the Millers. Like Harding, these three felt passionately, and they shared the view – one that Bridson described as perhaps the only opinion the self-mocking Harding took really seriously – that everyone's opinion was valuable. Although documentary programmes were being made elsewhere in the country, it was Harding's team in Manchester that was constantly breaking new ground, and it was for him that Jimmie Miller and Joan Littlewood began working in radio when they were in fact still teenagers.

Harding's producers had several key aims. They preferred to focus on issues of contemporary relevance, so were constantly nudging forward the borders of what their London masters would accept. They were keen to publicise what ordinary people had to say just as much as experts. Eventually, too, they edged tentatively towards allowing people's lives to be revealed by their own words (though largely through the voices of actors) in an era where tight editorial control from the centre dictated that virtually everything should be scripted. And they wanted to use sound imaginatively: they were strongly influenced by the photomontages of the German-born John Heartfield, and by the revolutionary early Russian film-makers. In particular they wanted to emulate in sound the topics and techniques explored in the cinema documentaries of John Grierson. (In 1929 he had made *The Drifters*, about North Sea herring fishermen, good enough not to wilt alongside Eisenstein's *The Battleship Potemkin*, with which it was first shown as a double bill. Grierson went on to head the imaginative GPO film unit, where he commissioned *Night Mail* and *Coal Face*.)

Harding's producers were also influenced by the so-called New Poetry of writers like TS Eliot and Ezra Pound. Pound, in fact, had written experimental operas for the BBC. As well as its music by Benjamin Britten, *Night Mail* was paced by a specially written poem by WH Auden, cut and pasted to the images, and matching the train in its driving rhythm –

> Here is the Night Mail crossing the border,
> Bringing the cheque and the postal order…

Harding consciously saw radio as a tool for poets. Bridson echoed *Night Mail* in his *Coronation Scot* of 1936. He had used his own poetry in the *May Day in England* that had launched Jimmie Miller's 'Northern voice', the programme contrasting the old English round-the-maypole tradition of May Day with its modern incarnation as a day of social protest. In his *March of the '45* Bridson wanted to evoke the tidal surge and ebb of the Jacobite Rebellion in a way that would 'make the listener become emotionally involved; make him grip his chair and be caught up in the action.' He co-produced it with London (with Laurence Gilliam, who had taken Harding's job there) and BBC Scotland. The Scottish readers brought his words 'down the line from Glasgow like a Highland river in spate.' Recognising by then that his normal poetry was hardly likely to appeal to a mass audience, he had switched to a fast-moving narrative verse in the Walter Scott style to trace Bonnie Prince Charlie's route today. The march moves on through a Northern English landscape, now rather altered since 1745, as had working conditions:

> Not many joined him, as it was;
>   And traces vanish as the years lapse.
> Very few would join him now –
>   Apart from the unemployed, perhaps …

When Harding was shunted off from Manchester to a siding as the head of Staff Training at the end of 1936, he used *March of the '45* as a key demonstration piece, one Charles Parker would have heard in his BBC training in 1947. But there were no genuine working-class people on radio yet, just a few actors like Jimmie Miller to give them the dialect they needed. The first working-class regional voices to be heard with any regularity appeared in Bridson's series *Harry Hopeful*, featuring a genial old Lancastrian clock repairer named Frank Nicholls. Now an actor, he was adept at drawing out working people in country villages from the Derbyshire Dales to the Scottish Border. Bridson jotted down their stories, noted their dialect and tricks of speech, and constructed a script whose parts he posted out to the original speakers. He then recorded them in their own homes, listening to the outcome in headphones in a car at their front gate, and inviting their families to criticise anything that sounded unnatural. In that laboured way he was able to create an approximation of the real thing that sufficed to make the programmes extraordinarily popular, and not just in the North. But these programmes didn't threaten the status quo, and there were still no genuine real and unscripted voices. As Bridson said:

> That the man in the street should have anything vital to contribute to broadcasting was an idea slow to gain acceptance. That he should actually use broadcasting to express his own opinions in his own unvarnished words, was regarded as almost the end of all good social order. Never once in history had the man in the street ever been consulted.

Even the magisterial playwright GB Shaw was not allowed to simply talk into the microphone – everything had to be scripted and vetted. Bridson was scathing: 'That spontaneous speech should have been banned by the BBC for the first 20 odd years of broadcasting is almost unbelievable.' It wasn't quite banned – the voices of the unemployed were heard in a programme in 1934 called *Time to Spare* – but the uproar it caused made sure repeats would be few and far between. In fact it didn't happen again to any extent until early in the war, when the Socialist Nye Bevan ran such rings round the stammering Conservative Quintin Hogg that Churchill decreed that no member of his party would ever appear live and unscripted again. Moreover, apart from the occasional 'character' speaking dialect, the voice of the BBC remained that of the Southern English upper middle class: not until 1941 was a non-standard voice allowed to read the news, when Southern listeners were jolted by the Yorkshire 'good neet' of Wilfred Pickles.

Mobile Recording

Before the war mobile recording equipment was scarce. This made it particularly hard to break through the effective ban on using real people, real regional voices. (The few outside broadcasting facilities the BBC owned were used to record royal visits and football matches rather than hunger marches.) Olive Shapley was another determined to get them on air, despite an unfortunate early studio experience. For Bridson's *Coal*, the 1938 programme for which he and Joan Littlewood spent a week down a Durham pit, Shapley was his fascinated assistant whose quote about swearing heads the chapter. She went on: 'These are not really swear words in the north-east, but for many people are woven into the fabric of everyday speech. The sight of these poor men trying vainly to form some sort of sentence without resort to them was enough to have me sent back into the studio to say "As you were". There was a terrible row about it.' That Bridson was nearly sacked as a consequence tells you all you need to know.

Olive Shapley was the first to use to its full advantage a massive outside broadcast van BBC Manchester had acquired, 27 feet long and seven tons loaded, maximum speed 20 mph. Needing a pair of technicians employed to work two turntables – which recorded alternately on four-minute discs – it was an expensive operation. It hadn't been intended for Manchester, but was too unwieldy to manage the narrow lanes of Wales and the South-West. Like Bridson she took it out to create programmes – scripted still, true – and recorded by the original speakers from a text using the language and vocal rhythms she studied from her recordings. But while Bridson had used his scribbled notes, she could listen again and again to the actual voices in assembling her script. Fifty years later on Radio 4, in her introduction to *Classic Features*, which included the second Radio Ballad, *Song of a Road*, she described how 'we wanted to wrest John Reith's BBC from the grip of the stuffed shirts by taking the microphone out of the studio and into the country at large.' As Scannell and Cardiff report in their *Social History of British Broadcasting*, as a contrast to her predecessors she was a breath of fresh air:

> She used a language that was informal, relaxed and intimate. Her programmes set up an equal relationship between speaker, subject and audience. That, combined with the sympathetic skill of the interviewer (a quite new technique which she had to learn for herself) led a contemporary critic to describe her programmes as little masterpieces of understanding and authenticity.

John Pudney came to Manchester originally on loan. He had been one of the first to use recorded voice actuality in 1934, hiring a film company's recording van to make the excruciatingly titled '*Opping 'Oliday*, about the London poor who descended on Kent in August to pick the hops. Pudney was the producer Ewan most admired:

> He was far and away the most talented producer I ever worked with in radio. He was a poet of some standing and was able to attract artists of the calibre of Auden and Britten to work with him. He had a nice sense of irony and an engaging schoolboyish sense of humour … Here was this upstart from the south, this effete poet who looked like a prosperous farmer up for a day in town, intent on riding roughshod over the well-kept pastures of the featureocracy … Pudney's approach to radio documentary was not aimed at subverting the classic feature but at humanising it. He was able to invest the dullest subject with humour and irony and one was never allowed to lose sight of the fact that a human intelligence was at work in even the most grandiose project.

At the outbreak of war, once over an initial startled paralysis, the BBC was galvanised to improve and professionalise its news gathering and outside broadcast capabilities. Producers of news and feature programmes from the War Reporting Unit followed the armies and brought the sounds of war and immediacy of battle into people's homes, conjuring up images in sound that newspaper journalists couldn't match on paper. Moreover, the war had brought to the microphone many ordinary people whose personal stories were a crucial part of the war effort and indeed were told by the people themselves. This could have been the pattern for the broadcasting of the post-war peace, when documentaries and drama flourished, but the imaginative use of real people in broadcasting dwindled. They appeared largely as 'characters', and were rarely allowed to speak on any serious issues.

During the war the separate BBC London departments of Drama and Features had been evacuated to Manchester and combined under Val Gielgud, elder brother of John the actor. Proximity there, combined with their distance from London, brought the best out of the talents thrown together, like Geoffrey Bridson, Laurence Gilliam, who was a huge flamboyant character known as Lorenzo (the Magnificent), and Stephen Potter of the later *Gamesmanship* series of books. Gielgud pursued a policy of encouraging established writers to write for radio, with successes such as Potter's *The Last Crusade*, Louis MacNiece's *Christopher Columbus*, and Dorothy L Sayers' brilliant 12-part series for Children's Radio about Jesus called *The Man Born to be King*, produced by Gielgud. This was a landmark in many ways. Sayers offended the ultra-devout Christians by using an actor to depict Jesus (some blamed that blasphemy for the fall of Singapore) and upset many more by using modern colloquial English. But she brought the dry text alive for many, and was among the first to humanise Bible characters.

After the War

In 1945 Drama and Features were split out again, with a London Features department under Laurence Gilliam, and Geoffrey Bridson as his number two. Imaginative radio continued to be encouraged, and the Italia Prize, created in 1948, became an additional spur to creative writing and production. Douglas Cleverdon (the man who would sympathise with Charles Parker over the criticism he received before *John Axon* was aired) produced several classics, including *Under Milk Wood*, written specially for radio by Dylan Thomas after years of Cleverdon's patient coaxing. That won an Italia Prize in 1954, the same year as did a play by Louis MacNiece. In fact between 1952 and 1960 the BBC won ten prizes, its winners including programmes by Jacob Bronowski, Henry Reed, John Mortimer, Samuel Beckett and John Arden. Only two of the winners, though, were radio documentaries: a programme about Mahatma Gandhi's last days, made in 1957, and the third Radio Ballad, *Singing the Fishing*, in 1960. Moreover, until the Radio Ballads, music was used only for scene setting and illustration, and there were hardly any voices other than those of actors.

Ewan recalls creating songs for *Lorry Harbour* for Denis Mitchell, who had been hooked on folk music after hearing Ewan, Bert Lloyd and Alan Lomax at a Theatre Workshop benefit concert. Mitchell had been amazed by their 'flyting' – trading songs competitively from subjects sent up by audience members on slips of paper.

> For Lorry Harbour we went to two or three places on the A1 and A5, truck drivers' all-night caffs. We recorded 60–70 truck drivers onto acetates. Denis Mitchell took it away and rewrote it and said could I still speak it like a lorry driver. None of us thought how crazy not to use the lorry driver! Then I remember auditions to see if people could sound like a driver.

By 1957 Bridson was getting disillusioned with the BBC's radio documentary output. For him the decline dated back to the appearance of independent television (ITV) in 1955, which 'had proved something of a shock to the BBC directorate, and was viewed with some resentment. To begin with, it was the love-child of the Conservative Party, which the BBC had done much to conciliate over the years. It posed a serious threat to BBC television.' ITV soon had double the BBC's viewing audience. Bridson was summoned to a meeting of senior programme staff in late 1954, where he argued in vain that radio needed to change radically to meet the threat. But 'Bow Bells continued to peal between programmes, and radio audiences continued to shrink.'

In an analysis of radio features that he made in 1962, after the sixth Radio Ballad, Ewan MacColl concluded that the imaginative pre-war 'documentary poetic epic commentaries on historical, industrial and political processes' had been replaced by 'journalistic, non-poetical, factual documentaries, with quotes from official documents rather than literature.' The Establishment was now rarely criticised. Bridson agreed, feeling that as far as serious listening went, apart from what was produced for the Third Programme's intellectual minority, 'cosiness was the watchword, where the real need was for trenchancy. In popular terms, radio stayed on the defensive – it never went on the attack.' In the 1950s, he felt, they merely balanced points of view until they cancelled each other out.

Radio Begins its Decline

Radio was becoming starved of income: the mother bird had eyes only for the fattening cuckoo in the nest: the cost of making BBC television programmes doubled in the two years after ITV arrived. There were more of them too, for the hitherto sacrosanct 6–7pm Toddlers' Truce hour was soon plugged. In 1957 the Third Programme's output was abruptly halved, which led to an ultimately useless protest by a deputation led by Ralph Vaughan Williams and TS Eliot. Elsewhere news and current affairs coverage was increased at the expense of drama and features. Gielgud and Gilliam saw their independence reduced by political manoeuvring. Bridson was affronted by the inevitable reduction in creativity and experimentation. The post of Controller of the Home Service was downgraded to Head of Planning, Home Service, and given to Ronald Lewin, an Oxford modern historian, which Bridson lamented: 'His personal interest seemed to veer towards the flood of war memoirs, would-be contemporary history, political testaments ... The result was ... painfully dull radio.' The audience research figures confirmed it.

Bridson lost his job and was sidelined as an independent producer. It was telling that when he started making programmes again, his greatest pleasure was to write and produce a 'ballad opera' in 1959 called *My People and Your People*. It was about a group of West Indian immigrants and the love affair between one of them, played by Nadia Cattouse, and a 'young' Scots skiffler... Ewan MacColl. 'The music, arranged for me by Ewan MacColl and Peggy Seeger, was lively and magnificent, the contrast between its Scots and West Indian rhythms being no less intriguing than the contrast between the two idioms and accents.' (One of the West Indian actor/singers was John Clarence, who worked on two of the Radio Ballads. Peggy Seeger learned about colour gradations in the black community. Pointing to a girl a shade paler than him Clarence whispered: 'I'd stand no chance with her. See, I'm <u>black</u> black.') Though it stood no comparison with Charles Parker's programmes – entirely scripted and without the music integrated – *My People and Your People* received good reviews. A last throw by one of the pre-war Manchester radicals. But now, 25 years after *May Day in England*, Ewan MacColl was back in radio, with the bit clenched between his teeth.

So when Ewan MacColl joins Charles Parker to go off to Edgeley to interview railwaymen, although BBC Radio features could demonstrate many <u>literary</u> successes since the 1930s, the original enthusiasm for allowing real people to tell their own stories has diminished. Actors are still making money out of dialect. The use of voice actuality is a rarity in radio again, though it's notable that someone trained in sound radio, Denis Mitchell, has been employing voice actuality in television documentaries. When in Charles's letter to Ewan in July 1957 he talks of using the railwaymen's voices, his caveat is: 'It will have to be actuality well up to Denis's standards before this could begin to work.' Mitchell's *Night in the City*, about a typical Manchester night, had been broadcast four weeks earlier, and his use of sound owes much to his radio training, as well as to Ewan MacColl's songs. Charles is galled that it's being done on television better than on radio, but after much strife he has shown what he can do. Real railwaymen, telling their own tale, a story enhanced by the music – and lauded by the critics. Now, will he get a chance to make another? Well, Ewan has made it quite clear that without Peggy he won't take part in any more. So Charles goes into battle with the BBC.

CHAPTER 8

Muck Shifting
Song of a Road

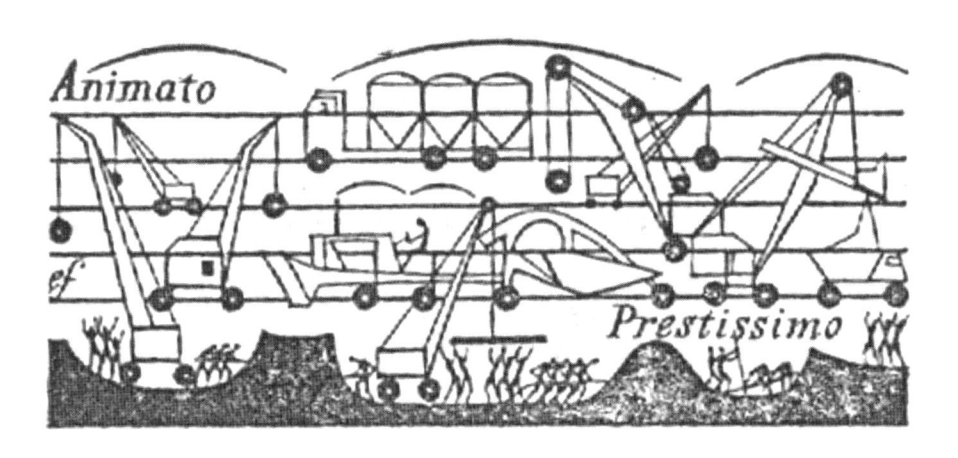

Are we jumping from the frying pan into the fire? From the thralldom of the 8.45, the limited flexibility of railways ... to an anarchic uncontrolled torrent dominated by self-interest and the dehumanising effects of power sans understanding. The cult of the motor car versus the old-style locoman. Why does the thought of the traffic on the Great West Road today inspire revulsion compared to Clapham Junction on Easter Monday?

CHARLES PARKER, FROM A 1958 IDEAS PAPER FOR *SONG OF A ROAD*

When you're up on the seat in the cold and the heat
You never think what you're lifting
You're bashing away every hour of the day,
You're working at the old muck shifting.

EWAN MACCOLL, 'CATS AND BACK-ACTERS',
FROM *SONG OF A ROAD*, 1959

Vindicated after his internal struggle at the BBC before *John Axon* could be broadcast, Charles Parker put the programme's success down to the way it allowed the listener to identify with the action. It hadn't won the Italia Prize in the end, but he was delighted with the way the songs and musical setting had helped to make the everyday experience dramatic. He craved more, but he would have to secure Ewan and Peggy if there were to be any more Radio Ballads. He knew the nature of the relationship between them, and he disapproved of it, as he'd told Peggy over tea in Heal's department store one day. So he was well aware that Ewan wouldn't come on board if she didn't, and Peggy was trapped on the continent by what we came to know as a Catch 22.

The US State Department had been against her trip to Moscow, where the CIA had monitored the US delegation, and was incensed by the subsequent visit to Peking against its heavy-handed 'advice'. Peggy had been warned that her passport would be impounded were she to return to the USA: she was told later she was on a blacklist sent to European governments. She was stuck. The problem was that the British government wouldn't issue her with a visa unless she had a BBC contract. But the BBC would only give her a contract if she already had a visa … So 12 days after the broadcast of *Axon*, and doubtless with Ewan's urgent encouragement, Charles went into battle. In an internal BBC memo to both his Midlands boss Denis Morris and the London Head of Features Laurence Gilliam he pressed for support in getting her back to England:

> She was responsible for the brilliant orchestration in John Axon, herself played the banjo in that production and she brings to her technical mastery of the banjo and guitar a unique understanding of the modal forms of popular music and their rhythmic and harmonic potential. I am hoping to commission a radio ballad series from Ewan MacColl, using Peggy Seeger if possible, and am at present negotiating for her return for the Italia production of John Axon. Douglas Cleverdon also wants her for Homer … How can we sort the hand-to-mouth work permit situation with the Ministry of Labour?

He draws a blank, and two days later his agitation increases in a further memo, his prose purpling as he goes. Worried that *John Axon* will prove a 'flash in the pan', Charles insists Ewan is essential: 'His finger is on the true pulse of the emerging music.' He tries to get a commitment for, say, a further five Radio Ballads, wanting to guarantee Ewan enough income to devote himself to it for a year. If he can get this, Charles is confident they will have 'a body of performed work unique and unmatched.' They mustn't miss 'a golden opportunity to write a new page in the history of broadcasting.' He goes on to press two buttons that he hopes will influence Gilliam – the potential income from TV rights, and the danger of losing Ewan to commercial television. But

Gilliam needs a stronger case if he's to tangle with unsympathetic government departments to get Peggy's visa, and asks for more facts to buttress the case. Charles gets yet more exasperated. He does exasperation well:

> Specific proposals for employment? Alas, I would need to be an expert in International Jurisprudence, The Laws of Contract and the BBC's staffing policy to be able to meet this request. Peggy Seeger is only allowed into the country by the Foreign Office for just so long as she has a work permit and evidence of income … Only on BBC urgent representations was she allowed to extend her last visit for a month to allow for the re-recording of certain passages of John Axon to meet your criticisms. This was in April, when she was on the point of deportation by the Foreign Office! She tried to return on June 4 to work with Ewan MacColl on *Homer* just on a student's visa, but was <u>arrested</u> at Dover, kept in the cells all night, and shipped back to France the next day. Her French visa is due to expire soon, and if we can't fix the problem, she'll be deported back to the USA. Under these monstrous conditions, it's unreasonable to talk of 'normal ad-hoc arrangement' …
>
> The 'undesirable alien' aura the FO seem determined to force on Peggy Seeger is quite outrageous. So I am asking the BBC to make up its mind whether it wants more and better John Axons, and if it does, to realise it won't get 'em without Peggy Seeger. More specifically I am asking the BBC:
>
> a To obtain agreements to her re-entry to work on the John Axon re-make for the Italia Prize – a supreme piece of irony!
>
> b Vide my previous memo, I am hoping to commission another five radio ballads from Ewan MacColl, a condition of which is the employment of Peggy Seeger. This really means a year's concentrated work for Ewan MacColl, but the c £250 that Peggy Seeger could expect to earn would not support her for a year, says the Ministry of Labour.
>
> So we need to have a staff contract. But how to frame it for so intangible an employment as Folk Style Instrumentalist cum Jazz New Popular Music Arranger and Developer of Emerging British/American Folk Song/Popular Music Idiom?

And with that he signs off with a brusque flourish: 'Over to you. Over.' It's no surprise that this doesn't work, even on a sympathetic ally like Laurence Gilliam. They meet a few days later, when Charles is put firmly in his place: you must enter Axon for the Italia Prize in its current form, because Peggy Seeger's not available for work in this country for 'the reasons stated'. As for Ewan MacColl, you can commission him for one or two new Radio Ballads but not a series. You 'took the point' – classic bureaucratic jargon to reflect that he realised Charles <u>didn't</u> — that it would be wise to look for other writers and composers to work with. No chance of that, of course, for Charles realises now that nothing can match the combination of the pair, who had shown on Axon how well attuned they were to his own intentions and sensibilities — let alone to each other's. To all appearances Charles is like a lover denied a chance to repeat a first ecstatic experience.

Denis Morris writes to Gilliam thanking him for 'the diplomatic and helpful way he has dealt with this.' Charles doubtless conveys to Peggy via Ewan that he's drawn a blank, so she and Ewan, communing in Boulogne on New Year's Eve over bread, cheese and a bottle of port, come to a simple if drastic conclusion. She'll marry a British passport. Another itinerant Paris folk singer, with whom she has been working occasionally, is Alex Campbell, tall and skinny, flamboyant, flame-haired, red-bearded. 'A complete and utter romantic, totally outrageous and a wonderful entertainer — full of jokes but also close to tears as well', as the singer Dolina McLennan recalled. Campbell had been singing with marked success in the streets of Paris since 1955 when he'd left a solid job in the Civil Service. Alex said that in Paris then there were no folk singers in the street: 'It was against the law. It was foreigners like myself who could do it. I was singing Leadbelly, skiffle numbers, occasional Scottish songs that I've known since I was a wee boy ... I was called King of the Quarter at one time.'

The romantic Alex was happy to oblige, and they were married by an American priest in surplice and sneakers in January 1959. Alex took his dressing-down for his new wife's now blatant condition rather well, thought Peggy, who was back in England next day, Ewan's 44th birthday. As she said: 'The following day I arrived unimpeded in London, six weeks before the birth of my first son. In the flyblown office of a Commissioner of Oaths, I swore allegiance to Her Majesty the Queen (and all her issue thereof into perpetuity).' So Peggy, or Mrs Alex Campbell as the BBC now punctiliously addressed her letters, was now a British citizen by marriage and the BBC was happy to employ her. (It would be some years, though, before the domestic arrangements were finally settled; Neill was born in March, but Ewan's daughter Kirsty was born to Jean later that year. Life was fraught for everyone.)

Meanwhile Charles had been casting around for the next Radio Ballad subject — he needed a strong follow-up. Among several topics that he touted were The English Labourer and Whaling (which was perhaps a fall-back alternative, using Bert Lloyd for his fund of whaling songs rather than Ewan). But when he returned from an apparently fruitless tour of the Midlands in October with Ewan looking at the labouring possibility, his next subject was presented to him. Whatever misgivings he might have had were suppressed because the idea came from his boss, Denis Morris. After hearing from its chief architect about the building of the M1 — the first stretch of Britain's first motorway was just being started — Morris felt it would make an ideal subject for a second Radio Ballad. A problem that would rear its head later was his view that it should involve everyone concerned with the road's making, not just the labourers. Charles was not going to demur, and started to get his head round The Road.

I shall dwell on this project at some length because it illustrates the problems Charles and other producers had (and still have) in getting their programmes off the ground. In early November 1958 he met a representative of John Laing, one of the two major contractors, and a Miss Phyllis Faulkner, who worked for the Information department of the Ministry of Transport. You can imagine their perplexed reaction from this quote from an ideas paper he wrote a few days later: 'I asserted my position as that of an artist and not as a reporter, and our principal interest being to convey the epic and poetic qualities in this immense project ... not to deliver ... a piece of high level reportage. After some astonished discussion they found this acceptable.' Or so he imagined. What Charles saw as a possible epic, Laing naturally viewed as a high-profile engineering project, absolutely crucial to their future, with a challenging deadline, and the last thing they wanted was highfalutin intellectuals tramping all over the route, probably inciting their navvies. Phyllis Faulkner, though, eventually turned out be an ally, and without her greasing of some very obdurate wheels the programme would probably have run into the M1 mud and stuck there. It wasn't just Laing who thwarted him either. He tried to speak to an eminent geologist, to find out about the strata the road would cut through, but:

> An approach to Dr Casey of the Geological Survey Museum as an acknowledged expert in the field ... was also denied me... I should stress that all I wanted was for a Geologist of Dr Casey's standing to wax lyrical on matters dating back 150 million years... This apparently was still not of sufficient antiquity ... to be considered safe for publication.

Charles put together an ideas paper. He mused about Sir Owen Williams, the road's chief engineer: 'the engine-artist figure transforming the physical world', and about earlier builders – the Romans, Offa, the canals, the railways – helping Civilisation to spread. Perhaps a River of Man approach – the flood of history, men flooding to work on it, a flood of cars on it? 'How to treat upon the automobile, civil engineering, the ruthless dominance of the machine, in a way that speaks of poetry and the epic, and its implications for man and civilisation?' Difficult. Especially when he felt he was facing the 'arrogance of technical advance without spiritual values, no sense of service to the community at large ... ruthless exploitation of labour, the ultimate objective profits not engineering achievement in the service of men.' You can imagine the boyish steam train enthusiast, fresh from the Axon footplate. Railway travel gives a sense of community, the car one of competition.

Doubtless the thought that it was his boss's idea in the first place stops him flinging his papers out of the window, and he goes on to produce a topic list that was close to the programme's blueprint. He carries out a recce along the line of the motorway and, energised, at last commissions Ewan on 27 November, 1958: 'I think we have struck oil with the London/Yorkshire motorway.' He'd met James Cryer, the project manager of the southernmost 12-mile section, a third-generation Rochdale builder, who had waxed lyrical about the surprising pleasures of 'muck shifting'. This is the kind of attitude he wants to capture. He books a trip for 8 December, anxious to start recording before the expected winter slowdown. But despite an encouraging note on 1 December from Morris, the following day he walks into a plate glass window erected by Laing. 'It's too difficult to proceed at present.' Laing have been stung by criticisms of the road's construction on BBC TV's *Panorama* and *Tonight* programmes, so the subtext is clear, and next morning Charles spectacularly loses his temper with a startled woman at Laing's head office, and writes to her hastily: 'I must apologise for tearing into you on the telephone this morning. I am afraid that the news that greeted me on my desk came as a shock to a flu-debilitated system and, plus a migraine headache, rather mitigated against quiet reasonableness.' Charles's tempests were becoming legendary, but neither he nor the recipients seem to have borne grudges.

The other contractor, Tarmac, is altogether more accommodating, but without Laing's support he might as well give up. Charles takes up a three-month secondment to television from January to March 1959 (where he's appalled at the poor sound recording facilities) but throughout the period he is wheedling away, tiptoeing round sensitivities, trying to get key mid-management figures on his side, to break down Laing's resistance any way he can. Eventually on 20 March he gets through to Sir Owen Williams, whose immediate support forces Laing to yield, and he and Ewan are allowed on site on 13 April.

So far so good, but, told to accompany them everywhere and vet the people they interview is a lady from Laing, deputed by a head of PR with the exquisite name of Captain Sir Aubrey St Clair-Ford. Charles and Ewan respond by trudging through the muddiest parts of the site they can find, and they shake her off after two days. They're under way. To Peggy, nursing baby Neill back in Surrey, Ewan writes of a homesick Irish lad of 16 crying his eyes out while operating a ferociously noisy machine without earplugs, and of the workmen eating great mountains of spuds but hardly any meat or green vegetables. (Well, the Irish, they're used to it.) They do a further recording stint in late April, and another in late June with Peggy riding a massive truck in the wind and rain for her first recording trip. Ewan recalls in his autobiography *Journeyman* that during 25 days of recording:

We patrolled the constantly changing length of the road, recording in hostels, dormitories, pubs, canteens and shelters. We recorded in the cabs of bulldozers and earth-moving machines and helicopters, in offices and plant headquarters. We found ourselves asking questions about bridge-building, about running a concrete batching-plant, about prefabrication techniques, about maintaining and running the Shavian Finisher and, in short, behaving as though our intention was to create a programme which would inform the listener how to build his or her own motorway.

Ewan makes clear here his distaste for what he saw as the concentration on machine over man. They wound up with a lively evening recording session in a pub with a party of Irish labourers on 10 July. Ewan and Peggy then spent over a fortnight wading through 120 quarter-hour tapes to select an initial 30–40 minutes of actuality, juggling it into the framework for a script. After another three or four weeks Ewan had written the songs and Peggy constructed musical arrangements, and on 3 September they presented Charles with a rough tape-assembly of actuality and related songs.

But Charles was unhappy with the balance of the material. He felt that his remit from Morris was to write about the <u>building</u> of the M1 rather than concentrating on the workmen who built it – to Ewan it meant that Charles wanted to tilt the balance crucially towards the work process, away from the working human. This fault-line led to the repercussions discussed in the next chapter that would ultimately settle their way of working: they were still fumbling towards it by trial and error. Charles, keen to finish the job so the programme could go out when the motorway was completed – a couple of months or so, but they had no date confirmed yet – selected some extra actuality. Ewan had to write new songs dealing with some pretty mundane stuff. He had a tight deadline, but he worked best that way and despite his reservations came up with several new songs in very little time, to which Peggy gave a fizzing jazzy orchestration that would give them the suitable air of pomposity Ewan felt they needed. Well, he could write a song about anything. A letter to the Ministry? Sure, and it trips along with Peggy's syncopating typewriter clacking in rhythm behind, carriage return and all:

> **Wrote a thousand letters to the Ministry:**
> **Dear Sir, your memo of August three,**
> **Your reference BL stroke CT**
> **Re alteration of existing drainage systems…**

And straight into some actuality about the nightmare of drainage. That doesn't read like a song, till you listen to it. Now Charles had to manipulate the revamped actuality into decent shape before rehearsals and recording, set for 28 September to 5 October in various not-entirely-suitable London studios. But it was a horrible job. The Midget tapes were the worst he'd ever had to use: of 120 at least half were marked by speed variation, amplifier crackle, induced echo and peak distortion. By his reckoning he spent over 250 hours (that's over six weeks of solid eight-hour days – so four weeks for Charles) getting the doctored actuality into 'tailored and polished actuality inserts' ready for the studio. And so they began:

> **Come all you gallant labouring men,**
> **Leave your family and your friends**
> **You're needed on the job again,**
> **On the London Yorkshire highway.**
> **A job to do, a job for you,**
> **And nineteen months to see it through,**
> **A chance to earn a quid or two**
> **On the London Yorkshire highway.**

The designation M1 wasn't yet commonplace, and it was as the London Yorkshire Highway that it was commissioned. Besides, it scans better. For this programme Ewan, Bert Lloyd, Isla Cameron and Fitzroy Coleman were joined as singers by Fitz's compatriots John Clarence and Big Thomas, who had just appeared with Peggy on the Bridson programme about West Indian immigrants. With them were the young Scot Jimmie McGregor, appearing on his only Radio Ballad. Jimmie found it fascinating:

> For me as a young fellow – I was really excited – it was wonderful to watch. I've got enormous studio experience behind me now on both sides of the microphone, but to watch someone like Ewan at work, he was very, very professional ... Bert Lloyd, lovely man. I was standing beside him – when we sang a chorus about the rhythm of the big scrapers – it went Dig and Scrape and Load – but I realised Bert was singing: Pig and Ape and Toad. When we finished the thing, he shrugged and smiled. It really amused me – the idea of these two very eminent men scoring these boyish points off each other. There were some great choruses in that, great work songs. Ewan would say 'Don't sing harmony', because I'd have instinctively sung harmony.

The harmonies he sang with Robin Hall made Jimmie a fixture on the regular weekday *Tonight* news programme on BBC TV, and very popular, so his diary was solid for the rest of the Radio Ballad period. The other singers would have included the luckless Bob Davenport, had he not been struck down by TB at the last minute and replaced by Louis Killen, another young singer from the North-East, who happened to be appearing at Ewan and

Peggy's Singers Club just the Saturday before rehearsals began. When Ewan casually asked him if he was free on the Monday, Louis needed no second invitation. He took the train back to a doubting mother in Jesmond, packed, wrote a sick note for British Rail who employed him as a clerk, and came back down. When he returned home it was to the sack. He had lost a job, but gained a life he loved.

Louis stayed in London in a bedsit with Rambling Jack Elliott and his wife. It was his first real professional engagement. 'It was lovely, a privilege taking part. I was in awe. I had a great time. Though it was quite beyond me at first – I couldn't sight-read – they would go over it all and I would pick it up quickly. This wasn't singing in the church choir, I was in a recording studio with professional musicians, plus the big guns of folk music. I did what I was told and kept my ears open.' He got one of the scene-setting songs with a cracking chorus:

> **The consulting engineer's the man who formulates the plan,**
> **The contractor gets it moving and he does the best he can.**
> **But the labourer's the bloke who gets the blisters on his hand –**
> **He's the one who keeps the muck a-moving.**
>> **With his dumpers and his scrapers and his ten-ton excavators,**
>> **With his rollers and his shovels, and his digs and lodging troubles,**
>> **He's the one, who fills the truck –**
>> **He's the one who earns his bonus shifting muck.**

That 'But' shows where Ewan's sympathy lies, but that dig is forgotten as the song rollicks along. Louis, though daunted in that exalted company, found a sympathetic drinking partner in another newcomer, a former merchant seaman from Devon, Cyril Tawney. The same core set of musicians was employed – Alf Edwards, Bruce Turner, Jim Bray, and Bobby Mickleburgh. They engaged two singers from Ireland because of the strong Irish flavour of some of the songs, reflecting the homeland of many of the labourers, forced to seek work across the Irish Sea for long stretches away from home. One was the BBC veteran Seamus Ennis, the other the uilleann piper Francis McPeake, who had mugged up the new songs back in Belfast before coming over.

The rehearsals took six evenings – it might with advantage have been 26, said Charles later, as he battled with obstinate tapes – and the recording three days. Somehow they got through it, despite a whole new set of technical problems as well as obstruction by a hostile studio manager, who Charles was convinced was tacitly encouraged by his London management to be difficult. Paranoid he had every reason to be by then, and he was probably right – don't let that bugger Parker get away with anything ... Charles expanded on this later in a vitriolic memo. When recording was over he took away two sets of 16 reels of 10½-inch programme tape, one of pure music, the other of music/effects mix. But programme assembly was once more a severe challenge and, with an uncertain deadline looming, to his intense frustration he took another three weeks lashed to the tape-editing wheel to overcome vagaries of balance and rhythm.

All through this fraught period he has to deal with other pressing concerns. Having commissioned and contracted the performers, just before rehearsals are due he gets a memo from one of Denis Morris's nervy assistants. Since a certain David Martin is making a TV film, he'd better suspend work on his radio ballad until they can see how it goes down. You can just imagine his appalled reaction to that, but he ploughs on. In the week after recording when he's now in 'a terrible post-production state of depression with the programme in bits on 32 tapes', he has to deal with some infuriating distractions. A tight-lipped memo from the Head of Engineering ticks him off for bypassing him and acquiring a scarce TR/90 tape editing machine from Staff Training so that he can do the first-cut editing himself, wicked man. Another complains about the amount of overtime he has extracted (willingly) from the engineers so he could get their wretched kit to work properly.

He'd already had to fight to get the programme broadcast for the road's opening, rather than at Christmas, as had been suggested. 'The future of this programme really hinges on its being broadcast when the motorway is opened – its whole dramatic point resides in the completion and achievement. To have this for Christmas is MADNESS (although a lovely repeat!).' The exasperated emphases are his. He gets his way, and on 15 October he writes in haste to the Editor of the *Radio Times* that the revised broadcast date of 5 November has 'caught us a bit on the hop', and asks for another boxed illustration to match the brilliant one Eric Fraser had produced for Axon. Fraser isn't available, so he gets something he loathes, looking like a 'dinky toy'. In his *Radio Times* article he writes:

> The main centrepiece of the programme which seeks to give the impression of the interminable pace and inexhaustible tempo of construction … is the Waulking Song, a direct application of a traditional Hebridean melody to which the women waulk [shrink] the cloth, endlessly repeating itself. We had to synchronise music to machine, which was very tricky. The inexhaustible movement of the final song is an adaptation of Galway Races, in which the singer sings each 4-lined verse and the first of the chorus in one breath. The effect of this is to lilt the suggestion of speed with which the motorway will be used.

Seamus Ennis still has the breath all right, and his brogue speaks for all the Irish labourers when he gives us:

> So when you're in the driver's seat and belting with your load
> Don't forget the casual labourers who sweated on the road,
> When you're racing under bridges, under clover-leaf or flyway,
> You can thank the roving boys who built the London Yorkshire highway.
>   With me whack, fol a doo, fol a diddley dum a day.

On 22 October Charles hears from the Tarmac Managing Director, who has been helpful throughout, that the road will formally open on 2 November. Laing hadn't bothered to tell him. He provides them with a draft script out of courtesy, but on 23 October they send him a letter saying that, provided two offending items are removed, 'permission is given for broadcasting the radio ballad.' They want a 'bloody' to be altered – collapse of stunned producer – and a reference to a workmen's hostel as a concentration camp removed. Charles is incandescent but contrives to write an emollient reply and takes no action. Laing evidently continue over his head, because Morris's deputy David Gretton writes to explain to them that 'Parker is over his boots in mud, so to speak', but he doesn't budge either. In fact the hostel that the diminutive Irish bulldozer driver Jack Hamilton refers to wasn't even run by Laing, or even on their section of the motorway, but they're twitchy about any further adverse publicity. If *Song of a Road* has a characteristic voice, it belongs to the jocular Jack Hamilton of Cork. He starts a roll call of a dozen labourers with different accents telling us where they're from – 'Jack Hamilton, yes, Cork City' – which at the end he sums up with:

> They're black men, white men, and they're all colours up there, brindle and all. Oh they're a good old crowd, oh they are yes. Oh they're a good old crowd. Oh, ah, we get on good.

The programme was broadcast on 5 November, Guy Fawkes Day, three days after the road was opened. Charles got his complete hour this time. Ewan and Peggy, who were off on a singing tour of Canada with their baby Neill, were not there to hear the broadcast and read the reviews. Their subsequent unhappiness with it, due to that lack of process/people balance which led to the summit meeting described in the next chapter, meant that they hardly heard it afterwards. But Peggy, listening to it intently again in 2007 after nearly 50 years, was surprised by its freshness and power. She concludes: 'This is much better than I remember it. I've always dismissed this as not working.'

Its last quote is from another Irish labourer, keen to get home at last: 'The motorway there. There's one thing I'd like to do when it would be finished.

I'd love to drive the whole length of it. Just, and that would finish me with it.' Charles, too, was finished with it, and can't have spent much time at home either. But he perked up somewhat when the first reviews came in. While it didn't achieve quite such universal approbation as its pioneering predecessor, for Paul Ferris it was:

> A near-triumph by *Axon* standards and an absolute marvel by any other. *John Axon* had a story and this only a theme, so someone should have weeded out the superfluous statistics, but it was when the writing and singing got away from figures and sizes that things began to hum in a very new-fashioned way. Men, recorded working and drinking and lovingly stitched into the programme, sounded just like men. Ewan MacColl's songs were charged with sadness and adventure. There was the feeling not that an artificial legend was being created for a minority audience, but that the sources of real legend were being tapped. If Joan Littlewood were still working for radio, this would be her kind of programme. These are certainly the most exciting pieces of pure radio you can find nowadays.

Robert Robinson though, who had loved *John Axon*, felt it was indeed an artificial legend. His was a criticism of the use of folk song at all:

> I felt that the producers were guilty of ... supplying a romance not inherent in the events. You felt that the producers had wanted to use such songs long before they ever met a contemporary worker on a contemporary road. In Axon the story gave rise to the treatment, in the later work the treatment was imposed. The abiding impression was not of a folk song but a folksy song.

An unexpected reviewer turns up in the Birmingham Post, and he was entranced. He seems to have missed *John Axon*, for he hopes 'this blend of song, music and speech' will be repeated:

> First, because it exhilarates by the emotions it deals with and its uninhibited way with them. There is a pioneer elation about it. The wonder is that it has appeared in a project so mechanised, up to date and unproductive as the M1 ... And the form it took was ideally happy ... Months were spent recording men talking and at work, months more editing and orchestrating and shaving off a scrap of speech, teasing it into place, adding new words to old work songs and ballads, employing, in the way Kipling loved, craft or trade terms, lists of machines, inventories, the whole part and parcel of engineering. Sixty seven miles may not seem much. But *Song of a Road* turns its achievement into an offshoot of the epic.

> Peggy Seeger set every scrap to music, with instruments like guitar, ocarina, banjo and trumpet, which a man might sling across his shoulders or stuff in his

haversack. Sea chanties, Dixieland jazz, a snatch of oratorio, the diddle-a-dum a day ceilidh jog-trot, even the authentic *musique concrète* of the mixers. It's all there, stimulating and ingenious ... It's equally apt for an Irish mother to be singing new words to an old separation song [sung by Isla Cameron]:

But remember lad, he's still your Dad,
Though he's working far away,
In the cold and the heat,
All the days of the week,
On England's motorway.

Waxing so lyrical was Alexander Walker, later a celebrated film critic. This will have cheered Charles, not least as sceptical views had been expressed after *John Axon*, by such as the poet and broadcaster Louis MacNeice: 'You have proved that the ballad and the idiom of traditional music can be a valid form of expression for the twentieth century, and for the mass media ... but only when it is applied to a simple black-and-white situation.' But Charles was stung to violent irritation by one of two articles in the same issue of *The Listener*, the BBC's own highbrow magazine. In the first Ian Rodgers had said that its approach to the treatment of a documentary subject raised problems which it solved most interestingly, and concluded that Ewan and Charles were working towards a new and exciting form. But David Paul scorned the end product in the second article, in which he compares it to:

a bomb made of ham ... as patented by Brecht and Littlewood. Good ingredients – splendid voices, exciting tape documentary, good tunes, nice musical noises. Why is the result so portentously unreal? The rigours of socialist realism balladry demand that the grass-widow sits at home rocking the cradle with her toe and crooning a lullaby, all about daddy away working on the roads ... For me ... the bits of real individual lives were lost inside the total concrete-mixer.

So Walker's meat is Paul's poison. Charles let himself get absolutely livid, and he blasted off a long intemperate letter to *The Listener*, piled high with towers of mixed metaphor. Perhaps it would have been published had he, as Denis Morris subsequently told him in a sharp letter of reproof, cut it severely. Perhaps it would have passed muster had he confined himself to assuring Mr Paul that 'the words of the lullaby that he so castigates did indeed emerge directly from words quoted by a labourer away from home for months on end', and to asking whether he 'really believes that the inhabitants of Oklahoma habitually sing "Oh What a Beautiful Morning" on rising?' But Morris liked the programme, fortunately, and sent him a congratulatory letter. So did Norman Corwin, who gratified Charles by writing that he even preferred it to *John Axon*.

The BBC audience gave it a more unanimous thumbs-up than it had offered for *John Axon*, though there were still plenty who wanted a story uninterrupted by music. A solicitor described it as confused, involved, repetitious, jerky and flippant, and a perplexed farmer's wife missed the point: she 'couldn't believe workmen sing while engaged in mechanical labour.' Some simply found it unintelligible. But a woodworker spoke for the majority. (Note incidentally the point about the writing: there was of course no actual writing at all apart from the songs, just selection and assembly.)

> Surely radio at its best. A joy to listen to such an intriguing story told in such an original manner. The writing was imaginative and clever, the music appropriate, the whole integrated into a most entertaining hour. The atmosphere was one of hustle and bustle in which one could almost see the road growing. The speech was authentic and moving, the words of the songs gloriously muscular and genuine, refreshing stuff compared to the ersatz neurotic slobbering of Tin Pan Alley.

Charles is soon back into his usual post-programme tidy-up. He writes praising the magnificent support he has received from the studio staff, especially his tape editor Mary Baker who has 'devoted herself unsparingly to the programme' and would become absolutely crucial to the Radio Ballads' success, and probably to his own sanity. He writes to every reviewer, replies to every letter whether of praise or criticism. He goes into battle with BBC bureaucrats on behalf of Louis Killen, whose fee the accountants were cavilling over – '£23 does the barest justice to his appearance and performance' – and of three singers without proper contracts (and thus not guaranteed repeat fees) to make sure they get them.

What next? As the *Times* reviewer had said, sympathetic but not entirely convinced: 'The idea which the authors are pursuing is fascinating; one hopes that they will next time hit upon a style which gives it the force of integrity.' This time he already has an idea. An achingly sad Scots voice on *Song of a Road* had said –

There's no work in Peterhead. I have to leave home for work you see. Travelling the fishing, working among the herring. Then when the war's finished you see, the steam went out and the diesel come in. So I had to take off somewhere else. Pick and shovel.

But before Charles can start on the Fishing he gets a nasty surprise in a letter from Ewan and Peggy on their return from Canada. An ultimatum.

CHAPTER 9

From Microphone to Broadcast
Engineering the Programmes

I am fairly clear that there are several members of your staff who have passed through the stage of finding Parker so odd as to be laughable, and have reached the stage of finding him so original as to be exciting. They forgive his demands because they have learned that it is a stimulating experience to do their best to respond to him.

CHARLES PARKER'S IMMEDIATE BOSS DAVID GRETTON
TO THE BBC CHIEF ENGINEER, 1959

Charles wasn't desperately good at explaining things and when we began he kept saying everybody must Create, all the time, and the phrase I've never forgotten is, when we were all punch drunk, he said we should be aiming at a mood of Controlled Despair. My only question, had I dared ask it, would have been 'How do we control it?'

GILLIAN FORD (NÉE REEVES), PLAYING IN THE SOUND EFFECTS ON
SINGING THE FISHING, INTERVIEWED IN 2007

An Ultimatum

At the end of 1959 Charles, Ewan and Peggy all wanted to make changes to the way they constructed the Radio Ballads before they started work on *Singing the Fishing*. Charles was exasperated by all the technical difficulties he faced before and after recording. They exhausted and dispirited him. But he was totally unprepared for a letter from Ewan and Peggy threatening to pull out of future collaboration entirely. They would only continue if <u>they</u> were allowed to make the final choice of the sections of actuality in the programme, and they stressed their view that the team should concentrate in future on working people and their attitudes to the job, not on the job itself.

As we saw in the last chapter, a disagreement had emerged between Charles and Ewan over the programme's main target. Because the idea for *Song of a Road* had been 'suggested' by his ultimate boss Denis Morris, Charles felt his remit was to mark the actual creation of the M1. It was, after all, designed to be broadcast when the road's first section opened. Ewan thought that the programme's strength lay in celebrating the workmen who had created it, their diversity of voice, background and job, rather than the process of road-building itself. He had been convinced of this principle as long ago as Bridson's *Tunnel* of 1934. It's tempting to conclude that this view was obviously because of Ewan's political convictions, but it wasn't quite as simple. The Radio Ballads aren't polemics: he does deliberately let working people have their say, rather than speaking for them.

Despite the difficulties of achieving his Radio Ballad concept, Charles was utterly convinced that they were pioneering the future of radio, so the letter upset him deeply. It was clearly an ultimatum, and once more he could see a potentially wonderful series foundering just as it was out of port. He dashed off an intemperate 12-page reply in longhand in which he charged them with putting at risk the entire future of radio, and condemning him to a 'life of professional drudgery and bleak mediocrity' if they abandoned the form. He waited for a reply, stewing, but none came for several days. Was that to be it?

In this chapter I want to step back to look at the key issues they had to resolve in late 1959 before they could agree on an approach to the programmes and a consistent workable method of making them. First we'll examine the gist of Ewan and Peggy's complaint, and how it was resolved, then look at the struggles that Charles faced and overcame in those pioneering early days of tape editing, when he was taking the process as far as it would go, then further still. At the outset it's worth reviewing the stages in the making of the first two programmes:

a) several weeks of recording in the field, usually by a pair or all three of them,

b) a short period for Charles to sort out the resulting tapes and send the voice tapes to Ewan and Peggy while he worked with the sound effects,
c) several weeks for Ewan and Peggy to painstakingly transcribe all the tapes, select the actuality, create the songs and a script, and produce musical arrangements,
d) a variable period for Charles to assemble the chosen actuality, get the sound effects recorded on acetate disc, finalise the booking of rehearsal and recording studios and times, contact, commit, and create contracts for the other performers, and manage all the tedious administrative grind that entailed,
e) a rehearsal and recording period in London of about a fortnight,
f) a protracted post-production period of several weeks for Charles while he wrestled with vagaries of tape quality and recording speed to make the final programme, which he was then forced to modify again…

Rules of Engagement

As with *The Ballad of John Axon*, for *Song of a Road* Ewan and Peggy had delivered to Charles an orchestrated script of songs and music, with their voice actuality choices marked. But when he'd come to run it through, Charles had felt that some of the work processes were neglected, and was clearly concerned that he would face internal criticism as a consequence. He had to make sure that he could continue to make such enthralling programmes (whether or not anyone else was enthralled, he certainly was), and he'd had a bad enough time with his BBC colleagues after playing them the first version of *John Axon*. So he had come back to Ewan with a further selection of actuality, and asked for more songs to amplify it. Ewan was not best pleased, but complied. As Ewan said –

> When Charles heard the tapes, he felt that we hadn't achieved the desired balance between 'the human expression of the job' on the one hand and work processes on the other. He decided, therefore, to choose some alternative actuality himself. This was the only occasion on which he did so in any of the Radio Ballads and the results were less than satisfactory. The introduction into the script of actuality dealing exclusively with technical matters meant that new songs had to be written, songs dealing with technical processes such as building cantilever bridges, songs explaining geological systems, songs celebrating chains of command in management…

A modern listener, hearing the surveyors and engineers often expressing, however awkwardly and flatly, their own enthusiasm for the job, can enjoy the contrast with the more piquant colloquial phrases employed by the workmen. But Ewan was convinced it was a mistake, and, when they returned from a tour of Canada soon after *Song of a Road* was broadcast, they wrote to Charles.

After receiving Charles's reply, Ewan and Peggy were still equivocating about whether to continue the collaboration – they had plenty of other work, as they did throughout the Radio Ballad period. A few days later an agitated Charles appeared at their house with peace offerings – 'a large bunch of flowers and a sticky mass of chocolate melted in the glove compartment', in Peggy's words. They made up, and in several meetings over the next few weeks they thrashed out some rules of engagement. They agreed in principle that the Radio Ballads 'should not be concerned with processes but with people's attitudes to them; not with things but with people's relationships with those things, and with the way in which those attitudes and relationships were expressed in words.' Charles bought into Ewan's view completely, and thereafter there's rarely a sign of anything more than a cigarette paper between them. (Although of course they would occasionally argue furiously over that cigarette paper thickness.)

The working method would change too. Ewan and Peggy would still sit down with the tapes and transcribe them all, make a first-cut selection, create songs, orchestrate them, and choose the final pieces of voice actuality. Now, however, they would send off sections to Charles to Birmingham as they were complete, with their actuality choices <u>plus alternatives</u>, so he could finalise the voice actuality and sound effect context for the songs while they were still working on the remainder. Indeed, Ewan would record a whole trial script for Charles, doing all the songs and dialect voices himself, with Peggy's rough accompaniment – and laughter. (The one for *Big Hewer* still exists, and it's very funny.) The alternative voice actuality gave Charles some freedom to manoeuvre if the original choice simply wouldn't work. This would clearly save time in the long run, though that would be offset by the sheer volume of tapes they brought back from the field, which increased all the time.

Mobile Tape Recording

So that was their combined working process sorted, but Charles's relationship to his own work process was still pretty unhappy. He had encountered fiendish technical problems. We've seen that the use of the mobile tape recorder was relatively new in 1957 when Charles started on *The Ballad of John Axon*. The technology was just over 20 years old, the first Magnetophon having been unveiled by BASF at the Berlin radio fair in 1935. No other countries exploited the new technology, but Goebbels' Propaganda Ministry used it extensively, and there were steady refinements through the war. (The Magnetophon and the accompanying Volksempfänger radio receiver, which was of deliberate short range to avoid Allied broadcasts getting through, allowed Hitler's long speeches to be recorded and heard in every German home.) In late 1945 Geoffrey Bridson found himself making a programme in Norway, using commandeered German recording gear, and was astounded by its sound quality. In London the BBC had a single captured Magnetophon machine to play them back on:

> Here was something that completely outclassed either wire or disc or film recording ... in quality of reproduction ... A single day's practice in editing them, snipping away with a razor blade, was all that I needed to convince me how obsolete all other mobile recording systems had become. I loudly sang [its] praises ... only to be told that it failed to come up to the exacting standards of BBC engineering!

Bridson was scathing about the administrators who 'never made a recording or ever entered a studio in their lives.' Philip Donnellan was amazed in 1953 to find that the tiny state radio in Copenhagen had eight tape editing channels at a time there was only one in the whole BBC. A conservative attitude to tape, together with a chronic money shortage, meant that by 1952 only six of Britain's long-gestated Magnetophon successor, the EMI Midget, were available to producers. By 1955 there were 100. After 1957 its valves were being replaced by transistors, the speed was halved so you could get 15 minutes on one tape running at 7½ inches a second, and a more robust version emerged, created for a Polar expedition. From then on there was constant aggravation between the engineering and programme production arms of the BBC. To the engineers the EMI Midget was 'small, light yet robust', as the BBC's official engineering history proclaims, and it 'held the field unchallenged for over 15 years.' Not unchallenged by Charles Parker. As he never tired of pointing out, they were heavy, boxy, sharp-cornered, poorly designed for the field. He was constantly nagging for a Nagra, a smaller, superior Swiss machine, but twice the price. They didn't even get him one in time for *Travelling People*, the last Radio Ballad – they used one Ewan and Peggy had bought. (She still has it, in perfect working order. She tells the tale of the BBC man arriving at Nagra's Swiss factory carrying a possible order for 2000. He wanted a few changes. Nagra's MD responded stiffly 'We don't make toys.' Hence no BBC Nagras. Eventually the German Uher emerged, a quarter of the Midget's volume and half its weight.)

Manipulating Tape

In 1957 nearly half of all recording was still done on disc. Cutting and splicing tape was still an arcane art, and only specialist editing assistants were allowed to do it. You couldn't possibly let a producer loose in the editing studio. At this time the young radio engineer Alan Ward was working for the BBC in London. Since getting his first radio set at the age of five, he'd always wanted to make programmes, starting on the RAF station where he did National Service. He joined the BBC as a trainee engineer in Birmingham in 1953, when everything was still disc-based, and was working in the Aeolian Hall in London in 1956 when the big 'BTR/2' machines were installed there, used for playing tapes for broadcast. Ward said that you were only rarely allowed to edit tape in emergency – 'it simply wasn't done.' An episode of the comedy *Take it From Here* had to be rejigged after its star Jimmy Edwards had arrived in the studio drunk, but that was an exception.

A radio fanatic, Ward had started secretly cutting and splicing tape for himself to examine the effects and was told he should listen to a programme made by this 'mad red-bearded producer in Birmingham, who cut up bits of tape that he suspended from clothes pegs in his office.' He listened to *John Axon* and was not ashamed to say he cried at the end, it was so powerful. And original: as an engineer he realised how many hours Charles must have spent working on the tapes to achieve the effect. Back in Birmingham, Ward was seconded to help Charles Parker on *Song of a Road*.

'He sent me out to record trucks on the A45. I spent most of the night doing it – the trouble was they kept stopping, thinking that I was thumbing a lift, the microphone stuck out like that.' He eventually got the job he craved. 'On Friday I was an engineer, on Monday a studio manager. I sat with my engineer friends in the canteen that morning and was told by my boss in no uncertain terms that I wasn't to any more. There was such a divide then.' Philip Donnellan said there was criminally little exchange of ideas between producers and engineers. 'To us the engineers were a class apart, like the … commissionaires or canteen ladies … the chief victims of the class system in the BBC … Charles changed all that by crossing the line.'

Charles Parker had incurred the wrath of the Head of Engineering when he was discovered at the end of his weeks of secret nightly editing sessions on *John Axon*. In an exchange of letters Charles pointed out that he could edit tape perfectly well, and was backed up by his assistant, who got a flea in the ear in consequence. Moreover, Charles was convinced that he simply had to do some of it himself:

> This is not in any way to criticise the capacities of orthodox tape editors, but simply that editing of this nature is ultimately a question of unconsciously applied rhythms and the achievement of an organic synthesis between natural rhythms of speech and the singer, and natural rhythms of the … piece of actuality … to be used. Such subtleties of rhythm can only reside in the fingers of he who feels the rhythms … It's like asking a painter to paint with a brush in somebody else's hands.

The BBC Engineering hierarchy clearly thought this was just so much bullshit, and they'd wanted to ban him from editing altogether. But a few months earlier Charles had got his Birmingham management to send him on the tape editing training course. He then managed to intercept one of the scarce new TR/90 playback machines, due for Norwich, and hang on to it for a crucial three weeks. Because of all the obstruction he'd encountered Charles was so infuriated at the end of *Song of a Road* that he fired off two scathing memos of complaint. In the first he wrote a withering piece to Denis Morris, his Midlands head, about 'political' interference and obstruction by Laing, the main contractor. It begins:

> *Song of a Road* was completed in despite of difficulties – not to say deliberate opposition – to a degree which all but stifled the work many times over. I hope personally that never again will I have to endure the frustrations, the deep rooted prejudices and ignorance, the desperate Philistinism which have marked virtually every stage in the production of this programme.

In a second fulminating memo he turned his attention to his technical problems. He was particularly exercised by his knowledge that commercial recording facilities were so superior to those of the hidebound BBC. 'I have so often expounded at great length upon the inadequacies of the EMI tape recorder that I am sick at heart to have to add to it.' But he overcame his nausea to launch another five pages of foolscap. He was incensed by several issues that were making the final assembly of the programme so infuriatingly complicated. First were the difficulties of speed and balance he frequently encountered when he came to play back the tapes, as well as the tape's sheer unreliability. Second was the time it often took to get the studio equipment working properly while he had the performers ready and waiting. His embarrassment at being made to look incompetent led to this engaging outburst:

> The original gelding of all Ferrograph machines by removing their control knobs and sealing them off at mid-position is an insult to intelligent use … The machine itself – with its vicious spooling hook wiping head guide and felt padded ironmongery – is a menace to tape joins. And the savage psychological effect of using inadequate inferior badly lashed-up equipment can be devastating especially while an expensive cast have to stand around kicking their heels and burning up rehearsal time. I was … in an office with no power points of any sort – which meant illegally operating the machine from the light socket.

Hmmm … A fusillade of memos ensued between Charles, his immediate boss David Gretton, and the obdurate Chief Engineer, who complained that Charles had worked two of his engineers for 13-hour days for over a week (including one Geoffrey Leonard, who Charles said 'wrought marvels' with the poor equipment). Gretton, though, was both sympathetic and a master of the deflating memo. To the Chief Engineer, following his complaint that Charles had 'worked alone in the principal tape editing channel, <u>contrary to regulations</u>' (original emphasis), Gretton wrote to point out that the engineers enjoyed working for Parker. On his memo copy Charles scrawled a biblical reference – Matthew XII 3+4 – which is when the hungry David eats the bread reserved for the priests (I've sorted out Goliath for them, now they fuss about <u>this</u>). Gretton's memo had begun with a crisp rejoinder:

> The regulations are based on certain propositions:
>
> 1. This expensive equipment might be damaged. But this hasn't happened.
> 2. The work might involve danger by electric shock. So might the submarine branch of the Navy.

A further difficulty Charles faced was in matching the music created in the studio with the voice actuality recorded in the field. In the studio while they were recording Charles was in charge, accompanied by a studio manager, and Peggy would direct the musicians and singers. Charles would listen through headphones to decide whether a particular take – on its own, or in combination with previous takes – seemed OK, then they'd move on to the next. In rehearsal they'd have decided what extra musical bridges and colouring passages to improvise, and often that would be altered in recording. The big problem was that in both *John Axon* and *Song of a Road* the musicians and singers recorded their pieces largely unaware of the vocal and sound setting in which they were to be placed.

The Studio Set-up

There had to be a better way, and Charles decided that if he could scrounge another scarce TR/90 playback machine to put on the studio floor, then an experienced assistant with a musical bent could play it on the spot so that the singers and musicians could hear what they were playing against, instead of in a sound vacuum. He managed to acquire another TR/90, a heavy three-foot cube, to install in the recording studio, where an operator could play back the actuality <u>live</u>, among the musicians and under Peggy's direction. It needed a soundproof housing cobbled together because the solenoid made a very audible clunk when it engaged, but after some trial-and-error it worked, helped by a tent of acoustic screens. So in the words of Alan Ward, who did the job on *Singing the Fishing*, 'I almost become a musician myself', and the singers and musicians could start to match their vocal and playing rhythms to the voices they heard, rather than doing it more-or-less blind (or rather, deaf).

The final crucial change was to where they rehearsed and recorded. As there were no suitable recording facilities in Birmingham, where Charles worked and lived, they'd recorded *Ballad of John Axon* and *Song of a Road* at different places in London, trailing between them. This was helpful in one key regard, because it meant Ewan and Peggy and the bulk of the other performers were closer and cheaper, but it left Charles prey to London restrictions and particularly the fearsome Engineering hierarchy there, about whom his paranoia was becoming acute. If only he could record in Birmingham, closer to home, where they knew him. In December 1959 Gretton suggested he use the cavernous Studio 6 in Birmingham, home of the Midland Light Orchestra (MLO), when they were away on tour. Although the orchestra was resident there through the year, they were away for three weeks in June, so Charles could use it if the third programme, *Singing the Fishing*, was ready in time. It would be tight, but getting the script in sections as they were complete helped him make it in time, and *Singing the Fishing* provided the working method they'd use thereafter.

The musicians were on the floor of Studio 6, along with Alan Ward playing the voice actuality through the TR/90. 'He was incredibly adept', says Peggy, who was slightly elevated and visible to the chorus and separated soloists. Up a set of stairs above in a control room with a view were Charles and the studio manager John Clarke, while behind them was Gillian Reeves on 'grams'. These were half a dozen machines that played the sound effects through on acetate discs, and Gillian would hop from one to the other like a Lancashire four-loom weaver to bring the requisite needle down at the right instant.

> One of the things I was having to do was cross-fade from one disc to another while fading up sea-wash. Not quite sure how I managed it. It was the only programme ever where I've thrown discs on the floor – there wasn't time ... One bit – you know the bit with the auctioneers and the Beaufort scale? I did cheat the auctioneers just slightly, once or twice, to get them so they sounded better against the pitch of the music ... speeded them up. Nobody ever commented on it, so it must have been all right.

Peggy Seeger says Gillian was quite brilliant, going for 10–12 hours at a stretch, never making a mistake. Because Charles had masses of 'wild sound' acetates, she had to lay instant hands on, say, 'the bit with the rattle of a chain when a man shouts Hoi.' Another faultless performer in the team was the fourth player, who wasn't actually there. Out of sight and mind was Charles's editing assistant Mary Baker, sat a mile and a half away from Studio 6, 'in the channel', the editing suite. John Clarke:

> Charles had made notes on each take and he decided which he would use for the first assembly, and he rang through at the end of sequence to Mary Baker: 'We'll use take 7, which I'm calling Blue Take.' He's making notes in different colour

crayons … Because Mary between takes has plenty of time to spare, she decided to compile the first assembly of the whole thing. So we were able, within five minutes of the last recording, to listen to the playback down the line from the studio of what we'd done the whole week. That was very unusual in broadcasting in any context. Ewan seemed bowled over by this departure from the previous ballad – to bring all the elements together into a live performance in the studio, like a concert, was something which they may have had their doubts about, but Charles knew it would be better in the long run to do it like that.

Mary Baker was vital in the post-production phase, for in practice she did most of the hard graft of splicing and editing herself. She was the backstop:

> It required very careful listening on my part to determine whether his decisions made in the studio were right. Sometimes only half a take was really good, and then an acceptable take of the other half had to be found and edited together at a point where a join could not be detected, not always easy if there was a thick mixture of sounds in the sequence. In the storm sequence one take was perfect, except that a singer's voice slipped off a note in the most dramatic part, and Charles was doubtful, but when I said 'He's one of those young ones crying below, like Sam says', he said 'Right, on to the next.' He was always ready to listen to ideas that came from involvement in the production.

Mary Baker was a selfless key worker in a seen-but-not-heard job, uncredited on the Radio Ballads. She it was who assembled stretches of silence from brief scavenged moments, as she did to get the right atmosphere for Sam's cottage – any old 'silence' just wouldn't do – and to disguise entry points. To Clarke it was unheard-of finesse. And Mary knew how to manage Charles. Clarke remembers her as 'a very caring lady, patient and kind. But she was also tough. She used to tell Charles: "No, you can't do that." And stand up to him, which was quite a thing.' His rages were famous. Alan Ward said: 'One day Charles was so dire that Mary phoned his wife to come and bring young Sara down. He'd been impossible, but it worked. He calmed down immediately.' She lived to 95, carrying his torch to the last. Late in life she had written a piece describing their editing methods. It ends like this:

> Charles Parker's work, especially on the radio ballads, was rewarding in many ways. The material and the way it was handled was an education in itself. He had taste and style and wit, and could make all concerned with him in a project give of their absolute best to it. He could create an exciting and stimulating atmosphere in which to work, and the result to me has been of lasting significance. I am glad I was there.

CHAPTER 10

The Big Catch
Singing the Fishing

I remember Charles looking down on the studio with Peggy in the middle on her podium and conducting and playing the banjo, and he said, 'Look – Peggy Seeger and her Amazing Performing People'.

JOHN CLARKE, STUDIO MANAGER, SINGING THE FISHING,
INTERVIEWED IN 2007

Course it's a wonder, too, you see, to pick one of these little fish up, the net's <u>vibrant</u> with life, rrrrrrrr, like that ... When you're doing well and catching fish, they talk to them all the time: 'Come on, spin up, my darlings, come on', and they absolutely <u>cajole</u> them into the nets.

RONNIE BALLS, RETIRED FISHING BOAT CAPTAIN,
SINGING THE FISHING, 1960

In November 1959, a fortnight after the broadcast of *Song of a Road*, Charles writes to Denis Morris and David Gretton suggesting they follow it up with a programme about East Coast herring fishermen, an idea he'd discussed with Ewan. It's a familiar theme, and although attracted to it Charles is worried that recently it had been heavily over-fished. In the past five years he had made *Harvest the Sea* with the playwright Willis Hall, and Philip Donnellan had discovered and used the old Norfolk herring fisherman and 'source' singer Sam Larner in a series of 15-minute programmes. Ewan is enthusiastic, but would prefer to look at a fishing community rather than fishing per se: he has recently been working with Scottish fishermen for Tyne Tees Television. Charles warily sounds out Denis Morris:

> I am sure a good programme could be done using Lowestoft and/or Yarmouth, and also possibly exploiting the songs and probably the voice of Sam Larner, but I know that MacColl is anxious ... to treat a small fishing community which would give a necessary discipline and cohesion to the work ... He met some fishermen from Gardenstoun on the east coast of Scotland and was wildly enthusiastic about their speech and the attitude of the community in which they live. I am therefore wondering if it would be at all possible for Ewan MacColl and me to trespass so far upon Scotland as to visit Gardenstoun and investigate the possibilities there? If we handled the East Anglian story we would not be breaking new ground, whereas the sort of treatment Gardenstoun might stimulate could be original and exciting.

To those who know *Singing the Fishing*, clearly identified with the crusty voice and salty laugh of the 80-year-old Sam Larner, it's a surprise to learn that at the outset East Anglia wasn't in the plans. But a visit to Gardenstoun revealed a problem. A Scottish features producer who knew the area had warned Charles that, while 'Gardenstoun is probably the most progressive small fishing community in the NE of Scotland ... like the others the people have strong religious views. I do not know the kind of treatment envisaged. What was done in *Song of a Road*, which to my mind was a fascinating, imaginative documentary, would probably give strong offence to the inhabitants.'

In mid-December Ewan writes a when-can-we-start letter: 'The storms last week and the [lifeboat] tragedy which they produced ... made me more convinced than ever that there is a great programme to be done on coastal seamen.' At the end of December Morris gives Charles the go-ahead (though he knows his man – he specifically bans him from making a detour to do a programme on the disaster) and Charles goes up with Ewan and Peggy in mid-January 1960. They find Gardenstoun fascinating but, as Charles writes to David Gretton: 'We didn't expect the village to be quite such a stronghold of Plymouth Brethren, and there may be problems with actuality recording. I think we should bring Yarmouth and Lowestoft in too.' Gretton's response is immediate and forthright: 'WHOA! May I acknowledge your note without accepting it? What you propose is so far removed from what HMRP [Morris] accepted that we want a fresh brief and fresh approval. Quite bluntly it raises the question of why we spent all this money on taking MacColl and Seeger to Scotland in the first place!'

Charles responds with a squirming justification, and eventually gets a reluctant go-ahead-but-I'm-watching-you. So Charles, Ewan and Peggy meet Sam Larner in the week of 7 February. This is where Ewan takes up the story:

> In East Anglia we hit pay dirt immediately when we met Sam Larner, an eighty-year-old ex-herring-fisherman from Winterton, Norfolk. He had first gone to sea in 1892 on board a sailing lugger and, in the course of his working life, had seen the sailing fleet give way to steam drifters. He had lived through the industry's golden age when Great Yarmouth had reckoned up the annual catch by the million barrels. Furthermore, Sam could sing. He knew dozens of country songs, traditional ballads, mnemonic rhymes for navigation and local legends. In the course of recording him, we set up a pattern which subsequently became our recording procedure.

In Sam's Winterton cottage, his blind wife Dorcas listening in – 'I been a wicked man in my time. Ain't that right, Dorcas?' ... 'You have, Sam, you have ... you been a wicked bugger, Sam' – they recorded him for an amazing 30 hours. Not surprisingly, he got irritable when they came back and asked him a question he had been asked before, but that became a technique used to project him – and others, later – back into the moment. After a while, no longer was he just telling the story, he was <u>reliving</u> it, and his verbal imagery became more rich and varied and often biblical. 'That come on a gale of wind, that came down the Sat'dy night and that blew for three or four days a living gale and we were in these little boats.' Ewan described Sam as sounding like Langland at times: 'Piers Plowman coming at you.'

When they'd begun, they only had a vague idea of the programme's eventual shape, beyond feeling that they had to find a novel approach. Charles wanted to avoid a 'mood' piece. Ewan suggested a pattern of tracking the fishermen as they followed the shoals round the coast, but that was a fishing method they discovered no longer operated. After meeting Sam, though, it was soon obvious that because 'he described his own life like a traditional storyteller telling one of the great Indo-European legends', a chronological treatment would work. They had originally thought that too trite. Sam had begun his working life on a 19th-century sailing boat:

> ... at 12 year old, cabin boy in the *Young John*. I done eight year in sailing boats ... There's something of a 'ooman bein' about a sailing boat, how they answer, and they talk to them, 'Go on, old girl, you'll do this, he'll do it.' They talk to them just so's they were a living being. But as regards the work, it were heaven when we gang to the drifters, the steam drifters, absolutely like heaven. I went in the *Larty*, that was the first steam drifter I went in, in October 18 and 99, and that was the first start of the good seasons. 1899.

'Ah, the steam drifter, the loveliest ship for the job that ever was built.' This was a second voice, Ronnie Balls, a generation younger, who takes over the tiller from Sam as sail gives way to steam. As Ewan said, to hear Ronnie 'describing the finer points of a steam drifter was to know tenderness and love in its purest form – and that's not exaggeration. Ronnie Balls loved steam drifters with the same kind of consuming passion that lovers in the mediaeval romances reserved for their mistresses.' They found Ronnie almost by accident, further down the coast at Yarmouth. Another articulate man, once the youngest steam drifter skipper on the Norfolk coast, he chronicled the terrible lean years between the wars. Throughout the first half of *Singing the Fishing* Ewan would dovetail their two voices, joining them with a third, George Draper, when they come to the storm scene, where Sam's 'living gale' alternates with George's 'she took a tremendous sea and I shall never forget that sea as long as I live.' The final section would move to the post-war diesel-driven, herring fishing of the Scots – Norfolk's moribund fishing was now completely dead – with the new echo-sounding gear for finding the shoals. Ronnie described it as 'if you were playing Blind Man's Buff, it's like taking off the handkerchief, isn't it?'

A second visit to the East Coast is followed by a long trip back to Scotland, where they experience the trawler man's life at first hand, working in shifts so at every instant one of them is available with a tape recorder. Charles, of course, is in his natural element at sea, but Ewan admits to being petrified, sailing in a seven-point gale through the Northern Minch on the *Honeydew*, which 'looks and feels like a toy boat lost in a grey wilderness of sea and sky. At one moment she is lifted to the summit of a great peak and the next she's ploughing through a deep trough ridged by banks of white-topped waves.' He clings onto a steel stanchion with his heavy tape recorder over one shoulder, with only a low gunwale to prevent him sliding into the sea, while 'holding up a microphone in a vain effort to record the storm.' By his side a Huguenot Scot called Lewis Cardno is 'trying to illustrate a theological point ... howling into my ear a lengthy quotation from Fox's *Book of Martyrs*.' Thus Ewan could readily identify with Sam Larner's view of Death:

That time he come for me in the North Sea, when he come in the storm, when all the young chaps were cryin' and prayin' down below. I done him then ... Ain't got long now, but when he come for me I'll look him in the eye. I ain't got nothing to be ashamed of.

By mid March they had what they needed. Meanwhile Charles's immediate boss David Gretton had been setting out how future Radio Ballads should be made. Having sorted out the location issue and swatted the engineering objections aside, he turned to the musicians:

> If you plan far enough ahead, surely they can take leave from their other occupations so that you can record when you like instead of having to do it when <u>they</u> like ... Lastly I must emphasise that this is a team enterprise or else it is nothing, and there must be an assurance that the team has been reconstituted and is going to work together, before we can put this big commitment of money and effort on to the conveyor belt ... You know my feelings on this and I cannot alter them.

Costs were capped. But now that Charles understood how much time he had to organise for the fiendish post-recording editing process, he was happy with that, and set rehearsal and recording dates for the first two weeks of June 1960, when the studio was free because the orchestra was on tour. With a huge map of the North Sea pinned up on the wall beside them, Ewan and Peggy started on the tapes:

> The final playback and transcription of the actuality took Peggy and me the best part of three weeks. After choosing and timing the actuality for the programme we compiled a tape of alternative actuality choices. We would categorise these choices by subject or idea, such as 'Hauling', 'The Catch'. The tape machine rolled and stopped as we put markers in the tape reel or correlated the transcript with the tape. The typewriter clacked on. Scraps of paper floated about the work-table: memos on which were scrawled odd words or phrases ('that night it blew a living gale') clipped to another scrap of paper with a couplet: 'In the stormy seas and the living gales, Just to earn your daily bread you're darin''.

> The scraps accumulated; 'we need a song with a refrain here'; 'how about the mandolin on this song?'; 'it's time for something up-tempo'. Or it might be an entire song text that would require only ten or fifteen minutes polishing. The writing of the songs took me about a month or maybe a little longer. Peggy spent another two weeks on the musical arrangements. We then made rough tapes of the songs and played them to Sam Larner, Ronnie Balls and anyone else who was

prepared to listen to them. Occasionally they would criticise a word or a line or a phrase or question a piece of information, whereupon I would rewrite the offending line or phrase and go on rewriting it until it met with approval. There were rare and wonderful occasions when Sam or one of the other fishermen would claim to have known all his life a song which I had just written. When this happened, we knew we had really come close to capturing the true effect of the fishing life upon these men.

They rehearsed and recorded in Birmingham from 29 May to 10 June 1960. The fishermen's voices were now played in by Alan Ward on the TR/90, down on the studio floor with the old hands Bert Lloyd, Bruce Turner, Alf Edwards, Fitzroy Coleman, Jim Bray, and a new fiddler, Kay Graham. Ewan as a solo singer was joined by John Clarence from *Song of a Road* and Ian Campbell, who later ran a successful folk group in Birmingham while still working as an engraver in the Jewellery quarter. Some of the Clarion choir, a Birmingham group with radical origins, were used to form a chorus under Katharine Thomson, and they included Gordon McCulloch, like Campbell an émigré Scot. The Clarion chorus singers, apart from the two Scots, found it difficult to unlearn their usual singing technique to sing in a style more suited to folk song.

Two young singers who had no such difficulty were Elizabeth and Jane Stewart, close sisters from a 'settled' Traveller family, whose mother had been a popular dance band leader in Peterhead. Ewan and Peggy had nipped over to Fetterangus while recording in Gardenstoun, and had been beguiled by their instinctive harmonising on 'The Back o' Benachie' to a jangling piano. Ewan would use the tune for one of two delightful songs written in Scots dialect for the women who came from Aberdeen to Yarmouth each summer for a 'holiday' gutting herring.

> **It's early in the morning**
> **And it's late into the nicht,**
> **Your hands a' cut and chappit**
> **And they look an unco' sicht,**
> **But you greet like a wean**
> **When you put them in the bree,**
> **And you wish you were a thoosand mile**
> **Awa' frae Yarmouth Quay.**

The women would spend all day with their hands in brine, where 'the rough salt breaks your skin, the pickle gets in', but they were days with no cooking, no domestic chores waiting when they got back. Elizabeth Stewart remembers coming down overnight, her first ever train journey, leaving

Scotland for the first time at the age of 20. She and Jane had a wonderful time, picking up the songs instantly, and dancing through the Birmingham streets serenaded by the fascinating Fitzroy as he composed impromptu calypsos for them to a guitar accompaniment.

Recording was long, intense, unremitting, take after take for some scenes: the complete storm sequence runs to ten and a half minutes. Here the fishermen's stories are interleaved both with a song whose rising tempo matches the coming gale and with the parallel crescendo of the auctioneer's hectic gabble on Yarmouth Quay. The prices rise with the wind as the men face mountainous waves, waiting for 'the one as is going to git us.' Ian Campbell found it exhilarating but exhausting. The Clarion chorus had been disconcerted at audition to find Ewan insisting they should sing unaccompanied. Not so Campbell. As he sang his solo audition piece he could see in the soundproof control room an enthusiastic Ewan, joining in his rousing 'Barnyards o' Delgaty'. When it came to rehearsal Ian found himself pulled out as an extra soloist, and he describes the recording process:

> I had imagined that we should have to learn the songs and record them independently so that they were ready for insertion in the programme … but the process was not to be so simple … MacColl had isolated not only obvious elements such as vocabulary and phraseology, but subtler elements such as speech rhythms and vocal patterns. It was not possible to regard the actuality and songs as separate components which could be created independently and then assembled into a finished product; they were overlapped and intertwined … musical rhythm was synchronised with speech rhythm or sound effects, and songs took their tempo and pace from the preceding actuality … The edited actuality was played through a loudspeaker into the control room above, and simultaneously to the musical director and her group in the studio. The producer was then able to combine and balance the two channels as he recorded them onto a master tape.

> Most of the music took the form of sequences which lasted anything up to ten minutes, and which might demand the rapid alternation of speech with solo song, chorus, instrumental music, sound effects, or any combination of all four. Each sequence had to be recorded in its entirety, and during the longer ones tension would mount to the point where mistakes were inevitable. But it seemed that nothing but perfection was acceptable to Parker; having recorded a sequence for the 24th time the studio would wait with bated breath for the producer's decision, only to be told that one of us had taken an audible breath in a silent bar … perhaps take 25 would be the successful one?

> Every day Charles became a little more dishevelled, a little more wild-eyed and a little more volatile, and it was easy to believe that when our work finished in

the evening he went home to work late into the night … MacColl also began to show the physical effects … though it had no visible effect on the intensity of concentration he brought to bear upon his work in the studio. The musicians in the instrumental ensemble, each one a prominent and respected figure in his own field … did all that was required of them, with an air of confidence and quiet enjoyment, and somehow they managed to adopt an attitude of responsibility towards the music …[while maintaining] a rather cool detachment from the music they were performing.

Perhaps one of the reasons Charles was so meticulous in the studio, even more determined for perfection, was that he knew two days into recording that the programme would be a candidate for the BBC's entry for the Italia Prize for radio features. The BBC hierarchy in London really liked the script, so he'd better make sure the final recording did it justice. He told John Clarke so, but no one else. Clarke had been surprised to be asked at short notice to be studio manager for the recording – it was only a couple of years since he'd started at the BBC, rattling the teacups for *The Archers*. He viewed Charles with the same kind of anxious awe that the singers had for Ewan MacColl. Campbell had regarded Ewan as a 'rather brooding and imposing presence' on stage, and said: 'I had heard report of him as a brusque and overbearing personality, so I was pleasantly surprised to find him friendly and relaxed and even, a description I am sure he would contemptuously reject, charming.' One key aspect, as Peggy pointed out, was that there in the studio she and Charles were in charge – Ewan was a major figure, certainly, but he was just a singer. Up there in the control room, above the action, Charles drove himself to the limit, said Clarke.

> He'd throw chairs about, and scripts … It was always theatrical with Charles. He knew that there were moments in rehearsal when an explosion is just what's wanted to focus the mind. In the *Fishing* on two occasions he'd say 'Right, it's time for an explosion' and he'd grab these scripts and go charging out the door and down the stairs onto the floor of the studio, ripping up scripts and throwing them about like snow, everywhere … Funnily enough, I met other producers in BBC Television who did exactly the same … It was so exciting, it was a rollercoaster ride through a wonderland. Everything was new … Charles quite often turned to me and said, 'What do you think we should do?' He's asking <u>me</u>? But I think that was part of the humility he had. Because although he was a raging burning brand, he was a very humble person.

At the end of that exhausting fortnight, which had included working all through the Whitsun holiday, Charles got everyone to stay behind, and Mary Baker came through with a completed rough-cut of the programme. It was the first time most of the performers had heard it: they were knocked out, and broke into spontaneous applause. Earlier there had been some grumbles, not surprisingly. At one point during a break in a rehearsal room which housed a grand piano, in Charles's absence there was some criticism of his obsession with perfection. A moment later they were alarmed to discover Charles emerging from under the piano, where he'd been asleep, perhaps waiting out one of his incessant migraines. But he affected not to have heard anything, and at the end of the week everyone's spirits were high. Indeed Peggy had the music still fizzing in her head when she wrote to Charles a few days later saying:

> We arrived back as flat as pancakes. Don't forget we love you … We had a wonderful experience these last two weeks even if it HAS left us feeling like husks, completely unable to face even moderate inactivity for the next week. Your patience was – I won't say unusual, but let's hope it is the beginning of what we may from now on refer to as 'your usual patience'. Would love to record it all over again. The tunes are gradually fading from my mind, letting me sleep.

After they got back from the Newport folk festival in Rhode Island Peggy added, 'Any chance we could start on the coal programme?' They were far beyond the doubts about collaboration that had followed *Song of a Road*. Katharine Thomson, whose Clarion choir had been mercilessly drilled, and who became a firm friend, wrote thanking Charles for a 'tremendous experience'. Bruce Turner used the same expression, adding, 'Alongside you and Ewan and Peggy I feel roughly on a par with some of those callow young jazzmen who ask to sit in with my band from time to time.' Hearing the fishermen's voices while they were playing had made a tremendous difference to their appreciation of their parts and how it all fitted together, as well as lifting their performances.

In speaking about the programme later, Ewan explained their aversion to commentary, or introductory statements like 'I was a herring fisherman from Great Yarmouth.' In fact Ronnie Balls comes in with an oblique entrance, as Ewan says, 'as though you are right in the middle of a conversation or argument.' Hence his opening words are: 'If you fish for the herring, they rule your life.' Ronnie's words alternate, line by line, with the opening stanza of 'Shoals of Herring', one of the songs that went into the bloodstream of the folk repertoire (two years later it turned up in Ireland, wonderfully, as 'Shores of Erin'). After its last line, Ronnie's 'Come on, spin up, my darlings, come on, and they absolutely cajole them into the nets' leads straight into the pulsating rhythm of the signature song –

> Come all you gallant fishermen
> That plough the stormy sea
> The whole year round
> On the fishing grounds
> Of the Northern Minch and the Norway Deep
> On the banks and knolls of the North Sea holes
> Where the herring shoals are found.

Having got the audience's feet wet, they drench them with spray – like Sam who as a lad would have a bucket of seawater thrown over him if he nodded off on his feet – with a driving going-to-sea-for-the-first-time 'recitative'. Twelve-year-old Sam recalls his first day at sea, his words interleaved as Ewan sings:

> It's up with the dawn
> With your sea boots on
> And down to the Yarmouth quay

Cabin boy in a little boat called the Young John, 1892 …

> To fish Smith's Knoll

… little sailing boat, about forty ton …

> Where the big seas roll …

And we're off, and we're living there with cabin boy Sam's 'dread, when you first go to sea.' Ewan's operatic recitative starts the listener on a breathless hour until the final plaintive, contemplative notes of:

Our ships are small and the sea is deep
And many a fisher lad lies asleep
In the salt sea water.
But still there's a hungry world to feed
So we go where the shoals of herring breed.
In the salt sea water.

It took Charles much less time to assemble the final programme than he'd spent hitherto. This time he got an Eric Fraser classic for his *Radio Times* illustration, 'absolutely first class'. His article betrayed his excitement, though it ended on this wistful note: 'The great days of the herring trade are over ... it is salutary for an hour or so to sit at the feet of the men who knew and lived through it.' The broadcast came on 16 August, and it was an instant success. Only Charles's detested *Listener* reviewer disliked it. Paul Ferris in the *Observer*:

> Without cant or hot flushes ... where the conventional documentary would have looked at effects of men on herring fishing, it cared only about the effects of fishing on man ... it could be the grittiest kind of corn but never is because of the intense dedication with which people have been observed, recorded and patiently embedded in music ... The programmes' style is now firmly established: humanist, unselfconscious, inevitably a trifle Left.

Charles was so anxious about the audience reaction that he wrote an internal memo trying to get the researchers to pose specific questions to listeners. He got short shrift from a Miss Langley, who knew her stuff: 'The fewer and more colourless the questions put, the more freely they respond ... I think you will find much more evidence will emerge than you expect at the moment.' In the event it earned the best response of any Radio Ballad until matched by *Travelling People*, the last. Although the usual minority thought it an 'utter waste of a wonderful rich source of material unintelligible or difficult to follow ... a garbled hotchpotch', they were fewer than for *John Axon*, most agreeing that it was 'a radio epic! ... masterly in conception ... a very exceptional listening experience', and that the 'rollicking mixture of unrehearsed voices and ballad is the product of great skill and method.' (Ian Campbell would have words to say about that 'unrehearsed'.) 'Many tunes were splendidly catchy, rousing and robust, and ... captured the spirit of this tough and dogged breed of men.'

The London BBC bosses agreed, so a 45-minute version was created for, and in due course won, the 1960 Italia Press Association Prize for documentaries. Before going off to Trieste Charles despatched effusive letters of thanks to the hard-driven technical team, saying to Mary Baker that if there had been any justice she would have been there too. (She wrote later that all she had hoped for was to have been on the credits.) Charles replied to a sheaf of letters from performers, fishermen – Sam Larner proud at being heard in so many countries – anonymous listeners, and old friends. Ian Mackintosh, who had commanded Charles's first submarine, wrote: 'You simply must keep this up, for God knows radio cries out to be used with sensitivity, imagination and comprehension instead of ... being brutalised by turgid banalities.' Charles returned from Italy with a prize that made him a lira millionaire (£500), and bags of presents, including a tie for his stepfather, who wrote thanking him, saying 'The characters portrayed came over still wet from the salt sea spray ... Am much better since I changed my job at the factory, having got out of the acids and anxieties and am in the stores mainly stock checking.'

Alan Lomax is thrilled when he hears it on WBAI-FM in New York, and asks for a copy to play to the American Anthropological Society. His plaudits on the Italia Prize award are shrugged aside by Charles: 'All that really owes more to Ewan and Peggy and above all to Sam Larner and Ronnie Balls.' To Ewan and Peggy he writes about issuing the Radio Ballads as records: 'We should get together and plan an assault [on record companies].' He has had many requests from listeners aching to hear the programmes again – no wonder, when they have so much to miss on first hearing, and need good reception and close concentration. Meanwhile he bemoans the prosaic work he's obliged to do in Stoke after returning from a three-week family holiday 'in a state of wildest confusion and contradiction.' To the violinist Kay Graham he confides, 'I have a quite terrible sense of lethargy and inadequacy which makes any sort of past achievement quite unrelated to me as I now am.'

After the family holiday Charles is eager to get started on a programme about Mining. Ewan and Peggy had been making programmes for the National Coal Board for over a year and are convinced they have their next subject. But despite the cachet of the Italia Prize Charles is by no means certain of internal support. He tells Ewan: 'I have not yet got the go-ahead to take on the Mining. Jobs have changed hands at the BBC.' His new bosses are startled by his programme costs and the length of time he takes to make them. However, while Ewan and Peggy are in the USA (Ewan has got a visa at last), he goes off to his first Durham Miners' Gala, and writes to Ewan: 'A folk dance group of us danced and piped until four in the morning – Ye Gods what people!' Ewan would assert that it was Charles's first experience of miners that changed his life.

CHAPTER 11

Another Bloody Working-Class Epic
The Big Hewer

Before we were half-way through the field-work he confessed to feeling utterly uneducated in the presence of miners ... how could one feel superior in the presence of men who appeared to have experienced everything and who could talk coherently about anything under the sun? For Charles it was a revelation and he was later to refer to it as the beginning of his education.

EWAN MACCOLL, ON CHARLES PARKER, IN JOURNEYMAN, 1990

My, he was a big man. Could you imagine? He was 18 stone. No fat. No fat – 18 stone of man. What they call the County Durham Big Hewer. Like a machine when he was hewing, you could hear the pick pick pick pick as regular as this clock. Never used to seem ever to tire.

THE DURHAM MINER JACK ELLIOTT, THE BIG HEWER, 1961

One morning in early 1961 the Newcastle folk singer Louis Killen, the late substitute on *Song of a Road*, answered a knock on the door of his mother's council flat in Jesmond. Standing outside, entirely unexpected, were Charles Parker and Ewan MacColl, loaded with recording equipment. 'Take us to some miners' was the gist of their message, and so he did. He took them to Johnny Handle, a mining friend who had discovered Bert Lloyd's collection of mining songs and began writing his own and singing them in clubs. Handle had been a miner till recently, but had given it up for folk song. Louis Killen:

> I sat in on the Johnny Handle sessions ... Six hours. They would just let Johnny talk ... they would interject to get clarification but mostly they would just let them talk on and on. Not an interview with set questions, not a BBC approach!

Louis took them to see the Elliott brothers, Jack and Reece, and was there for one of the several interviews they had with them. The Elliotts were wonderful at igniting those verbal sparks. Ewan: 'We had 12 people in the room at first and metaphor would top metaphor; it's like people firing proverbs at each other. It's the kind of speech that Swift would have been quite pleased to have written down.'

Charles had got the go-ahead for the programme on miners and mining late in 1960. He and Ewan decided to delve in three areas: South Wales, the North Midlands (DH Lawrence country), and the North-East, and all threw up fascinating characters. In the North-East it was Handle and the Elliotts: 'with Jack Elliott we got enough stories for an extra hour.' In South Wales they were put on to soft-voiced Ben Davies, known as Sunshine, a miner with a natural flair for language, to whom they returned for extra material, notably in the Dust section: 'a rare man, a very conscious artist ... [he gave us] tremendous passages.' Another South Wales miner was Dick Beamish. Peggy reflected on Charles's response:

> Dick Beamish staggered Charles. It shook him how articulate he was, a littlish man who took them on a long walk underground to a pile of coal where his friend had died in a fall. He made them turn their lamps out to experience total blackness. So dark, dizzy, nauseous. You could hear the earth creaking. Walking back, he suddenly said 'Stop', went very still, and over on the right there was the crash of a rock fall, which he'd sensed. And walked on.

Ewan elaborated:

> Meeting miners was, for Charles, a shattering experience. Up until this point he had managed to hold on to the somewhat Panglossian view that everything was all right (or nearly all right) in this best of all possible worlds. The coalfields

changed all that. We took our tape recorders into the pit-canteens, pithead baths, into pubs and miners' welfares. We dragged them through the galleries of drift mines in Northumberland and West Durham, down the deep shafts of East Durham and the hardrock mines of Wales, along the wide straight roads of East Midland horizon mines ... and we dragged ourselves along impossibly narrow passages into the hellish places where solitary miners lie on their sides and jab with short-bladed picks at the 18-inch coal-face.

Later Peggy was able to join them for a trip underground. Just like the fishermen, the miners would have ordered her out if they'd known, but in a pit helmet and clobber and with her hair tucked in she wasn't discernibly female as long as she kept her mouth shut. Her worst moment was feeling the claustrophobia while 'swimming' on her elbows in a three-foot seam. She dared not speak, and there was no going back.

Of course, Ewan and Charles were sent first to the 'characters', natural storytellers, and one's first reaction as an outsider is to assume that they're hardly representative. But Ewan stressed that there were many anonymous miners who became just as articulate, like the man who Charles bumped into outside Durham Cathedral. He was Ernest Black, a Nottinghamshire miner who became one of their best informants – once they'd found his lost false teeth. And as students of language, they had a field day. Ewan said:

> If you watch the miners as they come in the morning and wait at the pit top, they're talking and suddenly you realise you can't understand what they are saying, their talk becomes broader and broader as they stand there, they're entering into a new language as well, 'Pitmatic', where you never have to complete a sentence ... in its own way it's as economic as Cant [the Travellers' private language]. Completely different world.

> At the end of our field-recording stint, we had taped between two and three hundred reels of mining 'crack', the conversation of men who can make words ring like hammer blows on a face of anthracite, who, when they talk, enrich the bloodstream of the national vocabulary with transfusions of local Pitmatic – the bold, bitter, ribald, beautiful talk of miners.

It was a good job Ewan and Peggy had constructed a painstaking methodology for dealing with these tapes, for they'd come back with almost twice as many as for *Singing the Fishing*. In the circumstances, the programme came together remarkably quickly. So attuned was Ewan now to the process that he created the first-day-down-the-pit recitative in just half a day – it had taken three days of sweat to do the equivalent in *Singing the Fishing*. They rehearsed and recorded in two weeks, with the same method but with a little less intensity than last time. That didn't stop Charles throwing things, of course. One tantrum was ended abruptly, Alan Ward said, by the new woman on 'grams', the stunning Diana Wright, walking up to Charles, sitting on his knee, and giving him a resounding kiss.

Louis Killen was one of the solo singers who was used in the chorus, for they'd decided that folk singers would make a more malleable group than the classically voice-trained Clarion Singers. The 'Big Hewer' of the title was not in the original template. Louis pointed out that when they arrived in the North East they had been hoping to find a heroic miner, a real person, not a mythic figure. But everywhere they went they found a Herculean semi-historical figure, recurring like some creation myth. 'Whether he was real, or purely legendary, I never knew, even to this day', said Jack Elliott. In the Midlands it was 'Jackie Torr, from Derbyshire', in South Wales 'Isaac Lewis in the Anthracite'. This was a crucial device for Ewan, who could let his song-writing imagination loose on a super-hero:

> **In a cradle of coal in the darkness I was laid – go down.**
> **Down in the dirt and darkness I was raised, go down.**
> **Cut me teeth on a five-foot timber,**
> **Held up the roof with me little finger,**
> **Started me time, away in the mine – GO DOWN.**

And the chorus hammers in on the last Go Down. Later, Ewan and Charles were accused of naivety in using this archetypal figure. Dave Harker in his piece on the programmes in *One for the Money* says:

> It never seems to have occurred to Parker and MacColl that the mythic figure may have been a deliberate and grotesque caricature of the self-exploitative worker, the man who filled more tubs, dug more coal and worked more hours than any other. Doubtless a symbol of pride and virility to insiders … it could also be self-mocking caricature and an ideological stick to satirise men who undercut piece-work rates and are hence against the men's own interest. The limitation of production is one of the pitmen's few weapons … Parker and MacColl had a 'socialist-realist' prescription … and were going to <u>make</u> the miner an epic figure whether he liked it or not.

While there's an element of truth in this – in every industry when setting up piece-rates managers will go for the best worker, who then risks becoming a pariah to his workmates – here it seems that their informants were innocent and eager tellers of the story. To Peggy Seeger the miners quite clearly spoke as if immensely proud of their symbolic Hercules. 'They meant it. Down the pit the miners are a tight-knit community. Nobody shirks. There's no gaffer down there.'

For Louis, recording was no longer quite as nerve-racking as it had been for *Song of a Road*. He had more confidence in his own ability, not least because he had begun to replace the American songs in his repertoire with those from his own tradition. Moreover, at the end of the second day Louis saw tears streaming down Charles's cheeks as he sang for the first time his dialect stanza from 'Schooldays Over', the song that introduces that starting-out recitative, one that echoes but in no way copies Sam Larner's first day at sea:

> **Schooldays over, come on then John, time to be getting your pit boots on,**
> **On with your shart and moleskin trousers, time you was on your way,**
> **Time you was learning the pitman's job and earning the pitman's pay.**

(With some trepidation Louis had to correct Ewan's attempt at the tricky dialect pronunciation of shart, 'but he took it'). There were three similar stanzas, each introducing us to the sharply differentiated dialects of each region – Ewan for the Midlands, then Bert Lloyd for the Welsh:

> **Come on then Jim, it's time to go, time you was working down below,**
> **Time to be handling a pick and shovel, you start at the pit today,**
> **Time you was learning the collier's job and earning a collier's pay.**

I was 12 when I left school. As soon as I reached the age of 14 I went to the pit. The pit was the place.

> **Come on then Dai, it's almost light, time you was off to the anthracite,**
> **The morning mist is in the valley, it's time you was on your way,**
> **Time you was learning the miner's job and earning a miner's pay.**

When I was a boy, we all thought of the mines. When I was in school, I used to parade wearing my long trousers, and parading with my, my naked lamp on the road at night, as colliers – months before I had a job, you see. Oh yes.

Ben Davies, the last speaker here, has this exquisite Welsh voice, soft and sibilant. Later, when teaching, Charles would illustrate it by holding up an eight-inch strip of tape – 'Look, this is the length of a Welsh S.' Then it's down the pit, with an atmospheric murmur of Pitmatic against a background of zinging cables and clanking cages.

But you're away, you're bound below,
And your pit boots ring and clatter as you go, making sparks fly.
You're on your way, to the pit bank,
Where men riding cages wait, where the rusty cables lie,
Where the broken picks and shovels,
Where the heap of waste and rubble rises up against the sky.

And we're embedded in the miner's world, where for Ben Davies: 'Everything seemed to close in on me …the experience comes so horrible and terrible … the smell of horse manure … went through everything. I thought it was wonderful.' And where for another: 'The silence in the pit it's, it's like infinity, or the bottom of the ocean … And you can feel this pressing on you, the darkness.' And where: 'You hear a prop creak, and you … can see that little part just move that quarter of an inch. You know what's going to happen.' A rock fall, first a friend, then a widow:

> **Yes. He was working next to me. And a huge stone came down, and killed him … He was killed in the pit. He was killed on a Friday morning, on a Good Friday morning. I shall always remember … I see him now. Brought him in and brought him on a stretcher on the floor, there. In his pit dirt. The men bathing him like, on the floor.**

That image is strikingly similar to one in DH Lawrence's *Sons and Lovers*. Isla Cameron speaks for the widow in an aching slow lament before we're moved on to the hard times between the wars:

> In from the mine in his pit dirt they bring him.
> The neighbours they stand by the door.
> The fire will gang oot and the bairns will gang hungry.
> He'll walk to the pit no more.

> I was the only man working out of a street of houses. Forty houses. You daren't answer the bosses back. Because you know what'd happen, there's plenty of men waiting for your job … I had a sister living in the valley at that time, and oh, what a sight was to see, the pride that was there and yet, they were on the verge of starvation … A miner has always had the pride thing – he thinks, well if he can't make his living by the muscles of his arms and his legs, well he just doesn't want it.

> In every village in the Rhondda
> Children cry for want of meat
> Throughout the land their fathers wander
> Singing for pennies in the street.

This last a slow choral chant. And the Dust. A topic nowhere on their original list that emerged inexorably in interview after interview.

The curse of underground is the dust. Dust is the giant killer. But it doesn't strike all at once. But he likes his time. And he do takes his time, and he stealthily walks into your human system. Into your lungs. He is the real enemy, so minute in its form, yet so strong in its ravaging powers. I have seen victims of this terrible curse, this dust, I've seen victims of it, reduced to nothing. Couldn't breathe – no lungs to breathe. Only the beating of the heart, waiting for the time to be called away.

The Dust section is illustrated simply in song only by a chorus of Welsh miners. Moving enough, and yet even more on reflection when Peggy said: 'Twenty to thirty miners singing somewhere, not a pub because most were teetotal. Recorded by Dr Dafydd Thomas of Carmarthen. He said half will be dead within a year: Look at him, he's only 35. Incredible damage … Dr Thomas was an amazing man with a beautiful face, died of cancer himself.' (Ewan had a vivid memory of him among miners in the Theatre Workshop days, ministering to a company fatigued, under-nourished and ailing.) Jokes about death are constant. After one violent coughing fit: 'Shall I get the doctor? No, get the plumber.' Ewan told Peggy this story in a miners' welfare club, where she sat pregnant with her second son, Calum. He had to get her drink because no miner would be seen dead at a bar ordering milk.

They played their first draft of the programme to a group of miners and were taken aback to be told it lacked humour. So they went back and removed some song stanzas and a few voices, and pasted in a humorous section, without enough time to thread it through the rest, as doubtless they'd have preferred to do. One new song and a few jokes, but clustered together they tend to lose their impact, and they omit one (whether for reasons of good taste or poor recording quality is not clear) that would have capped the lot. It actually follows one of the occasional lines that sounds trite, as though spoken many times before, and comes from an old miner who suggests he has coal in his veins, not blood: 'I think if I cut my finger and it bled it would just come out black.' That's where the extract ends. On the original recording his daughter-in-law turns to her husband instantly and says, 'Well, cut his throat then, the fire's burning low.' Cackles of laughter round the embers.

ANOTHER BLOODY WORKING-CLASS EPIC – THE BIG HEWER

The Big Hewer was broadcast on 18 August 1961. In the *Radio Times* Charles extended the Big Hewer metaphor:

> In the programme we have taken [a mythical figure] and made the sounds of the pit speak for him – the uncanny whiplash of the steel ropes of the winding-gear speaking for his sinews, the deep pulse of the pump for his heart, the surge of the cages in the shaft and the constant flow of coal for his very blood ... I knew that only the epic could do justice to him as a subject ... For the sight of him underground in his helmet, with his blackened face and his insistent humanity in that most inhuman of environments – the coal seam – makes him an awesome figure, and the very proximity of the roof makes him of superhuman stature. ... Tough, forthright, politically aware – this we expected; but to find men and women so strongly imbued with a sense of history, of a long struggle shared, and above all who could talk brilliantly, and with an overwhelming sense of their real importance as human beings – this was a revelation.

The reviewers were nearly as enthusiastic as for *Singing the Fishing*. Mary Crozier in the *Guardian*: 'The miner has an intense and poetic awareness of the elements among which he lives and works. The songs, written out of the actual folklore, continually picked up and carried the movement from one theme to another. The technique of swinging rhythmical choruses, interspersed with recordings of the words of miners from coalfields all over the country, made this an impressive experience.' Her only criticism was that an hour of sustained listening to such intensity was too long – it could have been ten minutes shorter. The *Sunday Times* agreed: 'Although ten minutes off would help (it would help any hour-long programme) this stands out as one of the best of the year. "I lost a good man", her regret as hard and dry as the coal itself.' Paul Ferris in the *Observer*, usually an enthusiast, this time had doubts, feeling that some of the spoken phrases sounded too cute, too practised:

> In the Big Hewer there were uneasy signs of over-awareness. MacColl's singing was as effective as ever, and there were moments of intensity when no barrier of radio apparatus seemed to remain. 'I lost a good man.' But 'you're not burning coal you're burning blood'? Or still worse 'A miner's life is a mixture of tragedy and humour', it sounded as if the miners were talking on the record for any old radio feature. In *John Axon* that mixture of tragedy and humour was overheard, not stated.

The 'tragedy and humour' line was one of those added in a hurry later to preface the new Humour section. It just goes to show that when you have something near perfect you can't insert a new block. For Ferris by now the Radio Ballads were not just any old radio feature. Peggy pointed out later that these stock phrases – like 'burning blood not coal' – were mantras that many miners repeated. A later *Times* correspondent, reviewing a repeat, made a shrewd contrast with television:

> A medium that reduces the human figure to the size of a doll is not well adapted to creating heroes ... radio by contrast is a medium in which heroes flourish. It gives unfettered scope to the audience's imagination and moves naturally in worlds of legend and magic. ... Where the programme scores – setting aside the superb editing – is in its imaginative evocation of the mining life. The title is two-edged – the Big Hewer seems at first to be the archetypal collier, but he gradually comes to represent the mine itself, the factory that 'never stands still ... the ground moves all the time, you can hear it.' The total impression left behind is genuinely heroic. But doubts begin to creep in when it has the effect not of heightening the atmosphere but of simply inflating it. This happens in *The Big Hewer* when recorded statements are taken up by Mr MacColl as pretexts for a big-gestured ballad. The contrast is similar to that between a real working man, and a civic statue to the dignity of labour in the social-realist style.

There's a fine line between success and failure in songwriting, especially if you're trying to give a voice to someone else. A year or so later Ewan cast a critical eye at his earlier efforts. Reflecting on *The Big Hewer*, he concurred with the reviewer: he agreed he'd overdone some of the songs. But overall he felt that the recitative sections were even more effective than hitherto, partly because the whole cast of singers participated: 'It is at this moment that it becomes apparent that we are dealing with all the miners – the dead, the living and the future generations.' An admiring *TES* (*Times Educational Supplement*) reviewer, unnamed, stood back to look at the series, making the point that apolitical listeners didn't feel that they were being lectured to by Marxists:

> A new form, being hammered with richly extrovert energy into a fresh and revitalising sound-style, is the ballad-documentary ... To date all such features are not equally successful. Were they, one would suspect author and producer to be lacking in enterprise. The pioneer always has his defeats; they only make victory the sweeter. The Big Hewer ... managed to make a father-figure for its subject that was both ideal and human. The indirect approach, avoiding harsh proselytising, persuading the listener by first beguiling, then convincing him that he should accept truths he might at first be loth to accept.

So another 'bloody working-class epic', a phrase attributed to the BBC's Director General Hugh Carleton-Greene, who had enthused so much about *The Ballad of John Axon*. It brought another success for Charles and the BBC, but at a price – and it was the price of the Radio Ballads that his new bosses didn't like. What could he do about it?

CHAPTER 12

Radio on the Cheap
Birmingham Ballads and The Body Blow

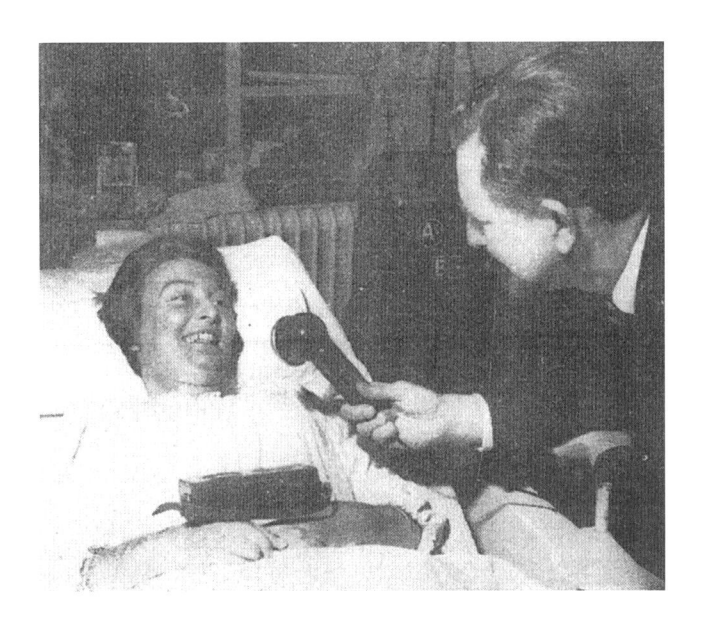

Scrubbing away and your mouth stuck up with toothpaste, tons more than you'd use yourself ... and you clench your teeth and say for goodness sake, it's not a doorstep you're scrubbing, it's my teeth. Come along dear, you know, open up. Talk to you as if you're a semi-idiot child and this vigorous scrubbing, on your teeth. Used to dread it ... When you're lying down you feel so much like a landed dab. You feel more like a moth on a pin down there, you don't feel equal to anyone.

NORMA SMITH, IN THE BODY BLOW, 1962

Charles told me he was in the shit. One hour of Radio Ballad was costing him as much as one hour of television. He'd done three of them. They cost as much as 20 normal programmes. Could I make one for nothing? It would bring the average down ...

IAN CAMPBELL, INTERVIEWED IN 2007

Let's take stock halfway through the Radio Ballad series. Radio reviewers love them, and Singing the Fishing has won the prestigious Prix Italia. But within the BBC itself there are complaints. Before getting the go-ahead for The Big Hewer, Charles Parker writes to Ewan MacColl that there are management changes in the corporation and that people have been muttering about how expensive the programmes are to make. He has received a body blow to his self-esteem. Invited to attend an important Harvard radio seminar, he has been refused permission to go by the BBC. Moreover, he's warned that if he continues to confine himself to a narrow sphere of work, his 'continued usefulness to the corporation will be in doubt.' It's a sharp tug on his reins, an unpleasant reality check.

Changes at the BBC

Radio was in retreat. During World War II its effect had been powerful: broadcast hours doubled and licence numbers tripled. Radio's impact was still immense in the early 1950s, and only Radio Luxembourg was then competing with the BBC. There was precious little television to compete with it either – what there was came from the same BBC stable, and could hardly be described as 'populist'. Moreover, most television sets in use were small, 14 inches on the diagonal, and in 1955 the cheapest cost the equivalent of £3000 in 2008; credit restrictions meant you had to find half of that up front. Not many could afford it – in 1955 fewer than five million households had television, while nearly everyone had a radio.

But the arrival of ITV in September 1954 sent shock waves through the BBC. Within nine months it had taken over 70 per cent of the BBC's television audience. The BBC was obliged to rein back radio expenditure and pour money into television. As the early TV pioneer David Attenborough said 50 years later, 'We laughed at those stuffed shirts and fuddy-duddies [in radio], at the same time taking their money because television was actually financed from the sound licence.' In 1954 three times as many households had radio-only licences than had television sets; in 1958 they were equal; in 1964 only a quarter as many. So money for radio programmes was being husbanded more carefully. Who in command, observing the audience shrinking as fast as its budget, would not look critically at programmes that cost substantially more than the average in money and time, and appealed to a minority audience? How many 'loss leaders' could they afford? The Radio Ballads were prime candidates.

If you examine the 'cost per broadcasting hour', as BBC leaders certainly did, you'll find that the first four Radio Ballads each cost £1500–2000, (£200–300,000 today). To make the 'average' BBC radio programme then cost about £150 per broadcast hour, and the typical radio feature was round £500 – so respectively a tenth and a third of a Radio Ballad. Charles Parker's bosses were happy to promote such features, especially if they won prizes, but they granted him no unquestioned right to make more. He was allowed a substantial amount of freedom in choosing his own subjects, but the Radio Ballads cost time as well as money. *The Ballad of John Axon* took ten days short of 12 months between his first letter to Ewan and its first broadcast. For *Song of a Road* the period was 12 months, for *Singing the Fishing* nine months, and for *The Big Hewer* another nine months. It wouldn't have been so bad had Charles been making enough other programmes in parallel. Some, yes, but many fewer – his 'broadcast' hours from 1960–3 were a third of what they had been from 1955–7. His 'productivity' had slumped. Never mind the quality, Charles, we can't feel the width.

So while he and his supporters were indignant, it's no surprise that he was under pressure to use less time and money in making the programmes. This led him in April 1960 – before *Singing the Fishing* had even reached the recording studio – to commission a programme from a local writer, the skilful and enterprising Brian Vaughton, who had been out and about independently with his own EMI Midget. Charles felt that Vaughton's first selected topic, Birmingham's old Jewellery Quarter, could appeal to a Midland audience. He decided it could be adapted to the Radio Ballad format – he was looking at everything with that eye nowadays. If he could make them quickly, with local amateur talent, and not Ewan, Peggy and a set of professional musicians staying in hotels for up to a fortnight, he might be able to slash both cost and time, and provide a riposte to the attack he was under.

The Jewellery

With this in mind, he approached two local folk singers, John Chapman and Ian Campbell. Ian was the Clarion singer picked out by Ewan as a soloist on *Singing the Fishing*. Like Ewan, he came from a musical Scots family, whose Aberdeen-born father (then still singing impressively) had been blackballed after leading a strike in a paper mill. Campbell had also worked with Charles on a Nativity play at the parish church in Harborne. After helping to create a Clarion skiffle group in 1958, Ian and his sister Lorna had transformed it into a successful folk group who were the regular hosts of the Jug o' Punch club at the Crown in Station Street in Birmingham, which Charles frequented, and Campbell's Radio Ballad experience had made him an enthusiast for the form. Throughout this period Campbell was still working as a skilled craftsman, an engraver, in the Jewellery Quarter, so he was flattered and delighted to be asked to come up with some songs for a cheap and cheerful programme about the history of his place of work.

Ian Campbell recalls Charles approaching him, before *The Big Hewer* was broadcast, and explaining the pressure he was under to reduce his programme costs. 'Well, I'd already done a lot of writing and I knew all the jewellery vocabulary. The actuality had all been collected by then.' In truth, *The Jewellery* was more a feature programme with songs, not a Radio Ballad. Campbell wrote five songs in three days, his group had only the weekend of 4–5 March 1961 to rehearse and record, and the programme went out just two days later. Little time for Charles to wield his tape splicer. The very few interviews were with old jewellers and the daughter of one: the mother of his engineer Alan Ward. Charles was tapping his contacts.

The Jewellery was restricted to Radio Midlands, in a three-part series on local industries. The response was mixed. There was a mediocre audience reaction, though those few critics who did write it up were in favour. Next day Charles wrote an over-optimistic assessment to David Gretton: 'I cannot sufficiently express my conviction that in a group of this sort there is tremendous potential for further actuality Radio Ballads of an absolutely regional character.' The Campbell group he used was certainly cheap – he pressed in vain for more money for Campbell, who got a mere eight guineas. No wonder the programme cost well under a tenth of the average of the first four Radio Ballads. Charles thanked Campbell effusively, but Ian wryly complains that his two programmes were always compared unfavourably with the MacColl/Seeger set, which had an investment of time, money and creative effort of an entirely different order. Charles did not at first mention them to Ewan and Peggy.

Charles had overplayed his hand – his bosses didn't share the reviewers' enthusiasm for the programme. Denis Morris wouldn't put it up for a national broadcast, nor would David Gretton sanction a Midlands repeat, deflating Charles with: 'A primitive piece of work ... poor narration ... cursory production methods. At most there are seven or eight minutes of compelling material ... It really is a museum-piece in more ways than one!' Well, of course. Charles <u>knew</u> that narrators should be done away with, and that extensive post-production work was necessary – that's what he'd been telling them! So it was galling that he was being criticised for it on a programme that cost next to nothing. He felt he couldn't win.

Cry from the Cut

Still, a couple of months later, while he was in post-production on *The Big Hewer*, Charles jumped at the opportunity when Vaughton came up with the subject of canals, of which Birmingham had a network on the scale of Venice. To make the songs for *Cry from the Cut*, Ian Campbell had just eight hours of actuality to work from, and three weeks to write five songs in any moments he could snatch – he was working all week and playing many evenings, and this time he wasn't familiar with the jargon. Recorded in a single day on 10 February 1962 and broadcast on BBC Midlands just three days later, *Cry from the Cut* was the same kind of radio-feature-with-songs as *The Jewellery*, with no time to dovetail words with music in the elaborate MacColl/Seeger manner. Nevertheless, perhaps partly because canal boating was a growing pastime that created enthusiasts, it was successful both with critics and audience. Indeed it achieved audience response figures that matched those for *Singing the Fishing*.

For creating the songs and performing them Campbell and his group had to make do with just over £50 in total: Charles wrote and told him he couldn't find more because of the budget. No wonder Ian felt sore when in 1963, after he'd played at the Edinburgh Festival, Charles reacted with horror when Ian told him he was going professional. With so much performing work Campbell could no longer manage to keep his day job as an engraver. 'I resisted it, and held out the longest ... Charles had this romantic idea of me as a traditional craftsman/musician, and he criticised me fiercely. I felt he'd used me.' Frankly, he had, and doubtless Charles was upset because he would no longer have a cheap local semi-amateur option.

There would be no more Vaughton/Campbell programmes. Between the broadcast of their two features Charles had begun preparing for a fifth Radio Ballad. In November 1961 he commissioned from Ewan and Peggy a programme on teenagers, but the following February, just after *Cry from the Cut*, an extra opportunity suddenly arose. David Gretton told him that he had some spare money in the kitty as the financial year drew to a close, so if Charles could make a programme before the tax year ended at the beginning of April ... He needed no further invitation, and immediately thought of an idea Ewan and Peggy had already lobbed at him. The year before, they had written and sung some songs for a half-hour television feature about polio sufferers, *Four People*. They hadn't particularly liked the result, largely because of the 'stagey' dialogue, and because the sufferers' own words hadn't been heard, but thought it would be an interesting vehicle for a Radio Ballad that broke away from the preoccupation with work. Could they succeed with such a subject?

The Body Blow

They had only six weeks. Charles consulted Guy Brenton, the director of *Four People*, and originally envisaged a 30-minute 'chamber' piece, with fewer instrumentalists, two singers (Ewan and Peggy) and possibly only two effects – the throb of a heartbeat and the wheezing of an iron lung. He did all the interviews himself, and used virtually the same subjects as the TV programme. He was certainly not aiming to skimp the post-production as he had with the Vaughton/Campbell pair, but the interviews affected him so deeply that despite the tight timescale he sought and was granted a doubling to an hour. As late as 27 February, a month before the broadcast, he had told Gretton:

The deliberate limiting of time to 30 minutes is another self-imposed discipline to see whether we can ... do it justice ... I am trying to apply the techniques of the Radio Ballad to the intensely personal experience of a group of polio sufferers, with the intention of purging the healthy person's somewhat atavistic fears of the grievously deformed or disabled.

It is clear that Charles himself held those 'atavistic' fears, a mix of repulsion and fascination. Poliomyelitis is a highly infectious disease that attacks the nervous system's motor neurons. It had been a rarity until after the war, when it struck a group of people in Kent, and spread. So devastating was it that when patients recovered a hazy consciousness in one of the specialist polio hospitals, like Rush Green in Essex, the experience was unearthly:

It is sort of dreamlike. I mean you've had a shock to the body, and of course then your mind, there's a shock to the mind as well. And ... you don't see anybody's face, I mean they haven't got any sort of identity to you. Just eyes, that makes it more weird. They're masked, because you're so infectious. You just see eyes, different sorts of eyes, peering at you.

Norma Smith, by the time of that interview recovered enough to be in a wheelchair, was a mother who had been struck down at a seaside resort: 'On the Thursday I was in one world. On the Monday and Tuesday I seem to have been thrown into a completely different world.' Day one, normal. Day two, flu symptoms, Day three, progressively weaker, Day four, paralysed from the neck down. The extent of recovery seemed to be a complete lottery. Scots housewife Jean Haggar, like Norma, managed to get back to looking after a home, a husband and a child. She had regained the use of everything but her left arm and part of her right. Heather Ruffell was completely paralysed still but had learned to 'frog breathe', an air-gulping technique that at least got her out of her iron lung. The two men were Paul Bates, an ex-army officer struck down on a patrol in Malaya at the end of his National Service, and Dutchy Holland. Each was still in an iron lung, flat on his back. Each had undergone an emergency operation (tracheotomy) to open the airways. Dutchy was the sole subject who could be described as truly working class, an assembly line worker at Ford's in Dagenham. His condition was so severe that he could only speak on the 'inspiration' phase of the iron lung's breath.

That word 'inspiration' acquired a genuine double meaning. Charles was awed by their suffering, courage and attitude. In a later letter he said: 'The robust no-nonsense self-confidence of Paul Bates, the ironic wit of Dutchy ... the serene objectivity of Heather Ruffell, the indomitable humanity of Jean Haggar ... bowled me over.' For once the usually anonymous subjects were named in his *Radio Times* introduction, as they would be at the outset of the programme. For him they 'revealed the flame of the human spirit burning with overwhelming clarity and brightness.' They were articulate, forthright, and almost entirely without self-pity, although Dutchy had lost his wife and daughters, Heather her husband, child and, most cruelly, an unborn child, and all of them their livelihoods. What's striking is that their language, while largely 'educated', loses little in comparison with the workers' speech which Ewan and Charles extolled. It's as though for those still paralysed speech was now hard-won, each breath an effort, and with its relearning came totally different speech patterns. Spare, direct, unwavering.

Charles spent a fortnight recording them, his interviewing empathy eliciting tremendous testimony. But how to assemble it? As early as *Song of a Road*, they had discussed the idea of cross-cutting several pieces of actuality from speaker to speaker 'and building them into montage blocks which would have something of the quality of the stream of consciousness passages in Joyce's *Ulysses*.' Since then Ewan had been excited by Alain Resnais's film *Last Year at Marienbad*, which used a similar technique in film. He went on to say that Charles was unconvinced until:

> We taped a montage block ... of 19 passages of speech from four speakers, each passage being a comment or part of a comment on the sensation of returning consciousness. The overall effect was overwhelming ... Charles found the technical challenge exciting. Tending to regard the montages as a surrealistic trick, he nevertheless became an expert at constructing them, and they appeared frequently, with electrifying effect, in *The Body Blow*.

With this extra complication, Charles has his work cut out in the time available. As well as the audio-montages he has the added task of connecting together Dutchy's chopped-up speech, but perhaps this necessity mothers his invention, for in those few days his editing on *Body Blow* is quite brilliant. And Charles is by now a complete master of the method, the machinery he uses is no longer fouling up, and he completes the first-cut audio-montage in time for a five-day rehearsal and recording stint on 19–23 March with just Ewan, Peggy and three other musicians, all of whom sign away their recording royalties to the Polio Research Fund. Recording is as intense as usual. Charles's secretary Norah Mash describes in a letter the calm that the slow, steady breathing sound of the iron lung brings to the studio when things get fraught. The finished programme is due to go out only four days later. Throughout this period Charles carries on a full correspondence with each of the five subjects, to whom he'd given copies of *John Axon* to indicate what he's trying to achieve. Heather Ruffell responds enthusiastically, ending: 'With All Best Wishes, Heather (All done with my own fair teeth.)' Heather uses her teeth to type, immaculately, on her own notepaper, headed with the hospital's address. While such aids are commonplace now, they certainly weren't then. Charles goes back to record Norma Smith at home with her daughter Carol singing and skipping, and arranges for Norma to sit in on one day of the recording. Peggy says she found Norma a 'fabulous' woman.

Their compelling stories punctuate a succession of montages from the moment they're struck down, through returning consciousness, realisation, resentment, resignation, back to the fight for movement and independence, and the determination to lead a useful life. They draw you inexorably into their world:

Sit up, your brain will say, sit up! And suddenly nothing happens, and you think – I didn't sit up ... And losing the use of my left arm and he says, go on, you're havering. I said, I'm not. And losing the use of it, I could feel the use going out of the shoulder. Right down to the fingertips. And I can always remember him lifting my arm and turning it round and round and round to try to put the life into it again ... You think, gosh, my legs are gone, I can't move my arms. Well you get such a shock. It felt, to me, it felt like all the muscles were being actually being knocked out of action. It was like electric light bulbs all burning out. One two three four, just one after the other.

Each of the five different voices assembled in this passage is clearly distinguishable to the ear. Jean Haggar's Scots, Dutchy Holland's East End, Heather Ruffel's soft refinement, Norma Smith's cheerful wit, Paul Bates's army officer, only 26 but with a voice like gravel after his tracheotomy, out of which he emerged, to everyone's surprise, with his voice intact:

They got me into an Auster to fly me down to Kuala Lumpur, down to the base hospital and I'm rather big, six feet four, which doesn't, you know, go easily into that sort of thing. Had to drag me out feet first. I got into the ward, was helped to undress and I sat on the edge of the bed, and then decided to ... lie down, be more comfortable, lay back, and I couldn't get my left leg onto the bed. And that was the last time I sat on the side of a bed or, or anywhere ... I was transferred to a tank respirator, and I had the form of polio which means the paralysis of the swallowing. It's quite simple – eventually you drown you see, in your own secretions, you can't cope with them. And they, then you can take them out of the iron lung, anaesthetise them, and then cut their throat, literally. Put a shortened tube straight into the throat, which I've still got eight years later, and breathe

them through that, respire them through it. Now unfortunately I was still fighting when they put this tube down my throat and I bit through it. I also bit the anaesthetist, when he tried to retrieve the, the broken tube … He's a good strong, strong Yorkshireman – I've met him since and we're extremely good friends, and he always sort of licks his thumb when he comes in … Anyway they did the operation in what I think they would claim to be a world record of about 28 seconds. No anaesthetics were necessary because I was out, and almost gone anyway.

No one had quite expressed on radio before so cogently what it was like to experience pain and paralysis. The pain, from Norma Smith and Heather Ruffell:

It's deep bone ache. It's in every muscle, and everything. Your whole body seems to shriek with pain. And your heels, little pains start and then they get like flames, then they get like worse flames, and unless somebody lifts them and rubs them to relieve that, it just gets, well it just nearly blots you out. But you just have to give in to it, just have to lie there and bear it, you can't do anything about it, just have to let yourself get carried away on the pain. To me it just felt like being crucified all the time … You have to know pain, to appreciate being <u>out</u> of pain. That's why the pain when I first got polio, and the no-pain now, that's why I'm happy.

Norma Smith, on trying to move:

And of course you have muscle charts … That means that they … sit there with a chart, and they've got every muscle listed down, and then they go through the motions of asking you to move these various muscles … Of course most of mine were noughts and the next month they were noughts and they just get tired of saying nought so they used to say zero, nothing, nought, nought, zero, nothing, you know, just to make a change, done in front of you. Whether they think of you as a human being while they're doing it I don't know … And you have to get over that embarrassment of lying stark naked while they all peer down at you … Somebody's probably got an elbow on your stomach, one end, while they're looking at your feet and saying, now waggle your big toe, and you go blue in the face trying to move your big toe, and you're sure it must be moving with the effort and

> you look down at the toe ... It's best not to look really because if you're not looking you're sure that your big toe's moving but if you open your eye, you see the ruddy thing's still stuck up in the air, it's not even moved an inch ... You feel with such concentration and willing everything, you know, you're saying, move, move, move! And you think that it <u>must</u> move.

They're not out of danger, either, not least because, believe it or not, the electricity supply to the Rush Green ward was metered. Dutchy Holland: 'I think you've got to be a polio to really understand. We have a saying in this ward that we live dangerously. And by golly you do. If someone's forgotten to put a shilling in the meter bang goes your air supply.' Or if Charles Parker, recording on his knees at the side of your bed, fails to notice that you're turning blue – though he (eventually) realises that he seems to have pulled out the respirator's plug!

And the start of recovery:

> I wasn't afraid while I was in the lung at all, ever, but I was afraid to come out. I can always remember Sister pulling me out a little bit every day. Five minutes, ten minutes, extended periods, and then she said to me one morning: Mrs Haggar we're going to take you out of the lung today and you're going to lie on the bed. I was quite happy with that, but when night came I got a terrific fear. I wanted back in it. And in the morning she said, well, you're still here, aren't you? So I said, yes, it looks like it.

The reviewers, supportive or critical, were all deeply moved. Patrick Williams in the *Sunday Telegraph* under the heading The Ballad of the Iron Lung: 'I doubt whether a listener with full attention on this programme can avoid sympathetic agitation in his own muscles. At a playback for the Press last week we all had trouble breathing ... There's no way of telling whether Charles Parker carefully judged the effect, or hit by accident upon the correct accumulation of stimuli to produce such acute discomfort.' The TES: 'It was more than a documentary, it was a tribute paid with aesthetic sense. Reality can move more deeply than a play; no actor could hope to convey the strength of such experience.' They're getting it.

But most disliked the songs. Ian Rodgers in the *Guardian*: 'The excellence of the cutting and the fact that all five were coherent and informative about their condition ... made me wish they could have been heard without the musical treatment. It ... too often tried to strike medals, to draw attention to bravery and fortitude which was obvious in what they said.' Peter Wilsher: 'The Radio Ballads have produced some of the most original and memorable radio heard in the last couple of years. But ... I could not persuade myself that the method was ideally suited to an illness ... They talked in flat unemotional voices about the onset of paralysis, its effects on mind and body, and its gradual slow partial retreat. But surrounding this was an elaborate framework of smug exposé and comment [in the songs] and doubts crept in.' The TV critic Victor Soanes didn't like the programme, while acknowledging that: 'It was extremely well done and technically brilliant. But the theatrical trimmings were superfluous – twanging guitars, superimposed troubadour voices, third-rate poetry.' Ouch. Peggy agreed later with some of this criticism, if not all: it was her own voice (too sweet, too <u>sweet</u>) that bugged her most. But the time and cost constraints prevented them employing another singer.

The voice actuality was so rich that the songs and music became a problem: we'll look at why in Chapter 18. This would have been an incomparable programme for its time without a note of music, and the combination of the stories, the montage sequences and the few telling sound effects were mesmerising. The programme in fact received stirring approbation within the BBC. An unsigned letter from Head Office in London called it '<u>staggering</u>, the best thing you've ever done. Technically brilliant and very exciting. It glued me to the edge of the chair for the entire 60 minutes.' Denis Morris wrote that 'Ronald Lewin and Laurence Gilliam both heard your polio programme this morning and were completely bowled over by it ... It should be considered as an Italia Prize entry.' Gilliam wrote saying 'I congratulate you and your team on yet another first class piece of work.' This must have been heart-warming for Charles, but you can't help thinking that among the reactions was an unspoken relief that it had no political edge: it wasn't 'another bloody working-class epic'. And it never did get selected as the Italia Prize entry.

Charles Parker and the Polio Sufferers

What about the polio sufferers themselves? Heather Ruffell, after recording her instant reaction in a telegram – 'congratulations to all concerned stop programme great success stop' – played the finished programme to her ward when she got a copy. Afterwards she wrote to Charles, while 'wearing her teeth down to the gums' writing the hospital magazine she and Dutchy had pioneered. While they all enjoyed it, she says, 'The criticism from polio sufferers was that there was too much on suffering in the first part, not enough accent on the many compensations we now have.' This was an analogous criticism to that of the miners when they felt *The Big Hewer* lacked humour. The polio sufferers had come out of the other side, and wanted to be reminded of that triumph more than to wallow in the nightmare they had – partly at least – escaped. Similar comment comes from polio sufferers listening to the programme for the first time today.

Charles had more letters from the general public after *The Body Blow* than for any other Radio Ballad. All but three of the 30 correspondents were deeply impressed and affected; the three loathed it. He replies to them all before going back to his planning for the teenager programme, then provisionally titled *On the Brink*, but his correspondence with the five subjects goes on for years. He has the idea of mitigating the boredom of those stuck in hospital with some of their faculties still available and time still on their hands, by using them as an auxiliary transcription service for the BBC. However, after letters to and from the head of the Polio Research Unit, and several hospitals, the idea runs into the bureaucratic sand. But he does employ one Pat Short to transcribe long interviews on old age and death. Short's husband is an amateur inventor who has rigged up for her all sorts of 'brilliant electronic devices, but ... is facing real obstacles getting them accepted.' Charles writes to electronics companies to see if they can help, with no apparent success. But windmills are for tilting at, and the prospect of failure never put him off once his emotions were engaged. He carries on a lengthy correspondence with Paul Bates, the six-foot-four army officer condemned to a supine existence... Well, no:

I hate to be lying flat, it's very bad for morale. And when people come and look at you as if you're a cabbage it lowers you even further. And if you suddenly sit up a bit, then here you are, independent, typing for yourself, saying what you want, with nobody else's assistance, it gave me satisfaction, pleasure, pride, self-respect.

Bates has a private income, so can afford round-the-clock support at home in Sussex. He had been chosen to pioneer an instrument called a Possum, which the patient could use as a typewriter 'finger' by blowing and sucking air through a tube. Heath Robinsonesque, maybe, but it worked. So did an array of other devices he had designed that allowed him to manipulate lights, radio, television and even a garden fountain, from the bed where he lay paralysed. Bates was tireless, wrote masses of letters, was a shortwave radio buff, and attracted the fascination of the 1950s motoring ace Stirling Moss. The immensely popular Moss, forever weaving his under-powered British machine through the field by daredevil manoeuvres, responded to Bates's desire for mobility by secretly arranging and paying for a truck to be converted so he could be driven. In fact, Stirling drove him round Silverstone racetrack in it just before he was due to race in his Vanwall in the British Grand Prix on Easter Monday in 1962. Bates watched him start the race, but not finish it, for it was the one in which Moss crashed so badly that he was in a coma for weeks. He made an almost complete recovery, but never raced again. Bates himself recovered the use of a single finger joint, somehow enough to write his story in a successful book called *Horizontal Man*. His mobility was complete when he had a milk float converted that he could drive himself with that one joint. It wasn't a Vanwall, but what a thrill. He married, and went on to father two children.

Dutchy Holland's story involves his two children, but there's no such positive ending. The correspondence that ensues reveals that Dutchy has tried a spell back at home, but with money and domestic worries (the disablement benefit was just ten shillings a week to add to his wife's eight pounds), he is back in hospital after a few months. Charles subsequently discovers, through his secretary's son, first that Dutchy's wife had taken up with another man by whom she has had two further children, then that she claims to be unable to cope with her two elder daughters, 13 and 9, and puts them into care. Dutchy's in anguish – he has lost his mobility, job, wife, and now children: 'I'm fed up just sitting here when I could be working for my children if only people would realise that there was some use left in folk just like me. I would sell my soul to the devil to look after my two kids.' Charles feels desperately for him and fires off letters, including one to Frank Cousins, general secretary of the TGWU, Dutchy's old union, but predictably gets nowhere. Cousins is 'keen to help the disabled get back to work … but can't help individuals.' Dutchy and Heather Ruffell had raised £1000 towards a van to transport polio sufferers, and another £1500 towards an ambulance, but can Dutchy play *The Body Blow* at the Essex Show where Rush Green Hospital has a stand? You want what?! Charles gets his knuckles rapped for even passing on the request within the BBC.

Heather Ruffell's father is an ex-brigadier, with whom Charles has an active correspondence on the possibilities of marketing simple affordable tape recorders for polio sufferers, and others disabled. Heather's life is gradually transformed. After Gwen Gibson, the head of Australian broadcasting's transcription service, moved by hearing the programme two years later, had sent her own money to be distributed to the five subjects, Charles gets in touch with them all again. He has a special soft spot for Heather, who tells him that she has won a scholarship with the Mouth and Foot Painters' Association, and is painting pictures for a book she has nearly finished. Her friends have given her a van so she's 'charging about all over the place.' The following year her sister takes her to America, though they have to wait for the ending of a national dockers' strike which prevents her specialised rocking bed from being hoisted aboard the liner. In September 1966 she remarries and settles at last in her own bungalow. Dutchy would have come to the wedding, but, in another savage little irony, can't make it because the van they were instrumental in acquiring for Rush Green has already been booked by someone else.

That gives an indication of how Charles became consumed with the plight of the people he met. It did not make for a conventional domestic life, as his daughter Sara recalls. Charles thought that Norma Smith and her daughter deserved a holiday, so he invited them away with his family in the summer of 1962. Sara remembers how Norma had to be carried upstairs in her wheelchair every evening. In fact, Charles was too busy to come on holiday. Just think of Phyl, on holiday without her husband, lumbered instead with a wheelchair-bound woman and her daughter – <u>and</u> his secretary too. Charles 'asked' Norah Mash to go on holiday with them to look after Norma: 'If you don't, Norma won't get a holiday … I didn't want to. Had to. Had fun though.' Norah at that time was another member of the hidden support team of women that kept Charles on the road.

Charles was in fact on the road for most of the second half of 1962, on a remarkable venture. The next Radio Ballad, about teenagers, would have to wait.

CHAPTER 13

Growing Pains
Centre 42 and On the Edge

> There were two or three moments where one literally feels a fire of a new vision, where one is touched and sobered in a profound way, where Haydn and flower-petals and gasworks perceptibly belong to the same world.
>
> MICHAEL KUSTOW, ON ONE OF CHARLES PARKER'S
> CENTRE 42 PRODUCTIONS, 1962

> Ewan is at last swinging into the mood of On the Edge. He closets himself for 14 hours a day, comes out at night looking like a toad coming out of a dark and slimy pool ... but this one is going to be the best one yet.
>
> PEGGY SEEGER, IN AN UNDATED 1962 LETTER TO NORAH MASH,
> CHARLES PARKER'S SECRETARY

Centre 42

The sixth Radio Ballad, about Teenagers, had originally been conceived for broadcast in November 1962, the 40th anniversary of the founding of the BBC. Charles commissioned Ewan and Peggy in late November 1961, but he was so busy in the following months that he left the collection of actuality almost entirely to them. Not only had he produced *The Body Blow* and the two Vaughton/Campbell programmes, he was working flat out on an extraordinarily ambitious project for the unions. Not for the BBC, and not paid. A short-lived but fascinating experiment in radical, actuality-based theatre, midway between the end of the travelling Theatre Workshop of Joan Littlewood and Ewan MacColl, and the explosion of radical theatre of the 1970s: it's worth a detour.

Resolution 42 at the annual congress of the TUC (Trades Union Congress) in September 1960 asked for 'greater participation by the trade union movement in all cultural activities.' But the TUC did little to bring about that lofty intent. It had involved itself with the theatre very rarely, notably in 1934 when it commissioned a play on the Tolpuddle Martyrs. This time, they set the ball rolling, but it had stopped by the time it was picked up by Arnold Wesker, the radical playwright, recent author of *Chicken Soup with Barley, Roots* and *The Kitchen*. *Roots* is a play in which a self-educated working-class girl tries to interest her parents in the culture she has come to love – and is met with blank bewilderment. So Wesker knew just what he was up against ... He campaigned for the construction of the first of a series of 'culture palaces' for working people, to be known as Centre 42. He formed an organisation, without any money at first but his own, to create a series of Arts Festivals in conjunction with the annual recruitment weeks of six different trades councils, designed to speak directly to working people. Wesker had a grandiose, if noble vision:

> You start off with a picture: orchestra tucked away in valleys, people stopping Auden in the street to thank him for their favourite poem, teenagers around the jukebox arguing about my latest play, miners flocking to their own opera house; a picture of a nation thirsting for all the riches their artists can excite them with, hungry for the greatest, the best, unable to wait for Benjamin Britten's latest opera, arguing about Joan Littlewood's latest.

Now, that seems to teeter on the preposterous, but back then it did fire a genuine crusading energy among many radicals. It was 'Pure New Left subculture', as Alan Filewod and David Watt say in *Workers' Playtime*, an analysis of community theatre. The New Left 'offered a Marxist intellectual context for the essentially middle-class dissidence of the activist theatre workers ... [which] gave them a grounding in left-wing politics.' (An early brochure even described it as the First Stage in a Cultural Revolution – if not entirely on the Chinese model.) Charles, his politics now transformed, threw himself with characteristic enthusiasm and almost manic vigour into creating a series of <u>six</u> plays in 1962, under the collective title *The Maker and the Tool*. He conceived each as a multimedia production, essentially live Radio Ballads with visuals – films, back-projected slides, recordings – with Haydn's *Creation* as a musical and structural underpinning.

The six Centre 42 plays were to be performed over an intensive and exhausting ten-week period in separate industrial towns – Wellingborough for Leather (where a pilot Festival had taken place in 1961), Nottingham for Coal, Leicester for Hosiery, Hayes in West London for Electronics, Birmingham for Gas, Bristol for its Docks. Beforehand he went to each town to investigate the industry and to collect actuality recordings, prior to writing an entirely new script for each, albeit with a standard template. While he was doing that he kept an eye out for promising teenagers, occasionally interviewing them himself before passing them on to Ewan and Peggy as useful material for *On the Edge*, as the sixth Radio Ballad would eventually be called.

As performers and technicians Charles used people he had first employed for a modern nativity play he'd written for St Peter's Harborne, *Dog in the Manger*, which had impressed Wesker. For that he'd augmented the church choir, some of whom had qualms about performing with the godless of the Clarion Singers. Similarly, most of the Centre 42 company were amateurs, including dancers from a boy's school. Few had acting training, most were under 30, and they went by the collective name of The Leaveners. When you consider the scale of the concept now it seems quite astonishing that they even got near to pulling it off. Michael Kustow, the playwright and critic, then one of a young band of festival organisers, reviewed the Wellingborough performance:

> Against the urgency of … recorded voices … Parker throws an apparently disparate complex of sensations, a choir singing extracts from Haydn's *Creation*, a narrator reciting Shelley, the foursquare fiddle and banjo of a folk-group singing industrial ballads, the dancing of 12 boys from a Birmingham secondary school, film of complex mechanical processes, slides of Blake engravings, of Gas Council cartoons, of flower petals magnified a thousand times. Often the result is confused and blurred, with the different elements fighting instead of fusing. But … there were two or three moments where one literally feels a fire of a new vision, where one is touched and sobered in a profound way, where Haydn and flower-petals and gasworks perceptibly belong to the same world.

Confused and blurred, two or three moments – it sounds like the damning of faint praise, but this was an imaginative attempt, many years after the wandering days of Theatre Workshop. Moreover, for the participants – from

Ian Campbell and his group, to Bob Etheridge, the motor mechanic who fixed Charles's cars when they'd been thrashed to death – it was tremendously exciting, as one performer recalled. Eileen Whiting:

> Of course there was a lot to go wrong and it sometimes did, but when it was all working together it was POWERFUL. Rehearsals – don't remind me – we joked that they were 10am till unconscious, and that wasn't far from the truth … remember we were all amateurs, which was a great strength but meant that we had to pack up and go to work on Monday. Many of us were young and resilient … but the older members … had manual jobs. They were valiant. Flower petals? They were beautiful close-ups of leaves photographed by Bob Etheridge while the narrator related: 'Two hundred million years ago the coal measures were laid down.' Songs were written by Clarion members … which generated a great rhythm exploited by the dancers to the full. They were ordinary kids from Lozells but their teachers got extraordinary performances from them.

> Charles would arrive at rehearsal with sheaves of paper saying: 'Throw out pages 14–56, 62–70 and 73–4 and replace them with these.' Charles would have written them late into the night as usual … His wife Phyl was an unsung heroine. She ferried him everywhere, she fed him and kept him sane. Charles had two modes – sparking with creativity and keeping everyone at full stretch and happy – and total exhaustion. I remember arriving in Wellingborough and seeing a car draw up. In the front was Phyl and in the back apparently a heap of old blankets. Then they moved and Charles appeared, groaning … We slept in various places – Bristol was a Civil Defence shelter which seemed to be converted from old air-raid shelters. Swarbrick was told off for playing his fiddle half the night, but I enjoyed it.

The Maker and the Tool was a qualified success, a heroic attempt by enthusiastic amateurs, which everyone participating believed would start a movement. Save for its delayed evolution into Banner Theatre (Chapter 20), sadly it prompted no cultural revolution, and nor did much else of the Centre 42 Festivals. Ian Campbell took part in the three closest to Birmingham, and wrote of the experience at length. As well as the performances, his group participated in the folk song concert which ended each week, with others including Louis Killen, Joe Heaney and Cyril Tawney, who all at some point took part in the Radio Ballads, as well as Ewan and Peggy. There were other events too. The linked series of Folksong in the Pubs, Painting in the Pubs, and Poetry in the Works Canteen was an attempt by Centre 42 to make sure that the Festivals should not be wasted on the middle classes and the intellectual minority of the working classes.

A forlorn hope. These Pub events with few exceptions were not a success. Ewan and Peggy didn't take part. Peggy says that (unlike her) Ian Campbell was an excellent pub singer, with the voice and the bottle to use it, but as he said later: 'I was determined that the people in the pubs were going to hear my message, the songs that I wanted to sing, whether they liked it or not. And they liked it not.' At best they were tolerated, in other places they were received, he said, 'with puzzled derision, cool indifference, or even hot resentment.' The concerts, though, were an unqualified success – but they were played almost exclusively to just the audience Wesker was trying to avoid. It hadn't worked. Wesker and his supporters struggled on, attempting to convert the Roundhouse in Chalk Farm in London, but couldn't raise enough money anywhere. The Arts Council was conspicuous in its refusal of support, as it had been for Theatre Workshop, and the TUC lost enthusiasm. In 1965 it pulled the plug on a brave but doomed experiment.

On the Edge

1962 was a whirlwind year for Charles, and *On the Edge* kept slipping. In February he had made *Cry from the Cut*, in March *The Body Blow*, and in April he was writing to Ewan and Peggy: 'I have just recorded ten hours of Else Rosenfeld, and a 19 year old for *On the Edge* … I'm desperate for tape – I've told Centre 42 I must have sixty 5" spools for *Maker and Tool*, but need another hundred for *On the Edge*. I lectured to BBC Staff Training yesterday and *Body Blow* had a tremendous reception.' (Else Rosenfeld was a concentration camp survivor with such vivid recall that Charles went on to make 23 quarter-hour programmes with her.) A fortnight later he tells Ewan and Peggy his planned itinerary: 'Nottingham May 8–11, Bristol 19–22 May. May 23 to June 9 on *Maker and Tool* script. 12–23 June *Not Known in Denmark Street*, 25 June to July 14 on the teenage programme with you both, 21 July to 4 August on holiday, then August editing and assembly of *On the Edge*.'

Charles was now continually trying to promote folk music. *Not Known in Denmark Street* was a programme about modern folk singers and writers, an attempt to counter what he and Ewan saw as the flood of debased culture arriving from America, exemplified by the pop music he loathed with a passion. These were the days of Elvis's imitators – Cliff Richard and the rest – singing ersatz American songs in ersatz mid-Atlantic accents – and I'm afraid the teenagers round the jukebox weren't listening to folk music or discussing Wesker's latest play, then or ever. This man Bob Dylan, maybe, but he would soon be vilified by Ewan and Charles, no longer a folk revival hero. (Ironically 1962, the year of Centre 42, saw the first volley fired in the British fightback, in thick Liverpool accents. That success was not one Charles liked at all.)

Throughout 1962 Charles is racing around, working all hours, driving himself and his cars into the ground. Bob Etheridge over the course of a few years replaced the engine in his Morris 1000 eight times. That was a resilient car, but: 'he didn't bother to do basic maintenance like oil and water.' In the event his planned timetable for *On the Edge* keeps on sliding. Not surprisingly it isn't ready for the performers until August, so Charles postpones rehearsal and recording to the week of 21 August, after his holiday. Ewan and Peggy have spent much of June and July talking to teenagers wherever their busy performing schedule takes them – hitch-hikers, coffee bar habitués, grammar school boys at bus stops – and following up with recordings at dance halls, folk clubs, jazz clubs, in their homes. As Ewan explained:

> Not that it was difficult – on the contrary, it was as if the teenagers had been waiting for someone to hold a microphone in front of them. We interviewed them singly and in groups, the sons and daughters of labourers and company-directors, of professors and railway-porters, miners and filing-clerks. There were schoolgirls, apprentices, mods and rockers, unemployed. There were 52 of them, from Glasgow and Stirling; Newcastle, Birmingham, Bristol and Reading; from Hackney, Poplar, Mile End, Hampstead, Camberwell, Brixton and the Old Kent Road. Once started, there was no stopping them. Like a stream of consciousness, everything poured out – their hopes, anxieties, bewilderment, fears, doubts, dreams, fantasies. Most of what they said was tremendously moving and we were really spoilt for choice when it came to choosing actuality excerpts for the programme.

Excited, but daunted by the prospect of the teenager programme, Peggy wrote to Charles describing their progress with the interviews, saying that the question that really turned on the tap was, 'There's a stereotype of teenagers in the newspapers. Is it true?' Later she added that he would go on: 'You're all on drugs … hate your parents … promiscuous? Is it true? Bang, wow, did they talk!' To Charles she went on:

> Writing about such things now gives me the feeling that a mountain climber must have, as he stands at the foot of the Matterhorn in a blizzard, ready to climb and terrified, yet pausing to plan what he'll do when he gets to the top. If he gets there. The title *On the Edge* refers to us, not the teenagers.

All that gorgeous material proved too much, as Ewan later recognised: 'The fact is, we had allowed ourselves to be overcome by its richness. We were glutted with it – we had swallowed it whole and still hadn't digested it by the time it went into production.' In explaining his reservations about the programme later, Ewan said that Charles's direction 'lacked the tautness and sense of excitement which had marked most of the previous Radio Ballads.' Charles was ill – Peggy described how he was afflicted during the recording: 'He had a continual migraine … I don't know how he operated – he was incapacitated for three, four, five days.' No wonder. His self-imposed schedule that year was brutal. He had to intersperse his post-production work for *On the Edge* with the preparation, rehearsal and performance weeks of the six *Maker and Tool* productions, in which he also acted, as if everything else wasn't enough. His first *On the Edge* effort is way over the hour. He writes to them on 26 November, a full three months after the recording, in something of a frenzy:

> Herewith the first assembly ... at 90 mins! Disappointed you were not able to see *Maker and Tool*, as I stand very much in need of your advice. Finished the 90 min version 15 mins before the playback arranged by David Gretton on 23 Nov. His response very enthusiastic but is very anxious it's not offered to London till down to 60, which is why I'm burning up the TR/90's at the moment. I think it's absolutely magnificent and really does constitute a new dimension in the work, and I do congratulate you. How you and Peggy have kept your patience while I have been dickering about on something else I will never know!

It's easy to see Gretton's disquiet at the prospect of a 90-minute version going to London, and hard to resist the feeling that he isn't quite as enthusiastic as Charles likes to think. The broadcast date is now set as 23 December, but in the week before, Charles writes to Ewan to say that his Head of Programmes isn't happy with the musical idiom. There isn't enough use made of the teenagers' own music, and it all sounds 'too much like the adult looking at the teenage world.' He's sensing 'the contradiction between the language ... and the lyrics.'

That's the complaint – how can a programme about teenagers in 1962, their lives heavily suffused with pop music, be effective in a musical idiom alien to their own, and much of it sung by a man of 47, as old as the teenagers' fathers? There were younger singers participating – Ian Campbell, Gordon McCulloch, Lorna Campbell and Ray Fisher as well as the (American-voiced) Peggy – but Ewan sustains a big chunk of it, and his powerful mature voice at times overpowers the message it's trying to convey. When Peggy heard it again over 40 years later, in places she cringed: 'It's montage gone wild ... This section is meant to evoke a bad dream but it only sounds pretentious ... Hate the whoever/whatever section.' In the end she was forced to conclude that it's 'about emotions not industry. There's no progression in the teenage state, just complaint. The other Radio Ballads had a chronology, a progression, this only had a state. You must have a chronology, or a person, or a profession.' Or ideally some combination of them working together: a community.

Charles was getting seriously edgy about the audience's response to using folk music by the time he came to write his *Radio Times* article, before *On the Edge* was eventually broadcast on 13 February 1963.

By rooting the action in the idea of a quest, and using the classic Quest Ballad form as the main musical thread, set to the mountain dulcimer, and sung in the austere nasal tone of the authentic ballad, Ewan MacColl and Peggy Seeger throw down a musical gauntlet to the pop song idiom so absolutely associated with teenagers.

The teenagers' 'Quest' is set out in the first song when Ewan sings a mournful lament to the sobbing notes of the dulcimer, which echoes the uncontrolled crying of Dot Dobby, whose wide-eyed Lancastrian innocence emerges vividly from the tapestry woven by the other 50 voices. Her words introduce the theme:

It's all new and like an adventure which you've got to face … well it could be a nice adventure. You never sort of know how it's going to be like when you go somewhere strange or turn a corner that you don't know what's on the other side. It could be something really beautiful or it could be a cliff edge …

A tale of the children of a troubled world,
The tale of a search and the long journey.
Leaving the safe and guarded fortress,
The searchers walk in the trackless places
From the world behind the wall …

The tune of this song, based on 'Queen Maeve', acts as a measured framing commentary to a parade of young voices from all over Britain. The contrast between Dot's language and Ewan's could not be greater. The triumph of method over content is evident immediately afterwards, with over 20 different voices all telling us their ages, similar to the trick that had worked, but much better, on *Song of a Road*. The cleverly designed and executed audio montage technique used in *The Body Blow* becomes overblown here, and the modern listener's irritation is constantly provoked thereafter. The dated jargon – 'with it', 'beat', 'man', 'dad', 'nit', 'square', 'nana' – jars too. Where the idiom of the miner or fisherman works, this doesn't. That is indeed how they spoke, but it grates, especially when Ewan sings it.

Some of the sequences are brilliant, as are some of the songs with younger voices (Peggy agreed that they should have used them more), but they can't rescue the overall impression of a fascinating failure. A driving back-of-a-motorbike sequence: 'I've got me tight black jeans, got me black leather jacket' does work, once Ewan hands the song over to others and a chorus. The best use of montage is in a long sequence when (only) two girls' voices alternate to a slow guitar as each relives a daydream:

> There was just this one boy, he's got a very weak heart, and I save him, you see and it's absolutely wild, triple blood transfusion, he's got a rare blood group, you see and I've got the same rare blood group …
>
> I'm walking down the street and I stop to cross the road and I go over a zebra crossing and a car draws up quickly. There's a young, very handsome man in the car and he really is a film director …
>
> He's got to have the blood immediately and the transfusion takes place in the main hall of the men's union at Glasgow university, with a great big long table with the Speaker's Mace at the end of it …
>
> And he says, would you like to make a picture for us? It's about a young girl. And I say, But I'm not beautiful. And he says we're not looking for anybody beautiful, we're looking for somebody with a face like you …
>
> And I end up, you know, having given so much of my precious life blood that I am in fact fighting for my life … [she dissolves in laughter]

Another sequence is triggered by Dot Dobby: 'And blokes have followed me home, but I've never given them a chance … Walking down the road, you know, sometimes, coming home, get the all-night bus, about twelve o'clock.' This leads to a mesmerising late-night walking home piece, with Ewan (why? – apart from his exquisite singing) as the boy, Alfie Kahn's lazy clarinet, and Dot telling us about her walk home with a lad trying to chat her up. Peggy: 'Fantastically good song, beautiful integration. Sounds like improvisation but isn't … but where does it come from? Something from Ewan's pre-war years?'

Ewan and Peggy afterwards felt that if the programme had just concentrated on Dot Dobby, whose inner feelings and memories simply flooded out, it could have been rescued, but it's hard to see now how. (Unless, for example, it had set out to examine the interaction between parent and child, which Peggy did 25 years later in her cleverly constructed song 'Different Tunes'. For that song she recorded mothers and their teenage daughters talking separately about their relationships with each other, and assembled the song from their comments.) Peggy later recalled that Ewan had been much moved by Dot Dobby. 'She just talked and talked, and cried. She sewed pockets on aprons in a factory. We sent her to Finland on an international schools festival, but she came back and got drowned in children.'

This is the Radio Ballad that has dated most, because teenagers' words always do, and because now we're far more used to hearing the views of teenagers canvassed and expressed. Back then it was more novel, and that attracted several of the reviewers. In fact they were divided, but the audience at home wasn't. (Inevitably, there's no record of what teenagers themselves thought.) First the critics in favour. Peter Wilsher in the *Sunday Times* appreciated the montages, and liked what the teenagers had to say:

> A remarkable study of youngsters poised between childhood and growing up. In the past I had thought the method tended to swamp the material. Here reservations are withdrawn – the match was near-perfect... MacColl and Seeger apparently talked to the kids till nearly dawn, when what they said was so personal and tender that it sounded as though the dialogue was taking place inside their own heads.

Patrick Williams in the *Sunday Telegraph* extols: 'marvellous bits of radio ... Charles Parker's technique is to edit the actuality like film, as exciting to hear as Grierson's documentaries were to see, and then thread them with song.' But he continues: 'This time the songs were pretentious.' Ian Rodgers in the *Guardian* agreed, after starting with a tag that Ewan will have appreciated:

> MacColl and Parker are among the Brechtians of today ... [but] some of his songs were tiresome because they pretended to express the spirit and attitude of adolescents and only succeeded in reminding the listener that the composer and singers were adults. They were demonstrably singing from the outside, but the attempt to convey with music the dilemma of the contemporary adolescent was worthwhile for it produced a few moments of great beauty: Colin Ross on the pipes accompanying loneliness, 'Where is the child that would climb on my knee?' A startling new version of 'Come Live with Me and be My Love'...

Paul Ferris in *The Observer*, usually a forthright supporter of the form:

> Abstractions loomed up from the beginning. This was a superior documentary in a superfluous setting ... Although many of the comments were sharp and valuable, they rained down like an actors' chorus in a slightly old-fashioned radio play. At times embarrassingly clever ... Their own fantasies are much richer than the studio fantasy composed of tarted-up recitatives. The beauty of these Radio Ballads ... has been that they are hot forgings straight from life, not statements about it.

So far, so mixed. But it's the audience research figures that really hurt. Usually scoring in the range 60 to 70 per cent, around the average for features or a little better, here it plummets to 50 per cent. This was dire for Charles. Most of the good burghers of the Home Service listening panel disliked it with varying degrees of intensity. Many were depressed, angry or both. The theme was unappealing. They were tired of the subject of adolescence, the perpetual glare of publicity on a natural stage of development.

> In my youth it was called the awkward age, and was got over with as little ostentation as possible, not flaunting and exploiting it in the present unhealthy manner ... Heard it all before, and this lot are unimpressive in their attitude to life, their power of expression – embittered, chips on their shoulders ... spineless half-wits who have rejected the wonderful educational opportunities available.

And so on, as Charles's gauntlet was flung back in his face. Actually Ewan and Peggy were at pains to point out that they really did have a broad cross-section, including university students. But most listeners didn't want to hear it, or the music, or to be reminded of the teenagers' preoccupation with the Bomb. For every 'Revealing – I had no idea this was the way young people are thinking', there were many who didn't want to know at all. For every one who found the music contained 'unusual, haunting and moving melodies with a strange beauty that heightened the effect of the speech' (just as the makers intended) there were many who found it a 'miserable caterwauling, all despair in a dismal tone.' And those who admired the 'novel, effective, apt presentation, with the telling repetition of significant words and phrases, skilfully blended, smooth, fast-moving' were outnumbered by those for whom it was 'disjointed, jerky, muddled, with no apparent plan, an Arty, gimmicky approach.'

It was their first major rebuff, not the 'best yet' they'd anticipated. They paused, and in an attempt to analyse why this was so poorly received, got together a group to listen to all the Radio Ballads again. What worked and what didn't, and why? And what next?

CHAPTER 14

Boxing Clever
The Fight Game

The problem of the artist is to direct the audience to the heart of the contradiction in its inhuman brutalising ... while asserting the positive virtues of the individual boxer's victory over adversity ... Boxing – damnable; Boxers – admirable.

EWAN MACCOLL, PRELIMINARY NOTES FOR THE FIGHT GAME, 1963

I heard the referee saying six, seven, eight. I thought, well, I'm going to get a right drubbing if I get up. But I get up.

PETER KEENAN, EX BRITISH COMMONWEALTH BANTAMWEIGHT CHAMPION, THE FIGHT GAME, 1963

Stung by the comparative failure of *On the Edge* with the critics, in early 1963 Ewan MacColl collects a small group of people together to listen to each Radio Ballad again. He then steps back and writes a thorough critique. He concludes that only the first four can be called 'ballads' in the strict sense of the word; he decides that *The Body Blow* and *On the Edge* can best be described as documentary radio features with incidental music conceived in the folk idiom. To succeed, he decides a Radio Ballad needs 'a carefully worked-out musical structure in which the actuality is set like the dialogue in a novel.' He wants *The Fight Game* to have an almost continuous musical line as in the *Fishing* and *Axon*.

Within a fortnight of the broadcast of *On the Edge* he and Charles put together an ideas paper on a programme about Boxing. Charles and Peggy hadn't been at all keen, but Ewan wins them round. He said:

> We had chosen professional boxing as a subject in an effort to escape from the huge canvas of industry and the intensely private world of the sick and the adolescent. I think we imagined that we were embarking upon a Radio Ballad which, for a change, would be gay and light-hearted. How naïve we were! It soon became apparent that we had entered a world inhabited by people who regarded the prize ring as a symbolical representation of the larger world in which we all live. Boxers, managers, trainers, sports commentators, all stressed this point over and over again.

Here was a sport coming under increasing scrutiny because of the number of boxers suffering from severe pounding in the ring, with an effect extending from minor brain damage (for which punch-drunk was the euphemism) to coma and worse. The death in the ring of Davey Moore soon after they began their interviews made it particularly topical. Since 1900, 450 boxers had died after fights, 200 of them in the 18 years since World War II, one a month. In Britain the doctor and Labour peer Baroness Summerskill was leading a campaign to ban the sport, which in her view exploited and damaged the most deprived in society to satisfy something little better than blood lust. Boxing since the days of Lord Byron had become entirely a poor man's 'sport', and one with little appeal to the middle-class spectator. A manager described the boxer's motive as:

> **Economic necessity. I never met one in my life that went into the boxing game for the sheer love of it. It's always that drive to get some money. Or perish ... All fighters have got to come off of poor families. Before you become a boxer you've got to be poor, you know, off a big family, or a poor family. But you don't get a doctor's son coming to be a boxer because he's, he's been spoiled, he's had a good upbringing, he's never wanted.**

So they would be taking a risk with a somewhat unappealing subject, however topical. 'What is happening out there?' they asked themselves, before they'd talked to any boxer. Ewan wrote in their preliminary notes:

> What is the nature of this activity of two men stripped to the waist confronting each other ... feeling no personal animosity but setting out deliberately to hurt each other? What is the balance between sentiment and sport, courage and stupidity, manliness and viciousness? Is it the stylistic representation of the inert struggle into which we are born? Do they personify good versus evil, science versus violence? [We must] explore the relationship between the two boxers, the insistence of it being a job's work, of having the responsibility to give the crowd its money's worth, the horrible fact that ... a man might contribute to the mental destruction of an opponent for whom he had a tremendous affection?

They put together a template of around ten different questions for boxers, trainers and fans. As usual after the interviews they debated and listed their ideas for musical themes: this is the Radio Ballad for which the most detailed record of their work-in-progress remains. They decided their opening song should have a lively tune – major, with chorus – one that can be used periodically throughout. Their plan for the song is followed by its eventual first two verses:

> It should underline the concept of boxing as a manly art, a character-building sport, an ancient sport, the final test of a man. A sport based on skill, on the ability to give punishment without taking it, a sport demanding the maximum physical fitness from the protagonists. Bring in the British fair-play idea ... The super-athlete with the killer instinct, the noble savage, the gladiator, the scientific fighting machine, the fighting monk abstaining from rich foods, the high life, women, drink, so as to provide the public with the last word in human spectacles – man against man.

> **There's a game some call the fight game and some the noble art,**
> **Blokes who play this game need bags of courage, bags of heart.**
> **It's a rough game, a tough game, needing guts and skill,**
> **And you'll never make a boxer if you haven't got the will.**
>
> **It's a noble sport, a manly sport, and there's no better sight**
> **Than two good boys in prime condition squaring for the fight.**
> **Eight rounds, ten rounds, round the ring they go,**
> **A-weaving dodging punching jabbing, dealing blow for blow.**

That's how it emerges – the last line repeating the rhythm of the ring. It's belted out with a jaunty tune against a musical background evoking fairground and music-hall, with a blaring trumpet component, a driving rhythm and a strong chorus backing up Ewan's voice at its harshest, interspersed with swelling crowd sounds and the weathered voices of old pugilists. Sonny Wilson: 'I loved the game, because everybody loved me, you see. They say I'm punch-drunk, but I can't say I am. It's just the way I walk, you see … I've had some real good tannings, and I've give some back. And I'm satisfied that I enjoyed every moment of 'un.' Then Ewan reflects the viewpoint expressed by the school-of-hard-knocks boxing manager:

> **Oh the boxing is a sport that sorts the men out from the boys,**
> **It's great for building character, it's marvellous for boys,**
> **It's a great game, a straight game, calls for discipline,**
> **Teaches you to give or take a bashing with a grin.**
>
> **Boxing to me is the greatest character builder in the world. Anybody can … press the button to blow a ship up … an atom bomb … whip you, anybody can stick a knife into you, anybody can pull a trigger. But where's the man with the character as can take a punch on the nose and keep his temper and keep control of himself?**

Ewan's voice in this stanza is just mocking enough. The notes they'd written in advance for this advise the singer to be 'astringent, ironical, but not too obviously so … somewhat bombastic.' Once he gets his teeth into an idea for a song, Ewan as usual churns out the verses, many of which didn't make the final cut. The idea for this verse came originally from a different song, with a discarded stanza that began:

> It's a great sport, a man's sport, a sport that's heaven sent,
> It sorts the men out from the boys and pays out ten per cent.

In the final version this idea of the manager's percentage (25 here is for fights with a bigger purse) emerges elsewhere as:

> **They'll punch and maul each other but of course no harm is meant.**
> **It's all good clean fun and pays the manager twenty-five per cent.**

This comes from the start of the culminating fight sequence, which lasts nearly nine minutes and apparently took over 80 attempts to get right. Charles had determined by now that he couldn't equal the best continuous take by cutting and splicing the best of the rest. In a later interview Ewan said of Charles:

> He was very insistent that the best work we did is where we had long runs and got into a rhythm of performance. He said there was no way the engineer could compensate for that rhythm ... The wear and tear on performers was tremendous. When we were doing it I'd see singers collapse – from standing up 7–8 hours without a break ... The casts got to know Charles very well and they knew if they'd done a take well they could tell from his expression. Though if he said 'that was a very nice take' everybody in the studio would shout 'BUT?!' And, sure enough, there'd be a but.

Ronnie Hughes remembers *The Fight Game*: he was one of the two trumpeters in it. The other was the classically trained Johnny Lambe from the MLO, who Hughes found for them. Still playing at over 80 in 2007, Hughes had in the 1950s been a member of Ted Heath's famous Big Band, and the Radio Ballad work was a real oddity for him. In fact he could remember very little about the experience, until, that is, he was played a few snatches of the trumpet from the recording. His lips began moving unconsciously with the muscle memory, and with that it began to flood back:

> I do remember it was a tough workout for a jazz trumpeter, no doubt about it, different phrasing. Especially the use of different time signatures. Everything we did was in 4/4, normal time, for the big band stuff, just sometimes 3/4. This was a completely different world, a challenge, kept us on our toes ... Ewan was quite a taskmaster. If he didn't hear what he wanted he would tell you. There's nothing wrong with that. He was a lovely man. But he was tough. Peggy was charming and professional ... but she didn't really understand the instrument ... consequently sometimes I'd have to say Peggy this isn't going to work, and we'd change it, work something out ...

After the introductory sections, the programme's shape is based on a boxer's typical upbringing, on through his weeks of preparation to the fight itself. Gordon McCulloch sings a song based on the childhood of the scrawny Scots boxer Peter Keenan, a bantamweight who was born in the typical two-room tenement, in which whole families were crammed, a Partick 'single-end'. 'As a kid I was a lump of wood, you know, wasn't very clever. When I started to box, and I found out this was something I was good at, I used to get a lot of medals, I would have done it for nothing just because I was good at a thing, I really loved boxing.' The song uses the traditional Scots tune 'Drumdelgie':

I fought the tears when the teacher's strap made stripes across me hands.
I dichted the blood frae my streaming nose when I fought with the rival gangs.
I had to fight to be recognised in the only world I knew.
I had to fight to prove to myself that I'm as good as you.
    It was come on Johnny, and put 'em up Johnny,
    I'll belt you black and blue,
    Stand up and fight, you dirty wee tyke,
    And show what you can do.

Then on to the first amateur fights, and the heady effects of success: 'I think when you're young like that, I think it's the glory, more than the money. Being a professional at sixteen, you think it's great, you think it's good, you know.'

When you're a fighter you're different.
You walk in a certain way.
Everybody's eager to shake your hand,
Everybody knows you're a fighting man –
There's Johnny boy, you hear 'em say.

Then it's on to the build-up to the fight, the long weeks of training, the early-morning runs, the speedball and skipping and sparring in the gym. Ewan went on a dawn run so he knew just how it felt, and came up with a song that mimicked the one-two staccato rhythm of the pounding feet, with each crisp syllable precisely bitten off:

Grab a slice of toast,
There's time to make a cuppa –
Mind you spread the butter thin,
Go easy on the sugar.

> That's it. That's the hardest part about boxing is the training. You've got to get up in the morning, you got to run three, four, five miles. You go back home, you clean up, and all the time you're working hard.

> **Lift 'em Johnny. Keep your knees up.**
> **Nice and easy Johnny, keep your breathing steady.**
> **How much longer? Must have done four miles already.**
> **Out and working at the start of early morning.**
> **Watch your breathing Johnny boy and stop your yawning.**
> **Past the Gaumont in the dark, run three times around the park**
> **Along the empty tarmacadam sweating.**

As read off the page, it hardly looks a song, but it works. The same rhythm takes us into the delectable syncopation of the skipping song that follows, based on the Scots 'Cam Ye O'er Frae France'. They imported a local ex-boxer, Bill Shreeve, one of the Centre 42 Leaveners team, as John Clarke the studio manager recalled.: 'It was a lovely sequence – we actually had a skipping rope in the studio, it wasn't just a sound-effect ... working up a sweat too ... The point about the way boxers skip is that they don't jump very high off the ground, their feet just clear about a quarter of an inch, because if they jumped high, like kids do, they'd be knackered in five minutes ... great fun.' As the trainer Joe Gans said:

> **I like all my boxers to be perfect skippers. Sometimes I do as high as 25 minutes with them without a break doing all sorts of exercises with the skipping ropes. It's not just a case of 1,2 1,2 1,2 – you skip, astride jump, and there's crossing rope, knocking them to the sides and flashing about from side to side, they're doing highland dancing, everything with a skipping rope:**

> **Every day we're here, busy at the skipping**
> **With the flashing rope, jumping leaping tripping.**

Peggy's tripping banjo follows the skipping feet, and Dave Swarbrick's fiddle comes in as they switch incongruously to Highland Dancing. As the trainer says: 'I said dancing, not clog-hopping!' Then on without a pause for breath to the punchball work, and the familiar confiding cockney voice of the British boxer Henry Cooper, who once put Cassius Clay on the canvas (before he changed his name to Muhammad Ali):

> **When you're training all right, you go on the ball, everything's going fine, you can hit speedball and keep it going, you feel good. I mean as you get fitter you feel better. You push yourself harder as well. And so it never comes easy. Your training for boxing never comes easy. You're pushing yourself all the time.**

In planning each song Ewan and Peggy would prepare a musical ideas sheet. For 'Wives and Mothers' they planned: 'a small song, striking a nice blend of humour and irritation, with a style somewhat in the manner of the song 'Fourpence a Day', in 2/4 or 4/8 time.'

The eventual song articulates their anxieties, bringing us to the boxer as he describes how each time he returns from a fight he finds the furniture rearranged: 'She cannae sit for a minute the night I'm boxing.' Finally he's off to the stadium, which has been a sell-out for weeks. He and we can hear the sounds of the earlier bouts as he waits like a condemned man for his fight to begin:

> **Wonder how the other bloke's feeling,**
> **Wonder if I'm in his class,**
> **Got the butterflies, cannae stop yawning,**
> **It's murder waiting for time to pass,**
> **Wished I'd never left the foundry,**
> **Wished that I was there the day,**
> **Wished I'd never put the gloves on,**
> **Wished that I was miles away.**

To prepare for the long fight sequence they all went to see the bout between Henry Cooper's less famous brother Jim and the local hero Johnny Prescott (again Ewan's archetypal Johnny – Noble, Axon, and the 'Johnny Come Back' of *The Big Hewer*). Charles had actually been to a fight earlier, when he was 'hag-ridden by failure to record the key moment' at the climax of the fight. 'I had to get to the ringside to recharge and was too shy to go while a round was actually in progress … a squeamishness that must be overcome.' At that fight he was much taken by the concern of a woman who had been:

> as a supporter … possessed with a frenzy for the victory, but when she called out 'Are you all right, Billy?', then the timbre of this woman's voice … her concern for the man she wanted beaten exactly captures the agony of contradiction of boxing. As an individual – even perhaps as a mother – she was in agony of mind for the boy on the floor.

That romantic notion was soon dispelled. There was no such sympathetic reaction when Prescott was knocked out by Cooper. Ewan and Charles sat with their recording equipment in the front row, at opposite corners, where the boxers' seconds were. Peggy said Ewan came out white as a sheet. He recalled:

Johnny Prescott was the local favourite, fair, good-looking, the girls surrounded him, nicely dressed, brought up in an orphanage. They cheered and cheered as he came in – we recorded it and it must have gone on for four minutes. A tremendous uppercut caught Prescott, and he seemed to float through the air in slow motion, and landed right next to me, on his side, like a wounded animal. His corner man was shouting 'Up up up up up up'. When he did get up Cooper's second right next to me said 'Right. Cut him down'. Just two blows, then a terrible silence, then the booing started. The man they'd cheered to the echo twenty minutes earlier.

Peggy, further back in the crowd, said:

> It was absolutely terrible… the women were horrible, cheering and slobbering, standing up ... Ewan said it was just like seeing a bull being slaughtered, stunned by a sledgehammer ...*The Fight Game* was meant to be about sport, wasn't meant to be political, but it turned out to be political, turned out damning of boxing. Ewan was brought up in the streets of Salford, and boxers came out of his street. His great friend Alex Armstrong was a boxer ... Ewan had been beaten up as a kid, and by the police: he hated, hated, hated violence.

The long fight sequence that results intercuts ring, trainer and crowd noises with the rhythm of the punchball, which Peggy said sounded much more vivid and effective than real sounds of punches landing from the fight. Over it comes the constant urging of the trainer, the snarling of Ewan's commentary voice, and the edgy tones of Gordon McCulloch as his young boxer:

Come on son. The left hand boy, come on fist him boy, box box box box.

> **If he's a fighter I've got to keep boxing him,**
> **If he's a boxer, I'll make it a fight.**
> **Got to see whether he favours his left hand**
> **Or likes to come in with his right.**

Jab him, son, come on, jab, jab, jab, jab. Come on. Get your right hand going now.

> **Come on, Johnny, make it straight from the shoulder boy,**
> **Come on, Johnny, in and give him the lot,**
> **Come on, Johnny, in and shake him and shatter him**
> **And whack him and crack him and wallop him round the ring,**
> > **Hit him with all that you've got.**

BOXING CLEVER – THE FIGHT GAME

You flinch as you listen, and you're meant to – how many savage words for physical violence are there in the English language? Ultimately our Johnny goes down, the swelling of the crowd's roar peaks, then shifts into booing – for losing so early and for curtailing their pleasure as much as anything. 'That is the fight crowd. They like you while you're winning. But as soon as you're licked, they'll like the fellow that licked you…The loser creeps out to lick his wounds, while the victor preens himself on the adulation of the mob.' And against the sounds of clearing up we hear:

When you came in you looked like a hero
There in the ring with your silk dressing gown.
We cheered you, we wooed you,
You failed us, we booed you.
   Johnny, you let us down.

We finish with a clearing-up song, a 'Dirty Old Town' mood piece based on the American tune 'St James's Infirmary', but slower, wistful, interspersed with a meandering small-hours trumpet, and ending with a sardonic twist –

The bars are deserted, the dressing rooms empty,
Stale with the smell of a thousand defeats
The pain and the glory are already fading.
What's left is the thrill when you count the receipts.

With the shape of the programme and their musical ideas firm in their heads, and fewer distractions for Charles, who had been working much more closely with Ewan than usual, they cracked on far more quickly than for *On the Edge*, and had the programme ready for rehearsal and recording for the end of May 1963. It was a particularly tough process this time, though rewarding in the end. As Ewan said:

> The demands made on the singers in *Fight Game* were enormous. The fact that each episode was so closely tied to a specific rhythm or a group of rhythms meant that the problem of getting everything working together was just that much more difficult. For the actual fight sequence, for example, there were 86 takes! A gruelling four or five hours for the singers. For the turntable operator, handling four machines and 8 or 9 acetates of effects it must have been a nightmare. My most vivid memory of that recording period is of a trumpet player with lips swollen into small balloons, saying that he had nothing left to give. I think we all felt like that.

The Fight Game was broadcast on 3 July 1963, and immediately gained the critics' unanimous approval. Here's a representative pair. Below is Peter Wilsher in the *Sunday Times*, but first Paul Ferris in *The Observer*, for whom the programme was a welcome return to form:

> The three people who made *The Fight Game* saw boxing in the round by getting inside it and recreating its highly-charged atmosphere. Charles Parker ... seems to be increasingly concerned with refinement and technical experiment – for instance marrying the rhythms of music and tape-recorded speech, or getting the right studio acoustics ... A boxer called Johnny and a fight (which he loses) provided a carefully under-emphasised story. MacColl and Miss Seeger and others sang with the usual spirit and precision. What emerged was a whole: excitement and involvement in boxing at the same time as disgust at the brutality and irony at the exploitation.
>
> Professional boxing of all sports probably lends itself to the epic approach. The angry hungry boy emerging from the slums, the cauterising ritual of training, a series of single combats, purple and gold rewards, the final hubristic downfall. All caught splendidly in the latest Radio Ballad. Their developing technique of crosscutting real dialogue with their own brand of racy vernacular half-mocking half-philosophical recitative fitted admirably. Some of the resulting sound-pictures are as effective as anything they'd ever done, for example early morning road work round the silent back streets of Glasgow and Liverpool, and the mounting rhythm and tension of the training gym. The choice of conversational snippets remains marvellously apt. My only faint niggling doubt is its apparently universal application. Though I passionately admire Ewan MacColl's metallic voice, whether he's singing about Eppie Morrie ... or the good clean fun of swilling the blood off the canvas, I suspect he'd sing equally eloquently about the groundnut scheme or a six-day international tiddlywinks contest. But of course there's always the chance that these might make excellent Radio Ballads.

Wilsher praises with faint damns. He and the other critics managed to suppress any antipathy they had about boxing in their reviews, but the BBC Home Service listeners had no such professional necessity. For a good half of them nothing could offset the distaste they felt towards the theme, and in fact the split between the responses was as marked as that for *John Axon* back at the beginning. Many felt it a wasted opportunity because they wanted to hear a scathing attack on the sport. The programme itself was much more subtle, as many recognised, 'No built-up glamour, no glossing over ... with some fine ironic touches ... the comments of the boxers themselves were startlingly and sometimes pathetically revealing.'

There's a curious but characteristic contradiction in the reaction of Charles and Ewan after the programme had finished. Charles wrote a long self-flagellating piece to Ewan, critiquing the production method, rhythmic failures in the music, failures in technical balance, how they use music behind speech. He was having a real downer – 'I realise how utterly ignorant I am of the overall form of the Radio Ballad and the theories behind it. Everything is still much too intuitive and mystical on my part!' Peggy is much more pragmatic about the 'theory'. She says briskly:

> There wasn't a theory. Each one happened. Certain things recurred: recitative, a classical concept, when you lay out your themes that you might use later on … You had these things but there was no theory. You were telling a story in two different ways, because the speech would say something different from the music. Charles is looking for a structure? We listened to the actuality and the structure came out of it. You don't impose the structure on it … I think we did hit the spot quite well in this, specially in the training and the gym – Bryan Daly's guitar creating what Ewan and I used to call a graph behind the cardio. A grid. Doesn't move.

Ewan, of course, did tend to theorise about successes and failures, but this for him was a winner. In all the other Radio Ballads there had been something that hadn't worked as anticipated; here there was nothing. Charles's finely tuned ear fussing about minor imprecisions didn't bother Ewan. In his view, everything worked beautifully. He adapted more of the tunes than usual from folk melodies, which he felt gave it a musical unity, and he himself sang superbly It's an irony that, though he wrote some of his very best songs for *The Fight Game*, most are now forgotten, for few could easily be sung away from the boxing setting. And who wanted to sing about boxing?

With the next programme, that was not a problem, so rapidly and permanently did his songs about Travellers enter the repertoire. Unfortunately, Ewan, Charles and Peggy, back on peak form, were about to be forcibly moved on. Just like the Travellers.

CHAPTER 15

Killed at the Crossroads
Travelling People

My great-grandfather, he looked at me one morning, we was sitting down, minding the horses, we was, he said, 'My son, years ago, when I was a boy,' he said, 'See that place there, that park?' I says, 'Yes, Grandfather.' 'We used to stop on that', he said, 'twelve month, two year at a time. Till a lord came along', he said, 'he put a bit of fence up and that's how they got the ground', he said, 'by pinching it, bit by bit.' That's how you come your squires and your lords. They've no more right to that ground than what you or I have. The ground don't belong to no one.

AN OLD TRAVELLER FROM *TRAVELLING PEOPLE*, OF HIS GREAT-GRANDFATHER, BORN C 1830

It was a perfect Radio Ballad subject. Apart from any other considerations, the Travelling People are now among the chief carriers of the English and Scots folksong traditions, a fact which made the choice of musical idiom a natural one. As custodians of many of the classic folk tales they number in their ranks storytellers of great skill. It was from these that the programme was to take its pace and overall style.

In this extract from *Journeyman* Ewan MacColl goes on to say that he and Peggy Seeger had been recording Scots Tinkers and English Gypsies since 1960, on field trips scavenging ballads and tales before they disappeared from memory. Soon after they finished recording *Fight Game* they spent a couple of weeks in the 'bow-tents of Argyllshire Tinkers; in harvest fields and roadside pull-ins in Aberdeenshire, Perthshire and Banffshire; around campfires where storytellers told tales of the dead returning to the land of the living to pay off old debts.'

After that trip in the summer of 1963 Peggy writes a long letter with advice to Charles, who's about to go off interviewing English Travellers. In the winter most by now are 'settled', sometimes with a caravan on a designated site, sometimes in a sparsely furnished council house that they simply up and leave in the spring. But in the summer finding them can be extremely difficult for 'gorgios', as they call the rest of the population. They constantly move on, or, as their interviewers come to discover, are forcibly moved on. She warns Charles that Travellers are extremely guarded with outsiders, and only relax – a little – once convinced of your sincerity. A 'source' singer and old friend of Ewan and Peggy's, who would sing on the programme, takes them in hand:

> We were really lucky to have had Belle Stewart with us. She got us into many places that we may never have known about and even had we known we might have just met distrust and hostility ... We found them to be like children, resentful of the way they've been treated the way a child is resentful, always saying 'We don't understand why?', instead of saying 'What shall we do about it?' They have no idea of organisation and although it might be easy to organise them it would be virtually impossible to <u>keep</u> them organised. Not only due to the fact that they are migrants, but because they compete against each other ... I really put my foot in it with a group of women by trying to get at ... [their] selling tactics. I asked 'What do you say when you go to a door hawking your soft goods?' Silence. So if they can't even combine their community knowledge, how to get them to organise?

This inability of Travellers to organise for their common good was still bugging her over 40 years later, though it wasn't for lack of will – on an earlier trip with them the American trade union organiser Bill Mencken was besieged by Travellers asking how to start a union. The unit of organisation was the family, often extending for generations down parallel lines – 'How a person like Belle keeps track of all her "cousins", as she put it, is beyond my understanding. But every person you meet is a cousin of hers.' One speaker, a reflective, well-spoken old man, Sylvester (Wester) Boswell, is asked about the origins of the Gypsies, and he says:

> **They took them many years to get to this shore, they believe, from India. But my father's teaching taught to me from <u>his</u> father, my grandfather Wester, and therefore he would get it from <u>his</u> father Tyso Boswell, and Tyso Boswell would get this information from his father again which was Shadrack Boswell. If you refer to Genesis in the Bible…**

So in his biblical 'begat, begat' preamble to telling the story of Abraham and Sariae he has returned to a direct ancestor born well before 1800 – a reminder of the way hunter-gatherer groups must have kept track of family lineages. That's what Travellers resembled, hunter-gatherers in a world that had moved on. Wester's son Gilbert Boswell invited Ewan and Peggy to the traditional annual horse fair at Appleby in the Cumbrian hills:

> There was only one entrance, really narrow. We drew up on the outside and got out and immediately there were about five or ten young men … What do you want? Mr Boswell … And they escorted us … Ewan said the last time that had happened to him was in the slums of Glasgow when he went to visit some activist in hiding. Appleby was a fantastic fair, caravans of all sorts. Gilbert's was pulled by a car. They had horse-drawn ones there, the old painted ones … furniture, beautiful painted wood.

A Boswell, Gordon, still in 2008 takes his caravan to Appleby each year, along the public highway, from his Travellers' Museum in Lincolnshire. Peggy advised Charles:

> On the whole, their main preoccupation is with stopping facilities provided for them, or rather <u>not</u> provided for them. Second to this comes the education of their children. Many of them cannot read or write. And the stories they tell about these two aspects of their lives and the discrimination they perceive through these two things are horrifying. Ask them to tell you about particular instances in which they've been 'moved on', or shifted. It'll be a river you can't block, the torrent of words and stories.

Typically unpleasant was the experience of Minty Smith, recorded at Cobham in Kent, on what Peggy described as a horrific piece of wet land they had been dragged to and dumped on, where a two-year-old had drowned in a puddle a month before. They chose to bring it into the piece early:

> **I was expecting one of my children, you know, one of my babies, and my husband's sent for the midwife and in the time he was going after the midwife the policeman come along. Come on, he says, get a move on. Shift on, he says, don't want you on here, on my beat. So my husband says: Look, he says, sir, let me stay, he says, my wife is going to have a baby. No, don't matter about that, he says, you get off. They made my husband move, and my baby was born going along and my husband's stayed in the van and my baby was born on the crossroads in my caravan. The horse was in harness and we was travelling along and the policeman was following behind, drumming us off and the child was born, born at the crossroads.**

The punctuation in that extract is for your benefit – there was none in the way she spoke, in a continuous stream. Her story led to the programme's original title *Born at the Crossroads*, which was only displaced at the last minute. It leads naturally to the opening song, one of several from *Travelling People* that has entered the folk song repertoire:

> **Born in the middle of the afternoon**
> **In a horse-drawn wagon on the old A5.**
> **The big twelve-wheeler shook me bed –**
> **You can't stop here, the policeman said.**
> **You'd better get born in some place else**
> **So move along, get along, move along, get along –**
> **GO. MOVE. SHIFT!**

Their treatment is emphasised by that blunt monosyllabic repetition from the chorus. The horse's measured clopping hooves beat out the time, and continue as we hear heartless moving-on stories between verses, in a range of voices. This is one of the songs that Ewan and Peggy often sang in folk clubs later on. On hearing this original version again, Peggy's reaction was: 'A bit slow, perhaps, but we had to set the pace to the horse's hooves. It wasn't yet sung-in.' This was a comment she made occasionally – with songs like this they practised constantly and made slight shifts in performance till they felt they had it spot on. The pace here in fact suits the steady slow days of the Travellers, no rush and bustle. Verses of this song punctuate the piece, just as being pushed from place to place punctuated their lives. A couple of verses are used to stress society's lack of Christian charity, as a Scots mother talks to her child:

Our Saviour travelled, didn't he, dear? Our Saviour travelled. He was born in a manger among straw. His mother's carried him on a little donkey's back, if it goes by the way of the world to the Bible. Must keep up that generation to the last of the world. It was the first of it and we're the last of it.

> **Born at the back of a blackthorn hedge**
> **When the white hoar frost lay all around.**
> **No Eastern kings came bearing gifts,**
> **Instead the order came to shift –**
> **You'd better get born in some place else …**
>
> **The winter sky was hung with stars**
> **And one shone brighter than the rest.**
> **The wise men came so stern and strict**
> **And brought the order to evict –**
> **You'd better get born in some place else …**

After a long internal struggle, Charles had by now become a Marxist, but he retained his Christian convictions, and what he heard and saw appalled him. Six years later, following a mass eviction from Balsall Heath, he founded and chaired a West Midlands Traveller Liaison Group. Brought up as a child to believe cleanliness is next to godliness, it did take Charles a while to adjust to the Travellers' lifestyle and courtesies. Earlier, while researching *Singing the Fishing*, he was berated by Ewan after refusing food and drink in the house of a settled Traveller, the aunt of the Stewart sisters. 'But they may be dirty.' 'You'll never do that again, or we'll finish the programme now.' You don't refuse Traveller hospitality: true, Travellers may look dirty, but their utensils aren't, and they keep pots for separate uses in a similar manner to Orthodox Jews. A story Charles told repeatedly from another Scottish trip is when, after an argument about God in the car, Ewan is riled enough to tip Charles out and tell him to ask <u>Him</u> to get him home … he relents and returns for him, of course. They debated hard, but they very seldom had serious rows, said Peggy. 'It's amazing how well two people so completely different could get on, but they did. I admired Charles utterly and completely. He came so far, so far.'

Before Charles sets off round the Midlands and South-West on his own trip, he fires off letters asking for help and interviews. Alderman Harry Watton is a Birmingham councillor with a special interest in Travellers, and his forthright comments in expressing the view of 'society' are so graphic – 'They seem to come almost from nowhere overnight. They're a bit like the starlings in Birmingham. They're here and they're making a mess' – that Ewan uses them as a counterpoint throughout the piece. Advice came from the Scots author Naomi Mitchison, Norman Dodds MP, and a Mrs Hugh McCorquodale, a Hertfordshire councillor. She writes back expressing her concern because Romanies are being turned off Colney Heath 'where they have been since the time of Henry VIII', and is one of the few helping them retain a remnant of their lifestyle. She's a romantic, of course – in another life she is the popular and virtually everlasting romantic novelist Barbara Cartland. Philip Donnellan, who, as with Sam Larner, had got there first, points Charles to the Travellers' 'Hopping' gathering in Hereford, if it still exists. 'If you go to an ironmonger ... and you can buy a heavy frying pan with a loop handle over the top for hanging over a hook, you'll know there are travellers still about.' The spoor of the Traveller.

Just before Charles sets off, David Gretton fires a warning shot: 'It is desirable, though not quite essential, that you should not upset the balance; your present intention to record one Tory and one Socialist meets this very conveniently.' In other words, don't come back with something that the BBC's political opponents can snipe at. Later, when *Travelling People* was circulated before broadcast, Gretton writes: 'After Lewin had heard this programme he was slightly bothered by Alderman Watton's remarks. He's not identified by name, but Charles can we justify it if challenged?' In other words, have you twisted it in the editing? Charles replies pithily by saying: 'From a 30-minute interview, the quotations are not merely fair, but are somewhat milder than what the alderman was driving at!' 'Not quite essential' and 'Slightly bothered' – such gentle understatement for 'don't you dare bugger it up, Charles.'

Charles finds the trip extraordinary and harrowing. He didn't know people lived like this. Advising for the illustration for his *Radio Times* article he writes that:

> The illustration must avoid a romantic Romany caravan image ... Most live in trailers drawn by small pick-up trucks or lorries, but many Scots tinkers still live in bow tents, tarpaulins stretched over bent saplings staked to the earth, and I saw shanty dwellings in the New Forest as bad as anything in Johannesburg. We discovered a people harried by the inexorable pressures and economic processes of modern life, progressively deprived of their livelihood as plastics, aluminium, motor transport, mechanised harvesters, and mass produced furniture, replace clothes pegs, artificial flowers, wicker work, tin pans, horses, cans, their traditional

crafts. They're driven now to scrap dealing with its attendant problems of litter and scrap heaps. The majority are desperate for permanent homes and acceptance by the community. We found what is virtually a breakdown in communications between them and society, public and private.

Ewan illustrated this in another song that has entered the repertoire, 'Thirty Foot Trailer', a song of farewell to the old travelling life, with a jaunty lilt and a characteristic rollicking chorus. (The title would have been different had Wester Boswell told Charles in a letter before, not after, the recording that the maximum permitted length of a trailer was 22 feet …) Ewan stresses this forced move away from natural materials in two of the middle verses:

Farewell to the besoms of heather and broom,
Farewell to the creel and the basket,
The folks of today they would far sooner pay
For a thing that's been made oot o' plastic.
    Goodbye to the tent and the old caravan
    To the tinker, the gypsy, the travelling man
    And goodbye to the thirty-foot trailer.

Farewell to the pony the cob and the mare,
The reins and the harness are idle.
You don't need the strap when you're breaking up scrap,
    So farewell to the bit and the bridle.

Charles goes on: 'Along the Wareham Road a convoy of Saracen armoured cars scream by … drowning out the voice of Caroline Hughes singing "Green Grows the Laurel". Seated at her feet are children and grandchildren in a bow tent fantastically hung with highly coloured cotton prints and smelling of stale bread and sour earth … Caroline Hughes sings songs old when Shakespeare was a boy.' Peggy still remembers vividly the fraught but spellbinding evening recording the tale Maggie Cameron told in another bow tent near Blairgowrie in Scotland:

There were about 20 people in there. Right in the middle there was a fire in an upturned bucket … and the kids were all there, everybody was there, they had dogs in there, every inch of space was filled. This was a better sound – we had the Nagra by this time – this beautiful machine. You could have sold everything that everybody had on in that room, all their old cars, and the tent and the pots and pans … for the price of the Nagra. There was so much poverty … they're singing and jigging away. Fantastic, the life in there.

Once a child had been hushed, in a silence you could cut with a knife Maggie Cameron told a story of two ghostly wee pipers in the night. Peggy was desperate lest the tape ran out – though fortunately the new Nagra had half-hour reels – while Maggie took her time, telling it the way she always did, and ending:

> **… But Mary she heard the pipes coming nearder and nearder and nearder till they come walking right in to the camp, and … she says, I lifted the side of the door and lookid oot Maggie and as sure as God's in the kingdom of heaven she said I nearly jumped into the bed. My heart went quicker she said than a traction engine. There was two wee men and they would nae be as tall she says as my Cairn terrier, wi' curled up shoes on them and peakit bonnets, lang whiskers on 'em and the size of their airms she says was like just the length of your hand. Two sets of pipes and they kept going in time round the fire and round the fire, one reel after another and she says I was even feared to blow breath, and they kep us waking she says till God sent the first streak of light in the morning before they disappeared.**

The last quarter of the programme focuses on the way Travellers are treated. A gorgio: 'They can't read or write.' A Traveller: 'I would like to read and write.' A catalogue of vile treatment through a childhood of intermittent schooling leads to a long 'Intolerance' section.

> **That brother of mine was kept seven years in one class. And my mother went to the teacher and asked why my brother wasn't able even to sign his own name, and the teacher, she says, 'Och I would never dream of learning that laddie on – he's the best message laddie I have in the school.' She's sent him messages here, messages there, message for this teacher, clean the blackboard, sweep the floor, and to this day he cannae sign his ain name.**

By the time they were ready for rehearsal and recording at the end of November 1963, Charles had been given the grim news he'd been half expecting, that this would be the last Radio Ballad. So there's a double meaning when he writes to ask for a pre-Christmas slot for the broadcast 'with its No Room at the Inn connotations.' Charles pours out the story of the ending of the Radio Ballads to Paul Ferris of *The Observer*, who bats on his behalf in an article. That can't have pleased his bosses and, moreover, he missed the Christmas slot by a long way.

The recording was difficult for several reasons. Ewan was going down with bronchitis, though he held himself and his voice together till he collapsed in the studio after the last take was completed. The fiddler Dave Swarbrick went AWOL for some of the rehearsals, which led to a fusillade of letters and telegrams to and fro, a rambling explanation from Swarbrick after the recording was over about getting his little finger caught in the car door, and a severe rebuke from a livid Charles. Especially for this programme a fiddle was a key instrument, and at the last moment Charles had to pull in the replacement fiddler Danny Levan, who managed with hardly any rehearsal. But the main problem was his decision to do the 'Intolerance' section in one long take, while recording music separate from actuality. Despite taking eight hours in the studio over that alone he just couldn't get it to work, so he had to cobble it together from bits as he had in the earliest programmes.

Before Christmas, furious with the world and himself, he expresses his frustrations across five foolscap pages, beginning: 'These notes are prompted by sense of confused indignation? Frustration? Helplessness? Misguided preoccupation with detail? Professional incompetence? A most complicated state of mind! Product of the pressures which operate on me during the final editing and assembly of a Radio Ballad.' The problem is that he can't sub-optimise, he can rarely bring himself to be satisfied with his editing or the standard of studio performance. 'It is agonising to hear superb performances so lost in a bad mix as to be unusable ... Why is it that we cannot create conditions in which the artists and technical team achieve a definitive performance which can be recorded in one [take]...?'

It takes so long. He belabours himself over the fact that he needs six days of six vocalists and nearly as much of eight instrumentalists, over £400 of a programme that cost £1700 in all. 'All this seems a most extravagant schedule by BBC standards ... The pressures of BBC policy by implication accuse me of unprofessionalism by utilising such methods, or lack of methods, and I accuse myself of this as the hours tick by.' He blames the acoustic of Studio 6, the inflexibility of its control desk and its studio managers. He argues himself into a corner. In the end he convinces himself that with the equipment and people at his disposal it is impossible to achieve the result he's striving for. 'In fact what we are trying to do is to achieve as polished a performance of a Radio Ballad that has only come together for a matter of days, as we expect from a performance of the [Beethoven] 9th Symphony that has been examined and worked at for a hundred or more years.'

Travelling People was not heard until four months after Charles's Christmas target, 17 April 1964, still called *Born at the Crossroads* until a few days before broadcast. Ironically, despite its troubles and the anxiety that, like teenagers, Travellers were a group that might alienate the Home Service audience, it elicited the best audience reaction of all. 'This really had the "feel" of the subject to a wonderful degree. One could sense the antagonism of both sides and through it all came the rhythm of movement, constant "moving on" ... Gay, plaintive and sad by turns, the songs were very evocative of the Gypsies' plight and very moving.'

The report summariser feels that 'listeners apparently have a soft spot for the travelling people', doubtless meaning in their romantic Romany incarnation. In his song 'The Gypsy is a Gentleman', decorated by mocking fiddle flourishes, Ewan has poked fun at those who thought that while the original Gypsy was colourful and welcome, his modern descendant was not:

Oh the gypsy is a gentleman and he always knows his place,
He never troubles anyone and he rarely shows his face.
He knows the ways of nature, he's reticent and shy,
And never pesters gorgios to sell or yet to buy.
   And the wind is on the heath,
   And the heath is far away
   From towns and private property
   Where decent people stay.

Oh the gypsy is a gentleman, he keeps well out of sight,
His caravan is picturesque, it's colourful and bright.
He's full of ancient wisdom and of wit he has great store -
Not like those thieving diddies who come knocking on the door ...

Two days after broadcast Paul Ferris in *The Observer*, despite feeling that it 'needed shortening and lacked pace in places, as though the style of the piece had been infected by the melancholy of the content', nevertheless concluded that it was 'one of the most remarkable of the Radio Ballads: full of bitterness and raciness, and appalling flashes of everyday inhumanity.' He takes the BBC to task for ending the Radio Ballads, which have been 'killed stone dead by the planners in London ... Since they didn't start till Radio was being eclipsed by TV they have never had the chance to become fashionable with the audience they deserve.' Exactly.

It was later largely assumed by their supporters that the Radio Ballads were stopped for political reasons. While Charles Parker's changing political attitude may have been identified by his bosses with his increasing (as they saw it) truculence and intransigence, it's clear, both in the internal BBC documents and Charles's own writing at the time, that it was the sheer cost and time – aggravating his loss of 'productivity' – that was their downfall, at a time when Radio was losing money and audience. Moreover, the 'industrial' Radio Ballads weren't overtly political – their Marxist authors didn't batter the listener over the head with Das Kapital. It's indeed ironic that the most vehement Radio Ballad, the one where the hearts of the authors are most visible on their sleeves, should be the last, and one where man's inhumanity to man extends across the class divide. Ewan doesn't shirk the parallels, reminding us what happens when Travellers are seen as pollutants:

> **Some of them were gassed at Belsen,**
> **Some at Buchenwald did fall.**
> **Others kennt the Auschwitz ovens:**
> **Men and women, bairns and all.**

You hear this and think: Come on, Ewan, you're going too far here, this is England. Then you hear the last words of this last Radio Ballad, and the complaint dies in your throat. They're spoken by Alderman Harry Watton, JP, a Birmingham Labour councillor. And you realise with a start that this is the only time Charles Parker ever allowed his own voice to be heard:

> **Watton:** How far does it come in your mind before you say I have done everything I possibly can and I will help the broad mass of these people. But there are some I can do nothing with whatever. Doesn't the time arise in one's mind that one has to say, all right, one has to exterminate the impossibles. I know all that leads to in one's mind, Nazism, who is it next: the Gypsies, the Tinkers, the Jews, the coloured man. I don't accept that really on these particular people.
>
> **Parker:** I don't think ... exterminate's a terrible word – you can't really mean that?
>
> **Watton: Why not?**

Silence, no credits.

CHAPTER 16

The Word Hewers
Finding the Voices

If you go into the nearest pub on a Saturday night and hear the story of Saturday's match, people don't tell the narrative in a linked line, like a short story spoken. They create a vigorous image, then they create another vigorous image right up against it and they clash … between those two little images is a 'spark gap' for you as the listener to jump in and fill in, so that you participate in the creative experience.

CHARLES PARKER, ARTICLE IN *FSU QUARTERLY*, WINTER 1975

There were times when the force of his memory was so strong in the old man that he would forget that we were present and re-enact conversations with friends and neighbours dead these fifty years.

EWAN MACCOLL, SPEAKING OF SAM LARNER, *JOURNEYMAN*, 1989

In Chapter 9 I examined how Charles Parker manoeuvred the Radio Ballads down the often potholed track from script to broadcast. In the next three chapters I want to return to the very beginning of the process. How did Charles, Ewan and Peggy go about interviewing someone (usually) working class, unfamiliar with and wary of the microphone? How did they extract such compelling testimony? How did they sift from that 'actuality' the extracts they'd use in each programme? How did Ewan conjure such fitting songs from the mass of voices, words, rhythms and intonations that they'd heard, and interleave them with the voices? And how did Peggy orchestrate a motley selection of instruments to bring the whole thing to musical life?

Back in 1960 Charles Parker wrote to Ewan MacColl: 'The astronomical expense of *Singing the Fishing* has made everyone run into the woodwork.' The BBC would increasingly be run not by programme makers but by those with an eye on ratings and costs. It's perfectly true that when you look at the Radio Ballads with an accountant's eye one of the immediate things that strikes you is the ratio of the minutes of actuality they recorded to the minutes they used in the end. Although the number and length of interviews varied, typically they would return with around 60 hours of recorded material. That means that in an hour-long programme they eventually used perhaps only one per cent of it.

This seems extraordinary at first. How could they justify that expense in time and money? Can they really convince us — let alone Charles Parker's bosses at the BBC — that, say, half that much would have given us an inferior programme? Ewan indeed says that the actuality recorded from miners for *The Big Hewer* was so rich that they could have made another equally good programme without taking any of the speech from the final version at all. While that may have been an exaggeration, it certainly suggests that they were distinctly self-indulgent in the time they spent on interviews. And everything they brought back they listened to and transcribed, a wearying dawn-to-dusk task that would take around a fortnight for two people. How many hours would a modern radio feature maker bring back? Vince Hunt and Sara Parker (Charles's daughter), who recorded much of the material for the 2006 Radio Ballads I examine in the final chapter, brought back a third to a half of the original team's figure. The 2006 total itself seems on the high side for most modern documentary features.

How did they go about persuading people, most of whose formal education ended at 14 or 15, to talk about their lives in a way that would capture a radio audience's attention? Only a few of us are naturals, instinctive storytellers. Most are not, so an interviewer has to know how to pan for the gold that he hopes is there in the stream somewhere. People often acquire a kind of verbal armour, a habit of speaking which is formulaic and unnatural, cliché-ridden or repetitive, and hard to penetrate. Middle managers writing reports tend to use a stilted third person and the passive, just as in school science we were taught to write up experiments: 'A solution of nitric acid was taken.' They replicate it in their speech. Ewan said that some of the people from the road contractors Laing sounded virtually incomprehensible, though the meaning was easier to figure out when read off the page. Working people were by no means immune back then, especially if they were union officials, as Peter Sellers illustrated in his wonderful creation Kite in the film *I'm All Right Jack*, released in the same year as *Song of a Road*. Ewan commented:

> The blokes in the mining industry, when they start talking at first, you get polemics from them, as if they're talking like a Union Branch meeting in gibberish. What we're constantly looking for is how much the speech is personal and how much an echo. The way the thing is said, not the information conveyed … Many workers are afflicted by officialese, but occasionally you can identify a gem. John Faulkner once interviewed Jack Dash [the dockworkers' unofficial leader]. First it was like a political harangue, but then he asked him about the comic characters on the docks and his language changes immediately. No longer has he to be spokesman for militant dockers.

One of the recordings for *Travelling People* wasn't used in the programme. In darkness, with 28 people in a tent, a woman speaks of the death of her daughter. As long as she's describing events in the camp itself, she automatically falls into her traditional language and mode of expression. Ewan:

> She dreams that a quarry is full of tears and she sees a small body put into a coffin and drawn through the water like a coach, but drawn by a team of rats – it's straight out of Webster. But when she gets to the hospital she begins to change her terminology and delivery style, and becomes pedestrian and very much infected by city speech, the words become … the clichés of hospital, and the whole thing falls to pieces.

Storytelling is an integral part of a Traveller's existence; brushes with 'gorgio' society might take the life out of their speech temporarily, but it would return. What of us, the 'educated'? The conflict after *Song of a Road* was based on Ewan's conviction that educated people, the managers, planners and white-collared staff, spoke in a boring and over-technical way. It wasn't universal – he later cited scientists he'd met, as in his preparation for *Uranium 235*, and some doctors. They were often brilliant in their ability to conjure up novel metaphors to help the layman's understanding, and equally to express themselves directly and simply when they needed to. 'A scientist in love with his work is quite as likely to get excited as a coalminer. It's not just a matter of education, but how closely the educated person identifies with his work.' But many, exemplified by the road surveyors whose language had been square-bashed into submission by their army service, are trapped by their profession's unconscious jargon and speech patterns, as in *Song of a Road*:

During that time the survey's been made to ascertain the amount of material to be moved, till the planning people decide how it is to be moved and where it is to be moved to. That results in a complicated graph called the mass haul diagram on which the whole of the earth moving is based.

The analysis Ewan and Peggy made of voice recordings after *Song of a Road* convinced them of the close match of 'ordinary' people's speech patterns to traditional song rhythms, compared to those of the educated, who Ewan described like this:

Listening to them, we found that our concentration would begin to dissipate after two or three minutes. To our 'uneducated' speakers, however, we could listen for long periods without any decline in concentration. Now this was odd since the soil-chemists, designers, planners and surveyors were (or so it seemed) getting far more job satisfaction from what they were doing than, say, the navvies, dump-truck drivers or joiners. We analysed the speech in several tapes chosen at random and came up with some interesting facts. Our managerial informants tended to use an extremely small area of the vocal effort spectrum. Their most characteristic effort was that of pressing, combined occasionally with short thrusts; or that of gliding or, less frequently, with subsidiary dabbing efforts. Irrespective of the subject under discussion they scarcely ever varied the tempo of delivery. Almost all of them made constant use of the impersonal pronoun. They were consistent in their use of tenses and rarely changed direction inside a sentence or phrase. Verbs were given no more vocal weight than nouns, and similes and metaphors were almost totally eschewed.

Now, Ewan's own language here needs some explanation, because he's using the terminology of Laban, the radical movement analyst and teacher whose methods became so integral to Theatre Workshop. Their actors were also trained to use a whole spectrum of vocal 'efforts', to keep the listener on the edge of his seat. Ewan applied them to the speaking and singing voice, and he employed them in the way he constructed both songs and (a key point) the Radio Ballads themselves. The eight basic Laban 'efforts' are Thrust, Slash, Wring, Flick, Press, Float, Dab and Glide, and their definitions are expressed by means of three opposite pairs of adjectives – direct or flexible, sudden or sustained, strong or light. In the paragraph above he uses Press (direct, sustained, strong), Thrust (direct, sudden, strong), Glide (direct, sustained, light) and Dab (direct, sudden, light). This is how Rudolf Laban expressed it:

Effort	Space	Time	Energy
Thrust	direct	sudden	strong
Slash	flexible	sudden	strong
Wring	flexible	sustained	strong
Flick	flexible	sudden	light
Press	direct	sustained	strong
Float	flexible	sustained	light
Dab	direct	sudden	light
Glide	direct	sustained	light

Read or sing something into a tape recorder, play it back, analyse your voice in those terms, change it, do it again. Essentially, Ewan is saying that variety is the spice of speech, and most 'educated' people don't vary theirs enough. It has been trained out of us. His road builders, on the other hand:

> used both similes and metaphors liberally. They changed tense constantly, often to emphasise a point or to sharpen an argument. They made use of extended analogies and emphasised verbs in such a way as to give every sentence an effort-peak. Almost all of them used the first person singular and the present historical with equal effect. Their single speaker would, in the course of an extended passage, sometimes use presses, thrusts, glides and dabs in much the same way that a boxer in the ring might use his body. A project manager drew attention to the two language groups in the course of defining the functions of a ganger: 'He's the link between us and them. I sometimes think we'd be no worse off if they were speaking Swahili.'

The grub's very poor. Some mornings there you couldn't touch it at all ... The beds, they've got bugs and all in 'em. The bed I'm lying in – has humps and hollows in it ... bejakers ... like a camel's back. It is. I tell you, I was up in the desert ... the first time I slept inside in it – looking at camels – humps and hollows. My arse was all blisters and carbuncles and everything ... In the morning I could hardly walk, I thought I wouldn't be able to go to work. It's an, it's an awful joint. Concentration camp. All they want is some gas chambers now and smother us.

That's Jack Hamilton again, the Irish dumper-truck driver, and it's the extract that so alarmed Laing. In *Song of a Road* you can compare these two languages readily. If you listen to it – it's hard to do it justice on the page – some of the programme's fascination lies in just that contrast. It's not that the planners and surveyors aren't enthusiastic about what they're doing, for they often are, but it's overlaid by the language and voice they employ. Every now and then a manager does get that feeling through:

> **I think one of the most interesting jobs of this class of work is the muck shifting. It's a wonderful job is muck shifting. Specially when there's plenty of it you know, and there's two and a quarter millions of it altogether. Oh yes I admit I enjoy muck shifting, better than anything.**

Charles and Ewan felt that children have an ability to express themselves naturally, but it gets suppressed by the need at school to become grammatically correct, in speech and in writing. Charles largely blamed the tyranny of the printed word, saying that the best recordings succeed by 'triumphantly reasserting the oral tradition after five centuries of submergence by the printed word and all the intellectual and literary pretensions of omnicompetence this has brought.' Ironically, Charles's meaning is often embedded in such word thickets, unconsciously making his own point. In *Travelling People* the most humane non-Traveller they met was named Strangeward, the county surveyor for Kent. Charles said: 'He talked for half an hour about the terrible conditions they lived in, very articulate, but nothing he said would make a listener sit up and think.' Then they met a 14-year-old girl who said simply 'To tell you the truth they treat us like animals, and I think of them as animals too.' In *On the Edge* the 16-year-old Dot Dobby was a rarity in that she could recapture her feelings so instantly and completely, then express them vividly. Ewan:

> We explained in great detail what we were going to do, and total recall took place, she went immediately to her feelings and all the conflicts inside her suddenly found voice, whatever we talked about. Occasionally the feeling was so tremendous she couldn't contain it: she wept uncontrollably. Every question got a purely personal response, a mechanism already perfected there, perhaps it's in all young people, and gets destroyed as they get older.

Peggy said Charles was cross with her for keeping the tape recorder running, but Dot's weeping got into the programme nevertheless. By contrast, said Ewan, some boys from Glasgow aged 18 to 21 were 'articulate as hell. There was anger, but there was a damp-course so to speak between their feelings and their language.' They didn't use a single phrase of it in the programme. That analysis of speech patterns increased the team's conviction that you had to be clever and patient to get a person to express, in direct and vivid speech, what you knew to be there. Feign ignorance, Charles said: 'If you convince people you're interested in them and really don't know anything, you can't go wrong. It's absolutely fundamental. You have to relearn how to listen. Someone's listening to them properly for the first time in their lives.' They concluded that you usually got very little in the first half hour of recording, very little active speech or metaphor, few verbs. But once you get people in full flight their speech is packed with them: the prosaic becomes poetic. Ewan: 'They have to be warmed up, taken to a different level. On TV you get only two and a half minutes, no wonder it's all cliché.'

Charles said that the best extracts derive from the times during the field recording when the particular speaker, 'under the pressure of the moment, relives in his or her own language some deeply felt experience ... and by intonation, rhythm, imagery or all three ... achieves a shattering degree of immediate communication ... and the living language, caught by the tape recorder, takes off and dominates the work.' Sam Larner was the perfect example of this. They had time to discuss overnight how to plan the next day. Often they'd return to something he'd said to make him open up further: 'That storm in 1910, that must have been rough.' He'd be tetchy but he'd go back and often emerge with something else, or a different expression, at some moments reliving a long-gone conversation, his eyes seeing a scene 60 years before, the room and his interviewers fading. Perhaps it's the daily proximity of death: Sam after the storm says, 'Same as miners, I s'pose ... you can't live with the dead, can you?' But they did, and the speech of both fishermen and miners were at times haunted by it.

With the miners for *The Big Hewer* they soon realised the trick was to get them to visualise the pit – as soon as they were back underground, they'd be away. Charles and Ewan hardly said anything after the first few scene-setting moments, just the occasional verbal nudge. Both could talk the hind legs off a field full of donkeys, but by then they had learned how to use silence. In the early days Charles would be too verbose, until Ewan told him he was fed up with listening to his voice on recordings. Thereafter they would both confine themselves to some prompting to bring out what's commonplace to the speaker but crucial to the programme. Then only interrupt when, Charles said: 'Occasionally someone in full flight says something extraordinary. Stop it, isolate the thought, and he or she will say it in a different way.'

The most difficult thing, as Charles realised and every interviewer knows, was to get them to say what they've just said, but in a way that could be spliced into the programme without a lot of fiddly work later. If you listen to a source tape, say, of a Sam Larner interview, in stretches there is constant coaching going on, a point stressed by Doc Rowe, the folk ritual collector who worked with Charles later. Moreover, Sam used his hands expressively, as many people do. Doc said Charles eventually told Sam to imagine a little man in the microphone who couldn't see him. Sam, arms outstretched: 'About this long.' Charles: 'Little man, Sam.' 'Oh, about three foot.'

The art of interviewing is to know when to interrupt and when to stay silent. If things were getting dull they'd sometimes resort to saying something outrageous, just to provoke a response. But at times silence was the best instrument. Ewan described anticipating moments of a subject's intense recall, and of how you could actually manipulate a pause:

> At first we used to abhor a silence, would butt in, supply a word they're looking for, but it's better to let them look [for it]. Long pause, they're breathing shallowly. Hold your breath. At the right moment a deep breath from you will produce one from them and that's often what's needed to set them off again.

Later they concluded that even flat monotone speech can be effective if used in the right way. In *Singing the Fishing*, after much debate, they deliberately alternated Ronnie Balls' excitable but sometimes unintelligible speech with the drier more informative tones of George Draper saying more or less the same thing. In *Fight Game* they realised that they could employ the often mangled uneducated-but-managerial speech of the boxing promoter, but use it ironically. In *Travelling People* two speakers from Cobham used what Ewan called a 'debased' form of speech, but its very monotony was perfect for expressing life just going on and on: '[If] the voice of one was dead, against him we put the other speaker who came from the same family but who had an upward turn in every speech he made. The two in juxtaposition really complemented each other.'

Listen to any of the Radio Ballads. *The Big Hewer* is a good example because of the rich variety of dialect. Listen to the brothers Jack and Reece Elliott from Durham sparking off each other, to Ben 'Sunshine' Davies from the Welsh valleys, to Ernest Black from Nottinghamshire. Imagine recording in their parlours, in the miners' welfare, down the pit itself. Charles was astonished, humbled, captivated. In a letter to Ronnie Balls, the herring fisherman, he said:

> I remember Ewan when we were doing *Big Hewer*, and I blenched … talking about how the hell we were going to match the calibre of this actuality of the miners talking and he dressed me down and said 'if we can't we'd better go out of business.'

Ewan would never blench – he just needed those words to trigger his song-writing imagination. This was a man who never used to see himself as a songwriter. At the age of 40 he had written few that weren't explicitly for theatrical productions. Then he took off.

CHAPTER 17

The Song Smith
Setting Speech into Song

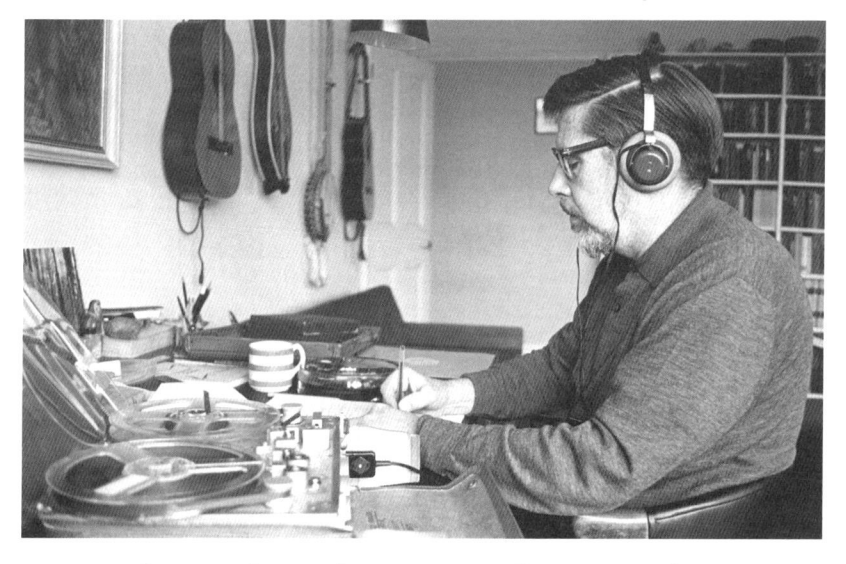

> He wrote deceptively simple songs as well as wonderfully intricate pieces. He loved the mathematics of poetry and would often play and juggle with the tumbling words. He used words exactly ... He would go to great lengths to learn the terminology of an industry before writing about it; or, as in the Radio Ballads, he would interview someone who knew the subject better than he ever could.
>
> PEGGY SEEGER, INTRODUCTION TO *THE ESSENTIAL EWAN MACCOLL SONGBOOK*, 2001

> I maintain that all the great periods of theatre – Greek, Roman ... miracle plays, morality plays, Lope de Vega, Commedia del Arte, Elizabethan – these were periods where there was no rigid demarcation between singing, music, acting. Music's easier to understand than the alphabet ... The trouble is that music has become this bloody special thing – music, the universal language!
>
> EWAN MACCOLL, TRANSCRIPT OF *LANDMARKS DISCUSSION*, MAY 1965

The creator of the Radio Ballad songs hadn't seen himself as a songwriter in his early days at all. From childhood, when he discovered a natural aptitude for writing lyrics, he had made up extra verses for the songs he liked. In the Red Megaphone days he wrote snatches he described as song-squibs, to advance a workers' cause or to bash the bosses. Some he fashioned on the spur of the moment; few were written down. He didn't think anything of it. For those he did compose, until he began to analyse his approach in the early days of the folk revival, he had no particular method.

In 1932 in the days of the Mass Trespass he wrote a song with that title to the traditional Scots tune 'Road to the Isles', and 'Manchester Rambler' to a tune thought to be his own. (Until, that is, someone spotted that it came from Haydn's 94th symphony.) It's the only wholly pre-written song in the Radio Ballads. He would make them up as he strode out on the Pennine Hills, or when driving over them in a theatre company van. In the Theatre Union days before the war he produced songs for several of the plays he adapted, including 'Jamie Foyers', whose title and tune he borrowed from a Peninsular War song of the early 19th century, for *Fuente Ovejuna*. After the war he churned them out in the same way for Theatre Workshop, but describes them as only minor elements in the productions, with just two exceptions: *Johnny Noble*, where they formed a more integral part, and *Blood Wedding*. For his adaptation of the Lorca play, in the event never produced, he sat down in the Pavilion Theatre in Felixstowe and spent all day making up Spanish-sounding melodies:

> That was the first time I ever felt that I was a real songwriter. The feeling soon passed and I returned to my role as actor-cum-scriptwriter, as one who could be called upon to cobble together a tune in between rehearsals. It didn't bother me at all that my songs were expendable, ephemeral pieces that could be dropped without trace from a production.

In 1938 he had listened to Alastair Cooke's 26-part *I Heard America Sing* broadcast from the USA, marvelling when he first encountered Leadbelly, Woody Guthrie, and Texas Gladden singing 'House Carpenter'. But it didn't inspire him to take songwriting seriously. Only 'Dirty Old Town', which had been dashed off about his boyhood Salford to an instinctively laconic tune of his own, simply to cover a scene change in *Landscape with Chimneys*, could be regarded as a song in its own right. Ewan said they sang the theatre songs for that and other shows with no accompaniment (or just a harmonica) not out of conviction but because they had no instruments. That had been in 1949. In fact one other song does survive from that production, 'The Trafford Road Ballad', a simple anti-war song which he resuscitated in some of his early concerts, based on 'The Sheffield Apprentice'. It was soon displaced in his repertoire by later anti-war songs of his own making.

Early Songwriting

Typically, once Ewan decided that songwriting was a craft that needed as much attention as writing plays or any other act of artistic creation, he analysed the process and emerged with a formula. He wanted his new songs to play a part in the folk revival, so they should follow the same disciplines as traditional song: no literary language, few adjectives, simple expressions that ordinary people used day-to-day. He was encouraged by the television producer Denis Mitchell to write truck-driver songs for *Lorry Harbour*, two of which were picked up by drivers: 'Twenty One Years' and 'Champion at Keeping 'em Rolling'. For a Mitchell programme about the so-called railway king, George Hudson, he wrote the narrative in the form of songs, pouring them out. Ewan's serious songwriting began tentatively, in the idiom based on the Irish street ballads he'd heard Seamus Ennis sing, then he became influenced by Bert Lloyd's singing and Alan Lomax's field recordings of English traditional singers. In this period came 'Cannily Cannily', a lullaby in Northumbrian dialect to a tune of his own, good enough to be mistaken subsequently for a traditional song. In 1954, on the way to a Christmas party, he wrote 'The Ballad of the Carpenter', which begins 'Jesus was a working man' and goes on for another dozen stanzas to identify him with the working-class struggle, introducing the word 'journeyman' in the fourth verse:

> He became a roving journeyman
> And he wandered far and wide,
> And he saw how wealth and poverty
> Lie always side by side,
>   Yes, always side by side.

Around the same time he wrote 'The Ballad of Tim Evans', a polemic about a simple young man wrongly convicted for the murder of his wife and child. Three years after Evans was hanged in 1950, his neighbour John Christie had been revealed as a serial killer, had admitted to killing Evans' wife, and was himself hanged. The song hit the headlines, featuring in news programmes and documentaries, but its last verse, which accuses the judge and jury of Evans' judicial murder, caused broadcasting officials acute anxiety. Describing their panic as a state akin to madness, Ewan said that after that time he never had any difficulty in believing that many of those who plan the nation's entertainment exist in a constant state of near-hysteria.

For *The Essential Ewan MacColl Songbook*, Peggy Seeger selected 178 songs out of a total approaching 300. Just four of them were written before the war, ten in the 1940s, and 14 in the period before Ewan and Peggy met in the spring of 1956. From that point his output leapt up, spurred on by the opportunity to collaborate with a brilliant musician with whom he was in love, and by the challenge of the Radio Ballads. He wrote over 70 songs for the Radio Ballads, of which 49 are included in the songbook, part of a great creative burst which produced 113 songs from 1957 to 1970 and several more that didn't make the cut. Peggy wrote this in her introduction:

> His best and most popular songs are based on traditional pieces, but even in his experimental works you can find the time-honoured motifs, usages, footages, forms and poetic constants that characterise the folk songs and ballads. When he employed slang he seemed to get stuck in the colloquialisms he had learned in his first 25 years, much of it classical and Elizabethan-based. He continued to use these terms in his songs – words like creep, flash boys, spivs, fakers and wide-boys, words that gave some of his songs a dated flavour. He also favoured the political clichés of the 1920–50 period. These turn up a great deal in the early songs and occasionally in the later ones. He didn't learn or employ new slang because he felt that fashions in language change too fast and that many terms (such as at the end of the day, cool, right on, no way etc.) are taken up solely so that those who utter them may appear to be in the swim. He drew most of his language from his own experience, from his reading and from people, and he was loath to take the easy way out when writing a song.

The paradox for Peggy was that such a 'tunemaster' was virtually illiterate in terms of formal musical knowledge. Jim Bray, the double-bass player who was in seven of the Radio Ballads and who had known Ewan before they began, said that jazz musicians originally used to scoff at him behind his back. In the early days of the *Ballads and Blues* radio series he would sometimes miscount bars and lose the thread. 'We soon revised our view – his was a remarkable talent.' Peggy felt that many of his earlier songs, set to traditional tunes without adaptation, could be stilted, formal and dogmatic, the least successful coming over as political speeches set to music, with the words sometimes ill at ease with the tune. But his approach was transformed by the wealth of the contributors' language he painstakingly studied before each of the Radio Ballads.

Journeyman has a chapter called Singing and Song-writing, but it contains nothing about writing songs at all, so you have to look elsewhere for enlightenment about his methods. In a programme called *Singing English*, recorded in 1961 halfway through the Radio Ballad period, Ewan, Charles and Peggy discuss their making, although little about either songwriting or musical arrangement. But in a couple of sessions at their home in Beckenham in 1965, recorded by Charles Parker and transcribed, he spoke at length about how he set about writing the Radio Ballad songs. (Ewan was inclined to exaggerate, but this is trustworthy because it was soon after the last Radio Ballad, and all three of them took part in the discussion.)

These meetings had been set up to help the writers of a new six-part series called *Landmarks* that Charles Parker was producing in parallel with a television version that Philip Donnellan was making (at ten times the cost). Newer writers were involved, interviewing in the Radio Ballad style, and the first programme in the series was stringently analysed by Ewan. Although he didn't participate in the series, he did provide a theme song, the wonderful 'Ballad of Accounting'. It starts amiably enough, and the timeless quality of the first stanza sets the scene for a series that looked at humanity from the cradle to the grave. But then it starts to bite, and you can just imagine the jolt it gave BBC executives when they heard the second verse unfold. But by then it was too late to stop it.

> In the morning we built the city –
> In the afternoon we walked its streets –
> Evening saw us leaving –
>   We wandered through our days as if they would never end;
>   All of us imagined we had endless time to spend;
>   We hardly saw the crossroads and small attention gave
>   To landmarks on the journey from the cradle to the grave
>   Cradle to the grave, cradle to the grave, cradle to the grave.
>
> Did you learn to dream in the morning?
> Abandon dreams in the afternoon?
> Wait without hope in the evening?
>   Did you stand there in the traces and let 'em feed you lies?
>   Did you trail along behind 'em wearing blinkers on your eyes?
>   Did you kiss the foot that kicked you, did you thank 'em for their scorn?
>   Did you ask for their forgiveness for the act of being born,
>   Act of being born, act of being born, act of being born.

Writing for the Radio Ballads

Ewan described to the *Landmarks* team how they listened to the Radio Ballad actuality. As they played each tape, Peggy would type the transcription on to foolscap sheets. They would mark up all the tapes with pieces of gummed paper to signify the kind of speaker – gender, accent, their breathing patterns, whether they were fluent or halting, had an upward inflection or perhaps were an emphatic 'finisher' – and to record the topic they had been discussing. When the transcription was complete, they'd cut up the sheets and assemble them in a script book under topic headings, each with a blank facing page (sometimes finding a subject they hadn't anticipated, such as Dust in *The Big Hewer*). This became their working book for the programme, with everything carefully timed from the beginning, which Ewan described as a crucial discipline. As a consequence they rarely overshot by more than five minutes. In the case of *Singing the Fishing* it was 30 seconds.

They would then call Charles in, and the triumvirate would spend two or three days of intense debate in Beckenham to settle the programme's shape. Often, Ewan said, the discussion would seem completely nebulous, almost a waste of time. But when he got down to work he'd realise what vital pointers it gave him, especially in what to avoid. Moreover, back in Birmingham, Charles would have a good idea of what he would be getting later, and there would be no unpleasant surprises. (Only for *The Fight Game*, in fact, did the Beckenham discussion radically alter the shape of the programme). Ewan would then take the rough plan and mould it into a working script where 'the script and songs complement each other and finally result in a work of art.'

Now to creating the songs. Ewan's approach to writing them changed radically after the second programme. For *John Axon* he started out with a number of tunes in mind that he felt would be suitable. (Later, he said, he began to feel that using old tunes unmodified was immoral – though it didn't stop him entirely.) He'd write one to suit the chosen actuality, but would often assemble it without any idea of what came next, even the actuality. Later he felt that this produced a series of disconnected musical episodes, with no organic relationship between them. In *Axon* too, he said, there was little variety, almost all depending on the rhythm of the train, from chugging uphill to charging down dale. Now, there are those who regard Ewan as reacting badly to criticism of his work. Often he certainly did, but he could be as scathing to himself as he was to others:

> It's true I said at the time that I was using the rhythms of the clickety-clack of the trains, but looking back I see that was just a get-out on my part, shirking the issue since a railway engine boils down to a single stroke, one-one-one-one indefinitely. You can divide it into threes, sevens, eights – anything – and still get music that's differentiated. But it still relates to the train, so in a way there I was cheating in my arguments.

He regarded the following *Song of a Road* as more scientific musically, though 'a bit of a mess'. The subject and nature of the actuality was often remote from the folk-song form, so he tended to use a 'bridge' type of music, the kind you get in the forerunners of the English music hall, before 1850. He settled for the rollicking sound found in the famous music-hall song collections like *London Entertainment*. At the time he felt all that was really necessary with that kind of lyric was a rather primitive knowledge of rhyming systems. Some worked, some didn't. His retrospective distaste for the compromises they'd been forced to make on *Song of a Road* persuaded him to wear a hair-shirt: 'The bulk of the material was shoddy in the extreme: on the whole it was bad work.' Fortunately, the sheer joie-de-vivre of the songs makes most of us more generous.

Analysing Traditional Music

It wasn't until he and Peggy sat down and reviewed their approach to folk song before *Singing the Fishing* that they figured out which songs didn't work and why. If it's to convey information, let's make sure a song will be good enough to carry it, 'still able to appeal to an audience in 500 years' time which no longer knows a herring boat or even fishing.' They took stock, too, of their limited knowledge of folk song, which they decided was patchy, had grown organically, and that they hadn't properly analysed. This was the start of their serious appraisal of folk music forms. Ewan: 'We had to learn a bloody sight more about folk music. We knew 300–400 songs but we hadn't explored them. Hadn't taken them to pieces as people do a Shakespeare play.' The research they did then was apparent in their exhaustive *Song Carriers* radio series they made within a year of the last Radio Ballad.

They set about breaking down *Singing the Fishing* into around a dozen episodes, with each highlighting a different facet of the fisherman's character and life. Just as they maximised the variety of the actuality, so they needed to vary the music, subject to the overriding need to stay within the disciplines of the tradition. Ewan asked himself what they were. 'I hadn't got it clear in my own head, and it's only recently I've managed to.' But he knew they had to make differences of tone for the singers, and in the instrumentation. Sometimes he'd make the singers excise all the harmonics from their voices, not an easy thing to do for the classically trained. 'If we used bel canto singers in the Radio Ballads they'd stand out against the actuality like ballet dancers in a pityard.' Moreover, they would have to learn an 'attenuated' style, using scoops and slides and other devices of the folk tradition.

Until then, he said, their concept of the folk tradition was a limited one. Provided a song was easy, intimate and relaxed, they thought that was enough, as long as the singers could sing in rhythm. But they decided for *Singing the Fishing* that the songs' variety must be much greater. How, then, to create interest and keep the listener engaged? Vary the melodic style: do what good traditional singers in Bulgaria will do, ringing the changes for all they're worth on time, pitch, rhythm, melody and mood. Apply the Laban movement approach to the shape of the whole Radio Ballad (just as Ewan had to the construction of his post-war plays). In *John Axon* the songs were mostly in a minor key, in *Song of a Road* largely major. OK, in future exploit the modes more thoroughly, use the change from major to minor to keep the listener alert. And the same with the time signatures – no longer use a preponderance of 4/4, as in *Song of a Road*, but try 3/4 and 6/8, 2/4 and 6/4 and 5/4, and associate these variations with changes in key. When a key change is needed, make a switch of time signature too, and sometimes pitch, to increase the variety from a number of angles.

Finding a Tune

A few years after the last Radio Ballad, Ewan described an exercise for members of the Critics Group (see Chapter 21) to help them find a tune for a new song they'd written. Start with a traditional tune that seems to sound right, he said, and whistle it to get it firmly in your mind. This is the jumping-off point. Then keep making variations, and choose the one that seems to fit best with the subject you're writing about. Switch on the tape recorder and continue whistling, varying it as you go. Then play it back, learn one that seems to work, number it Variant 1, then start again.

> Maybe after half an hour I'd say to Peggy: do you like any of these, and she'd say … not quite right, that's weak, that's strong, that third line weakens it, that cadence … And on I'd go. If nothing seemed to work, I'd say let's make the first movement in the tune down instead of up. And on through different iterations of scale, change of mode, whatever. By then you've either got something that works, or nothing at all. In that case, maybe you've got the whole concept of the tune wrong, and you need to start again: don't be afraid to, don't be lazy.

If he'd got nowhere, he might take a sentence from the accompanying actuality, often with a rhythm of its own. Like, in *Singing the Fishing*, '<u>that</u>'s at the <u>bot</u>tom of the <u>ocean</u>. Dar diddie diddie diddie dardar. Put that rhythm in your mind. Now, what ways can we ring the changes? Instead of that, how about Dar diddie diddie diddie dardar didar? It doesn't sound quite right, but it's unusual so it'll hold the attention. What if we were to convert the original tune in the same way, add an extra foot?' Ewan tried this first in a song for a film, putting an extra length of line in each verse. It had the effect of keeping the general feeling of the tune, but every verse was different. In *Fight Game* he successfully used this approach often, and even more in *Travelling People*. 'In fact by that time we were ridiculously preoccupied to see how far the traditional form could be extended without smashing up. We found to our amazement that it could be extended fantastically far. Anybody could do it, provided you're not afraid. Everyone's creative in some way.' The 'we' in these extracts indicates how important Peggy was as a sounding-board.

In *Singing the Fishing* Ewan had real difficulty with the song that became 'Shoals of Herring'. It comes in at the beginning of the chronological sequence with Sam Larner, an old man with a voice low in pitch, slow in delivery, speaking mostly in the present tense. They decided to contrast it with a song in the past tense. A phrase that emerged frequently from the actuality, especially from Ronnie Balls and the Scot Frank West, was 'the shoals of herring', so Ewan decided to write one closely related to their words and inflexions, mimicking the contrast between the Balls and Larner voices. He spent three days on the song, and says he wrote 62 different tunes to it, many, of course, closely related. He had written five versions of the song's text too, and was 'in despair' when he remembered 'Sweet William', an ancient ballad he'd tried to learn but abandoned because it didn't work for him as a singer. It's usually called 'Famous Flower of Serving Men'. In its original form it becomes a drag, he said, after a couple of verses. On his fifth variation it suddenly clicked. Its first line is a deliberate old ballad cliché, then it takes off —

**O it was a fine and a pleasant day,
Out of Yarmouth harbour we were faring
As a cabin boy in a sailing lugger
Searching for the shoals of herring.**

It worked perfectly for the voices of MacColl and Lloyd, who echoed the vocal styles of Balls and Larner, and *Singing the Fishing* is threaded through with eight 'Shoals of Herring' stanzas, alternating the two voices. He dredges up and integrates a mass of rhymes for 'herring' — Peggy said he had a perfectly good rhyming dictionary but preferred not to use it. The song is reflective in tone; when the pace needs to pick up we have the driving beat and lusty seaman's chorus of 'North Sea Holes', a further nine stanzas in several sections, which uses another new tune of Ewan's. This was what Ewan called a cumulative song:

> We said we'd start with the general information of where they go to find the fish — North Sea Holes. This form of song in musical terms is called cumulative — it has an accumulating chorus, you can add a line at any part and it will convolute and join the one before it. The convoluted line always gives a marvellous sense of time, not of rhythm but of time. It always sounds as though it goes back for years and years. We got herring fishermen to mark the main points of the shoals, the spawning grounds … it all says here's someone who knows his stuff.

His approach to variety in the songs was mirrored in his selection of actuality. The combination of opposing vocal styles, Balls and Larner, was one such result. It worked if it wasn't overdone: one for the information, one for the excitement. They used that technique in the storm sequence, in which it's almost as though we overhear Larner, Balls and Draper chatting together, recalling the worst storms they'd lived through. Of course, they were all recorded separately, and Charles Parker's skill comes in convincing you that they were reminiscing over a pint in a fishing village pub at the end of their days. Ewan describes how they tackled the storm scene, combining the need for variety in song styles with the voices available:

> After 'Shoals of Herring', we said we've got this song, very gentle, easy tempo, single voice. Now we need something else. We're going to a storm at sea. Sam Larner – 'it blew a living gale' – and Draper with this very flat and dull voice saying spectacular things, and all the more marvellous through its being juxtaposed against Sam Larner. And third we found this auctioneer selling the fish, extraordinarily moving and stimulating. It was Peggy's idea to set them against each other. Fisherman at sea making heroic efforts – like Ulysses getting back to Penelope – and all to earn his daily bread, represented by the auctioneer. OK, it makes sense, but what kind of music? We got another idea, that tremendously dramatic table of winds in Close's Fisherman's Almanac which all seamen knew, the basic language of the winds, the Beaufort Scale. The song for the storm sequence was built on a recitation of that scale.

By the time of the later Radio Ballads they weren't building the songs round the actuality so much as arranging the musical sequences first, then injecting whatever actuality would best fit. That would only work, of course, if you were already steeped in the voices and had a wide range of options. They were still working with their original actuality selections, which weren't finalised until the last minute, when the musical idea was elaborated. Ewan explained, holding forth in the *Landmarks* discussion:

> That's how we go through. In the next sequence [say] we're going to break down the verse form, we'll use recitative, the equivalent of free verse or prose poetry … we'll cut the actuality down … and use it in the present tense … [When] Sam Larner is saying 'And these old men would say – Come on, yer young buggers, rouse your feathers', we'd cut out the introduction, and go into 'Come on, yer young buggers' just as if he's saying it. Next episode we'd treat the same way – a tighter form of music, back to the verse form but verse and chorus now, two-line chorus, write it in 4/4 or 2/4 so it can be interrupted, because it's difficult to interrupt a 6/8 or 3/4. The point I'm trying to make is that each time there was a different problem, and each time we'd attempt to solve it in a different way within the disciplines of traditional music. And each time it worked.

Recitatives

The other distinctive feature of his songwriting for the Radio Ballads was what he called the 'recitatives'. He cut his teeth with the 'Iron Road' sequence in the loco shed for *John Axon*, based loosely on 'Poor Paddy Works on the Railway.' For *Singing the Fishing* he wrote the compelling 'Cabin Boy' sequence, which follows Sam Larner through his early days at sea in a sequence of nearly five minutes. It intercuts Sam, recalling life on a sailing boat in the 1890s, with a mixture of sung narrative and shouted instructions, all put together with some deliciously inventive musical accompaniment. For *Big Hewer* its equivalent is the 'Going to Work' section, the lad's first day down the pit, and it lasts almost an identical length of time. By now, Ewan said, he'd got so much on top of the method that once he was on a roll 'Going to Work' took him only half a day to produce. 'Cabin Boy' had taken him much longer. He described the recitatives like this:

> If this kind of recitative comes off you've created inside it all the themes you're going to use in the rest of the thing, and sure enough this is what we did. It's an interesting idea to take a form exclusively associated with classical music and conceive it in folk not operatic terms, in the actual technical idiom of folk music, conceive it in modes, never transgressing, moving from mode to mode, key to key, extending the rules but not breaking them. If a rule says that a pentatonic scale has five notes, and if you move outside it to another note you get another type of scale, then we'll join three more notes and we'll get an eight-note scale, and we'll have scale run into scale … It worked beautifully, much to everybody's amazement. This was not improvisation, it was written down carefully, and at this time I couldn't write music, I could only invent music in my head. I did this whole sequence on tape, words and everything; and as we were constantly moving from scale to scale it was a hell of a feat for me because it's almost like composing atonal music in one's head. Next time it was a lot easier.

Then there are the great Brechtian declamatory set pieces, often used as scene- or state-setting, or as a narrative mechanism. Not everyone takes to them. Piers Plowright, the eminent modern radio feature producer who was a Radio Ballad enthusiast, nevertheless says 'There were moments when you think, Oh God, Please don't come in again. I know where it's going … I don't need to hear you singing about it as well.' He felt Ewan signposted too much, but then not every listener 40-odd years ago was as attuned to the programme makers as Plowright became.

By the end of the Radio Ballads Ewan was rarely at a loss when searching for a tune, and he knew now how to adapt his own — in Peggy's words:

> He used his own tunes as jumping-off points too. Compare 'The Ballad of the Big Cigars' with 'The Gypsy is a Gentleman', and 'LBJ Looks After Me' with 'The Fight Game' … Like many songmakers he had a mode, a scale, he preferred: the Dorian. Start on D and run up the white keys on the piano. There were certain tune formats to which he constantly returned. So it wasn't surprising that he borrowed so much from himself — one tune, with minor variations, often carries three or four texts … Often, as in the case of 'Parliamentary Polka', he would

make the new song and be entirely unaware until later that he had plagiarised himself, from *Song of a Road*. He had an aquifer all his own!

Ewan used the same source tune as 'Shoals of Herring' in *Big Hewer* too, for 'Schooldays Over'. Peggy points out that there are elements of it in 'Freeborn Man', from *Travelling People*, but it's very difficult to spot the common origin. 'I used the tune consistently throughout all the Radio Ballads except *Fight Game*, did a variant of it, just to make it harder for myself, but as a matter of pride, to keep extracting fresh ore from an old mine.' Jimmie McGregor, who was on *Song of a Road* before his popularity with Robin Hall on the *Tonight* programme gave him so much work that was no longer available for the Radio Ballads, marvelled at how prolific Ewan was:

> His songwriting ability? Well, a year after Ewan died I made an hour-long programme about him. One of the points I made about him: if I'm writing, everybody who writes songs, you think – right, you get your idea, verse, chorus. You feel good if you manage to get three verses, four choruses, a reprise, a wee coda. You've constructed a song. And I made the point that Ewan, the roving journeyman, he just goes on and on and on and on and there's more, an embarras de richesses. There's just so much in the guy. He's not rationing himself – I'll save that for the next song? Oh no!

Until the end of his life the ore in Ewan's 'old mine' was never actually worked out. It's just that eventually the mine was forced to close.

CHAPTER 18

Trickling Marbles
The Sounds of the Radio Ballads

Peggy Seeger set every scrap to music, with instruments like guitar, ocarina, banjo and trumpet, which a man might sling across his shoulders or stuff in his haversack. Sea chanties, Dixieland jazz, a snatch of oratorio, the diddle-a-dum a day ceilidh jog-trot, even the authentic *musique concrète* of the mixers. It's all there, stimulating and ingenious.

ALEXANDER WALKER IN THE BIRMINGHAM EVENING POST, NOVEMBER 1959

The Ballad of John Axon

When Ewan MacColl presented Peggy Seeger with his disappointing rough-cut tape of *The Ballad of John Axon*, she had never tackled anything like it before. But then, nobody had. So she set to with her borrowed book on composing, and came up with some simple accompaniments for the songs. In the studio, though, some of the musicians pointed out patiently that there were one or two things that they just couldn't play:

> I was very inexperienced on *Axon* ... I didn't know that you wrote for the trumpet in the key it plays in, but for the clarinet a whole tone lower. Didn't know that the concertina wasn't like an accordion – Alf said you can have a melody or chords but not both. My mother had me transcribing music at an early age, and she used to take me to concerts with the score and say 'Look, the trumpets are going to come in here ... In five bars, wait for it, flutes here, now wait for it.' I remember a boyfriend of mine was King Vidor's son, and I transcribed some complex blues in three days for him while he was gallivanting with someone else. Gave me some ability. At college I had to write a five-part fugue out of my head, but that was very basic.

Moreover, once in the studio it was apparent that her orchestrations, some of which are very clever despite her inexperience, weren't enough. Charles Parker knew they would need musical bridges and he had a good ear for what would work. 'I discovered that he was getting the musicians to record some bits after we'd gone ... I didn't like them all but he knew what he needed.' She cottoned on quickly, and thereafter wrote musical links in advance herself, though some of the sections behind the actuality were improvised or composed in the studio. As we've seen, there was criticism that the *Axon* music was too American. Of course, British folk song was largely lying undiscovered, something they would soon help to rectify. And there were few home-grown instrumentalists – Alf Edwards was virtually the only concertina player available. Moreover, 'Ewan wanted that fast banjo to signify the train. He was still singing American songs at that stage: he loved Alan Lomax's singing. They were always trying to impress each other – and succeeding.'

Apart from Peggy's racing banjo, there are two 'signature' sounds in *Axon*. One was the steam train's chuff, from a slow uphill dragging to a headlong out-of-control downhill; the other was people whistling. The mechanical and the human. (In 50 years there has been a change of musical undercurrent – where working men used to whistle, they're now much more likely to sing. When there isn't muzak.) Everywhere the railwaymen went they whistled – you hear it in the Edgeley railway yard scene, and it's all over the programme once you start to listen. It was that whistling that set the pitch for 'You're on your own mate, you're on the footplate.' Charles did the incidental whistling himself, and it's almost worth billing as an extra musical instrument. His widow Gladys said of Axon: 'He loved dancing and was always whistling the tunes.' Ewan picked it up:

John Axon was a dancing man,
On his pins he was light and nimble,
And often he'd stand on the old footplate,
Whistling an old time jingle.

The train was both a blessing and a curse. It paced the programme, but it could be tricky to keep time to, and of course in both *John Axon* and *Song of a Road* the musicians couldn't hear the beat when they were playing. So it was all down to Peggy setting the pace from the engine in her earphones as she conducted in the studio. As she listened to it again in 2007 she picked up a few points where it caused a problem – 'When you've shovelled a million tons of coal' has to go hectically fast. On the other hand the musicians found it hard to match the measured starting-off-uphill chug of 'The repair was done', but Bert Lloyd handles the song beautifully, a perfect parallel for the flat voice of fireman Scanlon: 'After we'd had us breakfast we came off the shed in good time.' Peggy: 'Bert always smiled when he sang, with a perfect tone. If he wobbled a bit, it gave the song a natural feel: that's just how a railwayman might sound.' Peggy sums up their first shot:

> Towards the end it gets too overblown. The climax is dramatic in content and doesn't need to be so dramatic in form. We're imposing drama on it – nowadays I would do it more matter-of-factly. I orchestrated that jazz accompaniment before the crash. Does it sound too cheerful? It would have perhaps been better with a single drone behind it. But [overall] it was amazing as an experiment, considering we were making it up as we went along, pulled together out of several disparate elements. The use of the folk song types is very strong, it's ballads within a ballad, a story within a story. At points it definitely goes over the top and pulls out two handkerchiefs where it only needs one. But it has a vigour and a spontaneity. Very strong, very nice instrumental variety.

Apart from the intermittent chug of the train, which always brings us back to the story after a diversion, apart from the terrifying crash and the fierce hiss of the brake pipe fracture, Charles produced some telling sound pictures on *John Axon*. Those evocative steam train start-up noises – hoot, hiss, clank, chuff – are Parker heaven. The sounds of the engine shed, the clanking and whistling, the scraping of the shovel. And though he could have recorded anyone shovelling, he was a stickler for authenticity. Standing alongside a steam train in Loughborough 50 years after the crash, the old train driver Edwin Bolus recalled shovelling for Charles, who had come back to Edgeley for the effects to match the work song. 'I get there, he's in my cab, sitting in <u>my</u> seat. You didn't do that, you had to be <u>invited</u>. He sang this song and told me when to shovel – shovel, pause, signal – shovel, pause, and so on. Nice enough bloke.' Terry Burkitt remembers him coming into his signal box to ask him to repeat what he'd said when he sent John Axon on his way at six o'clock on the morning of the crash: 'He came in and sprawled down on the floor with his big black box and his microphone out. I thought, we've got a right one here!'

Song of a Road

For *Song of a Road* Charles had another set of engines to record, bulldozers and all the rest. He doesn't get carried away, using them simply as links and colour. He takes careful pains over the sound 'setting'. The Chief Engineer's 'I think it's the soil' is backed by birdsong and the distant lowing of cows. He added some faint rustling papers to 'The detailed design had to be done' piece. Machine shop sounds for the roving mechanic's 'A garage is all right but it's a rusty old life.' By now we're getting used to the rightness of a Parker soundtrack.

As for Peggy's music: 'In *John Axon* what I was doing was just instrumenting the songs; in this one there was more to do. It was a delight to orchestrate. Ewan had had no musical training, could barely read music, yet had an uncanny knack of creating recitatives with harmonies almost already in place, which I just had to dig out. He would know instinctively … where you transit into another key … He would write a song recognising that I would know what to do with it.' It's clear they didn't like some of the monotonous cliché-ridden voices Charles had chosen, but they made a subversively witty virtue of it at times by accompanying them with a sardonic trombone.

She was still learning when it came to the incidental passages, and especially the music sitting behind the words. But she and the musicians were hampered while recording because they couldn't hear the voices at the same time:

> I think I was beginning to learn what could go behind the actuality. There's too much happening in places – don't need the clarinet all the way along there, but … the musician has no idea what's going on. I simply gave Bruce Turner a chord pattern and an idea of what he was playing against. In the later Radio Ballads he would have the sound track in his headphones so he would have known when to stop playing and let the speaker speak, so it's a little intrusive here.

I was curious to know how Peggy would react when listening to a programme she and Ewan had written off because of the arguments over Charles's script changes. But because she'd barely listened to it since, it came to her fresh: 'This is much better than I remember it. I've always dismissed this as not working. But it does work, there's plenty to it ... full of life.' Except in the concrete train section:

> Charles loved that machine, moving along with great concrete turds dropping out of it, and a brush behind it smoothing it out ... But it's too ponderous. This sequence is too long, and badly instrumented. We're doing in the song what the words and machine are doing, too much emphasis. I should have stopped the background music while they're talking ... I could have instrumented it differently ... perhaps just used a piano.

Back then she never used to play the piano on stage for anything; she does now, though only for her own compositions. 'But then we had a thing that every instrument had to be portable. The concept was important to us. Where did we get that from?' It was part of what so attracted Alexander Walker in his review: 'instruments ... which a man might sling across his shoulders or stuff in his haversack.' The piano reminded Ewan of church and Scottish dance bands, and would rather spoil the idea of the wandering labourer-troubadour.

Singing the Fishing

Peggy: 'This is the first one that really worked. Some weaknesses in the chorus. It feels more English, with a banjo picked sounding more like a four-string.' This of course is the point where the musicians in the studio can now hear the voices with which they're dovetailing, and it shows particularly in some of the transitions. Peggy was getting steadily sharper with the incidental music, reflecting or anticipating the melodies, which now had a folk-style unity. But as she listened she wasn't short of aspects to criticise. The Clarion Singer chorus found it difficult to unpick their normal sound – a group of younger folk singers, as in *Big Hewer* and after, were quicker to get the effect they wanted. She felt she was still overdoing the incidental music at times. As brilliant as Bruce Turner's playing is, like his descending clarinet marble-slide that follows Sam Larner's 'coil the ropes so as you could trickle marbles down it', it's sometimes too compelling. Of Turner's improvisation behind Sam Larner's description of the rope room, a classically trained musician hearing it for the first time said: 'That clarinet piece was so interesting that I completely lost the words.'

The two most intriguing setpieces are the storm sequence and the going-to-sea recitative. This is the one over which Ewan struggled for three days.

He's describing Sam's vivid recollection of his first tough days at sea. The tone of the music here might have matched the 'poor little boy, had to answer everyone's call, you know – Boy, where have you got to, do this, go there, go on, get me this … and they were rough old boys, they were rough at you … my uncle used to flog me.'

> **And the rope drips water down your neck**
> **As the rope winch feeds it from the deck**
> **And the big new blisters hurt your hands**
> **And make 'em burn.**
>
> **Them were poor old times …**
>
> **And the biting cold has numbed your feet**
> **And you feel you'll die if you don't get sleep**
> **Hour after hour.**
>
> **… very poor**

Instead it bounds along at a jaunty pace, forcing us to look at it as a great adventure despite the hardships and the 'knuckle-bones of your arse' trepidation at going to sea again, with a bouncing chorus and an accompaniment that moves from guitar and ocarina to concertina, fiddle and clarinet. Sam recalls the misery all right, but he does it with such an intensity of recall as if saying, 'Ah – That was when I lived!'

The second setpiece is the storm sequence. Here we have three men, recorded separately but sounding as though they were jawing together in a pub over a pint, each taking us through his worst time at sea. Voices punctuated by the weaving of a contemplative concertina take us back to sea to relive their experiences. Imagine a storm at sea in a Hollywood feature film of the period. Masses of wailing wind and spraying spume and straining rigging, overtopped by thrashing music. How should they approach it musically? As we've seen, they decided to use the Beaufort scale of winds mounting from flat calm to howling hurricane, against the barely decipherable auctioneer. A bald juxtaposition: the harbour auction is what you're risking your lives for. A measured beginning, then a quickening of the pace as the wind mounts:

When the sea grows dark and the glass is low and falling ...

Quick rise after low indicate a stronger blow [Sam – sailor's tag]

When your nets are stretched out there two miles or more...

Winds south to south west force four to six, gradually veering north west and increasing to force seven tomorrow afternoon [classically intoned BBC shipping forecast]

When the wind is freshening to a gale
And climbing up the Beaufort scale
And the wind is streaming –
Your mind's not on the market then,
The buying then and the selling then
And the market prices.

Then Sam comes in with: 'They went in this boat and that come on a gale of wind, that came down the Sat'dy night and that blew for three or four days a living gale and we were in these little boats.' No storm sounds, no whistling wind. Just the double bass concertina to personify the threatening sea. The instrument now changes from its amiable ramble in the pub to a menacing growl behind Sam's words. Play the piece and simply listen to the massive concertina when all the keys are pressed down at once. John Clarke, who was upstairs in the control room, recalled that sequence almost with a shudder, so gripping was it:

> It needed maybe 12 or 15 takes. Ewan's 'sea and sky without division', it's really chilling. And every time I heard it ... when Sam goes 'there's one as is going to git us' and there's the sound of Alf Edwards' huge bass concertina going like RRRRRR, the big wave coming, and every time he did it the hairs went up on my neck: 'the big 'uns that come a-roaring at you, you can't get out on 'em ... You know there's death there if one of them gets you.' That instrument, Charles said, it's terrifying.

Though they'd been out to sea to record on a Gardenstoun vessel in heavy seas off the Scottish coast, Charles puts no storm sounds in that sequence, or any effects at all. Nor does he behind the cabin boy recitative. In fact he had a problem to solve: there were no longer steam drifters to record, and sailing boats are nearly soundless, so it's not until 15 minutes in that you first hear a sea sound – a gull. Having restrained himself until then, now he's away. In one place on his working script he scrawls MORE GULLS!! in the margin. Thereafter he gives us diesel engines, boatyards, gulls, winch and nets and chains, harbour sounds, the auctioneer, echo-sounder, radio – and more gulls. He uses gulls as the emblematic sound of harbour and net-hauling: 'Here they are, spin up lovely, bonny herring.' For a long time he resists giving us the sound of the sea itself, and even then just once. It was suggested by the fiddler Kay Graham, who was delighted when Charles adopted her idea when stuck for a link at the start of the pre-war 'poor old times' section. That piece has an exquisite throbbing sad sax and gentle guitar background behind a succession of tales of poverty and bankruptcy. Charles on the Fishing usually lets the instruments do the talking. And he did the same down the pit.

The Big Hewer

If the engine and the banjo are the signature sounds of John Axon, while Bruce Turner and Alf Edwards gave us the characteristic sound for the fishing, for Big Hewer it was the Mine. From the moment we hear the first pit-dry voices punctuated by the pneumatic drill, the soundscape is designed to take us down the mine and make sure we stay there. And that's done equally by sound effects, by a range of musical instruments – and by silence.

Within a minute of the drill and the metronomic tick, tick, tick, of the Big Hewer's tireless pick, we're going Down. 'Down in the dirt and darkness' we're descending with the cage: a crashing and clanking and rumbling, the echoing whiplash of the steel hawsers, to the hard black coalface of the opening song. Every instrumental trick is summoned to make sure we always remember we're down under the earth. After the haunting 'Schooldays Over', orchestrated sweetly and sparely with guitar and fiddle, the bass concertina's discordant downbeat diminuendo reminds the young lad what he faces, coupled with a deep sax. A companionable tin whistle evokes the constant whistling of the men as we move into the first-day section.

Ewan said that this recitative flowed out in one creative surge. Looking back, Peggy was once more 'amazed at its musical coherence', shifting between major and minor, with rising and falling chord sequences. Its driving energy takes the 14-year-old on his first day across to the pithead, listening to the miners' Pitmatic, their impenetrable mine-top banter, as they wait to go down to the Beaumont Seam. The interspersed old Welsh and Geordie voices are given space: either silence, or a simple melodic line on banjo, harmonica or concertina. This recitative benefits from a greater variety of singing voices and chorus: Ewan's dramatic voice doesn't over-dominate as it can do. Charles is sparing with the effects – only with: 'At last, I was going to see what lay below' do we get men's voices, a distant whistle, the signal bell, and into song with 'There's the signal bell, now the cage is coming.' That introduces several voices parading the arcane names of the jobs down the pit, from hewers and putters, brattice men and cutters, on down to the dilly bottom lads. Over 40 in all, which could sound dire en masse. But it doesn't, so well do the occupations fit the tune, and because the rhymes and the alliteration come in such profusion.

The pit sounds are deeply evocative, and Charles is careful to use them sparingly. There's a 20-second rockfall for the danger-underground section, there's the implacable monster machine cutter that 'drags itself along', coal boiling out like a wave, and we hear one final zing of the twanging hawsers at the end. He allows himself just a single echo effect. He recognises that deep underground is best evoked by the instruments. A range of concertina sounds for the hard rock that 'heaves and boils'; for the 'creaking' of the earth; for the 'breathing' of the mine; and a high-pitched edgy note for 'the darkness pressing on you.' The dry voices of the Dust section are accompanied by grim guitar riffs and the bluesy humming of a woman's voice. Fiddle and harmonica bring us back above ground to warmth and humanity in the miners' parlours and pubs. A strangely beautiful flute pastoral illustrates the days of poverty in the valleys when 'all they had was their pride.'

Peggy had lifted for Bryan Daly the blues guitar motif for Dust from a John Lee Hooker song she'd heard at the Newport folk festival, 'Flood at Tupelo.' She also wrote a verse of the signature 'Big Hewer' song, as she sat at the kitchen table feeding Neill, and created a new tune for 'Down in the Dark.' As she listened again there was much nodded approbation, and only occasionally did she frown – what's that banjo doing there? In some respects she felt it superior to *Singing the Fishing*: 'This has a far better chorus ... And it's a lovely ballad for transitions ... Charles did a beautiful job on production.'

The Body Blow

The fascination of *The Body Blow* is in seeing what happens when the team was chronically short of time, when things didn't work as well. They had six weeks: it had to be broadcast by the end of March, end of the 1962/3 financial year. On one level it's a gripping account of what it felt like to be suddenly struck down, to come to terms with it, and to drag yourself back to as active a life as your limbs and sheer bloody-mindedness can muster. It was subsequently used as a training programme for nurses so they could understand the psychology of pain and paralysis.

Where's the music in all this compelling stuff? Well, too often it's interrupting the flow without adding anything. It's overload. There are just two singers and Peggy later hated her own 'saccharine, sickly sweet' voice. Moreover, just three instruments, with less time to orchestrate them, naturally provided less than the usual variation in accompaniment. There are some good songs, but they're virtually all on one note – aching, plaintive, concerned, depressing. That partly reflects the nature of the suffering, true, and of course the shortage of time, but perhaps because Ewan hadn't recorded the actuality himself, didn't have the memory of it (a crucial catalyst) ticking away as he sat there composing. So the usual variety of ideas didn't come to him.

If you compare it with any of the previous four, you are promptly struck by the differences. The musical palette is pared down to what three musicians (Seeger, Edwards, Kahn) can play: concertinas, guitar, banjo, flute and harmonica. The sound effects are minimal. The songs lack variety of tone and pace. But there is a complex layering of the sufferers' voices, extremely cleverly assembled by Charles once he'd been convinced by Ewan that the idea could work. The resulting tapestry of voices braids perfectly the common threads of the patients' experience. What was crucial, too, was that the five voices, two men and three women, were soon instantly recognisable. Their stories mean the programme succeeds in spite of the songs' shortcomings.

The shortage of time meant that Charles didn't take what (few, true) opportunities there were to add effects. He had two kinds of respirator sounds, a child's skipping song, and that's it. With more time he'd surely have coloured-in effects at two or three points, notably when Norma Smith describes the system of pulleys fitted above her bed to strengthen her arms:

> **There was all little hangers and pulleys and rattles, and they used to call me Budgie, cos I used to look like a budgie in a cage, and I was always hooking from one to the other, like monkeys, and everybody had them, and it was rather funny. If anybody came into the ward we all hung on these things like a load of monkeys in a zoo, all peering forwards ... And I had lots of pulleys put above my bed, which I was told that I was to hang on to and help myself. This was a new angle for me, I used to be chomping all round that bed and all these darn things used to ding ding ding all the way down the bed, it was like a tram.**

The humour in it cries out for something, some effects-instrumental mix. In the event the limited instruments available suited Charles's desire to show he could produce a Radio Ballad more cheaply, at a third of the usual cost. The orchestration could be, and was, understated and simple. But the problem for Ewan and Peggy was that they couldn't escape from the view of the polio patients as 'sufferers'. There are fewer songs, and one or two are attractive on their own, but the cumulative effect is to drench the listener in pathos. Some of the songs had their origins in the half-hour television programme that prompted the idea, but they had no time to think through the overall shape. As a result the songs are all about suffering and all one-paced. They lift the mood only once towards the end when the recovering patients describe getting back into the real world, but the song doesn't really mirror that optimism, and lapses back:

> **Home again with the ones you love this morning,**
> **An end to the lonely months of hoping.**
> **Back to work and strife and the cares of normal life,**
> **Now you'll have to show your skill at coping.**

Strife, cares, coping. You feel that Ewan's songs are reflecting his own feelings about the grim life of polio victims, not their own ultimate view of 'great to be alive each new morning – let's make the most of it.' Of course, it's crucial that he had not recorded any of the actuality – in the time available Charles had to do it all – so their uplifting indomitability didn't make it through to his brain's song-creating factory. As a reviewer said:

> All those towering passionate declarations about 'stronger than pain is the human will to survive' all poured out in that splendid black voice of Ewan MacColl's … only seemed to trivialise and reduce to insignificance their experiences.

On the Edge

As we've seen, *On the Edge* is the Radio Ballad that was most criticised by (adult) audiences at the time, and the one that seems to have dated most. It's designed as a 'Quest' Ballad, constructed within a framing device of Ewan's narration song, which begins, 'A tale of the children of a troubled world.' The mediaeval Scottish bardic tune, Ewan's spare traditional singing style, and Peggy's wandering eight-string dulcimer accompaniment are designed to give it a timeless quality at the outset. This unique dulcimer is used early on again to counterpoint the sobbing of Dot Dobby, one of the programme's main speakers; thereafter we have the usual eclectic instrument mix.

The music is particularly variable and inventive, with liberal use of harmonica and concertina, piccolo and flute, clarinet and trumpet, fiddle and pipes, dulcimer and autoharp, either solo or paired with each other in unfamiliar ways. The music deliberately makes hardly any concession to what the teenagers themselves were listening to, although for the first and only time on the Radio Ballads we hear an electric guitar – but not for long. It comes in after 20 minutes, playing with bongo drums (drums of any kind were rarely used on the Radio Ballads) behind a collage of voices discussing street gang fights, then disappears again. It's replaced by the roar of a motorbike, the only non-musical sound effect that Charles Parker brought in, apart from using an echo machine for reverberation at one point. It wasn't the programme for effects, and in 1962 he was probably far too busy to collect them. However, the instruments and the many, many young voices fill the hour to the brim, and over the edge in places.

The glut of different voices gives us overblown collages, though when allowed to speak for more than a second they provide a wide range of tone and of regional accent, with for once a refreshing preponderance of female voices. If the four young singing voices that speak for the teenagers – Louis Killen, Gordon McCulloch, Lorna Campbell and Ray Fisher – had been used more, and if Ewan was confined solely to songs for narrator or parent, the outcome would have been more authentic. The music is there to create a mood that complements the speakers, which at times it does exquisitely. It's not at all predictable – throughout you have little idea of the sound that will come next. The meandering late-night walking (stalking) sequence is sung and spoken against Alfie Kahn's moody clarinet, similar to Bruce Turner in the depression-era piece from *Singing the Fishing*. It's brilliant, but it's sung by Ewan, not McCulloch or Killen, so it winds up being menacing rather than innocent, as this middle-aged man slows down for the girl to pass him. It's a four-minute dialogue between a speaker and a singer (Dot Dobby and Ewan), the instruments pacing along with them:

Walking down the road, you know, sometimes, coming home, get the all-night bus, about twelve o'clock.

> **Twelve o'clock,**
> **Dark, silent,**
> **Last bus gone,**
> **Drinkers gone from**
> **Pubs all closed and**
> **Streets all empty**
> **Streets all**
> **Empty streets**

It's not a busy place, but there's fellers all walking round, trying to pick me up. I say, 'No, thank you.'

> **Hear beat of shoes and feet on pavement, high-heel statement of shoes on –**
> **Slow down**
> **Wait till she comes abreast …**

Overall it's a frustrating piece, much less than the sum of some fascinating parts. Its design flaw, Ewan's (great but) intrusive and inappropriate voice, and that grating 1960 teenage jargon in some of the songs, mask some excellent individual and combined sections of voice and music. Listening simply to the music is fascinating. Some of the songs are just right – the programme comes alive in particular when the four young singers alternate and combine on songs contemplating first going out together, then getting married. True, the subject is certainly difficult for a Radio Ballad. Ewan wanted to follow his precept of letting the informants shape the programme, but, as Peggy said 'Teenage doesn't have a progression – it's all confusion', so he imposed a pattern that in the end didn't work.

The Fight Game

The team's reappraisal session after *On the Edge* led them to prepare for the next Radio Ballad with great care. It's Peggy's favourite, because 'everything we tried, it worked.' They felt that the actuality was by no means as compelling as some of the others, but there is a good mix of regional accents – Scots, Midlands, London, Liverpool, Black American. They set it carefully, and Peggy said the result was to her 'speech as music and music as speech, a totality.' Ewan explained its success:

> Everything worked beautifully and the reason why it did so is a simple one: the training of a boxer follows a series of rhythmic patterns: running, shadow-boxing, punching a speedball, skipping, throwing a medicine ball ... all actions done to a specific rhythm. Our task was to note these rhythms and incorporate them in songs, musical sequences and actuality blocks. By ringing the changes on a sequence of rhythms we could have a new episode without breaking the links with all the other episodes that made up the programme. I'm gripped every time I listen to the boxers. That is as near perfect as we got.

The key musical decision came from Ewan's research into the Roman gladiatorial contest, the metaphor used most often by the boxing fraternity: he found the gladiators were introduced by trumpets. They picked the two trumpeters from different backgrounds, jazz and classical. Their sound was augmented by Alf Edwards playing one of his other instruments, the trombone, whenever they needed the sound swelling or a sardonic raspberry blown after a manager's pronouncement. *The Fight Game* thus has the brassiest sound of any of the programmes, making us wince as much as Ewan's pugilistic sung commentary during the long and exhausting fight sequence.

There are two distinct sound patterns. For the fight the trumpeters' lips were as stretched to breaking point as the boxers' bodies. A trumpet fanfare signals actual boxing action – a punchball section representing training ring sparring, the weigh-in, the fight itself – and the trumpets blare and squeal at intervals throughout the fight action. For the remaining scenes there's a wide range of musical colouring, with alternating combinations of instruments giving constant variety. Concertina, fiddle, harmonica, guitar in several styles, piccolo, banjo, dulcimer – evoking fairground, Scots childhood, training run, skipping, the condemned-cell changing room. As with *On the Edge*, Peggy has the confidence now to try pairing unusual combinations. Take a small part of the manager's section, which describes how a fight is set up. Before the verse below come older voices paced by a trombone. 'I don't want any drones in my organisation' leads to a snatch of music-hall fiddle before piccolo and guitar accompany the promoter's refrain:

> **Give me the tang of liniment and the heavy smell of sweat,**
> **Give me the boy who draws them in, give me the certain bet,**
> **Give me the thud of leather and the music of the bell,**
> **Give me the clink of money and I know that all is well.**

The trombone then replaces the piccolo, pointing up a comically banal statement from a promoter that follows. For every scene outside the fight there's a different instrument mix, limited only by who plays what. In *John Axon*, ten musicians each play a single instrument. Now three of the eight employed here play nine between them, the versatile Alfie Kahn turning his hand to clarinet, harmonica, flute and the much-used piccolo. The spread of instrument and song style, as much as the songs themselves, keeps our interest alive in the breathers between each hectic skirmish in the ring. The songs are some of Ewan's best, now nearly all forgotten, and as many as seven are based on traditional tunes.

The singing is particularly strong, with the heavy North-Eastern voices of Bob Davenport and John Reavey punching their weight, and the lighter Scots voice of Gordon McCulloch for the young boxer. Peggy Seeger handles the wife-and-mother section in a way that pleases her more now, the men combine to provide old-boxer choruses, and the vocal action is shared out better than on the unbalanced *On the Edge*. Ewan's voice and acting ability are most impressive here, perfectly suited to anything from cheerful music-hall introduction to pompous manager to snarling trainer's second to world-weary summariser, as the piece goes from:

> **There's a game some call the Fight Game, and some the Noble Art …**
> **… What's left is the thrill when you count the receipts.**

Travelling People

After the sound-effect-rich Fishing and Mining programmes, Charles had needed to provide little for the next two Radio Ballads. In *Fight Game* he provided the sounds of training gym, the weigh-in, the fight itself, the shuffling-out and clearing-up at the end. For *Travelling People* he had two distinct sound profiles – outside and indoors. The dead sound of office and living room for those who found Gypsies intolerable; outdoor noises for the Travellers – the murmuring of voices, dogs barking, a snatch of birdsong, children's play. And the first noises we hear are set in sharp contrast: our world and theirs. The 'big twelve-wheeler that shook the bed' of Minty Smith as she gave birth on the move, replaced by the steady clop of the horse as it moseys along in harness, finding its own way as she does so.

Before Minty Smith describes giving birth in her 'carryvan', *Travelling People* starts without a shred of instrumentation or sound effect for nearly three minutes. A children's anti-Gypsy playground rhyme, prompting a roll-call of pejorative names for Travellers, is followed by Ewan's opening song. It's sung in the stark unaccompanied Gaelic sean-nós style, a vocal technique described by a practitioner as 'at once the most loved and most reviled' method of Irish singing. Ewan learned it from Joe Heaney, 'whose body shook when he sang.' With virtually every syllable ornamented, it's funereally slow, and can be hard to take if you're not familiar with it. The four minutes allowed the 'Terror Time' song is one of the few criticisms one can have of the piece's construction. Paul Ferris's otherwise admiring review picked this up, saying that it 'was infected by the melancholy of the content.' It was marvellously sung, nevertheless, by Heaney and the young Jane Urquhart (Jane Stewart from *Singing the Fishing*), unfamiliar though she was with the style.

Otherwise *Travelling People* is a near masterpiece musically. As well as Heaney, two new singers appear. One is the magisterial Belle Stewart, a Traveller whose voice appears several times, who like her distant Stewart relative, Jane, took immediately to the studio microphone – and went on to a successful singing career. The other is the young John Faulkner, who gives a fine rendition of 'The Gypsy is a Gentleman'. That, the 'Moving On Song', 'Freeborn Man' and 'Thirty Foot Trailer' are all sung today, often by people who don't realise Ewan wrote them in a fortnight for a radio programme. Although Peggy notes that 'Freeborn Man' hadn't yet been 'sung-in', when it was recorded for the Radio Ballad, Heaney and Urquhart work beautifully together. With Peggy as well there are even enough women to provide a rare women's-only chorus, and to do (some) justice to the key role of Traveller women as income earners. Belle and Jane duet on the hawking verse of 'Gypsy Jack of All Trades':

> In winter when the days are short, It's in the toon we're walking,
> Our baskets on our airms while we dae a bit o hawking.
> We dukker whiles and try and sell oor wares and bits o' laces,
> For every open door there's ten are shut hard in our faces.

This song, like 'The Gypsy is a Gentleman', is decorated with fiddle flourishes, performed with panache by Danny Levan, the last-minute substitute, who had little time to rehearse (and who didn't even make it to the credits). Once again, there's imaginative use of instruments to suit the mood: harmonica and guitar for 'Moving On Song', fiddle, piccolo and guitar for 'Jack of All Trades', concertina, fiddle, banjo and harmonica for 'Freeborn Man', concertina, banjo and flute for 'Thirty Foot Trailer'. A wickedly witty oboe joins the fiddle for 'The Gypsy is a Gentleman', at one point practising scales for 'towns and private property where decent people stay', at another dipping into a Bulgarian folk tune. It's the funniest piece of music in the entire Radio Ballad series, ending with a mock Palm Court Orchestra sign-off. One wishes Dinah Demuth's oboe had been recruited to the series earlier.

Travellers had their own musical tradition, of course. In a way, therefore, it's a pity bagpipes are missing – Belle Stewart's husband Alec was a piper who at that time was playing the pipes in lay-bys and switchbacks in the Scottish Highlands for American tourists. However, we do get some mouth music and a rattle of the spoons, weird but authentic sounds from an age-old tradition. Despite the tangible air of doom, Belle says defiantly right at the end: 'You'll never get rid of tinkers. They'll be there till Doomsday in the afternoon.' Ewan sums up the Travellers' dilemma succinctly in the final song:

> The hard-eyed men who guard the road,
> They bid us choose our way –
> And yet they will not let us go,
> Nor will they let us stay.

CHAPTER 19

Old Hands and Young Voices
The Performers

A folk singer is a guy who lies in bed all day and goes out at night to sing songs about work.

ANON, REPEATED BY JIMMIE MCGREGOR, 2007

Those guys could read fly shit.

ANON, REPEATED BY JOHN CLARKE,
STUDIO MANAGER ON *SINGING THE FISHING*, 2007

What gives us the Radio Ballad sound? It's a mix made up largely of highly skilled session musicians with years of experience, a group of enthusiastic and fast-learning young folk singers – and of course Ewan MacColl's stirring voice. The same core of musicians played throughout, though the disjointed nature of the series meant that they had to be re-assembled each time. Most of them had played with Ewan MacColl and Peggy Seeger at some time or other, and some had been part of the jazz band formed by the immensely talented Humphrey Lyttelton, born and educated at Eton College – a mile away in upbringing but not in politics from Ewan. Lyttelton had led the 'house' band for the MacColl/Lomax *Ballads and Blues* radio series in 1953.

Almost all the singers, apart from that 'toby jug', Bert Lloyd, were in their twenties, people who were starting to make a name for themselves as folk singers, but often still with a day job. Many became key figures in the story of the folk song revival, and many are still performing in their seventies. And with very few exceptions those who took part – and that includes the studio managers and technicians – speak with great warmth of the period, describing making the Radio Ballads, as does Peggy, as an unforgettable formative experience. So who were they?

Old Musical Hands

The only musician apart from Peggy to play on all of the Radio Ballads was **Alf Edwards**, a concertina player of genius at a time when the instrument was decidedly passé. In the late 18th century the appearance of a novel Chinese 'free-reed' instrument – where air is forced past a vibrating reed – led to a frenzy of invention in Europe. First came the harmonica and accordion, then the concertina and harmonium. Devised in the 1830s by Charles Wheatstone, a scientist and inventor born into a family of instrument-makers, the concertina sold in large numbers in the 1850s and 1860s. It was originally played only by the Victorian upper and middle classes – even dukes and earls, an Archbishop of Canterbury and Prime Minister Balfour took it up.

However, once the concertina began to appear on the second-hand market it became attractive as a cheaper alternative to brass instruments for village bands. As soon as it became common, in both senses, the middle classes stopped buying it, and in England it became a working man's instrument. For a time it was popular in dance bands and music halls as well as for traditional rural music. In fact it led to the growth of concertina bands, and with them the development of instruments with amazingly high and low registers. His proficiency on these enabled Alf Edwards to reproduce both growling storm and spooky pit to such wonderful effect. As a solo instrument it has been described variously as the electric guitar of its day and the successor of the one man 'tabor-and-pipe' of the Middle Ages.

Alf Edwards

All this enthusiasm was long gone by the 1950s. The complicated fingering, its buttons designed for chords and for rapid playing, with scales played by alternate hands, was a learning barrier when compared with the louder piano accordion, to which the piano-trained adapted more quickly. No musical slouch, Peggy spoke of how long it took her to learn the concertina when taught by Alf, who wouldn't let her play it in public for two years. He, of course, did himself no favours by teaching her, for now Ewan had Peggy to play the concertina. Her view of Alf is emphasised by everyone who knew him: a lovely man, calm, patient, always in jacket and tie like Bert Lloyd, and a wizard on a range of concertinas and other instruments.

Alf told Ewan that as a boy he had been paid sixpence by his mother for every instrument he learned. He grew up in the circus. His parents were 'Augustes', members of a traditional family of musical clowns, and he said his mother used to play the fiddle above (i.e. below) her head while balancing upside down on a tightrope. Indeed she did so while pregnant with Alf, which would have been around the turn of the 20th century. The trombone was his other major instrument, but he was proficient on many, such as the rarely played ocarina you can hear on *Singing the Fishing*. John Clarke recalls him being surrounded by an array of instruments on the studio floor. Alf was in demand whenever a concertina was needed, for films like *Tom Jones* and *Moby Dick* (when he appears as a seaman) and for Lloyd and MacColl on their groundbreaking early folk revival records. He too had a day job, a music printing business: Dave Swarbrick recalls seeing the Edwards basement full of Gestetner copiers. Lou Killen said, 'Alf could write music faster than I could write words.' But he wasn't good at improvising, though on the later Radio Ballads he did attempt it, playing, as he said, 'without the security of the dots.'

If Alf Edwards resisted improvising, **Bruce Turner** resisted reading the dots off the page. A brilliant saxophone player and clarinettist, he plays both instruments on the Radio Ballads, the first three and the last. He's responsible for many of the memorable mood pieces, his playing intoxicating the young Scot Elizabeth Stewart on *Singing the Fishing*, and his jazz background enabling him to come up with the right sound quickly. His reluctance to use a score, said Peggy, made him at first somewhat unreliable at timing his entry – 'on *Axon* I had to cue him in and count him down' – though he got better on the later programmes when he could hear the actuality over or after which he was playing. She recalls only ever writing out two complex pieces for him that needed precise timing. He found the crossover intriguing, as he said in a letter to Charles Parker after *Singing the Fishing*: 'It was at least as musically satisfying for us as anything we've done in the more accustomed idiom of jazz.'

Turner took up the clarinet before the war at school, and learned the alto saxophone when in the RAF. He joined Lyttelton's band at the beginning of 1953, and went to Romania with Ewan later that year. In 1957 he formed his own 'jump' band, which he led throughout the Radio Ballad period, and he provided several musicians for the programmes. **Terry Brown** was a trumpeter for the band when he played on *John Axon*, but declined to go abroad with them and was replaced by **John Chilton**. Chilton, later to lead the Feetwarmers band that backed George Melly, was co-opted by Turner for *Song of a Road*. Of this, his only Radio Ballad, Chilton wrote: 'The line-up that gathered under Peggy Seeger's musical direction ... [created] a highly unusual blend of tone colours. It was a fascinating endeavour, combining folk music and jazz.'

Chilton described himself in his *Hot Jazz, Warm Feet* as 'scuffling' for work at this time. Turner's band was popular, but like many others couldn't make a decent living for long, though Turner was well regarded enough to guest star with various bands in Britain and Scandinavia. He was famously disorganised and, because he didn't like buying manuscript paper, he used whatever came to hand, typically the grey cardboard of torn-apart cereal packets, tricky for others to read. Unlike most jazz musicians, Turner was a Marxist, a vegetarian and a teetotaller, and he had a notorious sweet tooth. He once outraged the Tories he was playing for at a party after a by-election, by liberating a chunk of their true-blue-iced celebration cake. He protested: 'It was not a craving – it was a political act.'

Turner was a talented musical impersonator, and to Chilton he was one of the best soloists European jazz has ever produced. Turner's band was featured

Bruce Turner's Jump Band with four musicians who were on the first Radio Ballad: Jim Bray, back left; Terry Brown, centre; Bruce Turner and Bobby Mickleburgh on the right.

in a film made in 1962 called *Living Jazz*, directed by Jack Gold. Turner was excited by the prospect of starring in a glossy Hollywood bio-pic of the 1940s, said Chilton, 'with silhouettes a-plenty, white suits for the musicians, and an audience in patent leather shoes ... Instead, Jack ... accurately portrayed us travelling in discomfort, staying in cruddy digs and playing a style of jazz that was not particularly popular.' The film was referred to later by the band as *Living Death*. Their brand of jazz was being overtaken in the early 1960s by the sudden, if brief, 'trad' revival exemplified by Acker Bilk, Kenny Ball and Chris Barber, then selling records in Britain in huge numbers. That craze overlapped with one for the Temperance Seven, which included **Bobby Mickleburgh**, who had played trombone on the first two Radio Ballads.

The usual driver for Bruce Turner's band was the laconic **Jim Bray**, a tall, balding double bass player. When he met Ewan he was in Lyttelton's band, with which he appeared in Ewan's Warsaw play in 1955. Bray shared with his instrument a taste for large cars. At one stage he acquired the Mercedes-Benz open tourer that had once belonged to King Zog of Albania (whose short-lived and Ruritanian royal throne had once been offered to the England sporting polymath CB Fry) and which still had Zog's coat of arms on the side. Peggy describes the extraordinary sight of Bray chauffeuring his double bass, which sat stiffly upright in the back. He had never played an instrument until he joined the Fleet Air Arm as a pilot at the end of the war. A tuba player initially, he switched to double bass and played it on seven of the eight Radio

Ballads. When jazz work began to tail off in the early 1960s and bands began to split up, Bray found a teaching job in Hyderabad, and it was from there that he spoke a few weeks before he died in 2007. What were Ewan and Peggy like to work with? 'Demanding, but Peggy was patient. They used to change their minds a lot, about the style they wanted things played in, so it was hard. But OK, that was our job. And they were damn good musicians.' He thought Alf Edwards the finest musician he ever played with.

Bray roomed for a while with **Bob Clark**, the 'best street fiddler' Peggy had ever heard, who went with Ewan to Moscow in 1957 and played on *John Axon* before disappearing onto cruise ships with a jazz trio (the one for which Spike Milligan had played guitar for a spell before finding fame with the *Goon Show*). The Radio Ballad violinists varied, and in fact they only used a fiddler on five of them, not least because it was a rarity early in the folk song revival. For *Singing the Fishing* they were to have used Dave Swarbrick, but fell back on **Kay Graham**, who carried on a correspondence afterwards with Charles Parker, feeling that she had been under-used. Perhaps her style wasn't right, but Swarbrick's was, and he was used on three of the subsequent programmes.

Dave Swarbrick has now acquired legend status in the folk world. Ian Campbell recalls how this young lad turned up in the railway carriage in which he and his group were practising on the way to the concert for Pete Seeger at St Pancras Town Hall in 1959. Ian Campbell: 'He asked if anyone could join in, got his fiddle out. Amazing. No matter what key we were playing in, he would just listen to one verse and then … straight in like

Dave Swarbrick

the clappers … Revolutionary idea to have a fiddler then. It was the days of skiffle, the three-chord trick, rudimentary.' After the concert's rehearsals he asked if he could play with them on their set. At first they were dubious, but not after their success that night – 'we tore the place up, standing ovation.' Swarbrick had given up the violin when taught it at school, but his mentor Beryl Marriott, the pianist in whose ceilidh band he'd been playing guitar, persuaded him to take it up again. Self-taught, he says he always had a 'flat' hand and held the bow half or even three quarters of the way up. He played with the Ian Campbell group for five years, a period when his life was somewhat anarchic, to put it mildly: Campbell recalls redeeming Swarbrick's pawned fiddle three times. But he was very young – rehearsals started for *Big Hewer* on his 20th birthday. Peggy remembers his brilliance and his foibles. They had to insist he wore no shoes in the studio, because he couldn't stop his feet tapping, and if they ever broke for a discussion they had to take his fiddle away – it was an extension of his arm and kept playing of its own accord.

After Swarbrick parted company with the Campbell group he teamed up with Martin Carthy, with whom he has made eight albums across 40 years, and in 1969 joined the 'electric folk' group Fairport Convention as they recovered from a terrible van crash. There he played among others with Richard Thompson and Ashley Hutchings, and recorded a dozen albums with them. Later, Swarbrick's health deteriorated rapidly and he finished up in a wheelchair with chronic emphysema, out of which he eventually and surprisingly sprang after a successful double lung transplant, defying his premature obituary in the *Daily Telegraph* in 1999. Back with Martin Carthy, they won the best duo award at the 2007 Folk Awards, and later that year he joined a re-formed Fairport to play the whole of their famous *Liege and Lief* album at the Cropredy Folk Festival. He recalled the enjoyment of playing on the Radio Ballads: 'I was earning two pounds seven and nine [about £36 at 2008 prices] doing 44½ hours a week at something I hated. Then the Radio Ballads, being paid musicians' rates. Marvellous. When I look back on it now I can't believe I was that young. I was an apprentice printer, would have been the worst in the world. It kept me from the call-up, then they abolished National Service two weeks before I jacked in the printing.' After *Big Hewer* he played on *Fight Game*, and rehearsed *Travelling People* before pulling out.

On the Radio Ballads they only used drums twice, an oboe once, and the brass was sparing too: trombone three times, trumpet four, though of course it was the boxers' signature instrument on *Fight Game*. They used two trumpeters: the Midland Light Orchestra's **Johnny Lambe**, and **Ronnie Hughes**. Hughes had learned the trumpet as a boy, and before settling down with the BBC Radio Orchestra he played with myriad bands, including Ted Heath's. Still playing in 2007 at 82, hearing *Fight Game* for the first time for 40 years brought it all back. He said it had been tough, a fascinating challenge to play, as Peggy acknowledged: 'I gave the trumpeters a really bad time in *Fight Game*. I gave Ronnie a high note he said he couldn't hit, but he did. He finished each session with swollen lips ... They were great, those jazz musicians – they'd play everything.' The combination of the trumpets' bellow and Ewan's unremitting commentary song brings to life the animal viciousness of the ring. And of the crowd.

Two others played on more than half the programmes, **Alfie Kahn** and Bryan Daly. Immensely versatile, Kahn had recorded on tenor sax with Fats Waller in London before the war, but it was harmonica, tin whistle, flute and piccolo he played on the last five Radio Ballads, as well as the clarinet after Bruce Turner had gone abroad. Growing up in the 1920s in a London Jewish family, Kahn armed himself against prejudice with a fund of self-deprecating anti-Jewish jokes. **Bryan Daly** was a classically trained session guitarist with immensely strong hands, playing acoustic guitar at a volume that once had the engineer telling him to turn the amp down. 'When I was a child playing a guitar was like a secret society. Now everyone does it.' Peggy said he was 'a vegetarian, incredibly solid ... hated performing simple stuff', as she recalled his playing of what they called the 'grid' behind the boxers in *Fight Game*. He accompanied Ewan for some years before Peggy's arrival. 'I improvised everything with Ewan. Went all over with him, but ... hated those Iron Curtain trips, armed guards on the trains ... Peggy? Very determined. Didn't know what she was doing at the start but she learned fast. But we were professional musicians, it was our job.' At any suggestion that vegetarians were wimps he would puff out his chest to be hit, and smile when the crumpled fist retreated. Later in life he found (comparative) fame and fortune when he wrote the tunes for a new children's television cartoon series, *Postman Pat*, following a chance meeting in the street with the animator's wife.

Peggy also played guitar, as well as autoharp, mountain dulcimer, and her characteristic five-string banjo, which she could play at awesome speed. A third guitarist was **Fitzroy Coleman** from Trinidad, where he lives on in retirement. He appears on the first three programmes, playing the guitar beautifully and singing the *John Axon* fireman's calypso. Fitz had secretly taught himself to play on the prized guitar of his father, who drove a steamroller. 'I started to invent chord constructions and rehearse the popular ballads of the day. It was only when he caught me and realised I could play without any teaching that he allowed me to use the guitar freely.' At the end of 1945 he came to England with Al Jennings' Caribbean All Stars Orchestra with just a guitar and the clothes he stood up in, and learned to read music on the boat. He barely survived that first English winter, but his playing style fascinated people, Peggy among others, and he was never out of work. 'What a player!' said Bryan Daly, and he would know. He was part of the Manchester Ramblers set-up, 'sailing through everything with charm and a

Fitzroy Coleman

beguiling sense of humour', as Peggy wrote in her *Songbook* introduction to the calypso she wrote about him, one of her earliest songs. He joined them on stage on Sunday nights at the Ballads and Blues Club. Those were the days when earnest young guitarists were eager to learn … Peggy remembers his performances vividly:

> We encouraged anyone with a guitar to sit in the front row and help with accompaniments. We hadn't yet realised that democracy and art have a hard time mixing: the first 40 minutes of every evening were devoted to trying to tune several dozen instruments. It was devotion on the part of the seasoned musicians and trying to all. Before you sang your song, you called out the key and the chords. The whole front row would glaze with concentration and left hands would search finger by finger for the correct string and fret. Now Fitzroy was a brilliant calypso guitarist … So he would reel off the number of bars to be covered by each chord – 2½ bars of A-Flat 13th, 6 bars of G 6th etc – and then launch into something impossible to follow. One by one we'd drop out of the race and Fitzroy would get happier and happier. He always ended the song by himself.

> 'But Fitzroy', I say,
> What are all those things you play?
> H-demented and Pi-R Square,
> Chords that make Segovia despair.
> And that formula you explain in a hurry
> Make Einstein worry.

Young Voices

With the notable exception of Bert Lloyd and Ewan himself, many of the singers were youngsters starting out in the world of traditional song. The most experienced of the rest was **Isla Cameron**, who forms a link with Theatre Workshop, for she had spent a short spell with them after the war when still a teenager. It was her voice singing 'Queen Jane' that turned Charles Parker on to folk music as he sat in the BBC record library. She was the foremost female singer in the early folk song revival, and sang impressively on the first two Radio Ballads and on *Big Hewer*. But film began to take over her career. Between 1958 and 1969 she had small parts in *Room at the Top*, *The Innocents*, and *Nightmare*, and a larger one in *The Prime of Miss Jean Brodie*. In 1967 her role in *Far From the Madding Crowd* was cut, but hers was the voice Julie Christie mimed to on the soundtrack (which also includes Dave Swarbrick), and she was the film's music advisor to composer Richard Rodney Bennett.

The singers came and went on the Radio Ballads, usually because of availability, and no one singer apart from Ewan sang on more than half. The eccentrically brilliant **Stan Kelly-Bootle** was a Liverpudlian who appears only on *John Axon*, on which he sings 'Manchester Rambler'. Stan was born a Bootle but acquired the Kelly while running the unrelated Stan Kelly skiffle group. He attended the Liverpool Institute several years before three of the four Beatles were there, and joined the Young Communist League at school along with his friend Alan Durband, founder of the Liverpool Everyman theatre and a key influence on McCartney. After becoming a radar expert during National Service, in 1950 Stan arrived at Cambridge to do a maths

Isla Cameron

Stan Kelly-Bootle, guitar and computer

degree, still only 20, yet with a pregnant wife and two children in tow... There with Rory McEwan he co-founded one of the first folk clubs in Britain, learned to programme the experimental EDSAC computer, and became Britain's first computer science postgraduate.

Thereafter, computing, song and soccer went in parallel. His love of Liverpool Football Club led him to manage several players in their 1970s heyday, and he wrote two sound-and-song albums in Radio Ballad style, about Merseyside and Liverpool FC, after 'lugging a Nagra recorder around the city' to collect the actuality. Stan wrote the Merseyside anthem 'Liverpool Lullaby' and much else. He was one of the first employees of IBM in the UK (slipping under their anti-Communist radar) and subsequently became an independent writer on computing. He wrote the famously witty *Devil's DP Dictionary*, a reprise of Ambrose Bierce's *Devil's Dictionary*, later called the *Computer Contradictionary*. Of Stan it was said that he had more columns than the Parthenon, and he still (2008) writes a monthly online column, where he is a scathing critic of computing pretensions, of which there is an ample supply, and of anything else that comes into his head. A polymath's polymath.

Stan describes **Dominic Behan** as someone who could only sing well if drunk, which is why Ewan expelled him from *John Axon* – he was paid but didn't make it to the credits. He and his more celebrated brother Brendan were from a formidable IRA family, archetypal roistering Irishmen. (Brendan was incarcerated in an English Borstal after trying to blow up Liverpool Docks in 1939, aged 16, and wrote *The Quare Fellow* and *The Hostage*, big successes for Theatre Workshop in the late 1950s.) Dominic was a talented writer and singer, creating a number of television plays, including *The Folk Singer*, and well-known songs like 'McAlpine's Fusiliers' and 'Liverpool Lou'. He was a key friend and supporter of Ewan MacColl in the early Singers Club days, despite their falling out at intervals, and with him released an early record of Scots and Irish street songs. Two further Irishmen on the Radio Ballads were **Francis McPeake** and **Seamus Ennis**, both uilleann pipers. Uilleann pipes are traditional Irish pipes, with bellows squeezed between side and elbow. Ennis was an early collector of Irish folk song, responsible for the early folk-song series *As I Roved Out*. Another destructive drinker, he appears just on *Song of a Road*, where he sings the rollicking 'Hot Asphalt'. Stan Kelly-Bootle quotes Seamus as ordering two treble whiskies at the Queen Elizabeth Hall bar, then turning to him to ask what he was having ... Philip Donnellan described his 'gaunt frame, like a clothes horse supporting a battered grey suit.' McPeake, who sang the 'Drivers Song', came from a famous multi-generation family of Northern Irish pipers, who among other things played for President Johnson in 1965.

As we heard in Chapter 8, **Jimmie McGregor** only managed *Song of a Road* before he was whisked off with Robin Hall to a hectic touring schedule and the *Tonight* television programme. They teamed up almost by accident:

Francis McPeake   Jimmie McGregor

We had just casually got together, Robin and me, and after Moscow we were carted off to the Budapest festival. Performed off the cuff. I could always sing harmonies and they threw us on together. Paul Robeson actually came round and said how much he'd enjoyed what we did – two young lads singing the songs of your own country and good luck to you ... I said to Robin 'Christ, that's something if Paul Robeson gives you a pat on the back. Maybe we should work on this.' We got an agent and a repertoire [not yet of Scots songs] and were asked if we were doing anything on Burns Night. Two Scots lads ... we found one traditional song we both knew, and I literally worked out the chords and harmonies in the taxi. On the strength of that they gave us a week's trial and we did it for four years ... Fantastic learning experience. It was all live – if it under-ran you might have to add a couple of songs. If it over-ran you'd get the signal to stop immediately, and we got telepathic at finishing together at the end of the verse we were on.

Song of a Road had an eclectic mix of voices. As well as Ewan and Bert Lloyd, and the Irish pair of Ennis and McPeake, there were the two West Indians **John Clarence** and **'Big' Thomas**. Ewan and Peggy had just met them on Geoffrey Bridson's Scots/West Indian culture clash programme earlier in 1959. *Song of a Road* was the programme that decided **Louis Killen** to begin a singing career. 'Lovely Lou', said Peggy, listening to his singing on that and *Big Hewer*, 'very biddable, quick on the uptake.' Louis: 'My family was Tyneside Irish, sang all the time – cowboy songs, church liturgy, everything.' On *Song of a Road*

Louis befriended **Cyril Tawney**, an ex-merchant seaman who 'had a hard time with Ewan, who hadn't picked him – Ewan thought he sounded too like Burl Ives, too sweet.' Louis displaced **Bob Davenport**, stricken with TB, another Tynesider from an Irish background, whose father and grandfather had been killed in an explosion before he was born. Davenport had an immense voice, and eventually sang (not enough, as Peggy subsequently reflected) on *Fight Game*.

Ewan's strongly held opinions tended to create both enthusiastic supporters and equally forthright denigrators, and both Davenport and **Gordon McCulloch** grew to dislike him. Like Ian Campbell, Gordon McCulloch was a Scot who had settled in Birmingham – and was an early member of Campbell's group – and both appeared in *Singing the Fishing*. Peggy admired the voices of both of them, such as in McCulloch's 'Up Jumped the Herring' in *Singing the Fishing*, and his portrayal of the young boxer Peter Keenan in *Fight Game*, born in a Partick single-end. Peggy: 'We asked him to sing in the fight sequence as if he was out of breath, and he got it instantly.' Both he and Louis Killen were under-used in *On the Edge*.

I've written about **Ian Campbell** and his experience of *Singing the Fishing*, the two programmes he made for Charles Parker, and the Centre 42 productions. His highly popular folk group at the Jug o' Punch had become the fulcrum of Midlands folk music in the early folk-song revival days. It began life as the Ian Campbell skiffle group, a spin-off from the Clarion Singers: 'It grew ... the policy was not to audition, so we ended up with 12 members, most of them playing something to shake and rattle. We had only two guitars – it was becoming ridiculous.' Re-formed as a folk group, they were soon very much in demand, not least to launch new folk clubs, their sound distinguished by intricate vocal harmonies and the unfamiliar fizz of Swarbrick's fiddle. For a spell they were residents with Martin Carthy on the highly successful Midlands TV *Hullabaloo* folk music programme, broadcast to every region but London. 'Right at the beginning of the Sixties we were virtually the only folk group in the country ... but we're forgotten now ... Everyone knows the Dubliners have been around since mediaeval times, but Luke Kelly was in Birmingham for three years stuck to us like a leech, copying out our songs. Everybody copied them back then without permission or attribution.' Peggy: 'Ian did a beautiful job on the Radio Ballads, his voice is true, absolutely true.' Campbell was a hugely talented man who had near misses with fame. In the 1970s BBC2 mounted an occasional series called *The Camera and the Song*.

> It was a kind of television Radio Ballad. I did the first one, *Here Come the Polis*. A singer/songwriter and cameraman on any subject they choose. Ralph McTell, Max Boyce, Victoria Wood, Jake Thackray, Alex Glasgow all took part ... I was paired with a cameraman I'd never met, brilliant, he found some wonderful stuff. A day in the life of Birmingham, starts at dawn ... Birmingham as the workshop

Ian and Lorna Campbell, with Dave Swarbrick behind them

of the world. I wrote new songs like 'Chocolate Paddies', Black Country men cursing black men for taking their jobs. The programme ends at dusk with the lights going out. It was broadcast at 9 p.m. ... the phone started to ring with congratulations ... then Charles Parker came on – 'Ian you bastard. It was wonderful – you learned a lot on the Radio Ballads. Nearly brought it off.' Nearly, oh well. Great reviews – 'a rare experience, a glowing picture' – thought it was one of the achievements of my life.

The Radio Ballad songs for women were scarce. After Isla Cameron came the younger generation, with **Elizabeth** and **Jane Stewart** on *Singing the Fishing*, then Ian Campbell's sister **Lorna** and **Ray Fisher** in *On the Edge*. Ray had been studying in Glasgow when she and her brother Archie were given a 13-week slot on Scottish television's equivalent of *Tonight*, called *Here and Now*. She recalls her lecturers giving her a hard time because she earned more in five days of television than they did in a month – such was television, though it was soon back to the shillings and pence of folk club appearances. **Colin Ross**, now her husband, came down to play the fiddle and pipes for *On the Edge*, pipes which he now manufactures in Whitley Bay as well as playing.

As we've seen in Chapter 10, the journey down to Birmingham was the first the young Stewart sisters had made south of Aberdeen. Jane appeared again in *Travelling People* with her older distant cousin Belle Stewart, the source singer who convinced other Travellers that Ewan and Peggy could be trusted as they traipsed round camps with a tape recorder in the summer of 1963. (The reverse was true too – Peggy said they could leave money and expensive equipment in a tent for days with no risk of being stolen.) Ewan and Peggy had brought Belle and her husband Alec, a piper, down to the Singers Club and launched Belle's (public) singing career. Peggy said of all the Stewarts that they took to the microphone instantly. Belle Stewart's family had settled in Blairgowrie where the raspberry picking gave summer employment. A singer, songwriter and storyteller, she came to notice through her song 'The Berryfields of Blair', after the collector Hamish Henderson sought her out in the 1950s: 'Collecting on the berry fields was like holding a tin can under the Niagara Falls', he said. Belle was nearly 60 when she sang with such unaffected pleasure on *Travelling People*. In Birmingham the Stewarts stayed with Dave Swarbrick's parents and in London later with Jimmie McGregor when they recorded for Topic Records:

> Some of my Muswell Hill neighbours ... they were astounded by them, as if they'd come from the Amazon or something – spoke a different language. When Belle was young she must have been an absolute stunner. Six feet tall, had these big Gypsy cheek-bones, statuesque woman, wonderful-looking person, even in her old age. And a store of the dirtiest, filthiest stories you've ever heard – and these people, middle class, we're sitting with, their jaws dropped. Never encountered anything like it, and of course Alec, Alec McGregor, her husband, a quiet wee guy, playing the pipes.

Joe Heaney   Ray Fisher and Belle Stewart

Two further male singers were recruited just for *Travelling People*, John Faulkner and **Joe Heaney**. Heaney was a source singer from Connemara, whose songs were sung in the Gaelic tradition of sean-nós, the style in which he sings the grim 'Terror Time' in *Travelling People*. He became close friends with Ewan, who he fascinated, and who interviewed him at length in 1964. For a time Ewan imitated the style, as in the unaccompanied 'There's No Place for Me' which opens *Travelling People*, though Peggy wasn't as sold on the sound as Ewan: 'He was experimenting. He stopped it after a while – not a moment too soon.' **John Faulkner** was a younger singer whom Ewan admired, and who became a key figure in the Critics Group (Chapter 21) set up by Ewan and Peggy just after the last Radio Ballad was recorded in late 1963. He and his then wife Sandra Kerr acquired fame ten years later through the immensely popular children's TV series *Bagpuss*. They wrote and performed the songs in the folk idiom, and each spoke a character. Faulkner later made a career writing film music as well as songs, which included the Nelson Mandela anthem 'Lion in a Cage'.

Bert Lloyd

At that first animated meeting with Bert Lloyd outside the Theatre Royal in Stratford East in the mid-1950s, Ewan's first impression was of a kindly uncle in Dickens who saves an orphan from a life of misery:

> A cheerful, minor, plump Dickens character, who looked cherubic but was anything but ... good-natured, yes, enormously skilled and intelligent ... high-pitched and artificial voice ... tremendous raconteur, a very good singer of traditional English songs, especially lyrical songs.

Bert was similarly many-talented, self-taught, a natural writer and an avaricious reader. Bert and Ewan didn't see eye to eye on everything by any means, and once fell out over the origins of folk music. Louis Killen recalled a workshop of Ewan's at Keele in 1965, when 'Bert stood up and questioned Ewan's theory of folk song.' Stan Kelly-Bootle described the disagreements as 'very donnish, historical arguments ... Ewan would date something as 1751, and Bert would say it couldn't have been written before 1815 because it talks of Waterloo porridge, stuff like that.'

But, in the great scheme of things, the differences they had over folk music and the working man were minor compared to their burning desire to champion both. Louis Killen described them like this: 'Ewan would bludgeon you to death, but Bert was more a stiletto man.' Their singing voices were very different. Peggy said: 'Many people don't like Bert's singing because he floats, pitchwise, but I always loved his voice ... He sang with a smile on his face, which gave it that sound.' Studio manager John Clarke liked it too, but, a Russian speaker, he couldn't share Bert's admiration for 'those proletarian work songs in which girls sing to their work tools.' The young Stewart sisters suppressed giggles as they watched Bert from behind, unconsciously rotating his bottom as he sang. Dave Swarbrick, equally young, 'loved him to bits ... Bert wasn't entirely happy with the Radio Ballads, thought they were too sentimental.'

Seven years older than Ewan — born on Leap Year Day 1908 — Bert had been sent to Australia for his health at the age of 16, odd-jobbing on farms for nearly ten years, and learning songs as he went. He was said to acquire languages 'the way some people collect postage stamps' — ideal for a researcher of European folk song. On his return home in the 1930s he found occasional work as a journalist, and translated Lorca's *Lament for the Death of a Bullfighter*. Spells at sea, including an Antarctic trip in a whaler, exposed him to sea songs, giving him material for a radio piece, *The Voice of the Seamen*, which led in 1938 to a BBC contract. Soon after the outbreak of war he collaborated on the series *The Shadow of the Swastika*, criticising Britain and America for their failure to stem the rise of fascism, just as MacColl and Littlewood were doing at the same time in their *Last Edition*. His Communist views made Bert suspect at the BBC, and at various times he, like Ewan, was effectively on a blacklist.

Bert's interest in folk song continued to grow and in 1939 he recorded East Anglian source singers in a Suffolk pub for Francis Dillon's *Saturday Night*

Bert Lloyd, the smiling singer

at the Eel's Foot, the first authentic English folk song broadcast. During and after the war he worked on articles for the *Picture Post*, but all his spare time was taken up with researching folk- and work-songs for his *The Singing Englishman*, published in 1944 by the Workers' Music Association (WMA). The first book of its kind, immensely popular and influential, its analysis nevertheless led to conflict with the English Folk Dance and Song Society (EFDSS). Bert detested what he called their 'sentimental travesty of lower-class life, with its poems and paintings of romanticised cottage scenes.' When he updated his work in 1967 with *Folk Song in England*, he apologised for the sketchy scholarship of its predecessor, 'put together in barrack rooms away from reference books … [and] like the okapi, not much to look at but cherished as unique.'

Bert realised that a folk song revival needed to appeal to a largely urbanised post-war society via industrial, occupational and political songs based on traditional forms. Hence his and Ewan's failed attempt to interest the Trades Union movement in the revival. As fellow Communists, song collectors and singers, they collaborated intensely for a few years until Bert was largely displaced as Ewan's singing partner by the arrival of Peggy Seeger. His floating tones were the ideal counterpoint on the first four Radio Ballads to Ewan's commanding authorial voice. Songs like the workman's 'Saturday Afternoon' in *John Axon*, 'Roving Rambler' from *Song of a Road*, recalling Bert's own itinerant days, and 'Shoals of Herring' in *Singing the Fishing*, all evoke perfectly the slightly world-weary labouring man who has seen it all:

Oh shift boys, shift, do the job and draw your pay,
When this road is finished I'll be moving on my way.
I'll clean my tools and wrap 'em in a pair of oily jeans –
You'll always find me working where you find the big machines.

It's that mix of voices – Ewan, Bert, and the young blood – as well as the great diversity of musical colouring conjured up from those experienced instrumentalists, that gives the Radio Ballads a sound that still fascinates today. All were assembled by Charles Parker's deft fingers, fine-tuned ear, and bloody-minded determination. The Radio Ballads had propelled Charles into a world that had delighted him, but that exciting time was now over. What would he do now?

CHAPTER 20

From Ballads to Banners
Charles Parker, 1964–80

> I've never met anyone with an ear like his. The way he made the programmes, every sentence was put together as a piece of art. He wanted to make Art ... He taught me the soft interview, simple questions, waiting, panning for that speck of gold among the dross.
>
> DILIP HIRO, WRITER AND JOURNALIST, INTERVIEWED IN 2007

> In the BBC, anyone who by his or her attitudes or behaviour was thought to be different, very easily got a reputation as an eccentric, or a person who was difficult ... Such a reputation clung year in and year out, was nourished and embroidered by the smallest incidents and was passed on, generally enlarged, until it could become a powerfully corrosive force which affected the prospects and possibilities of your work – and even your survival.
>
> PHILIP DONNELLAN, FROM HIS UNPUBLISHED AUTOBIOGRAPHY, 1980S

Radio 1964–72

Now a tireless documenter of English folk traditions, Doc Rowe was at his parents' house in Torquay when they put Charles Parker up in December 1966. At the time Charles was working with Philip Donnellan, his lifelong ally and friend, who was making a film on the blind, to be called BD8. Charles was helping him with some recording and doing his sound editing, but naturally got so emotionally involved with the plight of the blind that he decided to put together a radio programme on the same subject. Torquay on the English south-west coast held one of the two RNIB (Royal National Institute for the Blind) rehabilitation centres, and Charles was interviewing blind people and their carers. I shall dwell on this programme at some length because it marks the point at which Charles Parker's fortunes at the BBC go into a steep decline, and it illustrates his personality perfectly, as does this quote from Doc:

> He came to stay with us at Torquay while he was making it. We watched *Cathy Come Home* while he was here – that'll give you the date. My mother and sister always talked about this remarkable bloke. All night you could hear the sound of him going through tapes. Throughout breakfast he was reading the paper, working at the Uher [recorder] ... Cursing under his breath, scraping at the cheese. Charles – do you really want cheese on your toast? – Oh, bugger.

Donnellan and Parker were perturbed by many of the things they discovered about the treatment of the blind. In particular they were concerned by what they saw in workshops, where many inmates – a word Charles thought was apt – felt exploited. They had been institutionalised from a young age, sitting at factory workbenches for their subsistence and pocket money. Moreover, there was a general reluctance at the time to encourage the blind to move independently outside the home. In Torquay Charles met Lee Farmer, an American campaigner for the use of the 'Hoover' long cane, invented by an army sergeant in 1944 to help blinded soldiers. This is the now-familiar cane that blind people swing from side to side in front of them. Farmer discovered that Britain – the RNIB and others – was years behind the USA in adopting it, and lacked an ethos which encouraged self-help. The main researcher in Britain, the brilliant Dr Alfred Leonard of Nottingham University, emphatically agreed, and helped with the programme.

Philip Donnellan's television documentary went out in the autumn of 1967. It was welcomed by independent campaigners for the blind, but antagonised those responsible for their welfare, notably the RNIB. Lee Farmer wrote to Charles from Illinois saying that it looked as though 'Philip's arrows had hit their mark', and hoping that the programme had 'pinched the proper toes.' Its title BD8, incidentally, was the name of the form that blind or partially sighted people were required to complete before they could claim benefit. For various reasons it wasn't fit for purpose, and after years of campaigning it was eventually improved in the 1990s and finally replaced only in 2004, nearly 40 years after the programme was made.

Charles Parker pressed on to make an hour-long radio feature, which was originally scheduled for broadcast in late March 1968. But he was using folk song for illustration, and trouble with fixing recording dates delayed him. Recording eventually took place in Birmingham and London at the end of that month. With no London studio available, they went to Frankie Armstrong's flat to record. Frankie was a young folk singer with severely deteriorating eyesight whose experiences and voice Charles used in the programme: she wrote a song for it based on one in *The Body Blow*. Until recently a social worker for the blind, she had been forthright about her demeaning treatment. And, no, she didn't want to be a capstan lathe operator, thank you.

> I talked about the dire state of most of the non-statutory blind agencies, how in my experience those of us who had a visual impairment were stereotyped, and hence limited, by the very agencies who were supposed to encourage our independence … He … was appalled at what he found. Charles had the capacity to fire people's smouldering resentments into full-blooded anger. This led to the formation of the Blind Integration Group (BIG), which … was a crucial step in our moves towards self-definition and self-help.

When in June Charles had a rough assembly of what he wasn't allowed to call by his preferred title *Let Me See*, he submitted it to the then controller of Midland Region, David Porter. Charles felt that what he'd put together so far hadn't done full justice to the actuality, so he was surprised and energised when Porter said that he'd like to propose it for an Italia Prize entry. From that high point of optimism, Charles's work at the BBC began to come under increasingly critical scrutiny, and what happened when *The Blind Set* was finally broadcast on 9 October 1968 came as a terrible shock to him. It was bad enough that the director of the RNIB, then in its centenary year, should on hearing an advance copy promptly send an internal memo to RNIB staff forbidding them to listen to it, as representing only the 'lunatic wing' of the blind. Given that and a vehement letter of protest from the RNIB to the BBC's Director General it was hardly a surprise – but humiliating – that Charles should be carpeted by the same Porter who had encouraged him in June. But that the audience research figures were so poor? And, worst of all to a now-impassioned supporter of the blind, that most of the letters from blind listeners themselves – 24 out of 32 – were so critical?

Newspaper reviews varied. Jeremy Rundall in *The Sunday Times* said: 'A moving and skilful mixture of past and present, ballad and edited tape showed how we treated the man with the white stick as an alien … a horrific image of a

Dickensian set of attitudes.' The then *Guardian* journalist Gillian Reynolds, in one of her first reviews, realised what Charles was trying to do: 'I heard a programme one night about what it was like not just to be blind but to live inside a blind world. I had to write about that one.'

> It used the familiar and easily irritating collage form. Usually this form palls as efforts to pad out and brighten up a subject become glaringly obvious ... [It was] used here, in a far more subtle way, to break down the obvious emotional response to the subject of the blind, to allow the listener a more complex and yet more rational appreciation of what it's like to be blind... A picture was gradually built up of the gradual emancipation of a group from the whipped beggars of the 18th and 19th centuries to now. We don't want pity, we want help, would rather risk than rot. The impact was far greater because it was in sound only.

Reynolds, who 'then made all speed to get to know the rest of what he'd done', compared *The Blind Set's* approach and impact to that of Peter Nichols' recent play *A Day in the Death of Joe Egg*, about a couple with a mentally handicapped child. But it was the Birmingham Post's reviewer Keith Brace who expressed the listening public's negative majority view:

> The technique was like a tape-fiend's nightmare, so quick, mumbled, muffled, souped-up and electronically rained over that I must have missed every third sentence. The ear must be given time to absorb. The folk songs [organised, not written] by Ewan MacColl and Peggy Seeger had no contemporary relevance. These just got in the way of what sounded like fascinating off-the-spool comments on an often desperate state of life.

David Wade in *The Times* felt 'there is a terrible insistence about Mr Parker's productions and though his material was superb he ... could learn to slow down.' One of the audience research listeners said: 'There was a whining and self-pitying tone to the programme which blind people might resent.' They did. In essence, the programme revealed the unheard voices of the disadvantaged blind, often working-class, who had been shovelled into what was effectively a humane successor to the Victorian workhouse, their independence steadily institutionalised out of them. Hitherto inarticulate, they had truly been out of sight and out of mind. The programmes were largely heard, though, by the articulate blind middle class, who had fought their way out of dependence, were proud of it, and wanted that successful struggle celebrated.

Listening now, 40 years on, I was quite ready to find the programme a self-indulgence, an excess of method over content, akin to *On the Edge* in its over-use of collage. It wasn't – it was compelling, and indulgent perhaps only in its admixture of folk song, folklore and poetry when (as in *Body Blow*) its riveting actuality could stand on its own – and it is by no means hard to understand. Of course, Charles doesn't give authorial signposts at the start of his programmes, so listeners must be attentive from the outset, and join up the dots themselves. Moreover, Charles was indignant when he made it, and that comes over in the choice of content, if not in his surprisingly emollient voice, deliberately bland and detached. Pam Bishop played the guitar on the programme and recalls Charles's anger at the time. In the grounds of one centre, when walking together the blind weren't even allowed to do what was natural, to hold hands – they had to hold each end of a piece of string instead.

Charles's honest determination to reply to everyone who wrote in after his programmes, however critical their views, reveals a typical agitated self-criticism. He had forgotten, he said, that programmes have to make an impact on a single hearing. He told Lee Farmer it was a pretty devastating failure on his part that the programme had been 'almost universally abominated' by the blind themselves. They 'misconstrued about every element', particularly the irony, and 'one of the most terrible revelations for me was the cultural deprivation of the blind.' He took some heart from a few letters of warm appreciation, thanking him for drawing attention to the RNIB's chronic reluctance to take up new ideas, and to their tendency to portray the blind as 'deaf and daft as well' so they can raise more money, the need for which dominated their thinking. The newly formed Midlands Long Cane Club thanked him for his 'tremendous help to blind people in their struggle for independence.' But his supporters were not the people who mattered. A month after the broadcast Porter, in a volte-face from his original enthusiasm, wrote to him with this devastating conclusion:

> The controller of Radio 4 is critical of Radio Ballad style programmes in general, not just *The Blind Set*. It's an expression of his own judgment but also his assessment of the ordinary listener's view. I share his opinion on both points and would welcome a curtailment of the use of MacColl and Miss Seeger in contexts where their contribution appears unnecessary. Why spoil the taste of beautiful home-grown lamb by smothering it with an artificial Spanish onion sauce?

That first sentence wounds Charles deeply – it's now clear that he will be prevented from making anything in the way he passionately wanted. He said of his programmes: 'Reality tends to be fairly uncomfortable. I am not giving information about experience so much as communicating the experience. This is very disturbing because you make demands on the listener.' He writes a tormented draft paper, expressing fierce arguments for the form's retention; they were asking him to:

> Renounce techniques that have produced the most widespread and impressive body of Radio Criticism since the war ... the ideal marriage of vernacular speech and traditional song ... On available budgets the only alternative is straight jour-

nalism. If this is what's expected of me, then I must ask for an official directive to this effect, and the abandonment of radio as a significant form of expression.

But he doesn't pursue it. From that date in late 1968, Charles is on borrowed time, and he has to fight for most of the programmes he makes. Some of them are broadcast in the Midlands only, effectively marginalising him. Many come in for internal criticism, and few receive a favourable audience reaction, though newspaper reviews continue to provide plenty of solace. However, no broadcast gets the kind of plaudits the Radio Ballads received, and Charles gets increasingly despondent. But he won't compromise, continuing to make programmes about contentious topics that set his BBC masters' collective teeth on edge, persisting with the use of traditional song, and defiantly doing without a narrator's voice whenever he can. Philip Donnellan was withering about the BBC's preference for authoritative commentary:

> What has evolved is the pattern of the Front Man, the quintessential Whickerwork figure which ... the Controllers find most useful in terms of programme control (you can eat your dinner while they drone on) ... The alternative, a rejection of the mediating godlet ... means programmes must be labelled 'a personal view'.

From 1968 Charles began to work with a brilliant young journalist from India, Dilip Hiro, now an eminent writer and Middle East expert. His 1967 article on Asian teenagers in Britain in *New Society* led to two half-hour radio programmes – one of which went out the night before the UK cabinet met urgently to discuss how to regulate the flow of Asian refugees from Kenya – and Charles went on to make more with him. For the aspiring Hiro, Charles was the ideal mentor in radio:

> He was a genius with sound, a true eccentric genius. The most highly attuned ear I've ever met. His hearing was so sensitive, yet visually he was almost blind. Did one documentary, I saw it, I thought the man has no visual sense. But I've never met anyone with an ear like his ... And for him it wasn't 9–5, it was a 24-hour job ... He booked a studio all day for a 30-minute programme, using Stuart Hall for linking. He'd spend half a day on the first five minutes, notice the time ... then he'd have a migraine attack, and – literally, I'm not joking – he'd lie down on the studio floor till it was over.

They went on to make programmes on meditation, on black views of whites in the USA and Britain, and *No Surrender*, which looked dispassionately – without an authorial voice – at the views of Catholics and Protestants in Londonderry before the violence really exploded there. Hiro said Charles held the fervent simplistic view that his programme could make the ordinary combatants see the light, since 'they were all working class, after all.' Radio critics usually regarded the Hiro/Parker broadcasts more highly than did the audience, whose ears and radios weren't as finely tuned as Charles's. David Wade in *The Times*, in a droll review of an early 1972 programme about students in India, summed up one prevailing view about late Parker:

> I'm glad to say that *Snowballs in Calcutta* was one of Charles Parker's more restrained … Not only did he employ a soft-spoken narrator … but it was possible to understand almost everything everyone said: some of them were even allowed to utter several sentences on the trot. Mr Parker likes to apply his colours. He is by temperament an action painter, and some of what lands on the canvas would have been better scraped off before showing; but for all the mannerisms and occasional excess I look forward to his programmes. They have a vitality and an interest which is none too plentiful.

Alas, he wasn't going to be able to hear many more. In 1969 came *Broadcasting in the Seventies*, a BBC document heatedly deplored by most of its own programme makers. In both radio and television, imaginative producers were being allowed progressively less latitude. They complained in a public letter signed by a roll-call of brilliant young talent: Tony Garnett, Ken Loach, James McTaggart, Kenith Trodd, Jim Allen, Roy Battersby, among others. Paul Fox, Controller BBC 1, slapped them down in a briskly candid reply:

> If you refuse to take our gentlemanly hints we shall censor or ban any of your programmes which deal in social and political attitudes not acceptable to us. The odd rebel may be allowed to kick over the traces occasionally. Providing this is an isolated event, and not part of a general movement, it only helps to preserve our liberal and independent image. But enough is enough.

In Birmingham *Broadcasting in the Seventies* provoked a strike, with Charles and Philip Donnellan in the vanguard of a resistance which would mark their cards (in that small space still unmarked). A BBC reconstruction the following spring removed Charles's job as a Senior Features Producer. He rejected a demeaning offer to work for *Woman's Hour* at a lower grade – this would be known as 'constructive dismissal' to a later generation. He was given a year's grace, working directly for a new Controller of Radio 4, the young Tony Whitby. That he was not a Parker enthusiast was an understatement: in particular he disliked Charles's setting of music against words. He was incandescent at the opening of *Snowballs in Calcutta* because Charles had laid music behind 'difficult' speech – if he can't follow it, what chance do ordinary listeners have? 'Do the Network Controller's views not matter a damn?' was Whitby's rhetorical question. Charles was obtuse on the matter – often he wouldn't give listeners an easy lead-in to programmes before their less well-tuned ears could lock on. Whitby gave him a formula:

Here is the recipe that has proved palatable. Take a subject of immediate importance in British or International affairs, select a manageable aspect of it and throw the rest away. Clean and chop into small pieces. Add a large measure of intelligence, a general dash of wit, a tongue and a little heart. Allow to marinate for 2–3 weeks and serve very cool.

Whitby had already upbraided Charles the previous month over *The Iron Box*, a powerful programme about the treatment in San Quentin prison of the 'Soledad Brother', George Jackson, mostly in Jackson's own words. After ten minutes Whitby had turned it off in disgust, which left him at a (temporary …) disadvantage when attacking it. Of all the later programmes that Charles produced – it was written by Godfrey Hodgson, later a distinguished journalist and writer – it had quite the best reviews. Here are extracts from two of them, first from Jeremy Rundall in the *Sunday Times*, then Wade again in the *The Times*, this time finding no fault:

Rundall: 'Brilliantly produced by Charles Parker … the description of the treatment of the black prisoners in solitary confinement, forced to live naked among their own excrement … recordings of Jackson's own voice, the screams of hysterical women … and the gentle if melancholic Blues music … added up to superb radio verité.'

Wade: 'No cries of bias or axes-to-grind will explain away Jackson's appeal, because it lay in the voice and feeling of the man. He told a tale of prison life that made your hair rise up … [after which] we heard the prison staff describe some more-or-less benevolent institute of correction. Both were San Quentin, and with all allowances stretched to breaking, there was no connection. In that gap the listener detected something infamous.'

That gap was what Charles liked to leave the listener himself to bridge. What made Charles so indignant was that Whitby was in his view such a philistine that he wasn't even prepared to make the effort to listen. To Hiro, Charles seemed set on a collision course, determined not to change direction. By the start of 1972 he already knew he was facing redundancy. That November, the letter almost sealed, his programme with Hiro about Sri Lankan terrorism called *Siege of Ceylon* was refused because Charles wouldn't have a voice of authority to 'authenticate' the sounds of torture. It's sadly ironic that his best remembered late work is the superb *Long March of Everyman*, an immense 26-week series, intended by Whitby to show that radio could match television's cultural blockbusters, its Clarks and Bronowskis. But it wasn't Parker's. Michael Mason, a Parker supporter, had produced it with the young historian Daniel Snowman. It set out to tell the history of Britain through old documents and letters, read out by ordinary people. Charles's job was to manage the recording process, advise the researchers, and scour the country for the 800 speakers. That the programme was criticised for having too much incidental sound – it was actually assembled in the BBC 'Radiophonic Workshop' – is the crowning irony: Whitby was forced to defend it.

Charles Parker was made to leave the BBC on 31 December 1972 after two years of unavailing resistance to a BBC management tier determined he should go. The news of his sacking angered many within the BBC, and triggered a question in the House of Commons, but the outrage gradually fizzled. (According to Hiro, it did have one beneficial effect on the BBC – the fuss dissuaded them from sacking Philip Donnellan, 'more dangerous because his programmes were on television'.) Donnellan called it 'a shameful episode in the catalogue of BBC stupidity and malice.' Some Parker supporters in the BBC assembled an engagingly scurrilous spoof about the sacking, which they secretly turned into a black vinyl record and smuggled onto every BBC in-tray they could. Gillian Reynolds in *The Guardian* wrote a supportive piece about Charles and 'his' Radio Ballads, inadvertently provoking protests from Ewan MacColl. Afterwards Charles continued to pitch ideas to the BBC as an independent, but they were rarely taken up. So Charles turned to his other interests: he had many, and they were waiting to consume him.

The zipped-up Charles Parker cartoon by Richard Yeend that accompanied the Gillian Reynolds article.

Re-education

His re-education in life had begun, as he afterwards stressed, with the tape recorder. Thanks, moreover, to hours of debate with Ewan MacColl, to the knowledgeable and articulate miners, and to his exposure to the deprivation of the poor and outcast of society, his political views underwent an almost total shift. His humanism, said Philip Donnellan, was a mixture of Christianity and Socialism, one committed to the cause of the underdog. The shift was consolidated when in 1964 he attended a Marxist study group under the brilliant intellectual George Thomson, professor of Greek at Birmingham University. George, the husband of Katharine Thomson, who supervised her Clarion Choir members in *Singing the Fishing*, had spent some years in the remote Blasket Islands off the Irish coast. He'd made a particular study of their persisting Gaelic culture, in which he found echoes of society 'before property ownership'.

This, like most of Thomson's views, appealed to Charles, now a long way from the man who was stunned by the defeat of Churchill in the Labour landslide of 1945. He became first an energetic Marxist, then after the Sino-Soviet split of the 1960s he joined Thomson, MacColl and Peggy Seeger on the Maoist side of the fence. But Thomson, like Ewan, was an atheist, and this Charles found much harder to deal with. He had held off Ewan's arguments and sarcasm through the Radio Ballad years. 'Say a prayer for an old sinner, Charlie', from a smoking Ewan to a praying Charles, as they dossed down in a twin-bedded room after a long day's recording. But Thomson's subtle questioning was tougher to refute. Ian Campbell recalled an occasion at the Thomsons as far back as 1961 when Charles's belief in God was put to the test. Ian mimicked his anguished pacing:

> There we were at Katharine Thomson's house having a discussion, while out in the garden was the gardener, frail little old man, balding, came in, tatty pair of old flannels – of course it was George Thomson. Charles was pontificating. He was putting Ewan in his place about atheism. George came in to get a cup of tea. 'Very interesting' – he never made a positive statement – all he did was ask questions. 'Does that mean you believe...?' Bluster, flannel. 'Then how does that equate with what you said earlier?' Went on for about an hour. Ewan was looking at me – Ewan was not participating in this. Nobody in their right mind would interrupt George Thomson, one of the greatest minds in the world. So gentle, so hesitant about it. 'Well in that case...' Charles was pacing up and down. 'Oh for Christ's sake, George, I can't <u>disprove</u> it, but I <u>know</u> you're wrong.' He was never the same. Within six months – he was no longer a churchgoer. Had become active in the Labour party – active in CND. I don't think he stopped believing in God. I think he stops believing in the Christian church. The argument was about to what extent organised religion was responsible for wars. Of course George said God is a concept vitally needed by people, which is why we invented him – in our image.

Philip Donnellan illustrated this wrestling match between Religion and Communism by quoting from one of the scores of sixpenny notebooks Charles used, this from 1957: 'By the Grace of God I might do a tiny bit to move us as a people in the right direction … but how to avoid embracing communism as the only logical end of a growing concern for and understanding of the common man's potential?' He resolved his dilemma ultimately by deciding Jesus was 'the only true communist', and finally he came down to: 'The Church is a fantastic distortion of Christ's teachings. The communist party is I suspect of Karl Marx's doctrines, The Labour Party of the Webbs, The Bach Society of what Bach himself stood for…' So it was a plague on all your houses, and especially the BBC, who had fired in him a vision of public service broadcasting, then left him to pursue it as they chased viewing figures. Then fired him. Philip Donnellan, writing of his BBC masters, said:

> Incapable of fathoming the humanity of his technical ideas and arguments, unresponsive to the political implications and apparently quite unfitted to offer competent editorial guidance as to how the ideas could be more effectively communicated, they rejected the material and slammed him into a drawer labelled 'Expensive nuisances sub-category Marxist' and turned the key.

Life Outside the BBC

At the same time as he was taking part in George Thomson's study group, Charles was running a class on folk music at the Workers' Educational Association (WEA) in Birmingham. He hadn't lectured before, and he wasn't an academic, so at first he 'struggled to articulate his ideas', said Trevor Fisher, one of the eager young WEA group who found him inspiring. To Fisher, Charles was engaged in a war on imported American culture and pop music. 'Unlike a conventional lecturer he had no set body of knowledge, ideas or skills which he was seeking to criticise or impart.' He used the classes and a set of young enthusiasts to build up a thesis through polemic and argument, and they thrived on his inclusive approach. The culture he wanted to spread was one based on traditional song and true vernacular speech. He was confident enough after a while to propose that he front a series he'd planned with Ewan MacColl on British folk music, past and present, to be called *The Song Carriers*. In the event his boss felt it better that Ewan should introduce the series, which he did in a typically fluent style but with an atypically 'cultured' voice. It ran for 14 weeks in the winter and spring of 1964–5, overlapping with Charles's six-part *Landmarks* series, and each week's 45-minute programme was eagerly awaited by the new generation of aspiring folk singers, some of whom took part. To Charles's chagrin, though, it was only broadcast on BBC Midlands, not that it put off the enthusiasts. Karl Dallas cheered him up when asking him to write an article for his *Folk Music* magazine:

> I think the *Song Carriers* is bloody marvellous, and only wish it could be picked up more easily down here. A small group of keen young revivalists meets here every Thursday huddled round a radio tuned to BBC Midland: the atmosphere is rather like members of the Maquis tuning in to London during the war.

From this point on, Charles never seemed to stop. In practice he achieved increasingly more outside the BBC than he did inside it. His dedication to exploring folk music grew, inspired and reinforced by Ewan and Peggy's new 'Critics Group' in Beckenham. He would flog the car down there from Birmingham every week to take part. It led him to invite members of the local folk clubs to his home and to set up the Birmingham and Midlands Folk Centre. Out of this at Ewan's suggestion came the Grey Cock folk club, which began in 1967 at the Roebuck pub in Birmingham – 'Attracting a rag bag of anarchists, liberals and lefties and lots of young people like myself,' says Dave Rogers, 'with no firm political affiliation at all.' He was one of the Grey Cock habitués who began the experimental Banner Theatre. Charles's lectures 'blew his mind' with its mixture of politics, singing, ballad analysis and folk theatre, and soon helped to give Rogers that firm political affiliation.

Charles's enthusiasm for radical community theatre had been set back by the collapse of Centre 42. But it had been whetted again by his participation in the *Festival of Fools* (to be explored in the next chapter), which was a Grey Cock annual highlight – they used to take two coachloads down to London each year. The Grey Cock group had put together a number of projects based on folk song. *The Funny Rigs of Good and Tender-hearted Masters* used rediscovered songs from an early 19th-century strike of Kidderminster carpet weavers. *Of One Blood* was a powerful piece Charles assembled about racism. The shows were semi-staged in the folk club tradition, with little 'stage' as such, and an ethos of audience participation. This evolved into Banner Theatre more-or-less by accident. In 1973 Charles was struggling to fill the final slot in a series of folk evenings when Rhoma Bowdler suggested they do a staged version of *The Big Hewer*.

Rhoma Bowdler was a Shirley Valentine figure, an orphan who had left school at 13, by then a single mother with three children. She had been a 30-year-old comptometer operator when she went on a course on the 'New Maths' to help her youngest, and there discovered a latent appetite, first for learning, then for teaching. By 1973 she was an uninhibited drama and dance teacher, running an evening class in Martha Graham dance, and exploring the use of Commedia del'Arte methods. She'd learned Laban techniques at college, and had to drill the untutored Grey Cock singers, 'to get them from one side of the stage to the other without falling over.' She constructed a piece from the *Big Hewer* script and mounted it for a single night. Dave Rogers described *Collier Laddie* at the outset as a 'fairy-light production politically – it focused somewhat nostalgically on comradeship and craft pride in the industry.' (Later Ewan wrote some new material for them to toughen it up, reflecting the miners' growing militancy of the early 1970s.) But it still faithfully reproduced the sections on the dole, disasters and dust, and it was such a great success before an invited group of miners – some of them friends Charles had made on *Big Hewer* – that they were invited to tour South Wales with it. It was well received there, in an echo of Theatre Workshop's tours of 20 years earlier.

Banner Theatre

By now Charles had left the BBC. He divided his 1970's life between teaching, folk music and Banner Theatre – while constantly doing favours for anyone who asked. Though he was one of Banner's main instigators, and was very much the group's elder statesman and inspiration, he was aged well over 50 in a company most of whom were much younger. Their productions were painstakingly assembled by the group, though it took them a while to get Charles's persistent point about actuality, about using the words of real people and not constructing their words for them. Dave Rogers, who has been in Banner's engine room ever since:

> I couldn't understand when we first started what Charles was on about with actuality, and it wasn't until I got out and started recording some … that it actually made any impact. It seemed a rather quaint idea.

In 1976 Banner mounted a show about the 'battle' of Saltley Gate, a Midlands gas and coke plant that had held a huge reserve of coal during the 1972 miners' strike. The miners belatedly realised that Saltley was preventing the strike from really biting. The energetic young militant leader Arthur Scargill promptly deployed 400 of his new 'flying pickets', supported within a few days by up to 10,000 Birmingham workers. Their action forced the Gates of Saltley to close, and three weeks later the Conservative government of Ted Heath capitulated. In 1974 Scargill actually brought it down, in the heady days of worker power before new trades union laws and the Margaret Thatcher government broke the miners ten years later.

Saltley Gate set the pattern for the typical Banner show, based closely on Radio Ballad methods but using visuals as well. In this case the interviews had already been obtained by Charles Parker and others for a potential project that the BBC wouldn't countenance. After a painstaking transcription process the script and songs were put together by a group that included Charles, Rhoma, Dave Rogers and his wife Chris. It took the form of a series of games between workers and the forces of law and order, starting with a polite cricket match and ending with American football that becomes a pitched battle. The lines were given to performers who remained 'anonymous' so it was clear they were retelling the words of real people. The performance began with singers on a rudimentary stage, joined gradually by actors from the audience. Commentary was provided by a combination of slide backdrop, a jester figure, and a simple narrative linking song written by Rogers in MacColl style:

> In Birmingham City at five in the morning
> The streets are deserted, the air it is chill.
> A mile from the lights of the brash city centre
> The scarred face of Saltley is silent and still …
>
> … It's six in the morning, a cold Sunday morning,
> The bus stops deserted, no rush to clock in.
> A clatter of working boots shatters the silence:
> In Saltley a battle's about to begin.

At the end of the play the performers enter en masse from the back of the hall and encourage the audience to join their march onto the stage, singing:

> A solid wall are we
> Close the gates, close the gates,
> Our strength is unity,
> Close the gates!
> No power in the land can gain the upper hand
> When we united stand,
> Close the gates,
> When we united stand,
> Close the gates.

Strong simple stuff to stir the soul, and to summon the audience up onto the stage. The folk club ethos out of which Banner was born encouraged this audience participation and made *Saltley Gate* a popular show in Birmingham and on tour. And, knowingly or not (Rogers says not), it contained all the elements of the early agitprop theatre that Ewan MacColl and Joan Littlewood had pioneered before and after the war. Earlier, Banner had performed an agitprop show in support of imprisoned building workers, *The Shrewsbury Three*. They even did it on a train journey taking workers to a mass rally in London, playing extracts in every carriage in turn. The next year Rhoma Bowdler and the other women in the group mounted a women-only show,

Womankind. Between then and 1980 *The Great Divide* described racism in England; *Dr Healey's Casebook* attacked public sector cuts; *On the Brink* highlighted the troubled Midlands car industry; *Steel* fought closures in another declining British industry. *Steel* was their first production to use professional actors after Banner (praise be) had received some funding. Until then they were entirely amateur, though, like Theatre of Action, as professional as they could be in their approach.

Charles Parker played his part in these productions, though as an actor his part was almost always the authority figure, often from the police. He was dying to portray working-class figures, but was typecast by his voice and his gravitas. He helped to develop the shows when he could, and as with *Festival of Fools* finalised its soundtrack. Not just the sound either. Rhoma Bowdler:

> I don't know if I ought to tell you this … We wanted to use slides, you see … well Philip [Donnellan], he was doing the mining for television and he'd had a helicopter … so he could do some aerial shots of South Wales – and the camera hadn't been fixed properly … it was all shaky so he couldn't use it. We broke into, well, didn't break into the BBC. Charlie knew the bloke on the door … We went to this studio and we transferred the film onto slides and we were there all night. But you see, you'd start to do one thing, like the transfer, and then Charles would see something … which you knew was going to be of interest, but he couldn't resist making it there and then, editing, cutting it. Frame by frame. For hours. And hours and hours and hours.

Charles was by now over 60, living with Rhoma, and living as ever at a furious pace. His enthusiasm for Banner, and inclination to lecture for anyone who asked, often unpaid, wasn't helping his finances. After his marriage break-up he had signed his barely sufficient BBC pension over to Phyl, and of course was extremely concerned to make sure that he did right by her and their children. His financial affairs became a quagmire, one which Trevor Fisher waded through over a lengthy holiday, sorting out several years of unfiled tax returns for him. The only regular income was from teaching. Once a week for over ten years Charles set out before dawn for London to lecture on Radio to Tony Schooling's media classes at the School of Communication at the Polytechnic of Central London. His students there were split: he either bowled them over, or alienated them by his vehement dislike of pop music. Tony Schooling:

> I like teaching … it is even better if you can get a genius to do it for you … For me all this began in 1969 [at the BBC]. Charles Parker came to give a morning's lecture on Actuality. As so often happened with Charles, about half the members of the course saw a great light, including me: that morning I discovered I knew nothing. And about half were disturbed, discomfited, didn't see the point, and

what they saw they didn't like. Fierce discussion went on all through the lunch hour ... There are few who are neutral about the ideas and the programmes of Charles Parker.

He got up before 5 am as usual on the morning of 7 December 1980 to drive to London for his weekly lecture for Tony Schooling. Back after lunch, he had a meeting with Dave Rogers on Banner matters, then onto an evening rehearsal of *Steel*. Afterwards he was coming back from a meeting in a nearby pub when he called out that he couldn't see. Rhoma called an ambulance and followed it to the hospital in the car. 'And I took his boots with me, ridiculous. I had no idea of the seriousness of it.' She phoned Dave Rogers – 'If anyone brings him a typewriter I'll kill them' – and asked him to tell Charles's wife Phyl. Next morning Rhoma had to be at school for a crucial meeting. 'Dave and Pete [Yates] came over. I didn't know about his dying till then. I was so angry. He could never say no to anybody about anything.' He'd died of an aneurism. Later that same day John Lennon was shot. When Melvyn Bragg was asked a few weeks later which figure most important to him had died in 1980 he said Charles Parker, a brilliant innovator who had died unheeded. Michael Mason described him as:

> A real creative genius in radio, a passionately romantic radical, acutely sensitive to oral history. His editor's razor blade was like a sculptor's chisel, releasing the hidden poets in people.

Anne Karpf:

> Some people reckon that the decline of the BBC began when Charles Parker was edged out of broadcasting in a cravenly bureaucratic fashion and the whole innovative flowering of radio came to an end.

CHAPTER 21

Ballads of Accounting
Ewan MacColl and Peggy Seeger, 1964–89

> Aince mair the poet's fa'en swack
> And noo lies flat upon his back
> In Bromley hospice
> Whaur a' day, weel-faured sonsie lasses play
> At piercing him wi' lang syringes,
> And greet each new series of twinges
> Wi' eldritch laughter,
> And stroke the patient's head thereafter
> While thinking up new ploys
> And cantraips fresh
> Tae execute on his poor flesh,
> And here comes that auld wife Mistress Dracula
> The deevil's dam for mair o' my blood.
> Here, tak aff your dram.
>
> EWAN MACCOLL, ON A POSTCARD TO BRUCE DUNNET,
> WRITTEN FROM HIS HOSPITAL BED AS HE AWAITED HIS LAST
> OPERATION, 12 OCT 1989, TEN DAYS BEFORE HE DIED

Four weeks before Charles Parker died he wrote to Ewan MacColl and Peggy Seeger in praise of their new album *Kilroy Was Here*. 'I am at a loss for words as I always am when I try to express what all of us owe to you both.' Charles had admired Ewan from the moment they met, so amazed was he by Ewan's talents. In consequence Charles castigated himself severely after a forthright article by Gillian Reynolds appeared in his support in *The Guardian* in November 1972, as news was emerging of his sacking by the BBC. The article unintentionally raised Ewan's hackles by referring to Charles Parker's Radio Ballads, and occasional further occurrences in the years to come would generate more tension.

This wording was unfortunate, if understandable. It was all part of the campaign to persuade the BBC not to sack him, and radio reviewers then as now tended to cite the producer of programmes rather than the writer, as to a notorious extent do film reviewers, for whom writers seem not to exist. Charles needed all the support he could get. He was at a low ebb at the end of 1972, but so too was Ewan. Peggy – and it had taken a long time for her own crucial contribution to be credited – wrote to Charles on Ewan's behalf. Charles apologised promptly in letters published in two broadsheet newspapers, saying that if any one person deserved the plaudits for the Radio Ballads' success it was Ewan, but the damage had been done.

Ewan felt wounded – it was the second time he had been written out of history. The eventual success of Theatre Workshop after it settled down in East London had been built on the years of drive, energy, writing and ideas he had put into radical theatre with Joan Littlewood after they met in 1934. But now it was Joan's Theatre, and he had been forgotten. Now it was happening again. Just as Charles had put years into the BBC, only to see it eventually spurn his ideas, vision and methods, so Ewan had with the theatre. Now in 1972 he was recovering from seeing yet another imaginative venture founder – the Critics Group. This had brought him via folk music back to the theatre. It had begun in 1965 when he and Peggy were asked to provide study sessions for young aspiring folk singers. It was soon a superb weekly training ground in singing, songwriting and performance, but in early 1972 it had broken up with such acrimony that Ewan was, in Peggy's words, totally devastated. Its misjudged title referred to self-criticism, but by outsiders it wasn't seen that way.

The Critics Group

The folk revival that had begun in the mid 1950s was alive and thriving ten years after the Radio Ballad period ended. Ewan and Peggy had been running their successor to the Ballads and Blues, the Singers Club, since 1961. They had become virtuoso performers in great demand all over the country and in North America, giving concerts that were rigorously rehearsed and studiously staged. The combination of Ewan's voice and Peggy's musicianship was compellingly powerful. Moreover, they constantly researched, collected songs in the folk idiom new and old, and tried to find the 'right' way to sing them to do justice to their often unknown writers. They consistently sold out venues, they had a wide and widening repertoire, and they kept a record of what they sang and where, so their listeners kept hearing fresh material. If you go round folk clubs today people seem always able to remember when they first heard Ewan and Peggy, and what they sang, and which songs lifted the hairs on the back of the neck.

They were professional in the best sense of the word. But every movement which develops passionate adherents splits sooner or later, and the folk revival was no exception. Ewan became increasingly keen to focus on Britain's native folk song heritage. Always determined to stave off an American cultural takeover, he was irritated by the number of young singers affecting American accents (as he too had done before he saw the light). One evening in 1960 Peggy laughed so much at a Londoner singing Leadbelly's 'Rock Island Line' at the Ballads and Blues club that members of the audience got cross with her. This led to a vigorous debate that went on for weeks, ending when the club's members voted for a rule that singers there could only perform songs from their own nation's heritage. It applied only on their club's stage – of course you could sing what you like in other clubs or the bath.

Peggy is at pains to point out that this policy was not unilaterally decided by Ewan, as many people outside the club assumed. But because he was of Scots parentage and English upbringing, Ewan, of course, could sing from both cultures with impunity, which did nothing to soothe those who were affronted by the restriction. Hadn't music always ignored national boundaries, as Ewan, Bert Lloyd and the other researchers discovered? Ewan would often appear arrogant, and could easily alienate those whose enjoyment of singing was destroyed by criticism, or – worse – by being casually dismissed or ignored. Soon the folk world was divided into those who mocked Ewan and Peggy as the High Priests of the folk revival, and those who regarded them as quite brilliant, streets ahead of their rivals, and agreed with their insistence on instilling a professional approach. Why must folk music be so amateurish, when no other branch of music was? Why shouldn't singers train their voices as musicians did their instruments, for style and feeling as well as accuracy? Ken Hall, inviting them to be the first guests at a new folk venue in Bradford in February 1969, was first disconcerted, then impressed:

> First of all they sent a contract, which stipulated two straight-backed chairs and a stage. A stage? Well, we cobbled one together out of beer crates. They were the first folk singers I'd seen doing strenuous vocal exercises before they began. And they wouldn't start without dead silence. But what performers.

After their second son Calum was born in 1963, Ewan and Peggy invited the young folk singer Sandra Kerr to provide live-in childcare in exchange for musical tuition. Betsy Miller was nearly 80 by now, and though her mind and tongue were as sharp as ever – Peggy said, 'We got on when we weren't living together. We lived together for 16 years' – she couldn't cope much longer with two children when their parents were touring. They were away one night a week on average through the 1960s, as well as late at the regular weekly Singers Club sessions. Their workshops were increasingly popular. Sandra was bright and keen, and, with other singers eager to learn, the Critics Group was formed in Beckenham late in 1963. Young singers were given long reading lists, exercises in warming-up, voice production and Stanislavskian methods of approaching a performance, and above all learned to think about the origins of what they were singing. After an energetic singing and songwriting career Sandra Kerr now lectures on the only Folk and Traditional Music degree course in England, at Newcastle:

> Ewan was just amazing. I'd never met anyone who was so well read, who talked politics and literature and art and philosophy at the drop of a hat ... I know I couldn't do my job now anything like as well if I hadn't been in the Critics Group. The stuff they passed on to me, the ways of working, of sourcing material, looking at ballads – things he brought from Theatre Workshop ... like the Laban theory. He translated that into vocal terms and I still use it today with my students. I am working with second year students – they are collecting actuality from their grandparents ... the stories are extraordinary.

One of Sandra's own experiences illustrates what Ewan called 'The application and the idea of IF'. Imagine yourself as the original writer of a traditional song. You can't truly convince when singing a song about a seduced and murdered woman unless you can work yourself into it. As Peggy describes it:

> Sandra brought a problem to the meeting. She loved 'The Gypsy Laddie' but she was getting tired of it ... Ewan then launched into a ten-minute biography of the girl – it was all out of his imagination and it was like a short story ... he literally brought her alive, gave her a social class, clothes, feelings, hair colour, hopes and ambitions. Then all of a sudden he turned to Sandra and said, If you were that girl, how would you sing 'The Gypsy Laddie'? She immediately began to sing and it was electrifying. When she finished we all sat there, stunned. She'd never sung that way before. After a short silence Ewan began on another story. This time he described the girl but with *different* given circumstances. Instead of being poor she was rich. Instead of being young and lovely, she was older and disillusioned and plain. He spent another ten minutes on this new scenario and it was just as gripping and <u>detailed</u> (the detail is <u>always</u> important) as the first story.

Then he stopped and asked Sandra again: If you were that girl, how would you sing it? Damn me if Sandra didn't do it again. She floored us – and the song was quite different, had a whole new feel, a whole new aura surrounding it. Ewan did it twice more ... Sandra came through almost in a state of shock herself. She certainly wasn't bored by 'The Gypsy Laddie' any more.

Some of the first Critics Group 'students', like Gordon McCulloch and Luke Kelly (later of the Dubliners) had left early. They found it impossible to cope with the criticism, especially McCulloch when it was made publicly in the *Song Carriers* radio series. 'I didn't agree with him. Why did I have to take it?' Those that stayed largely agreed with Brian Pearson, that: 'It was compelling, enormously exciting. I learned an incredible lot. Ewan was the most extraordinary charismatic kind of person, he could talk ... absolutely beautifully.' A fierce taskmaster but generous with his time, blunt with his criticism but delighted by a good performance, Ewan was passionately determined that his young charges should bring the music of their past to life. He wanted them to share his vision of the world, so he added political classes. They were keen to learn, quick on the uptake, and they soon inspired him to resuscitate his latent first love – theatre.

Festival of Fools

In 1964 Ewan was asked to write a piece to celebrate the Co-operative Movement at the Theatre Royal Drury Lane, and although it only played once the multimedia show he produced restored his appetite. Within a short time he had the Critics Group performing and touring with his version of a mediaeval mumming play, with St George on a Harley-Davidson. The motorcycle motif recurs in the *Romeo and Juliet* for schools radio which followed it. The play, directed by Ewan and produced by Charles, was set in the East End of London among rival used-car dealers. The play uses modern language, its dialogue improvised in Critics Group sessions, and Romeo dies in a motorbike crash. Ewan wrote songs that included the lyrical 'Sweet Thames Flow Softly', and the result was much admired by teachers of working-class children for whom Shakespeare had hitherto seemed entirely irrelevant. From there they moved on to a New Year show, which ran most winters from 1965–6 to 1971–2, the *Festival of Fools*.

The show drew its inspiration from the mediaeval tradition of celebration at New Year. It tracked the past year's events month by month. The first attempt was tentative, but the performers (all initially amateurs) threw themselves into it with such gusto and growing skill that it became ever more elaborate and professionally drilled. Backstage support came from Singers Club volunteers canvassed each September. Ewan wrote the songs and skits from ideas assembled by the group from newspaper cuttings through the year. He directed, Peggy directed the music, scheduled rehearsals and as ever managed the masses of detail, while Charles, an assiduous participant in the Critics Group despite his full-time job and the long journey, went to town on the sound effects with his usual zeal. The early shows were variable, with 1967–8 severely criticised in *The Guardian*, but once it got into its stride the show always sold out, and its audiences were as passionate as its performers. It was expertly done, high speed and funny, unashamedly pro working class, anti-American, anti-capitalism, and the like-minded audience lapped it up. Peggy loved the shows, describing it as one of the four great things in her life (with falling in love, her children, and the Radio Ballads):

> All this was presented in the spacious function room of The New Merlin's Cave, a pub on Margery Street near King's Cross. We had three stages in this rectangular room: one tiny one in the corner, one larger one in the centre, and the third being the high formal stage at the end of the room. Every available space between these stages was taken up by chairs, 170 of them, set without a spare half-inch between them and always filled. Between the stages and between areas of the audience there were very narrow aisles along which the actors would run, dance, leap in the dark, always aware that someone's bag, pint or foot might send us sprawling. Often you had to run these aisles just after the lights had gone out, before your eyes got used to the dark – we'd practise running them with our eyes closed, counting the steps that took us from here to there, from there to there. Step down off Stage Three, then six stride steps and two stairs up onto Stage Two, manoeuvre past two chairs and a table in five steps, down two stairs on the other side, four stride steps to the four stairs of Stage Three, two small steps and sit down in your chair in typing position: I had ten seconds in which to do that run – in the dark.

At its best it had a surreal brilliance. The *Parsley, Sage and Politics* radio series by Mary Orr and Michael O'Rourke about Ewan and Peggy includes two sketches which illustrate it. The first picks up a news story about 'The Battle for the Smallest Room in the House', five companies competing for the toilet paper market. This becomes a 20-minute opera set in a Gents' lavatory, an exposition of monopoly capitalism performed by a row of business men in bowler hats at a urinal. Excuse for a scatological rhyme and pun fest:

> We've worked out the logistics and have accurate statistics
> In relation to the nation's pattern of evacuation.
> We have certain fundamental information …
>
> In this tight little island, and the Republic of Ireland,
> There are fifty eight million souls. Arseholes.
> All members are equal in matters so faecal …

Less flippant but even more surreally funny is a sketch that begins 'Once upon a time in the land of Groat Grooting Brit'. It was written with the kind of Joycean wordplay that a few years before had been popularised by Stanley Unwin – a Birmingham radio man who had worked with Charles Parker – and by John Lennon. A virtuoso monologue depicting ordinary people as nut gatherers, it was delivered like a children's bedtime story by Brian Pearson. Threaded into a dazzling Parker soundtrack that uses every sound trick in the book, it takes Britain from the origins of capitalism through its colonial empire (Oompah Oompah), via war, freedom movements, the devaluation of the (nut) currency, the rise of Armoricar, to the Vietnam War, waged against an enemy so ignorant of the rules that it doesn't know when it's beaten. Pearson was a natural as the *Festival of Fools* narrator:

> Ewan ran an efficient ship. It had to be – it was very complex, a tight timescale, all sorts of difficulties putting the show on … Charles produced the sound effects, quite complicated. It was in a nondescript London pub, with three stages, all that lighting, really elaborate. We bypassed the fuse box with six-inch nails, amazing the whole place didn't go up … all those chairs jammed in.

For Ewan it was 1940's *Last Edition* revisited. Young enthusiasts becoming slick exponents of radical theatre, espousing the causes he remained passionate about: the Vietnam war, apartheid and racism, nuclear weapons, the gap between rich and poor inherent in a capitalist system. As with most sketch shows – such as *That Was The Week That Was* (1962–4) and *Monty Python's Flying Circus* (1969–74) – the content was highly variable. Pearson: 'Some rubbish got through but the best bits were wonderful.' Attending it became a favoured relaxation for the many West End actors who tended to agree with its politics. Billie Whitelaw, Harry H Corbett and Nana Mouskouri were regulars, but few theatre critics deigned to come. This was before the London Fringe, so there was no *Time Out* to publicise it to mainstream theatregoers. Joan Littlewood overcame her irritation at Ewan's departure from Theatre Workshop to visit and approve. (Success had inevitably forced Theatre Workshop to become 'safer'. It was now partly funded by West End transfers so it had to respond to the critics, and the salary gap meant that company stalwarts like Corbett, George A Cooper and Richard Harris constantly moved on. Its strengths were being diluted.) Peggy looked back on the period like this:

> We got … actors and producers from the conventional theatre establishments, as well as some of the Theatre Workshop people, Ewan's old cronies. In fact, Ewan ran the Critics Group … as if it were a formal theatre troupe … He attended and scrutinised every single performance. He sat taking notes at the little bar while Calum sat clapping his hands and giving impromptu cues. Calum was four years

old and he would sit on the counter of the sound/lighting bar, rooted to the action. During one pregnant, dark silence in between sequences, his little voice piped up: 'You don't know what's going to happen next, but I do!' Then ... we would get those notes. My, would we get those notes! We had to sit, scripts in hand and take whatever he handed out. There was no debate, no defence, no excuse. He laced into Jim for milking his speech, into Pat for walking too slowly, into me for a wrong pace of song, into Sandra, into John, into Bob, into the chorus singers for messy cadences ... nobody ever escaped with a bad or tired performance and the show got better and better. The *Festival* was often so good by the time the run ended that we all felt that we should be moving it to a proper theatre and making it available to a lot of people ... but of course, we always took it off and started on our next venture: a recording, a series of clubs, a new look at some vocal style or other.

Those who stayed in the Group year after year were totally dedicated. I have often wondered how all those who had 9–5 jobs managed it ... getting up at 6, to work by 9, working till 5, travelling out to Beckenham or to Kings Cross by 7, working till 10.30 or 11, getting home by midnight, then starting the whole thing over again ... for two or three months. As each sequence rolled off Ewan's typewriter ... I'd make copies, make sure everyone had their parts, arrange a rehearsal schedule, arrange the music, train the musicians, get the singers to all sing exactly together – and on the recitatives, many of them out of the folk song style, that was murder. Our kids saw very little of us during those months, September till the end of February – for the *Festival* usually ran from the beginning of January for six or seven weeks.

It's unfortunate that the death of the Critics Group is perhaps better known than its life. Brian Pearson: 'That's the kind of thing that happens. Ewan acquires a family, trains them, and then is amazed that they want to leave home. But there were so many spin-offs for everyone.' Frankie Armstrong: 'The rhetoric was of democratic sharing and communal ideas, but ... he was in charge – he was keen to have all our ideas but he would do the writing. He was a genius ... and a great critic, but he couldn't take criticism himself.' Like many impassioned idealists of the Left (or anywhere), Ewan found it difficult to cede or share control, and in particular to accept criticism of some of his over-long sketches. Comic writing is often best done by more than one person, so variable is our sense of humour – Muir/Norden, Galton/Simpson, Feldman/Took, the Python team – and they do seem to need a screening process. (Spike Milligan as ever excepted.)

At the beginning of 1971 Ewan suffered a severe bout of depression. An exhausting year of touring at home and abroad in 1970 had been followed by the best ever *Festival of Fools*. But during the run, on his 56th birthday, there began the health problems that would dog him for the rest of his life. It shook him. He took stock, for once looked at himself critically, and decided he needed to devolve control of the Critics Group. He wanted to turn it into a professional revolutionary theatre group in the immediately post-war Theatre Workshop mould. He left the group to plan it while he took several months off everything but performing, for which he could always psych himself up. While he often didn't like what his erstwhile students came up with, they clearly enjoyed the independence. Though he and Peggy still kept up a demanding touring schedule in 1971, he decided not to risk the huge annual effort of preparing *Festival of Fools*, so it became largely a compilation of their best sketches. The strains began to tell, and at the end of the run the Critics Group collapsed in a rancorous heap. Many of the group went off to form a lively but short-lived East End experiment in co-operative theatre, Combine, before disappearing into new lives – sadder, wiser, and infinitely more skilled and knowledgeable.

Ewan retreated, nursing a sense of betrayal tempered with annoyance at his own shortcomings. The great theatre project had evaporated, but 1972 became an unsuspected watershed year for the family. In April and May Roberta Flack's version of Ewan's 'The First Time Ever' topped the US singles charts for six weeks. Within a year it had sold a million copies and the royalties made the family financially secure – for the first time ever. They bought a new car and a holiday cottage in Galloway in Scotland. In December Peggy gave birth to Kitty, who had to sleep on the dining room table because they were short of space. Betsy was still with them, with her own room in their two-floor flat in a large suburban house, but they never considered moving.

After his great creative period from 1957–70, Ewan now took an almost complete break from writing during the 1970s, returning to it at intervals when the spirit – or a Cause – moved him. Their performing schedule slackened a little, but the illness failed to diminish the power of his performances. Against the backdrop of a fading folk revival, Ewan and Peggy still often filled the clubs wherever they went, at a rate of nearly a show a week. Those who saw them in that period describe them as highly professional, courteous, encouraging and approachable, generous with their time and especially with their song archive in Beckenham. Twice in the 1970s they made successful tours of Australia. However, between the second at the start of 1979 and a projected American tour that May, Ewan began to suffer the health problems that would debilitate his last ten years. He had a heart attack in Italy in 1982, and another in America in 1984. They hadn't stopped travelling abroad – he sang in America again in 1986 and in East Berlin in 1988 – but his increasing physical fragility was making foreign tours perilous, though his vocal power barely diminished. All those years of heavy smoking, though he'd now stopped, were offset by the rigorous daily voice training.

In place of new creative writing came a series of projects that didn't tax him too severely. From 1971–3 he and Peggy worked with Philip Donnellan on television versions of three of the Radio Ballads (Chapter 23). Their record making didn't slow down either – from 1971–89 they produced nearly one a year, the same rate as before. Many were for their own new label, Blackthorne, recorded in the studio they constructed at home in Beckenham. In 1977 they published their long research into *Travellers' Songs from England and Scotland*, a real family effort in which the children took part (echoes of Peggy's childhood, if not the laborious transcription). They went on to publish *Till Doomsday in the Afternoon* (the title based on a quote by Belle Stewart from *Travelling People*), about a travelling family, the Stewarts of Blairgowrie.

Ewan made a brief return to playwriting. In early 1982 John McGrath of the radical theatre group 7:84 decided to incorporate *Johnny Noble* in a season of 'Clydebuilt' plays in Glasgow in early 1982. Directed by David Scase (who had played the lead in the original Theatre Workshop production which came to Glasgow in October 1945), it featured the young Scots singer Dick Gaughan singing the first narrator. This was Ewan's old part, and Gaughan managed to control his alarm when he found the original, his hero, sitting in the front row on the first night. A play set in the unemployed 1930s but playing in Margaret Thatcher's Britain, with steelworkers' livelihoods under pressure and the miners being lined up next, it was illustrated by the simple early songs that Ewan had later dismissed:

> In Durham County it is the same,
> The pithead gear is standing still,
> And men are filled with a sense of shame
> For idle hands and wasted skill.

Originally a BBC writer who had scripted some of the episodes of the influential *Z Cars* series, John McGrath had met Ewan when part of Arnold Wesker's original Centre 42 group. McGrath was a man after Ewan's heart, a communist Scot producing radical theatre in Glasgow for 7:84. Named because then 7 per cent of the population owned 84 per cent of Britain's wealth – figures that have barely changed since – it had helped to jump-start a political theatre that had been more-or-less stalled since the touring Theatre Workshop had settled in 1953. The prolific 'Fringe' theatre that we now take for granted had started in Britain at the end of the 1960s with groups like People Show, Portable Theatre, Welfare State International. In those years of student protest, a key factor was the abolition of censorship on stage in 1968, for no longer did companies have to submit scripts for scrutiny, and they could improvise with impunity. McGrath's 7:84 began in 1971, Charles Parker initiated the amateur Banner theatre two years later, and political and community theatre took off.

On and off, Ewan had been working on a play about an ageing sea captain made redundant by the switch from sail to steam, based on Ben Bright, an old mariner they had interviewed at length. Gratified and encouraged by the restaging of *Johnny Noble*, Ewan joined 7:84's board and finished the play, *Shore Saints and Sea Devils*. Although turned down by McGrath (as were two other of Ewan's plays which he modified and submitted) it played at the Library Theatre Manchester in late 1983 with David Scase in the lead. Ewan described it in *Journeyman* as 'Quite the best thing I have ever done.' However, reviews were mixed: Robin Thornber in *The Guardian* called it 'One of the most powerful plays I've seen for years [but] ... becalmed in the doldrums of its own verbosity.' If Ewan had written it in the Theatre Workshop days Joan Littlewood would have briskly sorted that out. Indeed, she ventured from her vagabond retirement to see it, liked the central premise, but was typically brusque about its shortcomings: 'I could put it right in a week.' But Ewan was a soloist now, no longer part of a theatre company.

Disheartened by the intimations of his mortality at the start of the 1970s, and so delighted by Kitty's arrival that he spent more time at home relaxing, Ewan wrote far fewer songs for a period. From the 1970s Peggy selects only five of Ewan's songs for his *Songbook*, though they include the coruscating 'Legal, Illegal'. There were six from 1980, but only one in the next three years, as his health deteriorated further. Was that seam worked out? No. The miners' strike of 1984 generated a further great burst of writing energy, in which he wrote small masterpieces of channelled rage whenever he saw a cause that needed an anthem, and the *Songbook* contains 24 songs from the last five years of his life. His son Neill recalls him being so powered with anger on behalf of the miners in 1984 that he would work 18 hours non-stop. The tunes are now mostly all of his own devising: from 1984 songs such as 'On the Picket Line', 'Holy Joe from Scabsville', and the blazingly indignant 'Daddy, What did you Do in the Strike?' with its varying chorus, the first and last of which follow.

> Daddy, what did you do in the strike?
> Did you tell the NCB to do its worst?
> Or did you save your lily liver,
> Sell the union down the river?
> A scab, a blackleg, one forever cursed!
>
> Daddy, what did you do in the strike?
> Did you scab and let your workmates fight the fight?
> How the neighbours stood and booed us,
> Said we had the stink of Judas,
> Daddy, what did you do in the strike?

He was not going out with a whimper. In 1986 came the angry/touching 'My Old Man' about his father, the anguished/angry 'Looking for a Job', based on one of the traditional Sicilian tunes that increasingly interested him; the angry/angry 'The Great Conspiracy', about deaths in South African prisons, and the puzzled/sardonic 'Public Unpublic'. In 1988 he wrote 'The Island', a rare song about Northern Ireland, where the conflict was one in which both sides were damned, and 'Nuclear Means Jobs'. In 1989, the last year of his life, he was stirred to write the wonderful 'Bring the Summer Home' to a tune of Peggy's, comparing the unpopular modern Poll Tax with its 1381 predecessor that led to the Peasants' Revolt. Three more songs that year – 'The Grocer', 'The Economic Miracle' and 'Rogues Gallery' – mocked the divisive 'successes' of Margaret Thatcher's government.

In 1986 had come his own epitaph, written when he was 71, after his legs for the first time refused to carry him any further on a tough moorland walk, and he let the family stride ahead. He saw the writing on the Pennine crags, where he'd trespassed and sung over 50 years before.

> I sat down on a rock, knowing that my mountain days were over. For the first time I was conscious of the full weight of my years. My desolation lasted for several days and then my grief and sense of loss gave way to nostalgia and I wrote 'The Joy of Living'. In an odd way it helped me to come to terms with my old age.

> Take me to some high place of heather, rock and ling.
> Scatter my dust and ashes, feed me to the wind.
> So that I will be part of all you see, the air you are breathing.
> I'll be part of the curlew's cry and the soaring hawk,
> The blue milkwort and the sundew hung with diamonds.
> I'll be riding the gentle wind that blows through your hair.
> Reminding you of how we shared the joy of living.

And, high among the Bleaklow Stones, that is exactly what Peggy and their children did.

CHAPTER 22

Different Therefore Equal

Peggy Seeger

My battlefield is the concert stage, the lecture hall. My job, like so many songwriters, is to place, in a memorable and enticing form, a message that, were it not hummable, might not be so easily remembered. Quite apart from that, it's enjoyable to write songs. And it's rewarding to hear other people singing a song you've written even though, as has happened a number of times in my life, they attribute it to (a) the 'folk' or (b) to another songwriter.

PEGGY SEEGER, FROM HER WEBSITE, UNDER *ACTIVIST WITH ATTITUDE*

So I become a typist and I study on the sly,
Working out the day and night so I can qualify,
And every time the boss come in, he pinched me on the thigh,
Says, 'I've never had an engineer!'
   You owe it to the job to be a lady,
   It's the duty of the staff for to give the boss a whirl;
   The wages that you get are crummy, maybe,
   But it's all you get, 'cause you're a girl ...

... What price for a woman?
You can buy her for a ring of gold.
To love and obey, without any pay,
You get your cook and your nurse for better or worse,
You don't need your purse when the lady is sold –

1971 had been labelled the Year of the Woman, so for that year's *Festival of Fools* (the last) they decided to celebrate women, and at the last minute Ewan MacColl asked Peggy Seeger to write a suitable song. Peggy, as usual up to her eyes in the show's organisation 'and the customary domestic chaos that came with it', rather reluctantly agreed. In the event the song came to her quickly: 'It appeared so fast on the page that it almost seemed to write itself – you'd have thought I'd been brooding on discrimination and prejudice all my life. Not so.' For the show she had her first-ever short haircut, and loved it – she said she felt like a new woman. Later she wryly reflected on how incongruous it was for a group of women to be singing 'I'm Gonna Be an Engineer' while wearing miniskirts. She was surprised when the song became a feminist anthem. Consequently it was increasingly in demand, and its success led to a gradual shift in her life, later accelerated by Ewan's illness.

Until then she had largely been defined in relation to other people – daughter-of, sister-of, partner-of. Before the 1970s letters usually arrived at Beckenham addressed to the entity 'MacColl-and-Seeger.' After 'Engineer' people began to write just to Peggy Seeger. She was increasingly asked to play for gatherings of women, which caused her problems at first because she hadn't really written any other feminist songs. The nearest was 'Darling Annie', a witty love song where the woman is happy to cohabit but not to marry – a slight stirring of a breeze of independence. Written earlier in 1971 in a rain-bound car next to Loch Lomond, it's in the form of a he/she dialogue, alternate verses sung first by Ewan, then Peggy. She has the last word with the song's final verse:

If you'll marry me I will give to you my name,
It will shield you from idle talk and envy;
For when you play the game you're secure from any blame,
Not ashamed to be my darling Annie.

Thank you, love, I'm grateful for the offer of your name,
But my own will serve as well as any;
I don't like the game and the rules would make me tame,
Not the same girl you married, not your Annie …

… I will live with you, and I'll be faithful unto death,
We will share all the burdens we must carry;
We'll always be free, me for you and you for me –
But when we're old, love, maybe we should marry!

Peggy and Ewan sang it together often, and marry they did when free to do so on his 62nd birthday in 1977. When they began performing together Peggy had been content to sing traditional songs and to accompany Ewan on stage, where they quickly developed instinctive musical reflexes. She was a skilful accompanist on a range of instruments. Her original five-string banjo was joined by guitar, mountain dulcimer, autoharp and English concertina (the piano on stage came much later). When she sang solo, traditional songs predominated at first: in the mid 1960s over 90 per cent of the songs she sang live were traditional. But by the end of the 1970s traditional and contemporary split roughly half and half.

In her songbook Peggy talks about her musical upbringing: 'Two traditions were ever-present and interlaced through my childhood, the formal and the traditional. They presented me with a vision of music that is wide and elastic.' Her formal music training got her hands in shape with endless scales and arpeggios. From very early on she could inscribe any tune on paper instantly, and has always been able to 'pitch' into an unaccompanied song with ease. The classical training means she readily switches between musical modes, formats and metres. But it's the folk tradition that continues to entrance her:

What a treasure chest of types and formats the folk tradition holds: catalogue songs, riddle songs, narratives, lyric songs, historical, funny, solemn, short, long, philosophical, nonsense songs … patient Griselda, the biter bit, the surprise ending … parody, satire, joke songs … the ACBC quatrain, the rhyming couplet, the repeated burden, you could go on forever. The old songs have given me so many ideas for new songs!

The Early Songs

Peggy is as dismissive of her early songs as Ewan was of his own – 'many 22-year-olds have written far better songs than this, so I can't use that as an excuse' – but prints them in the *Songbook* anyway, as she says, 'to use as cannon fodder when teaching songwriting.' After describing the 'clichés and Hollywood B-movie characters' of the *Songbook's* second song, 'When I was Young', she admonishes the reader: 'It sings well enough, but I hope you don't like it.' The book, whose full title is *The Peggy Seeger Songbook – warts and all: forty years of songmaking*, is an enticing masterpiece of clarity and exposition. With layout by Irene Pyper-Scott, it's illustrated by the craftily apt cartoons of Jacky Fleming, who under that song's text has a pensive schoolgirl querying 'Peggy, this bit where it says: I knew no greater pleasure than to follow where he led?'

The first song of which she (and Ewan) entirely approved was written when she was holed up in France in 1958. During that stay she watched on television as a Canadian mining disaster unfolded, the first gripping will-they-get-out-alive saga to play out in public view. After she'd written 'The Ballad of Springhill' – with one technical verse provided by Ewan – she sent a handwritten copy to one of the survivors, Caleb Rushton. She was very moved to meet him 40 years later.

> Three days passed and the lamps gave out
> And Caleb Rushton he up and said,
> 'There's no more water nor light nor bread
> So we'll live on songs and hope instead,
>   Live on songs and hope instead.'

Peggy's songwriting started tentatively – she cites 1967 as the first year she wrote any song that wasn't in some way derivative. Her songwriting gained impetus from the Critics Group period – nearly 60 of the published songs are from the 20 years after it began – and burst out with 75 in the period 1985 to 1997 when the *Songbook* ends. Since then she has written about 40 more. Her second song in the book is 'The Ballad of Jimmy Wilson' which tells the story of a black janitor sentenced to death in Alabama for stealing less than two dollars. Its final chorus line is 'Let men be free', and on the *Songbook* page Jacky Fleming's wild-haired little girl chides her by replacing 'men' by 'all.' Peggy's feminist sensibilities were not fully roused yet.

Her activist humanism was fully roused: from early on she wrote songs about issues of all kinds. She covered apartheid, poverty, the Profumo scandal, Oswald Mosley's re-emergence, Northern Ireland, teachers' pay, Vietnam, LBJ, Nixon, damage to the planet, exploitation of workers, including a garbage-collectors' song she sang on their strike picket line. If that sounds like a set of worthy polemics, they're leavened by wit and by her own understated singing. Her tunes seem always fresh and interesting, catchy without becoming irritating. She was writing and singing some of her own songs, but never performing alone – her concert appearances were always with Ewan. It was 'I'm Gonna Be an Engineer' which gradually began to change that from 1972 onwards. Although her personality could hardly be described as submissive, she was defined, in public at least, as a tireless supporter and protector of Ewan. Her faith in his ideas, and her expression of them, led her to be bracketed with him in the kind of criticism voiced by Gordon McCulloch, who wrote this in *Melody Maker* in May 1979 under the title 'MacColl – Out of Touch?'

> Ewan MacColl's polemical songs have about them a self-righteous hectoring quality, unfortunately magnified by the attitude of magisterial condescension which he unwittingly brings to his stage presence ... [Seeger] appears to share her partner's fatal weakness for homily.

Their early reviews had been almost universally positive, but later their political single-mindedness made them seem tiresome to some in the folk world. Ewan was Peggy's mentor, and provided her political education, and she went where he led. She subsequently recognised:

> I went from [my] father to a surrogate one, Ewan, to whom I practically apprenticed myself from the age of 21. Ewan was always on the move with ideas and projects and I was quick to follow. To *follow* ...

> ...When you've lived with somebody for a long time, you really start to share ideas. I was probably spouting a lot of stuff that ... that I had gotten second-hand. I should have thought WHAT?

Writing about Women's Issues

After the success of 'I'm Gonna Be an Engineer', Peggy was chastened to realise that at 40 she was as ignorant of women's issues as she had been of 'male-oriented, left-wing' politics at 20. In 1976 she started a project to write about women, with as much variety of song as possible. Typically, she set about it with the intensive research used in the making of the Radio Ballads:

> I sought out battered wives, single mothers, women who had been raped, women on picket lines, and many, many others. I interviewed them, listened carefully to their voices of experience and used their words, their tone of expression, even their breathing patterns and cadences ... In the process ... I discovered how other women live. It was quite a shock.

The 1976 album *Penelope Isn't Waiting Anymore* was the result. Beginning with the song of contraception (failure) 'Nine-Month Blues', she went on to the ever popular – and never outdated – 'Housewife's Alphabet'. It could be trite but isn't. Based on a traditional English song, it begins like this, and finishes with a double-take ending:

A is for altar where we go astray,
B for the bills that begin the next day;
C for the cuffs and the collars of shirts, and
D is for dishes and dusting and dirt.
E is my energy draining away on
F is for floors to be swept every day;
G is for girlhood, gawky and gone, and
H, fed-up housewife that's singing this song…

…**W** is for woman and washing machine
We both need attention (you know what I mean).

We've got no union, it's eight days a week –
They're crammed into seven, I'm out on my feet.
So much to do – where should I begin?
But I've got my lifetime to finish it in.
W is for wings, if I had them I'd fly,
X marks the spot where I sit down and cry…
Y–Z for yours truly, I've gone on too long,
And so has the system, and so has this song.

If this song was housework, you'd sing it and then
You'd go back where you started and sing it again
And again and again and again and again …

She calls this piece her 'soft' housewife song – not that its successor 'Lady, What Do You Do All Day' is particularly 'hard' in the often strident feminist terms of the late 1970s, but Peggy is rarely strident and never shrill – she usually prefers humour as her complacency-slicer: 'A nurse and a nanny until I'm a granny, But why is it nobody pays me?' This appears on *Different Therefore Equal* of 1979, which Ewan called her 'hard' feminist album: it's as angry as she gets. She writes songs about crucial current feminist issues – rape, abortion, marriage, wife-battering, sexual typing, exploited women workers. Peggy: 'I sat down to write the album as it stood, which is something I've never done.' Its syncopated conversational title song ends with:

If her and him are
Indispensable,
Treatin' em similar
Is only sensible.
Reason gives us
The logical sequel:
We're different,
Therefore equal.

Peggy chose to use Radio Ballad interviewing techniques to create many of these songs, recording people and echoing their words and vocal structures. From interviews with Jayaben Desai, a determined Kenyan Asian strike leader, she constructed 'Union Woman II'. Mrs Desai said 'I hear myself talking' when she first heard the song. For a spell Peggy assisted in a sanctuary for battered women. In her song 'Winnie and Sam', which begins with a deceiving upbeat and jaunty lilt, she derived the song's style from Winnie's taut body language as well as from her words. Its shock effect is increased when we discover 'Winnie is a lawyer's daughter, Sam's got a PhD', overturning any preconceptions of wife-bashers as drunken working-class men. As ever, Peggy varies the song style. The long, engaging 'Talking Matrimony Blues' mixes song and speech to a rhythmic accompaniment, and blames a patriarchal and capitalist system for exploiting everybody and keeping women at home. Written, ironically, in the year after she eventually married Ewan, it starts with a smile and ends with a kick:

Girls, don't hanker for bouquet and veils,
They soon turn to cabbage and nappies in pails.
The joys and the sorrows of conjugal life,
All these can be yours without being a wife.
Yes, a good life can come to fruition,
You don't need a licence to give you permission,
   You don't have to marry. You never get completely free choice anyhow. Too many people you can't marry for a start. I always fancied Paul Newman …

… So marriage is really to safeguard the boss,
'Cause without a workforce he'd make a loss,
And how could he rob 'em and screw 'em and twist 'em
Unless he had marriage to uphold the system
That supports the class
That exploits the man
Who exploits the wife
Who bears the kids
Who lives in the house that Jack built …
   AND JILL CLEANS.

Anger comes out most explicitly in the electrifying 'Reclaim the Night': 'If without consent he stakes a claim – call it rape, for rape's the name.' This album polarised opinion. At one end of the spectrum a reviewer said her lyrics deserved to be studied alongside the work of feminists like Kate Millett and Germaine Greer. At the other, many men couldn't take it. In a 1979 *Melody Maker* article Colin Irwin said:

> It's just about the most political record I've ever heard ... these songs are so ferocious, intimidating, and single-minded that it's not a record that inspires much sympathy in this admittedly male quarter, though doubtless the militants of women's movements will adopt it with a vengeance.

From 1968 to 1985 she produced *The New City Songster*, a pocket-sized songbook, in which she assembled contemporary songs of her own, from Ewan, and from many others. With no support it was hard work, and she constantly exhorted others to contribute, and to do some writing. She described her self-imposed task as a 'single-handed, infuriated response to the apathy of so-called dedicated folk people.' In the introduction to the 12th issue in 1976 she wrote cajoling women songwriters to come forward, which illustrated her own approach – everything is material for a song:

> YOU HAVEN'T TIME? Write a song about why you haven't time. YOU ARE TOO TIRED after your job as a mother, a student, typist, nurse, breadwinner or breadmaker, whatever? Write a song about that. Or perhaps write a song on the ploys being used by employers to get round the Sexual Discrimination Bill ... or on the need for daycare centres ... or about how difficult it is to get a pair of flat sandals.

Peggy was an active but not a campaigning feminist, nor was she on the extreme wing of feminism that excluded and despised men. She liked and admired many of them too much for that. In 'Dangerous Women' she reverts to sardonic humour to encourage men to imagine a reversed world: 'Cover your legs, remember to button your shirt ... the lawyers are women who say you were asking for it.' Her philosophy was well expressed in 'You Men Out There', a monologue written in 1995 for the 75th anniversary of women's suffrage in the USA, and constantly updated since. It takes pity on men puzzled by feminist anger, and explains in a kindly fashion how it all came to pass:

> Long before the time of books,
> Women were magic, women were mystery.
> Way before the start of history
> Before space travel and megacities

Females were heading planning committees.
Wise women (now called witches)
And powerful women (now called bitches)
Managed life and death and birth,
Cared and shared with Planet Earth ...

People and the Planet

The most constant threads that run through Peggy's songwriting and activism are concern for justice and for the planet, starting with that first Ban the Bomb song. Ewan took longer to awake to both feminist and ecology issues, and did so eventually through Peggy, who said in his *Songbook*: 'Ewan's songs are full of ... rearranging, conquering nature and bringing it around to doing what man wants it to do ... Ewan really talked only about mankind – that the earth revolved around men.' Compare Ewan's anguished 'Looking for a Job' from 1986 with Peggy's reflective 'For a Job', written six years later, and the contrast between them is clear. Ewan, writing of the desperation of the unemployed, sings: 'Just try me. I'll sweep the streets, I'll shovel shit, I'll do a bit of anything, willing to turn my hand to anything – anything, anything, anything. *Anything.*' While acknowledging that: 'without a job a man's not a man, a man needs a job', Peggy's song on the other hand questions any job that will lead ultimately to the Earth's destruction:

> He'd give the world for a job, he's running wild;
> Blindfold, brainwashed, self-centred, Pavlov's child –
> Turn forest to desert, turn heaven to hell,
> Turn home into nothing, will we live to tell
> How he gave the world for a job?

Always a fervent opponent of nuclear weapons and nuclear energy, she derived her influential 'Four Minute Warning' from a map printed in a newspaper showing the effects of a nuclear blast in concentric circles radiating from the centre of London. At the right pace the warning takes exactly four minutes to sing. Peggy was active in the early 1980s in the Greenham Common protest against the siting of US cruise missiles in the middle of the Berkshire countryside. She wrote the moving anthem 'Carry Greenham Home', the title song for the 1983 film documentary about the women-only peace camp. The following year brought 'Tomorrow', which she attempted to sing when she came up before a judge after being arrested at a sit-in on Parliament Square. But he choked off her protest and returned her to the cells, threatening to prosecute her for contempt of court.

In the 1980s issues ripe for songwriting continued to come thick and fast: El Salvador, Grenada, Chile, Northern Ireland, smoking, nuclear weapons, torture, abortion, the poll tax, more strikes by exploited workers, Margaret Thatcher, whose government Ewan didn't outlive. Peggy continued writing after he died in 1989, only slowing down slightly as she prepared both songbooks. There were still plenty of reasons for protest, most recently the second Iraq War, which led to 'The Ballad of Jimmy Massey', written after long hours interviewing a North Carolina man who left the Marine Corps in protest after a few months' active service. But the world's woes don't let up, and she writes increasingly about the planet and its greatest despoiler, her own native country. Having written about George Bush Senior's failure to take action on the environment at Rio, she adapted this neat squib for his even more culpable son, pausing for effect at the end of every verse pair:

Bush went to Kyoto with his bag of tricks,
Bush went to Kyoto with his bunch of –

PRIncipled diplomats who want to grab it all,
The thought of world democracy is just a lot of –

BALderdash and nonsense, what Georgie doesn't want
Is sharing what we've got with a lot of other –

COUNTries who are poor or black or just down on their luck,
So Bush went to Kyoto to tell them all to –

FUnd other solutions, 'cause he don't want to lose
The profits and the business, so he's prepared to –

SCREW the people, screw the climate, screw the earth and then
Make the world a safer place for Yankee businessmen.

A Life Change

Peggy's personal life underwent a major upheaval after Ewan died. At a time of disorientation, hardly surprising after over 30 years with him in an intensive hearts-and-minds domestic and working partnership, her friendship with the singer Irene Pyper-Scott was a crucial support. They originally met on stage as singers at a benefit for Nelson Mandela and Dave Kitson in the mid-1960s. Irene too lived in Beckenham, and much later they formed a local group called BANG, the Beckenham Anti-Nuclear Group, which tried to convince politically inactive local people of the dangers of nuclear weapons and the transport of nuclear waste. Irene often stood in for Ewan at concerts whenever his health failed him. In the aftermath of Ewan's death Peggy was devastated, and in her *Songbook* she described the next ten years as 'traumatic

– years of change, insecurity and adventure.' She and Irene fell in love, and they cemented their relationship by entering a civil partnership in 2007.

When they'd first met in 1964, Irene was a singer with a beautiful natural voice who had been called the Joan Baez of Belfast. They sang together for a spell when Peggy was having difficulty with re-establishing a solo career. One prospective agent had said that she was 'the leftover of a dead duo ... no spring chicken ... and not commercially viable.' So Irene and Peggy named their duo No Spring Chickens and in 1992 gave their album the title *Almost Commercially Viable*. Peggy's voice had been trained over the years to cross a crowded smoky folk club without amplification. Encouraged by Irene, she developed a solo career which led to a softer, more relaxed singing style, though she could still turn up the heat when needed. Her voice has stayed in magnificent shape, not least because she sticks to a daily half-hour vocal exercise regime.

At the turn of the 1990s Peggy re-examined her early performances (as she did everything else at that point) and issued *Peggy Seeger, The Folkways Years 1955–1992: Songs of Love and Politics*. An open willingness to criticise herself is apparent on the occasionally scathing assessments of the songs in the album notes, where she likened the selection process to 'going to a class reunion and seeing as grown-ups all those kids you liked and loathed.' She was encouraged by the reviews and, as the collection's title suggests, began to widen her songwriting targets, not that there's any let-up in the political song output whenever an injustice presents itself. She had written about Ewan and each of her children, now she wrote for and about Irene, for family weddings, for old and new friends. Her recent 'Bring Me Home' is a life-summarising song, which includes this verse echo of Ewan:

> Songs of love, tales of grace,
> Of flesh and blood and bone.
> The first time ever I saw his face
> His heart became my own,
> Then his heart became my home.

In 1994 she moved back to the USA after a gap of nearly 40 years. She is still (2008) carrying out concert and festival tours in North America, Britain and Australasia. She lectures, holds and participates in workshops, and runs a course on songwriting at Northeastern University in Boston: Some Perspectives on Songwriting. ('My perspectives', she stresses.) She gets a real kick out of teaching, starting with youngsters who know nothing of folk music, who are scared rigid of singing unaccompanied, then go on to startle themselves and their teacher with they can achieve.

Peggy, of course, has years of performance ahead of her to match Pete Seeger, who still plays and sings at nearly 90. Pete flew over with their brother Mike to join Peggy and her children, amid a battery of seasoned folk singers young and old, to celebrate Peggy's 70th birthday concert at the Queen Elizabeth Hall in London in 2005. Pete orchestrated the audience's participation as boisterously as ever. Mike, an accomplished and versatile folk musician, completes the set of Seegers still performing and recording. Peggy's sons Neill and Calum are both talented folk musicians and singers in the Seeger/MacColl tradition, appearing on and helping with many of Ewan's and Peggy's late albums (for which Kitty has sung and created artwork) as well as forging their own careers in music.

Looking back, Peggy regards the Radio Ballads as a wonderful creative opportunity, crucial to her development. After 1964 for a time she and Ewan worked on a possible Radio Ballad about the impact of nuclear energy called *Day Trip to Golgotha*. In the 1980s she researched a Radio Ballad on women. In 1983 she wrote to a friend:

> My programme is going very well. My problem is that I keep running into interesting women and the minute I do that it's out with the microphone and I have another three or four hours of tape which take about three hours each to transcribe and catalogue. It's going to be years before I finish at this rate.

Despite 50 hours of recording it never did finish. She needed a collaborator and by then Ewan was neither willing nor able enough, though he was horrified by some of the women's stories. She says she would definitely tackle another Radio Ballad if there was someone to work with.

We must hope there will be. For many years it did look as though the Radio Ballad form was consigned to history. There have been a few excellent songs-and-words albums made, such as Peter Bellamy's *The Transports*, but none with the dense texturing of the originals. Then, unexpectedly in 2006, an intriguing new series was made for Radio 2, which will be the subject of the final chapter. Until then, the only serious attempt at the Radio Ballad form had been for television. Philip Donnellan made fascinating films of three of the Radio Ballads in the early 1970s, with the help of Ewan and Peggy. Could a form designed explicitly for the ear, encouraging you to form your own images, work on screen, when those pictures are chosen for you and presented to you?

CHAPTER 23

Sound in Vision
Three Radio Ballads on Film

You may well 'assert' the relationship between the acceptance of violence in boxing and the tolerance of institutionalised violence in other fields – notably the military – but this is a personal view which is hardly acceptable when grafted on to an original script which, as far as I know, pointed-up no such relationship.

ROBIN SCOTT, CONTROLLER BBC 2, TO PHILIP DONNELLAN, ABOUT *FIGHT GAME*, 1973

When the last man leaves the pit for the factory floor,
Where the work is clean, the danger less and the pay is more,
When the last of the oil is gone who will
Remember the miners' rejected skill?
Who will – Go Down?

NEW VERSE BY EWAN MACCOLL FOR *THE BIG HEWER*, 1974

The impact of the Radio Ballads on documentary makers in both radio and television in the 1960s was immense. While no one attempted to copy their dense texturing of words and music, and few entirely dispensed with a narrator, it became increasingly unthinkable to reassemble the words of real people in actors' mouths. The programmes were used in the BBC for training courses, where later radio feature makers like Piers Plowright were fascinated by them. But, apart from *The Camera and the Song* (p. 213), there was really only one attempt to do something comparable on film, and that was a set of direct adaptations of three Radio Ballads made by Philip Donnellan, Charles Parker's old friend from BBC Midlands radio in the 1950s.

Donnellan's *Joe the Chainsmith* had been made in the same year as *John Axon*, and in television was just as influential. But by the end of the 1960s the BBC regarded their producers with an equal degree of exasperation. Both made brilliant programmes but they insisted on embedding their own viewpoints, they wouldn't do what they were told, and they ignored any rules that obstructed them. Their talents were complementary – one had an amazing ear, the other a keen visual sense but less feeling for sound. They had collaborated, and each created controversy, on their programmes about the blind. Donnellan was unstinting in his praise for the way Charles created sound pictures: to him it was as though Charles shared with the blind their super-sensitive aural ability.

In making a film version of a Radio Ballad, Donnellan faced a question akin to one you must ask of any radio programme that adds music to words. MacColl, Parker and Seeger had to make sure that their songs augment the power of the message inherent in the words, not diminish them. Is it a better programme than with the words alone? When it works, yes. Music taps into the mind at a different emotional level (researchers increasingly believe that song in humanity's early history was a precursor of speech) and can slip in under our guard to manipulate our feelings. But you have to be careful – how much more careful do you have to be, then, if you have something that already works really well with sound only? The majority of our sensory input arrives through the eyes, so the images, still or moving, must be chosen with great sensitivity if you want to heighten the emotional impact of the original rather than dissipate it. Especially if the original is brilliant.

Shoals of Herring

Does Donnellan succeed? In 1963 he had tried a TV version of *On the Edge*, to reviews no better than for the original. Then in 1971 he approached Ewan, Peggy and Charles with a view to producing a film version of *Singing the Fishing*. (Charles had incidentally tried to put together a film of *John Axon* in 1959, but had been thwarted by copyright issues.) It was Donnellan who had first encountered the man known locally as 'old Funky' Larner, who was fetched to the Mariner's Arms at Winterton 'in his carpet slippers, to sing unstoppably till midnight.' East Coast herring fishing had declined dramatically in the dozen years since the radio programme, something Donnellan wanted to illustrate. His approach shines a shrewd sidelight on the original tack taken by Ewan and Charles. For Donnellan, the romance needed a counterpoint:

> Their programme is charged with human force and energy and poetry but it does not tell enough of how fishermen are exploited. It gives no indication, however brief, of the structures of ownership and labour. It lacks political edge. They had ignored the most fundamental reasons why the English fishing had collapsed and the Scottish survived. The Englishmen were wage-slaves, they worked for big industrial firms – Ross Group and Boston Deep Sea and others. When the profits dried up for all the usual English reasons the boats were laid up, the men laid off, the industry crumbled. But the Scots families by tradition owned their own boats: they might be up to the neck in mortgage debts but they alone determined how and when and with what they went to sea; and it was they alone who decided whether they would survive or not.

One can imagine Ewan's reaction at finding someone who thought he hadn't been political <u>enough</u>. Donnellan's is a fair criticism, but after the *Song of a Road* ruckus Ewan and Charles had determined to make a programme that looked at fishing explicitly from the fishermen's viewpoint. Hardship and rough times are illustrated throughout the original, but the piece discusses a way of life without examining closely the state of the industry. The ownership/exploitation question seems to have been one they didn't probe. Those who criticised the Radio Ballads for their political stance were off-beam: looking back now, and especially in view of some of Ewan's political songs, the programmes are remarkable for how polemical they could have been but weren't. But Ewan, despite his political stance, was wedded to the idea that their subjects' words should tell their own story, and they didn't set out to find union activists, for example. A dozen years on, Donnellan used the far-sighted fishing vessel owner Gilbert Buchan, who explained why East Anglia had lost its fishing, and who would later help Britain negotiate the EEC's Common Fisheries Policy.

How do you go about translating a Radio Ballad about fishing onto film? On the one hand it's trickier than starting afresh, because you're constrained by the pre-existing story; on the other at least you do have a structure in place. You can go out and film modern fishing, but that would catch only the last third of the original programme, the Scottish diesel-engine era. You could use still photographs up to a point, and what could capture the era better than the evocative images of late 19th-century Whitby fishermen captured by Frank Sutcliffe? 'Those rough old boys, boy', came alive in their craggy features. Moreover, there is marvellous old film of sail and steam available, and Donnellan chose to augment his new material with extracts from three pre-war classics – Grierson's *Drifters*, Harry Watt's *North Sea* and Campbell Harper's *Caller Herrin'*. He showed parts of each against segments of the original *Fishing* soundtrack. The storm scene is halved in length but works remarkably well against *North Sea*, with those 'great seas a-coming' and pouring over man and deck as the Edwards concertina roars them on. Moreover:

> There was often a startling rhythmic identity between sequences of a film like *Drifters* and sections of the music-voice montage that had been created for the Radio Ballad. In several major sections we only had to find a single point of synchronisation between soundtrack and archive film and then let it roll, to see at once an extraordinary affinity which might continue for a minute or even longer: the protracted storm sequence is an outstanding example, set against footage from *North Sea* and running one minute thirty-eight seconds.

Sam Larner and Ronnie Balls were now gone – Sam had 'looked Death in the eye' – and while Donnellan could still use their voices, embedded as they were in some of the best sequences, he needed to film substitutes. The ones he found were apt. The erect and articulate Bill Solomon of Oulton Broad stood in for Ronnie Balls, and 'Crabpot' Rushmore was an even more theatrical Sam. You can't manipulate film-plus-speech as you can speech alone, so there could be no pinpoint sound selection in the Parker style, but some of their testimony was in the Larner/Balls tradition. Crabpot was a man who had clearly fished on both sides of the law. He faltered at one point, while listing his boats just as Sam had, and his wife prompted him with: '*Kessingham*, that was the last boat you was skipper on, that was when you were had up for smuggling tobacco.' Her face breaks into a slow smile.

These modern equivalents work well, and the filmed interviews dovetail easily enough with the voices of the originals. Donnellan has his own 1950s film of Sam Larner too, singing 'Sailing over the Dogger Bank, Oh wasn't it a treat', before we cut to his grave. Film from *Caller Herrin'* shows us the women gutting fish at a fearsome rate (even allowing for old film speeds) as the Stewart sisters sing of 'lassies at the pickling, and others at the creels.' The Scots women are represented here by Magsie Buchan, the shrewd mother of Gilbert, with expressive face and darting eyes as she tells us how 'there's nae content noo, it's money, money.'

After a day with Donnellan Ewan rewrote extra song stanzas to reflect the industry's decline, in part due to domination by huge Russian and Norwegian factory 'klondikers', their power-hauled nets stripping the last herring from the North Sea. So, intercut with voices from the original Radio Ballad and some new ones, we get several extra verses for 'North Sea Holes' to illustrate the changed times:

> The mair fish that are ta'en the day
> The less the mornin's catch will be.
> And when the seas are a' fished oot
> How will fishers earn their fee?
>
> Wi' your power block and fancy nets,
> Your mortgage and your heavy debts,
> And an overdraft that must be met,
> We're bound to plunder the herrin' O.

Plunder it is. The film ends with a new 'Shoals of Herring' stanza, in which: 'As we waste the wild crop of the ocean … We may see no more the shoals of herring.' Peggy's banjo complains angrily as the titles roll over waves crashing in Gardenstown Bay. She constructed the musical arrangement for the new sections, using two new instrumentalists, and Alf Edwards, for whom she wrote a new piece to back a replacement Depression section. Three old East Anglian fisherman talk about the end of their livelihoods as they pick their way through a deserted boatyard.

The film works. Shown on BBC 2 in September 1972 and again a year later, it was well reviewed: 'as much a delight to the ear as the eye, a rare combination.' Philip Whitehead in *The Listener* got in a dig at a BBC management which at the time was leaning on Donnellan as much as Parker:

> The producers of both the radio and television versions are talented men often at odds with the Corporation over their ideas for future programmes. It is the bite and zest of the individual with something to say … that transforms the schedules from mere competence to something more.

Because BBC 2 coverage was as yet only patchy in the very region where herring fishing was still hanging on, Donnellan took a copy of the film to Scotland and showed it for a week to eager audiences in fishing towns. The BBC, far from being pleased that its reach had been extended, gave him a 'final warning' interview for flouting the rules: 'It was clear the heat was still on, but now I was on my own.' The interview took place five days after Charles Parker had left the BBC.

The Fight Game

Philip Donnellan, often at odds with his BBC managers, had found a more sympathetic boss in Robin Scott, then Controller of the new minority-audience BBC 2. (One way of minimising Donnellan's influence from the late

1960s was to keep him off BBC 1.) A crucial ally too was Scott's predecessor, David Attenborough, whose successful stint in BBC management now tends to be forgotten. Scott enabled Donnellan to make two more films of the Radio Ballads, choosing *Fight Game* and *Big Hewer*. Of Irish extraction, he had recently been on an eye-opening visit to Northern Ireland, and decided to use his boxing film to imply that the acceptance of violence in sport is linked to its excessive use in society at large and by the military specifically. Nevertheless, of the three films he made, this sticks most closely to the pattern and script of the original.

He has to find a new set of boxers to film, and he follows three in particular, who are due to fight at the Royal Albert Hall on 31 October 1972, two of them future world champions. Both are helpfully named John: the charismatic young John Conteh, and the thoughtful John H Stracey, who talks reflectively of 'the animal in people'. On that night Stracey loses by a low-blow disqualification to the swaggering Bobby Arthur, that bout and the others filmed to provide the setting for the original's fight sequence. It's a match that works perfectly: the boxing footage and editing is often brilliant, the effect repulsive yet fascinating, and its techniques foreshadow what we see in *Rocky* and *Raging Bull*, which were made in the following ten years. It's shot from several angles, with slow motion, successive stills, snatches of the raging crowd turned on by what they see, and – tellingly – a slow pan round a dinner-jacketed front row. The tricks are not overdone, and follow the soundtrack without strain, as for:

> **A little breather now they're off again,**
> **Swapping punches, taking punishment,**
> **The swollen lips – the angry bruises – it's a lovely fight.**
> **See where the blood shows each time the glove lands.**
> **Three minutes heavy punching both the hands two-fisted fighting**
> **Hard slogging.**
> **Gloves thudding.**
> **Eyes bleeding.**
> **HE'S DOWN!**

Throughout the film Donnellan intersperses images in subliminal flashes. They include soldiers in Northern Ireland, bullfighting, a machine gun's cartridge belt, a joust re-enactment, a poised trigger finger, a Northern Ireland crowd pelting the Army. None lasts for more than a second until the end of the fight, when we see longer cut-aways of wounded soldiers and civilians. The final credits run over a shot of a blazing building and the sound of bullets. Cleverly assembled, powerful and disturbing, the film inflamed many, not least the Ministry of Defence, who provided some of the film. The BBC weren't too happy either – they can't have enjoyed reading the *Listener* critic: 'The motto of BBC 2 is becoming "Charles Parker Lives" … An almost unbearable climax of jolted heads and flying gumshields.'

The Big Hewer

Despite his irritation, Robin Scott allowed Donnellan to film one more Radio Ballad: his memo at the head of this chapter continues: 'I am glad to know that in *The Big Hewer* there will be less problems and that its treatment can be more closely related to *Shoals*.' Scott was prepared to back Donnellan who, though his gratitude was genuine, was still exasperated:

> It may seem gratuitous to celebrate anything so simple which should have been supported without question by all our routine claims to a free and independent television service. But my consistent experience of 12 years in that medium had been of censorship, management intervention and threats. It also has to be remembered that at exactly the time when these programmes were being remade for television, the BBC management was preoccupied with firing the man who had made them possible.

Donnellan decided that because of what had occurred in the mining industry in the past 12 years he would have to change *The Big Hewer* far more than he had the other two. Then, when it was ready, he was obliged to delay its screening until after the 1974 miners' strike – lest it inflame the already inflamed, or allow viewers to judge the miners' case for themselves. He included some film of the Saltley Gate picket line that Charles subsequently employed in the Banner Theatre production of *Collier Laddie*, and added footage from the (then and now) forgotten coalfield at Betteshanger, an unlikely colliery to find in the quiet Kent countryside near Dover: 'A couple of thousand people crowded into a cramped and cracking council estate between sea and farming acres', in Donnellan's words. Initially he was forbidden by the NCB (National Coal Board) to film underground, but it relented under pressure from the union. Ewan again wrote new verses, and even more than in *Shoals of Herring* Donnellan decided he had to tackle the politics.

It's in the film of *The Big Hewer* that the distracting effect of the all-powerful visual image is clearly felt. The most atmospheric moments in the Radio Ballad come when it evokes the intense feeling of being underground – or how we imagine it feeling, because few of us have been down there. Radio does the dark well (you'll recall that the first specially written radio drama was set in a coal mine), but film can't. Old still photographs work better, but the first part of the film fails to achieve the impact of its radio original, despite some imaginative shots. That changes as soon as we get above ground: you can't evoke a pit disaster, but you can show its aftermath: the cluster of anxious wives and men at the pithead, the roll call of the dead – as many as 80 in 1973 – and old black-and-white film of a winding funeral procession. You can hear of the effects of pneumoconiosis – 'He's got inside his lungs a good tombstone of solid coal dust' – while a doctor goes dispassionately through the scarred X-rays. You can see the painful walk of a 50-year-old as he spoke of the fate of his four brothers and two stepbrothers, in whose footsteps he would soon be shuffling.

In its last ten minutes the film jumps out of the original and into the 1974 present. We see miners debating, balloting, striking. Arthur Scargill persuades a lorry-driver to turn back at the Saltley Gate plant, and its gates close. Miners are triumphant. It's halfway between 1962 and the miners' apocalyptic year of 1984, and by this point Ewan needs no persuading to write more stanzas to reflect the current state of the industry. First the new kind of pit, a living factory, men serving machine and each other. Then the effects of an industry in crisis, North Sea oil coming, pits closing.

> **A mine is a body with coal flowing through its veins:**
> **Men are the hands and muscles and nerves and brains,**
> **Where surface workers and face teams labour,**
> **Each man dependent upon his neighbour,**
> **One of a team that serves the machine, Way Down.**
>
> **Sweated in the hot pit, lay in the dark wet seams and froze.**
> **Been locked out, known despair when pits were closed.**
> **Agreed to the deal on power loading,**
> **Watched the terms of the deal eroding –**
> **Again we're betrayed, and seeing our pay Go Down.**

Rather to Donnellan's surprise it was well received within the BBC – Scott's replacement as Controller BBC 2, Aubrey Singer, called it 'enthralling'. Charles Parker would have been pleased that the reviewers hadn't forgotten its radio origins either. Here are three extracts, from *The Western Mail*, Peter Lennon in the *Sunday Times*, and from Shaun Usher in the *Daily Mail*, who ends with a point just as relevant today:

> Any appreciation of the programme should not make one forget that it was radio, with its reliance on the all-important spoken word, which provided its origin.

As one would expect from Charles Parker sound was used interestingly. A statement from a miner was stopped to allow a burst of expressive music and then allowed to continue: a tricky device which could go absurdly wrong in insensitive hands, but it worked well here.

Hopefully many documentary makers watched this implied tribute to radio – if only because it would encourage them to listen to words with as much care as they devote to weighing film quality.

It's clear that, despite the inevitable loss of aural impact, his versions were a success in television terms because Donnellan understood entirely the rationale of the originals, they provided him with great source material, and his updating was sympathetic. He was a skilled film-maker, had fine editors, and kowtowed to no one. He managed to cling on at the BBC, pushing the borders of 'balance' in a number of films. Many of them were never shown, such as *The Irishmen*, an impressionistic portrait of Irish immigrant building workers in London. It features songs written by Ewan, including 'The Tunnel Tigers', which used the Irish tune 'William Taylor' to describe them building the Victoria Underground line. Peggy produced the music, wincing later at the editing, which sometimes chopped up the songs oddly. Sandra Kerr later said Donnellan's ear was subordinate to his expert eye. She produced the music for *Gone for a Soldier*, a moving and pointed film which intercut letters from the 'common' British soldier in past wars with film of new recruits being trained for Northern Ireland. One of his last films, it adapted the *Long March of Everyman* technique by employing modern squaddies to read letters home from soldiers long dead. Its broadcast went ahead in the teeth of virulent opposition from the Army at the height of the Northern Ireland conflict.

For another 30 years after Donnellan's films no more was heard of the Radio Ballads until Topic re-released all eight on CD in 1999. Then in 2006 came an unexpected series on Radio 2, with new writers, singers and musicians, on six fresh subjects. How did that happen, and did they work?

CHAPTER 24

A New Generation
The 2006 Radio Ballads

We couldn't get it through the door it was so big. We mike up the drum outside because the control room's inside, no line of sight, so John Leonard and the engineer are inside and I'm in the doorway cueing the drummer. Boom, boom, boom. We're alongside a lake that goes on to the Irish border, and that <u>sound</u> – well, lights go on everywhere ... On the journey home, the drummer told me later, driving back through Newry, the back doors of the van swing open and the drum comes out and rolls across a roundabout. Out they went to get it, everyone stopping. Ten years earlier, no way, they'd have been away.

VINCE HUNT, IN 2007, ON USING A PROTESTANT LAMBEG DRUM IN A CATHOLIC AREA WHILE RECORDING FOR *THIRTY YEARS OF CONFLICT*, 2006

A NEW GENERATION – THE 2006 RADIO BALLADS

Thirty years after Philip Donnellan's film, and 40 years after *Travelling People* ended the original series, the concept of the Radio Ballads was unexpectedly revived. A Sheffield-born radio executive and one-time folk singer, John Leonard, who for years had nursed a desire to produce a modern equivalent of the original series, came to the BBC (repeatedly) with a proposal. For years they weren't interested, but remembered him when they launched a new initiative, *RealVoices*, which aimed to illustrate the richness and diversity of regional accents. Consequently Lesley Douglas of Radio 2 asked Leonard's company Smooth Operations to produce a new set of eight; she later described it as one of her best-ever commissions. Another enthusiast who had been egging Leonard on from the beginning would be musical director, John Tams.

Tams had much in common with MacColl, through a kind of convergent evolution. Born into a working-class Derbyshire family, he was radical in politics, he had been a journalist and presenter on radio, and he had acted, sung, and written songs. He, too, had been a folk song collector, in Ireland, North and South. He had been musical director for the National Theatre for 15 years, working for Bill Bryden on memorable productions of *The Mysteries* and *Lark Rise to Candleford*, before taking the part of rifleman Hagman in the Napoleonic War series *Sharpe*, for which he wrote and sang the songs, and through which he became known to a wider public.

Tams did *Six Men of Dorset* at Sheffield's Crucible Theatre for 7:84, opening two days before the police cavalry charge at Orgreave during the 1984 miners' strike. (A year later, after a play about miners' wives, the English 7:84 lost its Arts Council grant and folded. The Scottish 7:84 battles on to this day.) One of Tams's songs was sung on the 1984 picket line just as Ewan's were. Here his life and Ewan's intersected: 'Just imagine Ewan doing a Ballad of the Strike.' Tams's public success as a singer came late in his career when Folk awards began. He won Album of the Year in 2001, three awards in 2006, including Folk Singer of the Year, and one in 2008. He has recently worked on the songs for *Warhorse* at the National Theatre, and shows as little sign of slowing as Ewan did in his 50s.

In the end there were six Radio Ballads in the new series, with two, on football and teenagers, dropped from the original proposal, the latter after interviewing was well under way. They were made during 2005 and broadcast in early 2006 in successive weeks on Monday nights from 27 February to 3 April on Radio 2 – so the equivalent of the 1950s Light Programme rather than the Home Service. The six final subjects were the steel and shipbuilding industries, both in terminal decline, HIV/AIDS, foxhunting, fairgrounds and Northern Ireland. So, while there is some mapping onto the original subjects, it's hardly slavish. Nor is their adherence to the original approach, though what is eloquently clear is their desire to honour the original makers, pioneers who went before them, in Tams's words from his stage act, 'carrying tape recorders so massive they needed batteries powered by wood-burning stoves.' And to do justice to the new generation of informants that Tams preferred to call the life-tellers: 'At all costs we must honour their stories, moreover we must honour their lives.'

The 2006 Radio Ballads were *Song of Steel*, *The Enemy That Lives Within*, *The Horn of the Hunter*, *Swings and Roundabouts*, *Thirty Years of Conflict* and *The Ballad of the Big Ships*. The first thing to stress about them is that they take place in a completely different broadcasting world. The differences can be expressed simply like this:

Comparators	1958–64	2004–6
Timescale	8 in 7 years	6 in 12 months
Timing	Sequential	Overlapped
Budget	Open-ended (sort of)	Set in advance
Makers	Inside BBC	Outside BBC
Actuality collectors	CP+EM+PS (pairs, mostly)	VH/SP (singly)
Hours recorded for each	average 60–70	average 25–30
Songwriters	One	Many
Writers did interviews?	Almost always	Almost never
Recording medium	15 min reel-to-reel	70 min DAT/Minidisc
Music arrangement	PS, integral	JL, 'framing'
Musicians and singers	Jazz and folk	Entirely folk
Sound mixing	Tape splicing	Computer-based

(VH and SP are Vince Hunt and Sara Parker, Charles Parker's daughter).

That gives some idea of the enormous differences in the way they were put together. The response of audiences was excellent, though there's a split into two populations as with the original BBC research audiences for *John Axon* – only, for the 2006 series, it depends on whether you had heard the originals. The vast majority, people new to the concept, on the whole found this series extremely striking. They had rarely if ever come across anything quite like its combination of the use of song and avoidance of formal commentary. That enthusiasm was reflected in the British domestic equivalent of the Italia Prizes for Radio, the Sony Awards, where *Song of Steel* won the prize for documentary features – a real rarity for Radio 2 – and *Thirty Years of Conflict* a third place in the community programme category. But, so entrenched in their minds had the original series become, that most of those who loved them instinctively found the 2006 programmes difficult to like. Part of their reaction is understandable, 'ooman nature', as Sam Larner would say, and part a reluctance to accept that <u>anything</u> could be as good as the programmes they fell in love with (and they unconsciously tend to discount those of the originals they didn't much like). We'll have a look at how the two series compare at the end of the chapter.

Collecting the Voices

How was the new series made? First, the actuality was collected by two people separately, Vince Hunt and Sara Parker, and – a particularly crucial point – rarely by any of the songwriters. In Peggy Seeger's view that was bound to be a drawback for the writers. In the only exceptions, John Tams went to Nottingham's annual Goose Fair for *Swings and Roundabouts*, and sat in on an early *Steel* interview at the Magna museum, formerly Steel, Peach and Tozer, the 'Steelos' of the resultant song. It's telling that the songs he wrote after the Steel visit came extremely quickly: 'I watched their hands, saw how they carried themselves, let it gestate for a while, then it poured out.' But the rest of the interviews were carried out by the interviewers on their own, so the other songwriters didn't have that advantage. As with the originals, once the interviewer had got the recall started the testimony became unstoppable. As Tams said:

> Some of the questions Vince put had never been asked or answered out loud before. The common spirit of a community that knows itself so well doesn't always have the need to talk about it – but now it could.

Vince Hunt had been a newspaper 'legman' who had moved into radio in 1990. He could remember the days of tape splicing, so he knew how hard it was: 'Both me and John started with quarter-inch tape. Hands all covered with blood.' He found Parker's assembly skill almost impossible to believe: 'What he achieved with that kit is incredible.' Nowadays, tape editing uses computer software, of course, where you can even see the shape of the sound's wave-form as you listen. Hunt started on the *Steel* programme and went on to the *Shipbuilding*, to industrial sites built on a massive scale. They were unforgettable experiences, and his response to the sounds of the steelworks has echoes of Ewan MacColl in his father's foundry, and of Charles Parker's childlike joy in the railway yards:

> I took a trip round the steelworks – amazing education it was. Amid all those different sounds I could hear a faint tinkling, I couldn't fathom it. It was from a roll of steel turning on a lathe, the tinkling of shavings off the lathe, a great chisel thing, a waterfall of shavings. I went back and back and back for those sound effects. The processes are the same as the old steelworks. Red-hot steel on a conveyor. Dark cavernous place, enormous scale. Great castings in heaps everywhere. That Sheffield Vulcan image … there's something primeval about steel making. It's called a cathedral furnace, and it's that size. A huge furnace with

blazing hot fire. Dante's inferno. Can I watch? Yes, but keep against that wall. But what about my recording levels? Steel crashes on the anvil. I'm standing 20 yards away, face boiling, puffer jacket starting to melt.

A statue of Vulcan sits atop Sheffield town hall, so a dialogue between Lucifer and the blacksmith of the Roman Gods cried out to Tams to be used. The Lucifer of his song has 'signed up another demon … Maggie says his name's McGregor' for Dante's Inferno. That's the way Ewan described his father's workplace, voiced again by Hunt. By contrast, when he went to Swan Hunter's shipyard on Tyneside – there are no ships made any more on Clydeside – 'My hands were sticking to railings as I went up, it was so cold'. Hunt did the bulk of the actuality collection in an intensive period, trekking over the country to record foxhunts and saboteurs, and to Northern Ireland. That had a special intensity for him: 'I was there when the [1992] Manchester bombs went off. The second was under a bush and it blew me off my feet. When I was recording the Irish bombing stories over there my heart was going like this …'

The second interviewer was Sara, Charles Parker's daughter. She had become a radio producer by a roundabout route: it was never in any career plan. It began by accident when she was working as a journalist and did some recording on the Thames for a friend, and she has wound up years later making programmes as her father did, with the same sensibilities. It's not, she thinks, that she absorbed it as a child, but she unconsciously uses an identical approach. When she read about her father's early recording days she was genuinely taken aback to find how similar to hers his mental processes and method had been – the tricks needed to put people at ease, and for shaping the interview to cajole out speech in a form you can use.

> Like going fishing. The same question time and time again. I do remember watching him edit … tiny pieces … these little bits of tape, all stuck along the edge, a word on each … I am supposed to be quite good at getting people to talk … I think now it must be inherited … My father really listened – a lot of interviewers don't.

She is now a highly regarded radio feature maker in her own right, and, though for several years she didn't let on within the BBC who her father was, John Leonard knew of her work and it was for that reason and not out of sentiment that he approached her. She has a formidable ability to coax out sensitive information, and her HIV interviews with patients and parents had people in tears in the studio, said Hunt – 'We do it quite differently, and she's brilliant.'

Making the 2006 Radio Ballads was a cottage industry. Vince Hunt and Sara Parker were jobbing interviewers and voice collectors. For Vince that was no problem: 'The final cut? Not my job. My job's to dig through the earth for the gems ... Listening to nine hours of material for a 15-second clip. Speeches by Ian Paisley and Gerry Adams. Awful lot of shit to wade through.' Used to making complete programmes from start to finish, Sara found it more difficult to hand over interviews, and lose segments of speech she liked on someone else's cutting-room floor. But she was in Kent, the songwriters were dotted all over the place, often on the road. Leonard and a small production team were up in Manchester, Tams close to them in Derbyshire with a studio, which they used because the BBC's was too expensive.

Writing the Songs

The actuality – on average a bit over 25 hours for each programme, less than half that for the originals but still a huge workload in their timescale – came back to Manchester and was listened to by Annie Grundy, who did an initial selection, transcription, and aggregation by topic. Often, enthralled by what she heard, she stayed into the small hours, and she was not alone in burning midnight oil. John Leonard further selected and assembled chunks of actuality which were put onto CD for the songwriters. When the songs came back, Leonard and Tams worked on their integration into each programme with Andy Seward, a gifted engineer and producer. Essentially it was five songwriters who created the songs. Tams himself wrote 19, Jez Lowe 18, Julie Matthews 10, Karine Polwart 6. Each wrote for four or more of the six programmes, while the Irish singer Tommy Sands came up with 6 songs for *Thirty Years of Conflict*.

Half of Tams's contribution was for *Song of Steel*, which was the programme on which they tested out their method. But he had no intention of trying to emulate Ewan by writing everything himself, and so commissioned modern songwriters in the folk idiom whose work he knew. While Tams does write songs, his wide canvas – including theatre, television and the screen – means that he has written less for concert stage and folk club. Moreover, to write them all in just eight months? That would have taxed even Ewan. No:

> It's too big a barrel – I'd scrape it if I wrote the lot. MacColl's ego was sufficient to the job, he wouldn't want another writer on. There's only so much vocabulary, only so many chords ... I couldn't write the AIDS show. Women wrote most of that, plus Jez. So underrated, Jez, indelible lyrics. A proper songwriter.

Jez Lowe was introduced to the Radio Ballads at college, unlike Leonard and Tams, who heard the songs first without knowing their origin. Moreover, he was used to writing songs 'from the actuality'. From an Irish family settled in the North-East, like many singers in the folk revival, Lowe was commissioned in 1997 by the BBC to write and present a seven-part series on the music of his region, *A Song for Geordie*. His evocative song 'Coal Town Days' was written for the BBC to accompany the announcement of the plan to close the last coal mines in England, and he'd written others for local celebrations:

> I did a sort of Radio Ballads thing called *Banners* for the local council, with local musicians, 120 people … Easington, listening to people talk. I went back to the *Big Hewer* to refresh my memory, but I'd heard them at the Poly in Sunderland where they were in the library, so I was aware of the technique. The originals were much more theatrical too, more visual, this was more pure radio … Using actuality recordings was telescoping my process anyway. It was easy for me to visualise, listening to the actuality CD, all pre-edited, and many of the songs came straight out at me. The shipbuilding stuff was (literally) riveting. But I had to accept that I was being a hack, had to let it go when I was finished, hand it over like Fitzgerald when he did film scripts while writing his novels. Hard to accept, that, having no time to work on a song later, refine it.

Julie Matthews, on the other hand, was less used to that style of songwriting. Indeed, although her father like Leonard's had worked in the Sheffield steel industry, she had never written about her own background. She was in the back of the van between gigs on tour when she first listened to her CD of wartime women working on the steelyard cranes, tears on her cheeks:

> To hear those old women – they sounded like my relatives – and they blew me away … It was an emotional thing for me, coming from Sheffield, all those beautiful accents … I put them on the iPod and immersed myself in all the voices for six weeks, wrote seven songs in a rush and the rest in a trickle. The AIDS song, 'Sum of What I Am', was a line from a woman who happened to be HIV positive, but 'I'm all these other things too.' Totally inspiring. I wrote 'Crane Drivers' very quickly. It was a weird way of working for me … for that first song I literally took some lines word for word. It's the first time I've ever written and sung in my own dialect.

Me brother said I don't believe it still -
They're taking on women at the rolling mill.
So I went down and I put in me name -
When I turned 18 I was a crane driver,
Turned 18 I was a crane driver.

So taken was Julie Matthews with the whole process that she now finds it somewhat unsatisfying to sing the songs <u>without</u> the actuality. So in 2007 she took on tour a concert of ten of her Radio Ballad songs, singing them with the original voices embedded, and will do more. For the Scottish singer Karine Polwart, too, it was an unfamiliar way of working. Insulated from the assembly process, as they all were apart from Tams, it took her a while to key into how her verses would dovetail with the voices with which they were interspersed. Her comment on writing 'Luck Money' for *Swings and Roundabouts* emphasises that, like the original team, they were all learning as they went, but over a truncated timescale. They could do it, of course, through modern technology.

> It was the last song I wrote, so I was much more conscious of what was required to make it thread in with the speech ... I recorded the song with very much a full structure in mind of where the speech was going to come in, in and out of the melody ... I was right to the wire with the deadline, so I sent the lyric then literally sang the melody down into an answering machine ... and mercifully the length of the bars and the verses fitted perfectly with the bits of speech John Leonard wanted to convey in that section ... It was good fun to do it that way.

The compressed timescale meant that at one point they were working on all six programmes in parallel, something Charles Parker never had to do. (He'd have been delighted by the computer tools available, and you can't help feeling that he'd have been touching up every programme right up to the last minute.) Throughout the exercise the team was conscious of the legacy, and determined not to let their predecessors down. One early decision Leonard and Tams made was not to try to emulate the musical complexity of the originals. Keep it simple, drop in the actuality between verses. Tams said, 'We adopted the form but adapted the way we approached it ... tried to make it unbroken, so no gaps in the music ... we fought over the music throughout, had a good ruck, all good-humoured.'

John Leonard started with *Song of Steel*, a subject he knew. His father had been an engineer in a Sheffield steelworks and had his own small foundry. He vividly remembers carrying molten metal around, stoking a cupola furnace, going past Steel, Peach and Tozer in the bus feeling the heat through the bus windows. A mile-long plant either side of the road, the massive forge hammer shaking the centre of Sheffield:

> I wanted to get the hammer going, keep it going, so it irritates, then keep it going on ... The song's in rhythm, but ... I couldn't get the start of *Steel* right. I'd start with the hammer, then the music, then the speech, then the song. But it distorts on radio. I went back to *Big Hewer* which starts with the drill – deliberately didn't listen to them again, but I did just this once. *Hewer* has this exciting beginning. Ah, yes I see, easy – establish it, take it down – I sat at the feet of the master for half an hour. Otherwise I wanted a free mind, so I stopped listening to them.

> [My] old man used to sit reading t'Star, and this bang bang bang bang going on, then all of a sudden he'd put his hand out and catch t'clock … that had vibrated off t'mantelpiece … he said he could gauge the number of bangs …'

> Going down to Steelos, get mesen a start.
> Dunna let it cobble, it'll tear the place apart –
> Catch it as it's coming, throw the bugger back,
> Keep your tongs upon the metal and your eyes upon the track.

Tams was well placed, as Ewan was in Scots, to write in the local dialect. The actuality in the steel and shipbuilding industry is as compelling as anything in the original Radio Ballads. A shipbuilding worker came in from nowhere, sat down in front of Hunt, and spoke non-stop for an hour. 'I usually have to prompt a bit, but there was never a "Go on" in that conversation.' He's the Glaswegian in *Ballad of the Big Ships* who tells a story about chucking the job in – literally:

> One day I thought I'd had enough – I just cannae take this any more. And it was off with the boots and I threw them into the Clyde. Off with the overalls, threw them in, and I swung the toolbag over my head – Splash, into the Clyde. And I walked off and swore that you'd never get me back in the shipyard again. Tick tick tick tick tick tick tick. Time goes by and needs must and I ended up going back a second time. First day back, the first person you see is the last guy you worked with, and he'll say to you, 'You were a long time at the toilet' – as if you'd been away at the kludgie for 11 years!

I, you, he'll… all those pronoun, tense and viewpoint switches that Ewan and Charles loved in traditional storytelling and ballads. One novelty which they would have admired was the use of a muscular local poet, Ian McMillan. His was one of a shipyard load of industrial dialects from Tyneside and Clydeside, especially from those working in the 'Black Trades', as they called those down in the dirt and dust in the depths of the freezing ship. The list of trades and implements was an opportunity Ewan would have relished, and Jez Lowe came up with a beautifully crafted song that used the trade list as a background chant. 'Whose idea was that?' said Peggy, 'Brilliant!' Interwoven are descriptions of life deep down that recall the mining:

A NEW GENERATION – THE 2006 RADIO BALLADS

Your family needs you to do as needs must,
To the mercy of metal and madness you're thrust,
And the keels and the girders of darkness and dust
And a deadly concoction of sweat, fumes and rust –
   'Cos you're Black Trade, you're just Black Trade –

All you welders and riveters and boilersmiths and platemen,
You gaugers and pipefitters, sparks and sheet metal workers,
You riggers and coppersmiths, red letters, hard drinkers,
Cablers and laggers, you pullers and dabbers ...

The bane of your life lies there snug in the slips –
She's round at the stern and she's wide at the hips,
And she's proud at the bow and the pout on her lips
Says this country's an island and an island needs ships,
   And you're Black Trade ...

You can be working in confined spaces, sometimes no bigger than a cupboard under the stairs ... Generally you're working in the dark on your own. Once you put your head down all you can hear is the crackle of the arc.

The two heavy industry programmes mirrored their original equivalents, the railways and the mines: the archetypal Radio Ballad recipe of a tight-knit community of labourers (yes, men). But whereas in 1958 and 1962 the makers could celebrate the courage, hard work and camaraderie of the working man – in nationalised industries – now steel and shipbuilding were in private hands and in terminal decline. The comradeship and the crack were still there, but articulated by old men reflecting, as Sam Larner had, on a tough life that had gone for ever. Like Bill Senior, the cracked-voice steel man who died of the effects of dust before the programme was broadcast. The political component in both is inevitably more explicit now, just as *Big Hewer* became in Philip Donnellan's hands. Here Karine Polwart takes an idea of Jez Lowe's to create a song comparing the fragility of man engaged in dangerous work (as in *John Axon*) with the massive metal structure he inhabits, except that now the vehicle was <u>designed</u> for destruction. The only two ships being built in Britain when the programme was made were warships.

> You crafted and caressed her with a careful hand,
> But the lady didn't understand,
> And you riveted and plated her till morning.
> But with a coil or a careless spark
> Or a tumble in the dark
> She'll leave her mark upon you without warning.
>
> You can float a boat of steel upon the ocean,
> You can fix it up with nuts and bolts and toil –
> But you can't weld a body when it's broken.
>
> On a cruiser that was fitted by your father
> You anchored in San Carlos harbour,
> But the lady at the helm she was not for turning,
> And in your bell bottoms blue
> In April Eighty-Two
> You bid adieu and watched all you knew burning.

The HIV/AIDS programme *The Enemy Within* was a *Body Blow* equivalent, with the same inherent problem. With the moving testimony that Sara Parker brought back, how to avoid the songs simply doubling the emotion without adding anything new? The result was similar – some of the songs were fine on their own, but doleful en masse, and one was left thinking the same: what a marvellous programme it would have been without the music. One difference, of course, was that the modern sufferers had to confront a stigma and hostility – sometimes spoken, sometimes not. This made it as affecting as *Body Blow* but in a different way. Julie Matthews:

> Give it a label, call it by name,
> But the life I made before this
> It cannot claim.
> That life was so much bigger than
> The enemy that lives within
> The shadow underneath my skin
> Is not the sum of what I am.

As with *Travelling People*, *Swings and Roundabouts* looks at a group who were almost a separate community. They have a stigma to confront too, for the general public is inclined to lump them together with 'dirty Gypsies'. The response, uncomfortable to hear, was that modern fairground families (though many came from the same background) prefer to distance themselves from Travellers. While it, too, has some good songs and great stories, the actuality seems stretched, and John Leonard feels they should have gone back to more sources. It was perhaps the one programme that became the victim of the rush to the line. In fact, it was only added late on, suggested by John Tams, who had worked on fairgrounds as a lad nearly 40 years earlier, and had a ready-made moving-on song of his own, the atmospheric 'Pull Down Lads':

> Pull down, lads, the sets are cooling down, lads,
> The ark's all packed and the dodgems stacked, a bite of scran then go,
> We'll leave it as we found it, they'll soon forget we've been,
> For we trade in fun and we go and come,
> We're often scorned but seldom mourned,
> I hope you'll know what I mean.

A justified criticism of the original Radio Ballad series was that women were depicted almost totally as wives and sufferers. The only exceptions were the Scots fishgutters in Yarmouth. Even on the modern series there's still little to show that there has been a feminist movement, with just the woman crane driver in Sheffield whose job went as soon as the men came back from war, and one formidable woman running a fairground company. This time, though, they did try a rural programme, tapping into the controversy then current about hunting with hounds, about to be banned by law.

On the face of it, *Horn of the Hunter* was a tricky subject, bound to draw the ire and fire of both sides in the dispute. Moreover, they were certain to have difficulty finding any modern folk singer keen to write a song in praise of hunting. But somehow, through a combination of new songs and old – there were several old hunting songs to draw on – it worked. Vince Hunt scoured the country, and it helped the feel of the programme that he went to many hunts not populated by the classic squirearchy of the popular imagination. Many of their participants came across with down-to-earth North Country voices, their pockets unlined with inherited money. And the soundscape was particularly effective. Jez Lowe came up with a song for the fox (no actuality to call on from him), and swallowed his distaste of hunting to use a strange traditional hound-christening rhyme to baptise each of the hunt-followers, from huntsman to saboteur:

Next to come the houndsman and that I'm bound to call you –
Know your pack by name and mark, their ways and whiles and natures.
Pair the couples, old and young, but pick the babblers too –
Come the houndsman come, be a good dog and true …

Next to come the saboteur and that I'm bound to call you –
Risk a life to save a life, with the strength of the law behind you.
Rituals, traditions, all but killing fields to you –
Come the saboteur, be a good dog and true.

The final 2006 programme, *Thirty Years of Conflict*, parts company further from the originals by looking at the Troubles in Northern Ireland, over 30 years after Charles Parker and Philip Donnellan examined them in the early chaotic days. They risked controversy this time as well, though somewhat less than if they'd been making it before the Good Friday Agreement brought an end to (nearly) all the violence. Although Sara Parker was wary – the conflict had surely been observed from every angle – she realised while listening to Tommy Sands' stories of a pre-Troubles childhood that they could use the warring communities' shared love of traditional music. Killing musicians was beyond the pale: song was 'where the orange and the green are just colours on the spotlit stage', as Lowe summed it up succinctly in 'The Miami', referring to the Miami Showband murders that shocked everyone. This story and that of Bloody Sunday were framed by the flat-voiced tales of pub bombings and friends killed. The gut-wrenching songs are from Tommy Sands, powerful in the understatement of his quiet conversational singing voice, a man who has lived through and seen it all:

Someone died on Sunday, the funeral was today.
Tonight there will be trouble: someone's going to pay.
Don't go out tonight love, it's better that you stay,
For anything can happen in these Troubles …

No sanity, morality, humanity, no mind,
There's no meaning there's no feeling, there's no reason, there's no rhyme
It's an eye for an eye till everyone is blind –
And anything can happen in these Troubles.

At this stage in history they received no interference from BBC or government, though it didn't prevent some disconcerting moments. 'Different

Drums' was Julie Matthews' song, talking about the distinctive drumbeats that pounded out the quite specific rhythms of the two communities. The Protestant Lambeg Drum is a monster. Vince Hunt gives the background to the chapter-head story of the recording and return of the drum:

> We went over to see Tommy, give him the gist. 'Don't Go Out Tonight' he did in front of me in his study, just like that. I recorded it on to minidisk, not via a broadcast-quality mike. Didn't matter, he was perfect straight through ... I interviewed an IRA member about Bloody Sunday – he'd never spoken before. We got two groups of kids from a teacher promoting cross-religion harmony who assembled a mixed choir. We were in Tommy Sands' studio, in a Catholic area. A Protestant with a Lambeg Drum drove over after work, a bit nervous ...

Though it was the *Song of Steel* and *Ballad of the Big Ships* that captured most attention, and were broadcast first and last, the Irish programme is in a sense just as successful because it was the one that could most easily have foundered. As it was the music and songs enhance the actuality in the way the best of the originals did. It signally fails to include women – they were leading peace campaigners, after all – though all the voices are gripping. And one can't imagine this Tommy Sands song ever getting through, 30 years earlier:

> Some were chatting with their lovers
> Some were walking holding hands,
> Some were dreaming of a greater future dawning.
> But who could tell that darkness would descend upon their dreams,
> All upon that Sunday, Bloody Sunday.
>
> Screaming, then a burst of blood,
> 'Oh Jesus' someone cried –
> A lad of seventeen is lying dying.
> And thirteen more would follow him before the day would end.
> Oh cursed be that Sunday, Bloody Sunday.
>
> They were walking, they were talking,
> They were laughing, they were singing
> And calling out for civil rights and freedom.
> But now it was a flag of blood that fluttered in the breeze –
> A curse upon that Sunday, Bloody Sunday.

In Conclusion

So how do the two series match up? It depends entirely on your standpoint. Is a comparison even fair? This is what John Tams had to say:

> It is my belief that song-making has changed – MacColl was a pioneer of that also – and while imitation is the sincerest form of flattery why produce an entire series of MacColl pastiches or rewrites over 40 years on, for a community of listeners who have moved on and who've never heard of MacColl or the originals? ... Those who had heard the originals are now probably well into their 70s, or had bought the vinyl versions, and would possibly through the mists of nostalgia see the new work as perhaps Radio Ballads Lite. But we saw it as part of our role to back-announce the originals in the hope that [we] would introduce the listeners to the very source that had so inspired us.
>
> Consider also this was Radio 2 – not Radio 4 ... Radio 2 won the Sony awards over Radio 4, who are defined by their documentary output, and ... [so] maybe the 2006 Radio Ballads had a majority of 'first-time' listeners. For those new listeners the 2006 Radio Ballads were the <u>originals</u>. They were never claimed as such but the listener is the final arbiter and I've come to think in fairness to both pieces of work they should be considered entirely separately and on their own merits ... We made six radio documentaries also with songs and music. That's all we did – we claim no origination – we simply focused on our subjects and tried to serve them.

I don't think they should be compared as in a beauty contest. But using the same title as the originals, which were made nearly 50 years earlier under very different conditions and timescales, probably made that inevitable. The new series has been a great success: one reviewer said that it was years since he had been so educated by music. Had they not been billed as 'Radio Ballads', the old folkie reaction might well have been something like this:

> Well, they're not the Radio Ballads of course, but there are some wonderful stories in there, and some of the songs are great. Took less than a year to make the series, you say? That's tough. Guess they did a good job, considering.

Instead, those who grew up with the originals, like Sandra Kerr, whose pedigree as a folk singer, songwriter and teacher is impeccable, start automatically on a straight comparison. It all begins with the notion of the Radio Ballad (a somewhat confusing title for the layman anyway) as something that tells a story in an hour of ballad-form, and these aren't quite like that. From the originals' perspective much of the actuality is as spine-chillingly good as in the originals. Some of the songs indeed match up to Ewan MacColl's, but to admirers of Ewan's songwriting you have to be a paragon to come close. They point to less variety of pace in the music. They go on to compare unfavourably the formulaic song-speech-song-speech, plus a simple instrumental line taken on behind the voices, with the complex tapestry of musical sound of their predecessors. (When that worked in the originals it was absolutely brilliant, but, as Peggy says now, it was sometimes overdone.) Sara Parker, who of course has a loyalty to both series, makes the pertinent comment that nowadays it's anathema in radio programmes to have music behind speech. (Her father knew all about that by 1972.) The 2006 'house musicians' – built around John McCusker and Andy Cutting – do a superb job, though overall there's a smaller range of instruments. Apart from the iconic Grimethorpe Colliery Band in *Song of Steel*, there isn't the injection of other musical influences, jazz and classical, which enlivened the originals. But, as John Tams said 'Jazz, in 2006?' It's a different world now.

My own stance is this. At their best the originals are, and continue to be, enthralling, but I can see the flaws, notably when they attempted subject matter unsuitable for the method. Some of the new series too are superb, but I do think we should look at them in a separate light. Overall, I'm delighted that the Radio Ballad form has been renewed and reinterpreted after a long wait of over 40 years, and with such skill and attention to the spirit of the originals. Let's have some more: there's a host of topics waiting out there. The Leonard/Tams team has been looking among other things at Cotton, Homelessness, The Armed Forces, The Minimum Wage and Old Age. Ewan himself would be salivating at the prospect of those, not least Cotton, which goes back to his Red Megaphones of 1932. Gratifyingly, all will bring women more to the fore.

I'll leave the last word to a distinguished journalist who has listened to radio since the days of Charles Parker, whose work she admired hugely. Gillian Reynolds is Chairman of the Charles Parker Archive Trust. Through the Trust, which looks after a mass of his interviews and other material, she helped to secure a Lottery Grant to digitise and catalogue the collection. They are an incomparable resource for oral historians, as I well know. She, too, might be expected to prefer the originals, and she indeed believes they were magnificent imaginative radio, which moreover opened programme makers' eyes for ever to what could be done with tape recorders and real voices. Yet she admits that at times she resented being preached at. A generation later she called this new series the best radio of 2006. That's just how Paul Ferris described *The Ballad of John Axon* in 1958.

Listen, and decide for yourself. And let's not have to wait so long next time.

Endnotes – Major Sources

The Radio Ballads themselves

The Radio Ballads are available on CD from Topic records, www.topicrecords.co.uk, and from the book's website www.setintosong.co.uk. The records each differ slightly from the broadcast programmes, and in the case of *John Axon* by a quarter of an hour, because it was broadcast originally in a 45-minute version. Incidentally it was a (modified) version of that length that was entered for the Italia Prize, and the entry for *Singing the Fishing* two years later was similarly truncated. Here are the eight Radio Ballads with their first broadcast dates and CD numbers:

2 July 1958	*Ballad of John Axon*	TSCD 801
5 November 1959	*Song of a Road*	TSCD 802
16 August 1960	*Singing the Fishing*	TSCD 803
18 August 1961	*The Big Hewer*	TSCD 804
27 March 1962	*The Body Blow*	TSCD 805
13 February 1963	*On the Edge*	TSCD 806
3 July 1963	*The Fight Game*	TSCD 807
17 April 1964	*Travelling People*	TSCD 808

The Life of Ewan MacColl (Jimmie Miller) before Peggy Seeger – Chapters 2 and 5

Ewan MacColl's biography *Journeyman* covers his early years in great detail, the theatre and radio before and after the war, and the folk revival. About the war years he is silent after mid 1940, and he writes little about the period after 1971. As well as providing additional recollections of their pre- and post-war life together and in the theatre, Joan Littlewood's *Joan's Book* covers his call-up, return, arrest and release. Further details are available from Jimmie Miller's MI5 file (started when he was 17…) in the National Archive at Kew and now partly available online, and Army Personnel Records in Glasgow. The two autobiographies are essential and vivid reading, though for both authors telling the story is more important than absolute precision (and we would not wish it otherwise), and neither is very good on dates. Where they matter the most rigorous arbiter is Ben Harker's recent biography *Class Act*, essential reading for those interested in Ewan MacColl's life. Charles Parker's interviews with Ewan's mother Betsy Miller in 1962 and 1969 are a crucial added source for his childhood. For the background to conditions in pre-war Lancashire the first port of call for source documents is the Working Class Movement Library in Salford.

The excellent 1985 radio series by Mary Orr and Michael O'Rourke, *Parsley, Sage and Politics*, provides a good general background and includes extracts from interviews with his pre-war friends. Transcripts of the original interviews, especially the lengthy one with Ewan himself, are held in the MacColl/Seeger Archive and are particularly fascinating. Ewan talks about his early life in the TV programmes *Daddy, What Did You Do in the Strike?* and the posthumously broadcast *Ballad of Ewan MacColl*, and on several radio programmes.

For Ewan's theatre work before and after the war further sources are *Agit-prop to Theatre Workshop*, edited by Ewan MacColl and Howard Goorney; Goorney's *The Theatre Workshop Story*; *Theatres of the Left 1880–1935* by Raphael Samuel, Ewan MacColl and Stuart Cosgrove, and the Theatre Royal Archive at Stratford East. Derek Paget was helpful in reviewing the (belated) development of radical theatre after Theatre Workshop settled in Stratford.

For Ewan MacColl's pre-war radio work see Geoffrey Bridson's *Prospero and Ariel* and Olive Shapley's *Broadcasting a Life*, and the extensive BBC Archive at Caversham. For Alan Lomax see *Ruth Crawford Seeger* by Judith Tick, and *Alan Lomax: Selected Writings 1934–97*, by Ronald Cohen. To disentangle the often unrecorded early years of the folk revival see *Dazzling Stranger* by Colin Harper, and, of course, the exhaustive resources of the library of the EFDSS (English Folk Dance and Song Society) in Camden, London. Brian Shuel's magnificent photographs, of which I reproduce only a small proportion in this book, provide the perfect picture of the early folk clubs for one who, alas, wasn't there.

The Life of Charles Parker – Chapters 3, 12, 13 and 20

The major source is, of course, the Charles Parker Archive, set up after his death by his wife and children, and I'm indebted to them and to those at the Archive and the Charles Parker Trust who have assiduously developed it since. That has culminated in a project to digitise the great collection of interviews of which he went to extreme lengths to keep copies. The unpublished autobiography of his late friend and colleague Philip Donnellan, provisionally entitled *Corporation Street*, is immensely valuable in illuminating his working life at the BBC, as well as being an absorbing read. There are some important letters in the MacColl/Seeger Archive, and further career record information is available at the BBC Archive. There is little documented about his pre-war life, while his war record and experiences come from the National Archive and various interviewees, notably his university friend Philip Cox. His post-war career in the North American service was brought vividly alive by his old boss Peggy Broadhead and his one-time secretary Rosemary Fitch.

Further sources for his BBC Midlands career come from a lengthy recorded interview with Trevor Fisher from 1971, who subsequently wrote the summary *Charles Parker, Aspects of a Pioneer: A Personal View*. Dilip Hiro, Doc Rowe and others gave a picture of his personality and working methods in the period after the Radio Ballads, while Daniel Snowman and Michael Mason discussed his work on *The Long March of Everyman*. Particularly helpful too were the interviews for Sally Flatman's 1995 radio programme *The Ballad of Charles Parker*. His teaching and involvement in the early days of the Grey Cock Folk Club were recalled by Eileen Whiting in letter and interview, and by meetings with Joy Ashworth, Bob Etheridge, Pam Fisher, Trevor Fisher, Barbara Miller and Doug Miller. His involvement in the founding and early years of Banner Theatre was explained by Dave Rogers and Rhoma Bowdler, and there is a detailed case study of Banner in Alan Filewod and Davis Watt's *Workers' Playtime*. His work as a lecturer in Birmingham and London was described by Trevor Fisher and Andy Cheal. His lectures themselves were painstakingly assembled, edited and introduced by the late Anthony Schooling, and lie in the Charles Parker Archive, awaiting a publisher still. There are many other unpublished articles, lectures and discussion transcripts in the Archive, and extracts from some of them are on this book's website.

The Life of Peggy Seeger – Chapters 4 and 21

The principal sources for Peggy Seeger's early life have been Judith Tick's biography of her mother, *Ruth Crawford Seeger*, and Peggy Seeger's substantial unpublished writings, augmented by several conversations. Her life, too, is well illustrated in *Parsley, Sage and Politics*. For Pete Seeger, see *How Can I Keep from Singing: Pete Seeger* by David Dunaway. Peggy's life in England is covered extensively by the MacColl/Seeger archive. An invaluable study of her later song writing and life after Ewan's death is Amber Good's prizewinning 2002 thesis *Lady, What Do You Do All Day*. Peggy's informative website is a model of its kind, as is her *Songbook* and its introduction.

The Radio Ballads themselves – Chapters 6, 8, 10–15 and 19

The prime sources for the details of the creation of the Radio Ballads are the documents in the Charles Parker Archive, with some extra material in *Journeyman*, the MacColl/Seeger Archive and the BBC Archive in Caversham. Peggy Seeger went through each of the Radio Ballads with me over a three-day period, and without her insights the book would be substantially poorer. The following living participants all gave interviews (those asterisked spoke over the phone): Jim Bray*, Ian Campbell, Lorna Campbell, Bob Clark*, Fitzroy Coleman*, Bryan Daly, Bob Davenport, Rae Fisher*, John Faulkner*, Kay Graham, Ronnie Hughes, Stan Kelly-Bootle, Louis Killen, Jimmie McGregor, Colin Ross*, Elizabeth Stewart and the back-from-the-dead Dave Swarbrick. Interviewed for research into *John Axon* were the retired Edgeley railwaymen Edwin Bolus, Terry Burkitt, Jack Moores and Johnny Smith, and I'm indebted to the film-maker Andrew Johnston for finding and interviewing Ron Scanlon, Axon's fireman.

Further information on the musicians with a jazz background comes from John Chilton's *Who's Who of British Jazz* and his *Hot Jazz, Warm Feet*, and Bruce Turner's *Hot Air, Cool Music*. An interview with Dave Arthur was particularly helpful on Bert Lloyd's life, ahead of his forthcoming 'Bert' – *A Life of AL Lloyd*. I have drawn heavily on Ian Campbell's unpublished articles, in particular that on *Singing the Fishing*, but also his piece on Centre 42, which was reinforced by Eileen Whiting and Bob Etheridge. The section on the 'Birmingham Ballads' was brought to life by Ian and Lorna Campbell, Brian Vaughton and Alan Ward.

Many people have written articles on the Radio Ballads, and while I haven't quoted from these directly their articles have all been of considerable benefit, notably those of Lawrence Aston, Karl Dallas, Fred McCormick and Ian Parr. Ian, secretary of the Charles Parker Trust, has done pioneering work researching the Radio Ballads and other Charles Parker programmes.

BBC Voices – Chapter 7

Again, *Prospero and Ariel* and *Broadcasting a Life* are excellent on pre-war broadcasting in Manchester, and in the former Geoffrey Bridson brings the story of BBC radio features up to the Radio Ballad period. For general histories see in particular *A Social History of British Broadcasting* by Paddy Scannell and David Cardiff, Sean Street's *A Concise History of British Radio*, and Asa Briggs' *History of Broadcasting in the United Kingdom*. There are two books both entitled *Life on Air*. David Attenborough's covers the period when television was on the rise, and David Hendy's history of Radio 4 takes us into the modern radio era. Interviews with Sean Street, Piers Plowright, Gabi Fisher and Sara Parker shed light on present-day radio feature making.

Creating the Radio Ballads – Chapters 9, 16, 17 and 18

The Charles Parker Archive contains his voluminous writings on the difficulties of early recording, in field and studio, and editing. John Clarke, Gillian Ford and Alan Ward, who all worked in the studio with Charles Parker on several of the programmes, were immensely helpful in unravelling the mechanics of the recording and editing process, and bringing the studio to life. So, too, was the late Mary Baker, Charles's editing 'assistant' – a word that does scant justice to her immense contribution – whose explanation of her working life with him is now in the Archive. Edward Pawley's *BBC Engineering 1922–1972* is a solid factual history of engineering in the BBC: other views from the users come from *Prospero and Ariel* and *Corporation Street*.

Both Charles Parker and Ewan MacColl wrote and spoke at length about interviewing methods: for example in their *Singing English* discussion broadcast in 1962 and Charles Parker's paper on *Field Recording Techniques* of 1965. An important source for Ewan's elaborate approach to song writing for the Radio Ballads is their 1965 *Landmarks* discussion in Beckenham, held in the Parker Archive: *Journeyman* has nothing to say on his precise methods. For the songs themselves and the background to their writing *The Essential Ewan MacColl Songbook* is indeed just that. The principal source for Chapter 18 was Peggy herself, while Tessa Murray improved my negligible musical education.

Ewan MacColl and Peggy Seeger – Chapter 21

Their lives together are covered in copious detail in the MacColl/Seeger Archive. Peggy Seeger's introduction to Ewan's *Songbook* is compelling and honest, and their early years together are also covered by her own unpublished writings, which extend to the Critics Group and *Festival of Fools* period. That was amplified by interviews with Frankie Armstrong, Bob Blair, Kathy Henderson, Sandra Kerr, Gordon McCulloch, Jim O'Connor and Brian Pearson; conversations with Jimmy Carroll and Denis Turner; and an email exchange with Michael Rosen. *Journeyman* is very selective about Ewan's later life, with some areas completely unmentioned, but I've had much help from Jacquie Dunnet, Karl Dallas, Richard Humm, Neill MacColl, Geordie McIntyre, Ian McDeson, and Alison McMorland – and above all Peggy Seeger herself.

Sound in Vision – Chapter 23

The major source is Philip Donnellan's *Corporation Street*, willingly provided by his widow Jill: I hope it soon finds the publisher it deserves. I'm indebted to Paul Long for providing me with an electronic version, and to Ken Hall for copies of and advice on the three Radio Ballad films.

A New Generation – Chapter 24

The story of the making of the 2006 Radio Ballads is based on interviews with John Leonard, John Tams, Vince Hunt, Sara Parker, Jez Lowe, Julie Matthews and a conversation with Annie Grundy, and the views of Peggy Seeger, Sandra Kerr, Gillian Reynolds and several others. The 2006 programmes are available from Gott Discs.

Bibliography, Sources and Footnotes

Note that a full bibliography, list of sources, and footnotes are available online at www.setintosong.co.uk, together with a complete transcript of the text of the programmes (as recorded, rather than as broadcast).

List of Illustrations

Back Cover:
Charles Parker interviewing for Singing the Fishing, 1960
Ewan MacColl and Peggy Seeger at the Newport Folk Festival, 1960

    1 Eric Fraser's Radio Times graphic for *The Ballad of John Axon*, 1958
    4 The young Jimmie Miller, and Coburg Street where he was brought up
  19 Charles Parker interviewing a herring fisherman, 1960
  28 Mike and Peggy Seeger at Swarthmore College, 1955
  36 Ewan MacColl in his play *Uranium 235*, c 1951
  49 The wreck of John Axon's train, Chapel en le Frith, 1957
  61 Peggy Seeger with her motor scooter, 1957
  62 Joan Littlewood and Geoffrey Bridson, 1939
        Fougasse cartoon from Punch, 1941: 'A talk on the larvae of the common logarithm'
  72 Radio Times graphic for the December 1958 repeat of *Song of a Road*
  86 Bryan Daly, John Cole, Peggy Seeger, Bob Clark, and Charles Parker recording *The Ballad of John Axon*, 1958
  96 Sam Larner, and Eric Fraser's Radio Times graphic for *Singing the Fishing*, 1960
108 Eric Fraser's Radio Times graphic for *The Big Hewer*, 1961
117 Charles Parker interviews Heather Ruffell for *The Body Blow*, 1962
130 Heather Ruffell mouth painting, c 1977
131 Young motor-cycle riders in the 1960s
142 Paul Pender and Terry Downes in a world title fight in 1961
154 A young rider in a Travellers' encampment
165 Charles Parker interviewing at Saltley Gasworks for *The Maker and the Tool*, 1962
173 Ewan MacColl working at home in Beckenham, 1965
185 Rehearsing for a Centre 42 concert in Wellingborough in 1962 – Alf Edwards, Peggy Seeger, Bert Lloyd and Ewan MacColl
201 Louis Killen and Bob Davenport at the Singers Club, 1962
203–17 Radio Ballad performers, see captions for names
219 Charles Parker running a workshop at the Keele Folk Festival, 1965
227 Charles Parker zipped-up, cartoon by Richard Yeend, 1972
235 Ewan MacColl and Peggy Seeger at the Singers Club, 1970s
247 Peggy Seeger in 2004
259 Philip Donnellan at the opening of the Charles Parker Archive, 1986
268 John Tams and Jez Lowe at the 2006 Radio Ballad concert in Glasgow, 2007

Picture Acknowledgements

My particular thanks are due to the generosity of Brian Shuel, whose photographs are a magnificent record of the early Folk Revival years; to the family of Eric Fraser, for permission to include his iconic Radio Times illustrations; to Charlotte Tucker at the Birmingham Library digital laboratory; and to Peggy Seeger and Kitty MacColl for their help with the family collection.

Specifically : Eric Fraser family pp. 1, 96, 108; Bryan Ledgard and Mike Harding p. 268; Charles Parker Archive: cover and pp. 19, 86, 165, 234; Punch p. 62; Seeger family collection: cover and pp. 4, 28, 36, 61, 96; Brian Shuel pp. 173, 185, 201, 203, 205, 206, 209, 210, 212, 214, 215, 217, 219, 235, 246; Richard Yeend p. 227.

Simplified Timeline

	Ewan MacColl	Peggy Seeger	Charles Parker
1915	born Salford		
1919			born Bournemouth
1931	first street theatre		
1934	first radio work		
1935	marries Joan Littlewood Theatre of Action	born New York	
1937			National Physical Lab
1938	Theatre Union		
1940	joins and leaves Army		joins Navy
1945	Theatre Workshop, Uranium 235		Cambridge University
1949	marries Jean Newlove		joins BBC
1953	Ballads and Blues	Radcliffe College	
1954			BBC Midlands
1956	Ewan and Peggy meet – Ramblers		
1957	Ballads and Blues club		
1958	——————————— First Radio Ballad ———————————
1961	Singers Club		
1962			Centre 42 plays
1964	——————————— Final Radio Ballad ———————————
1965	Critics Group starts, first Festival of Fools, Song Carriers		
1967			Grey Cock folk club
1968		first New City Songster	
1972	Critics Group ends, final Festival of Fools		leaves BBC
1974			Banner Theatre
1976	Blackthorne Records		
1977	Ewan and Peggy marry		
1980			dies
1989	dies		
1992		No Spring Chickens with Irene Pyper-Scott	
1994		returns to USA	
2007		teaching songwriting in Boston	

Index

2006 Radio Ballads **267–82**
7:84 theatre company 244–5

'A Wee Drappie O't' 7
Almanac Singers 31
Almost Commercially Viable 257
American Folk Songs for Children 31
American Folk Songs for Christmas 34
Animal Folk Songs for Children 31
Armstrong, Alec 16, 150
Armstrong, Frankie 221, 242
Arts Council 40, 135
As I Roved Out
As You Like It 21
Attenborough, David 45, 118, 264
Axon, Gladys 50–1, 56, 59–60, 187
Axon, John 50, 56, 187–8

'Back o' Benachie' 101
Baker, Mary 85, 94–5, 103, 106
'Ballad of Accounting' 177
'Ballad of Jimmy Massey' 256
'Ballad of Jimmy Wilson' 250
'Ballad of John Axon' (song) 55
Ballad of John Axon 49–61, 63, 69, 73, 75, 81, 83–5, 88–9, 91, 93–4, 115–6, 119, 123, 143, 149, 152, 178–9, 182, 186–8, 204, 206, 208, 210–1, 218, 260, 270, 277, 283
'Ballad of Springhill' 250
'Ballad of the Big Cigars' 183
Ballad of the Big Ships 270–1, 276–8, 281
'Ballad of the Carpenter' 175
'Ballad of Tim Evans' 175
Ballads and Blues 45, 50, 176
Ballads and Blues Club 236–7
Balls, Ronnie 96, 99–100, 104, 172, 180–1, 262
BANG (Beckenham Anti-Nuclear Group) 256
Banner Theatre 134, 230–4, 244
'Barbara Allen' 35
'Barnyards o' Delgaty' 102
Bates, Paul 122, 124–5, 128–9
'Battle Is Done With' 151
Battleship Potemkin, The 65
BBC Radio Midlands 25–6, 49, 73, 94, 120, 146, 221, 229–30
BBC Radio (other) 11–15, 22, 26, 27, 45, 57–8, 62–71, 81, 135, 140, 152, 162, 207, 210, 223, 227, 269, 282
BD8 220

Beamish, Dick 109
Behan, Dominic 54, 211
Bellamy, Peter 258
'Berryfields of Blair' 215
Big Hewer 41, 64, 89, **108–20**, 127, 149, 166, 171–2, 177, 183–4, 189, 192–3, 207, 210, 212, 230–1, 264, 274–5, 277
Big Hewer (film) 259, 265–7
'Big Hewer' (song) 111, 266
Bishop, Pam 223
Black, Ernest 110, 172
'Black Trades' 276
Blackthorne Records 244
Blind Set, The 221–3
Blood Wedding 44, 174
Blue Blouses 10
Body Blow 117, **121–30**, 132, 135, 138, 143, 193–5, 221–2, 278
Bolus, Edwin 188
Boswell, Gilbert 156
Boswell, Gordon 156
Boswell, Sylvester (Wester) 156, 160
Botkin, Ben 31
Bowdler, Rhoma 230–4
Brace, Keith 222
Bray, Jim 47, 53, 80, 101, 176, 205–6
Brenton, Guy 121
Bridson, Geoffrey 8, 11–12, 14, 38, 44–5, 62, 65–9, 71, 79, 87, 90, 212
'Bring Me Home' 257
Broadcasting in the Seventies 225
Broadhead, Peggy 22–3
Broonzy, Big Bill 45, 48
Brown, Terry 204
'Browned Off' 17
Bruce Turner's Jump Band 204–5
Buchan, Gilbert 261
Buchan, Magsie 262
Bumgarner, Samantha 30
Burkitt, Terry 188
Butlin's 37, 41–2

'Cabin Boy' 105, 182–3
Caller Herrin' 262
'Cam Ye O'er Frae France' 148
Camacho, George 57
Cambridge Footlights Revue 21
Camera and the Song 213
Cameron, Isla 26, 45–6, 54, 79, 84, 113, 210, 214

291

Cameron, Maggie 160–1
Campbell, Alex, 75
Campbell, Ian 101–2, 106, 117, 119–121, 132, 134–5, 137, 206–7, 213–4, 228
Campbell, Lorna 119, 137, 196, 214
'Cannily Cannily' 175
Cardno, Lewis 99
Carleton-Greene, Hugh 50, 116
'Carry Greenham Home' 255
Carthy, Martin 207, 214
Cartland, Barbara (Mrs Hugh McCorquodale) 159
'Casey Jones' 26
'Cats and Back-Acters' 72
Cattouse, Nadia 71
Centre 42 131–5, 148, 244
'Champion at Keeping 'em Rolling' 175
'Children of a Troubled World' 138
Chilton, John 204–5
'Chocolate Paddies' 214
Christopher Columbus (radio) 69
Clancy, Adrian 59
Clarence, John 71, 79, 101, 212
Clarion Singers 101–2, 104, 111, 119, 133–4, 189, 213, 218, 228
Clarion Skiffle Group 119, 213
Clark, Bob 53, 206
Clarke, John 94–6, 103, 148, 191, 201, 203, 216
Classic Features (radio) 68
Classic Soil (radio) 15
Cleverdon, Douglas 58, 69, 73
Coal (radio) 67
Coal Face (film) 65
Coleman, Fitzroy 46–7, 54, 79, 101–2, 208–9
Collier Laddie (play) 230, 265
Collins, Shirley 47
Columbia Broadcasting System 23, 50
Colyer, Ken 46
Combine 243
Come All Ye Bold Miners 45
'Come Live with Me and Be My Love' 140
'Come, Me Little Son' 84
Communist Party 18, 38
Cooke, Alastair 174
Cooper, George A 241
Cooper, Henry 148–50
Cooper, Jim 149
Corbett, Harry H 241
Coronation Scot 66
Corwin, Norman 50, 84
Cotten, Libba 31, 32, 46
'Crane Drivers' 274
Crisis in Spain 65
Critics Group 180, 216, 230, 236–43, 250
Crozier, Mary 115

Cry from the Cut 120–1, 135
Cryer, James 77
Cutting, Andy 283

'Daddy, What Did You Do in the Strike?' 245
Dallas, Karl 230
Daly, Bryan 47, 153, 193, 208
Danger (radio) 64
'Dangerous Women' 254
Dark of the Moon 35, 46
'Darling Annie' 248–9
Dash, Jack 167
Davenport, Bob 79, 198, 201
'David of the White Rock' 7
Davidson, Bill 39
Davies, Ben 'Sunshine' 109, 112–3, 172
Day in the Death of Joe Egg 222
'Day of the Fight, The' 149
Day Trip to Golgotha (projected) 258
Delany, Shelagh 42
Demuth, Dinah 200
Desai, Jayaben 253
Different Therefore Equal (LP) 252
'Different Therefore Equal' 252–3
'Different Tunes' 139
Dillon, Francis 217
'Dirty Old Town' 5, 9, 151, 174
Dobby, Dot 138–9, 170, 195–6
Dodds, Norman, MP 159
Dog in the Manger 133
Donegan, Lonnie 31, 46
Donnellan, Philip 22, 26, 90–1, 159, 177, 211, 219–20, 224–8, 233, 244, **258–67**, 277, 279–80
Douglas, Lesley 269
'Down in the Dark' 193
Dr Healey's Casebook 232
Draper, George 99, 172, 181–2
Draw the Fires 13
Driberg, Tom 59
Drifters, The 65, 262
'Drivers Song' 211
'Drumdelgie' 146
Dunnet, Bruce 235
Dylan, Bob 48, 135

'Economic Miracle, The' 246
Edinburgh Peoples' Festival 40
Edwards, Alf 46, 54, 80, 101, 186, 191–2, 194, 197, 202–4, 206, 262–3
Eisenstein, Sergei 13, 65
Eliot, TS 65, 70
Elliott, Jack 108–9, 172
Elliott, 'Rambling' Jack 80
Elliott, Reece 109, 172
Enemy That Lives Within 270, 278

INDEX

Engels, Friedrich 7–9, 15
English Folk Dance and Song Society (EFDSS) 218
Ennis, Seamus 27, 44-5, 80–1, 175, 211–12
'Eppie Morrie' 27, 152
Essential Ewan MacColl Songbook, Sixty Years of Songmaking 173, 175, 245
Etheridge, Bob 134–5
Evans, Tim 175

'Famous Flower of Serving Men' 179
Far From the Madding Crowd 210
Farmer, Lee 220, 223
Faulkner, John 167, 199, 216, 242
Faulkner, Phyllis 76
Ferris, Paul 49, 58, 83, 106, 115, 140, 152, 161, 163, 199, 283
Festival of Fools 230, 239, 242–3, 248
Feuerbach, Ludwig 7
Fight Game 142–53, 155, 172, 178, 184, 197–9, 207–8, 213, 264
'Fight Game' 144–5, 183
Fight Game (film) 263–4
'Fight, The' 151
Fire Sermon 13
'Fireman's Calypso' 54
'Fireman's Not For Me' 54
'First Time Ever I Saw Your Face' 48, 243
Fisher, Archie 214
Fisher, Ray 137, 196, 214-5
Fisher, Trevor 229, 233
'Fishgutters' Song' 101
Flack, Roberta 243
Fleming, Jacky 250
'Flood at Tupelo' 193
Flying Doctor, The 40
Folk Song in England 218
Folk Song USA 31
'For a Job' 255
Ford, Gillian (née Reeves) 86, 94
'Four Minute Warning' 255
Four People (TV) 121
'Fourpence a Day' 149
Fox, Paul 225
Fraser, Eric 81, 105
Frayman, Natt 11
'Freeborn Man' 184, 199–200
'Freight Train' 31, 32, 46
Frow, Eddie 10
Fuente Ovejuna 174
Funny Rigs of Good and Tender-Hearted Masters 230

'Galway Races' 81
Gans, Joe 148
Gaughan, Dick 244
Gielgud, Val 69–70
Gilliam, Laurence 57, 66, 69–70, 73–5, 127

Gladden, Texas 174
'Going to Work' 183
Gone for a Soldier 267
'Good Dog and True' 280
Good Soldier Schweik 16
Goodman, Bob 9, 16
Goodnight Irene 31
Goorney, Howard 38
GPO Film Unit 65
Graham, Kay 101, 107, 192, 206
Grassic Gibbon, Lewis 38
'Great Conspiracy, The' 246
Great Divide, The 232
'Green Grows the Laurel' 160
Greenwood, Walter 10
Gretton, David 26, 82, 86, 92–4, 97–8, 100, 120–1, 137, 159
Grey Cock Folk Club 230
Grierson, John 25, 65, 140, 262
Grimethorpe Colliery Band 283
'Grocer, The' 246
Grossman, Albert 48
Grundy, Annie 273
Guthrie, Woody 31, 44, 174
'Gypsy is a Gentleman' 163, 183, 199–200
'Gypsy Jack of All Trades' 199–200
'Gypsy Laddie' 239

Haggar, Jean 122, 124, 126
Hall, Robin 79, 184, 211–12
Hall, Ken 237
Hall, Stuart 224
Hall, Willis 97
Hamilton, Jack 82, 169
Handle, Johnny 109
Harding, Archie 11, 14, 64–6
Harker, Dave 111
Harper, Campbell 262
Harrison, Charlie 8
Harry Hopeful 66
Harvest the Sea 97
Heaney, Joe 134, 199, 215-6
Heartfield, John 65
Hell is What You Make It 40
Henderson, Hamish 215
Hiro, Dilip 219, 224–7
Hodgson, Godfrey 226
Holland, Dutchy 122–9
'Holy Joe from Scabsville' 245
Hooker, John Lee 193
Horn of the Hunter 270, 279–80
'Hot Asphalt' 211
Hot Jazz, Warm Feet 204
'House Carpenter' 46, 174
House Un-American Activities Committee 33
'Housewife's Alphabet' 252

293

Hughes, Caroline, 160
Hughes, Richard 63–4
Hughes, Ronnie 146, 207–8
Hullabaloo 213
Hunt, Vince 166, 268, 270–2, 273, 276, 279, 281
Hutchings, Ashley 207

I Heard America Sing 174
'I'm Gonna Be an Engineer' 248, 251
Ingersoll, Robert 7
International Brigade 16
'Irish Washerwoman' 32
Irishmen, The 267
Iron Box 226
'Iron Road' 182
Irwin, Colin 254
'Island, The' 246
Italia Prize 60, 69, 73–4, 103, 106–7, 221
Ives, Burl 34, 50, 213

Jackson, Aunt Molly 31
Jackson, George 226
'Jamie Foyers' 16, 174
Jewellery, The 119–20
Joan's Book 12
John Bullion 13
John Laing 76–7, 82, 92, 167, 169
Johnny Miner 45
Johnny Noble 40–1, 44, 245
Journeyman 10, 38, 52, 77, 155, 176
'Joy of Living' 246
Jug o' Punch 119, 213

Kahn, Alfie 194, 196, 198, 208
Karpf, Anne 234
Keenan, Peter 142, 146, 213
Kelly, Luke 213, 239
Kelly-Bootle, Stan 54, 210–11, 216
Kerr, Sandra 216, 238–9, 242, 267, 282
Killen, Louis 79–80, 85, 109, 111–12, 134, 196, 201, 204, 212–13, 216
Kilroy Was Here (LP) 236
Kustow, Michael 131, 133

Laban, Rudolf 12, 41, 168–9, 179, 230, 238
Labour Party 228–9
'Lady, What Do You Do All Day?' 252
Lambe, Johnny 146, 207
Lampell, Millard 50
Landmarks (radio) 177, 182, 229
Landscape with Chimneys 40, 174
Larner, Dorcas 98
Larner, Sam 95–9, 100–1, 105–7, 112, 159, 171–2, 180–3, 189–91, 260, 262, 270, 277

Last Crusade (radio) 69
Last Edition 17, 217, 241
Last Year in Marienbad 123
Lawrence, DH 109, 113
'LBJ Looks After Me' 183
Leadbelly 31, 44, 75, 174, 237
Leaveners, The 133, 148
'Legal, Illegal' 245
Lennon, Peter 266
Leonard, Dr Alfred 220
Leonard, Geoffrey 92
Leonard, John 268-9, 272–5, 279, 283
Levan, Danny 162, 200
Lever, Harold 16
Lewin Ronald 57, 71, 127, 159
'Lion in a Cage' 216
Littlewood, Joan 12–16, 27, 29, 38–42, 62, 65, 67, 83, 132, 218, 232, 236, 241, 245
'Liverpool Lou' 211
'Liverpool Lullaby' 211
Living Jazz 205
Lloyd, AL (Bert) 44–7, 54, 60, 69, 75, 79, 101, 109, 112, 175, 181, 187, 202–3, 210, 216–18, 237
Lomax, Alan 31, 34–5, 40, 43–7, 52, 69, 107, 175, 186, 202
Lomax, John 31
London Column (radio) 25, 27
'London Yorkshire Highway' 79
Lonesome Train, 16
Long March of Everyman 226
'Looking for a Job' 246, 255
Lope de Vega 16, 173
Lorca, Federico Garcia 37, 40, 44, 217
Lorry Harbour 69–70
Lowe, Jez 273–4, 276-7, 279
Lozells School 134–6
'Luck Money' 275
Lysistrata 17, 38
Lyttelton, Humphrey 45, 202, 204–5

'McAlpine's Fusiliers' 211
MacColl, Calum 114, 238, 241–2, 258
MacColl, Ewan and:
 acting 11–12, 14–15, 40, 46–7
 Ballads and Blues Club, 236–7
 childhood 5–7
 Critics Group 180, 216, **236–43**
 early education 8–9
 Festival of Fools 239–43, 248
 folk music 7, 11, 37, 43–8, 179, 216–**7**, 236–9
 illness 235, 242–3, 245–6
 interviewing 51–2, 77–8, 97–9, 109–10, 136, 140, 155–6, **165–72**
 Littlewood, Joan 12–17, 38–42, 245

INDEX

Lloyd, AL (Bert) 44–5
Lomax, Alan 43–7
National Service 17–18
Newlove, Jean 38–9, 42, 48, 75
Parker, Charles 27, 50–1, 53, 78, 87–9, 107, 109, 146, 158, 236
plays 13, 15–16, 36–41, 244–5
politics 8–10, 14–17, 239–40, 242, 244–6
prison 38–9
radio 11–16, 45, 69–71
Radio Ballad creation 52–3, 78, 87–9, 100–1, 110, 114, 123, 131, 136, 138–9, 143–6, 149
Red Megaphones 10–11
Seeger, Peggy 35, 37, 46–8, 75, **235–46**, 249, 251, 256, 258
Singers Club 80, 236–9
singing 55–6, 121, 134, 138, 145, 147, 151–2, 157, 195–6, 198–9, 216, 236, 248, 251
songwriting 16, 48, 50, 52, 55, 69–71, 78, 83, 100–1, 110–11, 116, 121, 127, 138–140, 146–9, 151, 160, **173–84**, 188, 192, 194–7, 236, 239, 244–6, 251, 259–60, 262–3, 265–6
television 45, 47, 50, 259
theatre after Theatre Workshop 239–45
theatre direction 13, 239–42
theatre pre-war 13–14, 16–17
Theatre Workshop 37–42, 45–6, 236, 238, 241
MacColl, Hamish 43
MacColl, Kirsty 75
MacColl, Kitty 243, 258
MacColl, Neill 75, 77, 82, 193, 245, 258
McCormick, Fred 287
McCulloch, Gordon 101, 137, 146, 150, 196, 198, 213, 239, 251
McCusker, John 283
McDiarmid, Hugh 40
McEwan, Rory 210
McGrath, John 244–5
McGregor, Alec 200, 215
McGregor, Jimmie 79, 184, 201, 211–12, 215
Mackintosh, Ian 106
McMillan, Ian 276
MacNeice, Louis 69, 84
McPeake, Francis 80, 211–12
Maker and the Tool 133–5, 137
Man Born to be King 69
'Manchester Rambler' 11, 54, 174
March of the '45 (radio) 66
Marriott, Beryl 207
Martins and The Coys 44
Mash, Norah 123, 130–1

Mason, Michael 226, 234
'Mass Trespass 1932' 11, 174
Matthews, Julie 273–5, 278
May Day in England (radio) 66, 71
Mencken, Bill 155
Mickleburgh, Bobby 80, 205
Miller, Betsy 4–6, 10, 13–14, 17, 37, 39, 238, 243
Miller, Will 5, 7, 10, 13–14, 39
'Miner's Wife' 113
Miracle at Verdun 16
Mitchell, Denis 45, 50–1, 69–71, 175
Mitchell, Warren 47
Mitchison, Naomi 159
Moorsom, Sasha 57
Morris, Denis 26, 73, 75, 77–8, 81-2, 84, 87, 92, 97–8, 120, 127
Mortimer, John 69
Moss, Stirling 128
Mouskouri, Nana 241
'Moving On Song' 157, 199–200
'My Old Man' 5, 246
My People and Your People 71

National Coal Board (NCB) 107, 245, 265
New Merlin's Cave 240
Newlove, Jean 27, 38-9, 42, 48, 50, 75
Newport Folk Festival 104, 193
Newsboy 13
Nicholls, Frank 66
Night in the City 50, 71
Night Mail 65–6
'Nine-Month Blues' 252
No Spring Chickens 257
No Surrender 224
Norman, Frank 42
North Sea 262
'North Sea Holes' 105, 181, 262–3
Northeastern University, Boston 257
Not Known in Denmark Street 135
'Nuclear Means Jobs' 246

O'Casey, Sean 36, 40
Odets, Clifford 13
Of One Blood 230
On the Brink 232
On the Edge 131, 133, **135–41**, 143, 151, 170, 195–8, 213-4, 222, 260
'On the Picket Line' 245
Other Animals 40
Our Singing Country 31

Paine, Thomas 7–8
Pan American Union 33
Parker, Charles and:
    Banner Theatre 134, 230–4

BBC management 26–7, 57–8, 75, 77–8, 81–2, 92–4, 97–8, 100, 106–7, 118–22, 127, 137, 159, 163, 221, 223–7
BBC North American Service 22–5
Birmingham Ballads 117–21
Bowdler, Rhoma 230–4
Cambridge University 21–2
Critics Group, 230, 239–240
Donnellan, Philip 22–3, 26, 159, 220, 224–5, 227, 260–1
folk music 26–7, 135, 221, 229–30
Grey Cock Folk Club, 230
interviewing 22–3, 51–2, 77–8, 97–9, 109–110, 121, 123, 126, 133, 159, **165–72**, 188, 272
MacColl, Ewan 27, 50–1, 53, 78, 87–9, 107, 109, 146, 158, 236
Maker and the Tool 133–5, 137
Navy career 20–1
Parker, Phyllis 21, 23, 25–6, 130, 233–4
polio sufferers 127–30
politics 133, 158, 228–33
Radio Ballad production 52–3, 56–8, 76–82, **86–95**, 101–5, 123, 136–8, 140, 146, 152–4, 161–2, 270
Radio Ballad sound 186–8, 191–6, 199
radio programmes (other than RB) 22–7, 135, 220–7
radio technology 24–5, 49, 51, 53, 56–7, 66–8, 80–1, **89–95**, 162, 271–2
religion 22, 26, 228–9
Seeger, Peggy 54, 61, 73–4, 104, 155
studio recording 53, 79, **93–5**, 96, 101–4, 111, 123, 152, 207
tape recording 24–5, 51, 89–90, 150
teaching 112–13, 229–30, 233–4
Travellers 158–60
Parker, Phyllis 21, 23, 25–6, 95, 130, 134, 233–4
Parker, Sara 25, 66, 95, 130, 166, 270–3, 278–80, 283
'Parliamentary Polka' 183
Parsley Sage and Politics 240, 285–6
Paul, David 84
Pearson, Brian 239, 241–2
Peggy Seeger Songbook, warts and all: forty years of songmaking 209, 250, 255–6
Peggy Seeger, The Folkway Years 1955–92: Songs of Love and Politics 257
Penelope Isn't Waiting Anymore (LP) 252
'Peter Keenan's Song' 147
Pickford, Jack 59
Pickles, Wilfred 14, 67
Playfair, Nigel 63–4
Plowright, Piers 183, 260
Polar Bears' Picnic 26
Polio Research Fund 123, 128

Polwart, Karine 273, 275, 277–8
Polytechnic of Central London 233
'Poor Paddy Works on the Railway' 182
Porter, David 221, 223
Prescott, Johnny 149–150
Prometheus the Engineer 14
'Public Unpublic' 246
Pudney, John 15–16, 65, 68
'Pull Down Lads' 279
Pyper-Scott, Irene 250, 256–7

'Queen Jane' 27, 210
'Queen Maeve' 138
Queens' College Cambridge 21

Radcliffe College 34
Radio Ballads:
  audience reaction 60, 85, 106, 141–2, 153, 162–3
  costs 100, 118–19, 162–3, 166
  interviewing 51–2, 77–8, 97–9, 109–10, 121, 123, 126, 136, 140, 155–6, 159–61, **165–72**, 188, 271–3
  methodology 50–1, 53–4, **86–95**, 153, 162
  music 52–3, 78, 127, 146–8, **185–99**
  performers 53–4, 79–80, 101–2, 104, 111, 137, 146, 148, 161–2, **201–18**
  press reviews 49, 58–60, 83–4, 106, 115–6, 140, 152, 163
  songs 54–6, 72, 78–80, 82, 84, 101, 105, 111–3, 126–7, 138, 144–5, 147–51, 157–8, 160, 163–4
  songwriting 52, 78, 100–1, 110, **173–84**
  speech and speakers 52, 82, 85, 88, 98–100, 102, 104–5, 109–10, 112–5, 117, 122–30, 136, 138–40, 142–3, 145, 148–50, 154–61, 164, **165–72**, 177, 180–1
Raffles, Gerry 38, 41
Ramblers 46–7, 208
Reavey, John 198
'Reclaim the Night' 254
Red Megaphones 10, 13, 174, 283
Redgrave, Sir Michael 40
Reed, Henry 69
Reith, John 11, 14, 63–4, 68
Resettlement Administration 29
Reynolds, Gillian 222, 227, 236, 283
'Road is Done, The' 82
'Road to the Isles' 11, 174
Robeson, Paul 16, 212
Robinson, Earl 50
Robinson, Robert 58, 83
'Rock Island Line' 46, 237
Rodgers, Ian 84, 126, 140
Rogers, Dave 230–2, 234
'Rogue's Gallery' 246

INDEX

Romeo and Juliet (radio) 239
Rosenfeld, Else 135
Ross, Colin 140, 215
Rotha, Paul 25
Rothman, Benny 11
'Roving Rambler' 218
Rowe, 'Doc' 171
Royal National Institute for the Blind (RNIB) 220–1, 223
Royal Navy 20–1, 93
Ruffell (Strudwick), Heather 122–5, 127, 129
Rundall, Jeremy 221, 226
Rush Green Hospital 122, 126, 129
Rushmore, 'Crabpot' 262
Rushton, Caleb 250

'St James Infirmary' 151
'Saltley Gate' 232
Sands, Tommy 273, 280–1
'Saturday Afternoon' 218
Saturday Night at the Eel's Foot 217
Sayers, Dorothy L 69
Scanlon, Ron 56, 187
Scargill, Arthur 266
Scase, David 245
Schlumberg, Hans 16
'Schooldays Over' 112, 184, 192
Schooling, Anthony 233–4
Scott, Robin 259, 263–5
Seeger, Charles 29–34, 44
Seeger, Constance 29
Seeger, Mike 29–34, 258
Seeger, Peggy and:
    Ballads and Blues Club 236–7
    childhood 30–3
    Critics Group 180, 216, **236–43**, 250
    Europe 34–5, 60–1, 73–5
    feminism 248, 251–5
    Festival of Fools 239–43, 248
    Folk Music 33, 47, 179, 236–9, 249
    interviewing 77, 110, 136, 139–140, 155–6, 160–1, 251, 253
    MacColl, Ewan 35, 37, 46–8, 75, **235–46**, 249, 251, 256, 258
    musical upbringing 28, 31–3, 54, 186, 249
    Parker, Charles 54, 61, 73, 74, 104, 109, 155, 158
    performing music 32–3, 186, 195, 203, 208–9, 249, 263
    politics 250–7
    Pyper-Scott, Irene 256–7
    Radio Ballad music 52–4, 59–60, 78, 83, 126–7, 145–6, 148–9, **185–99**, 204, 263
    Singers Club 80, 236–9
    singing 33, 35, 47–8, 121, 134, 152, 157, 193, 247–51, 257

    songwriting 209, 247–57
    teaching 238, 242, 257
Seeger, Pete 7, 28–31, 33, 44, 206, 257–8
Seeger, Ruth Crawford 28–34
Seiber, Matyas 45
Senior, Bill 277
Seward, Andy 273
Shadow of the Swastika (radio) 217
Shapley, Olive 14–15, 17, 20, 62, 65, 67–8
Shaw, George Bernard 40, 67
'Sheffield Apprentice, The' 174
Shoals of Herring (film) 260–3
'Shoals of Herring' (song) 104, 180–2, 184, 218, 263
Shore Saints and Sea Devils 245
'Shores of Erin' 104
Short, Pat 128
'Shovelling Coal Song' 55
Shreeve, Bill 148
Shrewsbury Three, The 232
Siege of Ceylon 226
Sinclair, Upton 8
Sing Christmas and the Turn of the Year 52
Singer, Aubrey 266
Singing English (radio) 176
Singing Englishman 218
Singing Jailbirds 8
Singing the Fishing 69, 85, 87, 93–4, **96–107**, 110, 115, 118–9, 121, 158, 166, 172, 178–82, 189–92, 201, 203–4, 206, 213-4, 218, 228, 260
'Sixteen Tons' 48
'Skipping Song' 148
Smith, Minty 157, 199
Smith, Norma 117, 122, 124–5, 130
Smooth Operations 269
Snowballs in Calcutta 225
Snowman, Daniel 226
Soanes, Victor 127
Solomon, Bill 262
Song Carriers, The 179, 229–30
Song Hunter 45
Song of a Road 68, **72–85**, 87–8, 91–4, 97, 104, 109, 112, 119, 123, 138, 167–9, 178–9, 184, 187–9, 204, 211–12, 218, 261
'Song of a Road' (song) 80
Song of Steel 270, 273, 275–6, 281
Sony Awards 269–70
Stanislavski, Constantin 13, 41
Steel (play) 232
Steel Peach and Tozer 271, 275
'Steelos' 271, 276
Stewart, Belle 155–6, 199, 200, 214–5, 244
Stewart, Elizabeth 101–2, 204, 215, 217, 262
Stewart, Jane (Urquhart) 101–2, 199, 214, 217, 262

Stracey, John H 264
'Sum of What I Am' 274
Summerskill, Baroness 143
'Sunday, Bloody Sunday' 281
'Surveyor's Song' 78
Sutcliffe, Frank 261
Swarbrick, Dave 134, 148, 161–2, 203, 206–7, 210, 214–5
'Sweet Thames Flow Softly' 239
'Sweet William' 179
Swings and Roundabouts 270–1, 275, 278–9

'Talking Matrimony Blues' 253
Tams, John 269, 271–3, 275–6, 279, 282–3
Tawney, Cyril 134, 213
'Terror Time' 199, 216
Theatre of Action 13, 233
Theatre Royal, Drury Lane 239
Theatre Royal, Stratford East 27, 42, 44, 216
Theatre Union 16–18, 37–8
Theatre Workshop 37–46, 59, 70, 114, 132–3, 135, 168, 174, 210–11, 231, 236, 238, 241, 243–5
'There's No Place For Me' 216
Thirty Years of Conflict 268, 270, 273, 280–1
'Thirty-Foot Trailer' 160, 199–200
Thomas, 'Doc' Dafydd 41, 114
Thomas, 'Big' 79, 212
Thomas, Dylan 69
Thompson, Richard 207
Thomson, George 228–9
Thomson, Katharine 101, 104, 228
Thornber, Robin 245
Threepenny Opera 37, 47
Till Doomsday in the Afternoon 244
Time to Spare 67
Toller, Ernst 13
'Tomorrow' 255
Tonight 77, 79, 184, 211–12, 214
Topic Records 57, 215, 267
Trades Union Congress (TUC) 132, 135
'Trafford Road Ballad' 174
'Training Song' 147–8
Travellers, The 40, 45–46
Travellers' Songs from England and Scotland 244
Travelling People 90, 106, **154–164**, 167, 170, 172, 180, 184, 199–200, 207, 214–5, 244, 269, 278
'Troubles' 280
Tugwell, Rexford 29
Tunnel 12, 87

'Tunnel Tigers' 267
Turner, Bruce 46–7, 54, 80, 101, 104, 188–9, 192, 196, 204–5, 208
'Twenty One Years' 175

Under Milk Wood 69
'Union Woman II' 253
United Europe (radio) 11
Unwin, Stanley 241
'Up Jumped the Herring' 213
Uranium 235 35, 37–40, 167
Usher, Shaun 266

Vaughan Williams, Ralph 70
Vaughton, Brian 119, 121, 132
Voice of the Seamen 217

Wade, David 222, 225–6
Waiting for Lefty 13
Walker, Alexander 84, 185, 189
Wallace, Nellie 10
Wanamaker, Sam 40, 47
Ward, Alan 57, 90–1, 93–5, 101, 111, 120
Watt, Harry 262
Watton, Alderman Harry 159, 164
Weavers 31, 33, 44, 47
Wesker, Arnold 132–3, 135, 244
West, Frank 180
Western Treasury 31
'When You're a Fighter' 147
Whitby, Tony 225–7
Whitehead, Philip 263
Whiting, Eileen 134
'William Taylor' 267
Williams, Patrick 126, 140
Williams, Rosalie 37–8
Williams, Sir Owen 76–7, 188
Wilsher, Peter 126, 140, 152
Wilson, Sonny 145
'Winds Of Change, The' 200
'Winnie and Sam' 253
'Wives and Mothers' 149
Womankind 232
Workers' Educational Association (WEA) 229
Workers' Music Association (WMA) 46, 218
Workers' Playtime 132
Wright, Diana 111

Yates, Pete 234
'You Men Out There' 254–5
'You're a Miner' 113